JOSEP PLA

Seeing the World in the Form of Articles

Josep Pla

Seeing the World in the Form of Articles

JOAN RAMON RESINA

UNIVERSITY OF TORONTO PRESS
Toronto Buffalo London

Toronto Buffalo London
www.utppublishing.com

ISBN 978-1-4875-0184-6 (cloth)

(TorontoIberic)

Library and Archives Canada Cataloguing in Publication

Resina, Joan Ramon, author
Josep Pla : seeing the world in the form of articles / Joan Ramon Resina.

Includes bibliographical references and index.
ISBN 978-1-4875-0184-6 (cloth)

1. Pla, Josep, 1897–1981 – Criticism and interpretation. I. Title.

PC3941.P54Z65 2017 849′.985209 C2016-908083-8

University of Toronto Press acknowledges the financial assistance to its publishing program of the Canada Council for the Arts and the Ontario Arts Council, an agency of the Government of Ontario.

Canada Council for the Arts Conseil des Arts du Canada

Funded by the Government of Canada | Financé par le gouvernement du Canada | Canadä

For Eliana, my morning star

Contents

Illustrations

Acknowledgments

This short book has been a long time coming. Pla's work is extensive and all-embracing. It grows on one almost organically. But like strong nutrients, it needs to be broken down and absorbed with the help of other substances. And I do not mean only or necessarily Pla criticism, of which a fair amount exists. Rather, I mean readings that help expand the Pla universe and understand the complexity of a deceivingly simple writer who was also a thinker, even if that term is often pronounced with a solemnity he would have derided. I mean, especially, conversations with persons who share my admiration for the writer from Palafrugell. The list is long and running through it would risk unpardonably forgetting someone, but one person stands out for the intensity and range of our conversations: Xavier Pla, the other Pla, a conspicuous specialist with whom I have been "talking Pla" for years. I owe him bibliographical and biographical details that have proved useful at more than one turn in the writing of this book. I am also grateful to the graduate students in my Pla seminar at Stanford in the fall of 2009 for vivid discussions and illuminating comments. And to Robert Davidson for inviting me to deliver the keynote address at the meeting of the North American Catalan Society in Toronto in May 2013. There I presented the substance of one of the chapters in the book and thereby profited from the questions of the audience. Last but, indeed, not least, to my colleague and good friend Hans Ulrich Gumbrecht for reading the manuscript and giving his blessing. Although friends are rarely the most reliable critics, his intellectual generosity is, in true Californian style, all natural.

In the order of institutional gratitude, I wish to acknowledge the team at Internationales Kolleg Morphomata of the University of Cologne for welcoming me as fellow in the spring of 2014. In the context of the Kolleg's annual theme, "Figurations of Death," I elaborated the corresponding chapter in the book. The final push toward completion was possible through the generosity of Stanford University by way of its Humanities Center, where as 2014–15 Donald Andrews Whittier Fellow, I was able to devote myself exclusively to the book.

Preface

On 7 April 1967, one year after the original publication of Josep Pla's *The Gray Notebook*, Jill Jarrell, Madrid-based literary correspondent on Spanish and Latin American literature for Farrar, Straus and Giroux, sent to Lila Karpf, of the department of subsidiary rights of this New York publisher, a report intended to introduce Pla to American readers. The report had been prepared by Gabriel Ferrater, a poet who acted as literary adviser for Seix Barral, a Barcelona publishing house. In her acknowledgment of 19 April, Karpf praised the report, declaring herself impressed by its author's intelligence and saying that she was forwarding it to the editorial board. On the next day, Roger W. Straus, Jr, wrote to Jarrell again praising the quality of the report but turning down the proposal. The reasons for the refusal had nothing to do with the quality of Pla's literature. Given the speed of the rejection (it took less than twenty-four hours), it is safe to conclude that no one at Farrar bothered to check on Pla or asked for a second opinion. Quite likely, the decision was based on the absence of Catalan literature from the American intellectual horizon and the corresponding difficulty of marketing an author without a clear national adscription. In other words, the rejection had nothing to do with Pla or his work and everything to do with the prejudice that, even today, despite the existence of sporadic translations and notwithstanding the inclusion of Catalan authors in the appendix to Harold Bloom's influential *The Western Canon*, hinders the publication of critical work on Catalan literature at university presses, not to mention commercial ones.

In a carefully crafted report, Ferrater had recommended deep cuts to the English version of *The Gray Notebook*, eliminating lengthy passages dealing with Barcelona personalities unknown to American readers and bringing down an eight-hundred-page book to a condensed five-hundred-page one. But even this playing up to publishers' fondness for economy failed to sway them. Pla would have to wait forty-seven more years before *The Gray Notebook* finally appeared in English. Posthumously but integrally. Why the long wait? The answer does not lie in the circumscribed universe of literary values but in the wider one of political ontology. By 2014, the year before *The Gray Notebook* was finally published in English, Catalonia had made news and come to be widely regarded as a nation of sorts. And Pla was, and remains, the most read Catalan author.

What makes the delay particularly distressing (and so telling about dynamics in the so-called World Republic of Letters) is that it reveals an unusual hardening, a protracted stiffening of the initial resistance to Pla's international projection. And responsibility did not lie solely on the foreign publishers. Why had it taken so long for someone to write on Pla's behalf to an American press? Pleading Pla's cause in 1967, when the writer was already seventy years old, Ferrater anticipated an objection in the form of suspicion: "Why, a foreigner might ask, has Pla been 'Discovered' by so many people so late in the day?" (132–3). Having pre-emptively formulated the question, he proceeded to meet the publishers' predictable scepticism: "The answer is that Pla was discovered, and greeted enthusiastically by everybody that had a bit of brains, back in 1924, when he published his first book [...]. But later, he fell into two traps: he was *in* the side of Franco during the civil war (I said *in*, not *on*: I mean simply that he found himself in the Franco-occupied part of the country), and after the war, to earn his living, he was forced to write in Spanish, not in Catalan. You know how people are here, and will easily imagine how vicious such traps can become" (133).

No, the New York publishers did not know "how people are here," nor could they easily imagine which traps Ferrater was talking about. That last sentence was written in code internal to the Barcelona literary establishment. Nor was he entirely candid about Pla's only having found himself *in* and not *on* the Franco side, a matter than has not been put to rest even today and that I try to disentangle in chapter 9 of this book. As for the necessity of writing in Spanish after the Civil War, it is true that, with the Catalan press outlawed, Pla had to write for periodicals in Spanish. But it is also true that after the Second World War he was able to publish books in Catalan, beginning with the reissue of *Viatge a Catalunya* (Voyage to Catalonia) in 1946, followed by *Cadaqués* in 1947. With these precisions or, better, imprecisions, Ferrater sought to explain Pla's marginalization in post–Civil War Catalan literary circles and the critical establishment. The odium endured in fact long after his death. He was denied the Premi d'Honor de les Lletres Catalanes, Catalonia's highest literary award, which no one had merited as much as he. But if political prejudice might explain why no one had tried to export Pla before; it did not explain why no one *outside* Catalonia had done so either.

The problem was not merely "how people are here," but why Catalan culture remained invisible in the new order that had emerged from the defeat of the enemies of democracy in the Second World War. The answer, or at least part of the answer, lies with the Allies' accolades to Franco, the US treaty with Spain, and the hardening of monolithic, monocultural nation states as the basic structure of the West. With the official suppression and even negation of the Catalan language in Spain, its literature also disappeared from, or failed to appear on, the international horizon. There was no context for Pla's reception. Worse yet, if one had been provided, it would have been the lethal one of "regional" or "provincial" literature. Failing to write in a "world" language, he would not have qualified for the transfiguring albeit deceptive description of "minor" literature. When Gilles Deleuze and Félix Guattari launched this antipodal category, they found no better illustration for it than a consecrated, perhaps *the* consecrated author in one of the major European languages. Pla, a major author in a marginalized language, would not have fit the bill.

When in his 1961 *Theatre of the Absurd* Martin Esslin wrote that Manuel de Pedrolo would "be better known outside his native country but for the fact that he writes in a language – Catalan – that is little understood by those in the English-speaking world who would normally have access to French, Spanish, or German" (246), he might have been speaking of Pla. Ferrater was certainly right, even if somewhat restrictive, when he asserted: "That now, in Europe, there are not more than five or six prose-writers as good as Pla, I believe this is undisputable fact. But, of course, it is not easy to say *why*, and to describe *how*, he is such a good writer" (132). A critical book that aims to introduce an author to a new audience should strive to say why the writer in question merits the attention and to explain in what ways he reaches the high-water mark. I am not sure that I have achieved this basic purpose, but I am confident that at least I have debunked the myth of a vernacular, linguistically simple, and culturally insular author.

The fact is that when Pla published his first book in 1925, he was immediately recognized as someone with a style of his own. From that moment and until the Spanish Civil War, his reputation solidified and he was widely acknowledged as a major writer and as one of the finest journalists. From the start of his career, then, it was obvious that he was no mere reporter, but a writer who could not be easily subsumed under the existing categories. He wrote narrative – his first three books gave evidence of a skilled narrator that was, however, aborted (as chapters 4 and 8 argue) – and sent back reports from all over Europe that, going beyond the standard of the trade, constituted engaging essays on social psychology, the political intricacies of the moment, and the cultural life of the countries he visited. All of this described from a distinctly situated point of view that claimed objectivity through the power of (real or alleged) presence to the events. Such writing had no distinct designation in inter-war journalism – it did not fit the rubric of "spiritual chronicle," which Miquel dels Sants Oliver fumblingly applied to Gaziel's reportage about the early days of the First World War in Paris – (Gaziel, *París 1914*, 14). It would eventually come to be known under the vague and generic classification of literary journalism (discussed in chapter 1). Of this genre, Pla was, without a doubt, one of the unacknowledged legislators.

In the course of his life he published 120 titles and thousands of articles, which in the mid-fifties he started reworking and reorganizing into the thirty-eight volumes of the Collected Works that appeared before his death in 1981. This already large oeuvre continued to grow with the edition of unpublished materials until it reached the current forty-seven volumes, comprising over thirty thousand pages. Sundry materials and the bulk of the correspondence fell into the hands of his publisher, Josep Vergés, and of Pla's heirs. This mass of unpublished documents is caught up in a legal dispute and, for the time being, remains inaccessible to researchers. There is little doubt that one day it will throw light on parts of his life that remain dark and thus the object of rumour and malicious hearsay.

Josep Pla i Casadevall was born in 1897 in the town of Palafrugell, in the Empordà region of Catalonia, in the area that, in the 1950s and with a view to developing its touristic potential, would be renamed Costa Brava. Being the older son of well-to-do farmers, he was sent to university in Barcelona, where he took a law degree that he would never use, having discovered a writer's vocation and found employment in the grimy world of the press of those years. At twenty-two, he was sent to Paris as foreign correspondent for the daily *La Publicidad* (later to be renamed *La Publicitat*), a decisive experience in his life (discussed in chapter 2), from where he submitted penetrating chronicles on all aspects of French society. In the 1920s he travelled throughout Europe reporting from inflation-ridden Berlin, where he also wrote stories about the desperate lives of the low middle class; from Italy, where he claimed to have covered Mussolini's March on Rome; from Portugal, or from Madrid, where he witnessed the proclamation of the Second Spanish Republic and wrote a provocative little gem of a book with characteristic sarcasm. In 1924, he visited the Soviet Union, invited by fellow Catalan journalist Andreu Nin, who was Secretary of the Red International of Labour Unions and a member of the Executive Committee of the Communist International. Pla, the future conservative writer, wrote then favourable reports of his visit for the daily *La Publicitat*. These articles were then reissued in 1925 as a book, his second. From each of these destinations and from many others, he sent articles that he would eventually collect into the volumes of his Collected Works.

At the start of the Civil War, an anarchist patrol showed up in Palafrugell asking for Pla with unambiguous intentions. Reasonably fearing for his life, he escaped from Barcelona in the company of Adi Enberg, his alleged espouse. They sailed to Marseilles, where she worked as a secretary in an office of espionage on behalf of Franco. Pla's role during this time remains tangled in gossip. There is some evidence of his involvement with this clandestine outfit, but there is no clarity about the nature of his collaboration. Soon, however, he left for Italy, where he redacted an infamous account of the politics of the Spanish Republic commissioned by his Maecenas, Francesc Cambó. This was hackwork, which Pla refused to reissue and did not include in the Collected Works. Shortly after the war, he withdrew to his family's ancestral farm in Llofriu, where, donning the peasant's beret, he spent the rest of his life as a twentieth-century reincarnation of his beloved Montaigne. From there he travelled throughout the region, writing on the landscape, the climate, the sea, local customs, tastes, and histories (chapters 5, 6, and 7), fleshing out a practical philosophy of proximity and of life's embodiment.

Pla had a stinging tongue but was surprisingly reserved, almost puritanical, when it came to his personal life. Adi is never mentioned in the entire body of work, and neither are most of the other women in his life, aside from his mother and grandmother. There is little or no intimacy in his diaries, and this reticence has been considered to limit their interest. This reserve, said Ferrater, contradicting the grandiloquent assertion made in his report for Farrar, Straus, and Giroux, is what keeps Pla from being a great author on the European level (119). Ferrater missed in Pla's texts the racy confessions of a Paul Léautaud, ignoring the insurmountable fact of the censorship. Also, he could not have known that, after Pla's death, Vergés would expunge the materials for the posthumous volumes of passages he considered risqué or off-colour. And there is reason to believe that Pla's heirs do not give access to the remaining papers out of similarly prudish considerations. But women existed in his life, and crude or bawdy allusions do in fact crop up in the notes for diaries he would never write. Notes concerning a certain "A," who seems to have been Pla's real passion and, at a distance of ten thousand five-hundred miles – since she emigrated to Argentina in 1948 – an object of regret, an obsessive memory, the pen pal of an erotic correspondence, and the occasion for wet musings during Pla's waning years (chapter 10).

There could hardly be a less metaphysical writer. The literary epitome of Berkeley's *esse est percipi* principle, Pla eschewed all considerations of transcendence, practising a strictly observational writing. Religion appears in his works only as a fundamental, and useful, social institution with profound formative consequences, but never as the framework of a subjective leap in the style of Kierkegaard. Likewise, death, when it turns up in his books, is always an external event, loaded with social drama, and described in anthropological detail with a touch of the grotesque or a macabre humour that renders it ridiculous. Naturally, it is not death itself that is ridiculed but society's puny defences and beliefs intended to quarantine the inevitable, erecting a buffer zone between individuals and the consciousness of their finitude.

It is absolutely fitting that the first book of Pla's to appear in English was *The Gray Notebook* (to which chapter 3 is devoted), and fortunate that the publishers, New York Review Books, if they exhumed Ferrater's report for Farrar, did not follow his recommendation to abridge the diary, for it is a great book through and through. The allegedly superfluous passages about Barcelona's cultural milieu of the second decade of the twentieth century amount to a wonderful canvas of a period in which figures like Josep Maria de Sagarra (also recently translated to English), Eugeni d'Ors (an author awaiting the honour), and Francesc Pujols interact under the critical, sardonic gaze of a young Pla who, of course, wears the lenses of his much older, mischievous, and experienced namesake. Since the translation of *The Gray Notebook*, a second volume containing Pla's best narrative work has come out in English with the title of *Life Embitters*. Other books are on the translator's desk and will be appearing by and by. When that happens, it is to be hoped that the availability of his work, coupled with its brilliance, will place Pla in the tier of foreign authors familiar to the Anglo-American public. At that point some readers may look for analysis and exegesis of that eminent body of literature. Anticipating that need, this book aims to break the ground and set up the critical substratum for a lasting reputation.

JOSEP PLA

Seeing the World in the Form of Articles

1 Journalism as Literary Praxis

This book is about a great writer. A trivial claim, to be sure. Critical monographs routinely pin their interest on the real or perceived excellence of their subject. So why make such a claim? Perhaps because the object of this claim was never sure of belonging among the great, since he considered himself a hack journalist and limited his claim to fame to having done a conscientious job. There was a great deal of sincere or feigned modesty in this self-assessment, but it is true that the strictures of the newspaper article disciplined Josep Pla's writing and gave his mind a concrete bent. He regretted that they prevented him from fulfilling his early dream of becoming a "creative writer," as people call writing that is undisciplined by the daily event and the evening deadline. With characteristic self-irony, Pla said that in his youth he had made the mistake of writing lyrical papers with absolute personal freedom. "And what are lyrical papers?" he pretends that a young lady had asked him. "Lyrical writing," went the answer, is a paper that has nothing to do with a commercial letter" (5:7). In this reply we can see Pla's trenchant, more often than not sarcastic, categorization. There is writing that consists of personal effusions and writing that merely communicates unadorned intentions or information, writing that has commercial value and whose performance is regulated by specific requirements like those of any other job. Perhaps, he goes on to say to the hypothetical young lady, this explanation is too crude and vulgar. Perhaps he should have rehashed the "generally obscure and incomprehensible written lucubrations" on lyricism put out by the usual academic pedantry (5:8). In any case, he made the mistake of writing lyrical papers instead of the usual commercial ones. To practise the second kind of journalism decently, he adds, one needed to meet a lot of people, to take many cabs, to go many places. It was neither easy nor pleasant. To write lyrically, on the contrary, it was enough to look at the world unconventionally, with complete candour (5:8). This form of writing was economically unproductive; the other generated great personal inconvenience. Although Pla admits to having practised both kinds of journalism, he claimed that most of his output was made to order, something he believed to have been ultimately helpful. "All the great ancient literature and much of the modern was made to order" (5:8). In this he was staking his claim as a writer on a bold contrarian view about literary excellence. If the great authors from the past were essentially craftsmen who turned out products on demand, then he could insert himself into a prestigious line of descent. He could stake a claim for his journalistic production as literature. To support this claim, he rejected romantic notions of genius, of self-originating writers. Apparently exempt from anxiety of influence, he emphasized the learned aspects of the craft, admitting freely to the necessity of borrowing, even of plagiarizing. Writing, he said, is not a trade of voluntary intentions. It is a trade of necessary things. He considered himself lucky to have written always under the baton of necessity, to be a writer of made-to-order texts. Abandon the notion that such products cannot be well done, following all the rules of the art, he says. They can be done conscientiously, because that is the way a professional undertakes concrete, limited actions. Tackling the unlimited, the vague and fuzzy, leads to shaky results (5:9).

Pla was at the intersection of two forms of writing. Not just two styles but two sharply distinguished categories that appeared irreconcilable at the time he began to do newspaper work. In fact, they were getting farther apart, as the modernization of journalism relegated the more "lyrical," essayistic journalism of the earlier twentieth century in favour of a more austere, information-focused communicative style. In this newer, news-focused form of reporting, Pla was arguably less skilled than some of his colleagues in the Catalan and Spanish press, notably Eugeni Xammar, the top foreign correspondent in the 1920s and 1930s, arguably one of the best on the European scene. But whereas the sharp, brisk, and in every respect brilliant reports Xammar telephoned from Paris, London, or Berlin were effective in conveying economic circumstances, diplomatic manoeuvring, or political mood in the space of a newspaper column, they lacked the polish, wealth of image, and originality of simile and metaphor that raised Pla's article to the realm of literature. One could say that the difference existed from the beginning. The young Pla published travel books composed of descriptions of the cities he visited as foreign correspondent, as well as a narrative, *Relacions* (1927), exhibiting a literary vocation that was weak or absent in Xammar and other contemporary journalists such as Gaziel, Manuel Brunet, Carles Sentís, Augusto Assía, Manuel Chaves Nogales, or Julio Camba.

So much, at least for now, for the claim that Pla, who in his lifetime was known primarily as a journalist, belongs in the higher ranks of twentieth-century literature. But before I turn to his work, it will be useful to situate literary journalism in historical perspective. The choice of qualification, the adjectivation of "journalism" by "literature" rather than the other way around, indexes the relation of prestige. "Journalistic literature" means something entirely different. "Literary" ennobles, while "journalistic" debases. And yet, as products for middle-class consumption, the novel and periodical literature emerged at about the same time in the eighteenth century, when both were of dubious respectability and associated with a predominantly female readership. Ionia Italia points out that the majority of the writers who turned to journalism then did so for economic reasons, but strove to divest it of its bad image (7). Let us pause on this bad image *ab origine*. It would take journalism a long time to shake it off, whereas the novel, also suspect at first, was soon admitted to the domain of fine letters. The reward, it would seem, for distancing itself from action. Literature was to become part of the realm of art by turning to sentiment, the taste for adventure, aristocratic or bourgeois passions, and to the empyrean of values deemed eternal. Journalism had the odour of sweat about it, the ooze and grime of the lowly places where men congregated and news sprang up. News preyed on the moment, on the raw present, on the fleeting event. It called on the writer to make instantaneous decisions on the newsworthiness of phenomena, to stake his livelihood and reputation on a perishable commodity and to fret about the judgment not of posterity but of the next day's readership. This went against the grain of received wisdom: Péguy's "Homer is new this morning and there is nothing perhaps so old as today's newspaper" (1323) had a sacramental effect. It posited (and demanded) the production of instantaneous classic works, losing sight of the fact that Homer – or the various epic singers in ancient Hellas – rhapsodized on demand. Bards performed on commission at the courts of petty kings. Demodocus, poet in residence at the court of Alcinous, is given free choice of song but the muse (i.e., the spirit of the occasion) urges him to intone a popular and much expected recitation of the *Iliad*. At Odysseus's palace in Ithaca, Phemius sings – allegedly under compulsion – for the suitors. And this time there is no leeway. They impose the theme on him. Much to Penelope's chagrin, they want to hear a song about "the wretched Achaeans' struggle to make it home from the battle at Troy." Ancient epic was, as Pla contended, a made-to-order product.

For a long time, "literary journalism" would have sounded like an oxymoron. We probably owe it to postmodernism's challenge to the categorical separation of discourses that the oxymoronic quality dissipated and became all but imperceptible. But that was not yet the case in the first half of the twentieth century. At that time applicants for posthumous fame despised journalism. And at the beginning of the second half of the century, the gap still seemed to be growing wider through journalism's conversion into an academic discipline closer to the social sciences than to the humanities.

Although in the United States journalism had been taught at university since 1879, until the 1940s a degree in journalism prepared the candidate for doing what journalists had been doing all along. It was vocational training. Joseph Pulitzer summed up its purpose as to "make a better newspaper, which will better serve the public" (cit. Winfield 8). Then, in the 1950s, with Wilbur Schramm journalism embraced social scientific methods and became a branch of communication studies, first at the University of Iowa and after 1955 at Stanford. As John C. Hartsock explains in *A History of American Literary Journalism*, "the behavioral emphasis based on quantifiable empirical evidence has continued to dominate much of this study, despite calls since at least the 1970s for other approaches, particularly cultural and qualitative" (237).

Through this metamorphosis, journalism, which had been denied admittance to English departments, obtained academic respectability but was divorced from the literary disciplines. It was embedded in departments of "communication," often focused on "data journalism," which in today's technological environment sounds more reassuring than "writing." The term "data" suggests something hard and substantial beyond the confines of language; something that escapes the troubled field of metaphor and lends itself to quantification, graphic charts, and statistical analysis. "Writing" was left to the soft, troubled literature departments. This split between aesthetic – Pla's notion of "lyric" – education and quasi-empirical social science – his simile of the commercial letter – replicated the Platonic distinction between philosophy and sophistry, that is, between a metaphysical belief in a truth to be arrived at by peeling off all the layers of myth, and awareness that truth is a matter of contextualization in specific language games.

Literary journalists – and by extension all those aware of the social effect of metaphor – belong in the party of the sophists, while the data crunchers who expelled the poets from their republic of communication science believe, like all metaphysicians, in the ascetic reduction of the beautiful to the useful and conflate the latter with the real. Richard Rorty put it elegantly: "After the scales are rubbed off a butterfly's wing, you have transparency but not beauty – formal structure without sensuous content" (152). Transparency, that is, as the unproblematic structure of the event through quantification and analysis of data. Journalism as science has rubbed off the genre's sensuous content. No wonder it can no longer fly.

As experts in the art of swaying opinion, the sophists understood sensuous impressions and what people today call emotional intelligence. They were the media men of the fifth century BC. Their quick, articulate minds turned with the urgency of influencing the decision makers. They fluttered around the agora. They travelled in search of business, adapting their teachings to local need. In contrast, the philosopher withdrew to the Garden of Academus to project a republic founded on necessary truths, the sort of truths we call scientific. Considering the existing partition of the universe of discourse between the practical and the theoretical, the public and the arcane, the influential and the irrelevant, it is tempting to assign journalism and literature to different sides of that divide. And the temptation has often been indulged. Who would have thought in 1962, when Northrop Frye delivered "The Educated Imagination" in the Massey Lectures series of learned radio talks broadcast on the Canadian Broadcasting Corporation, that some day it would be impossible to hold, as he did, a mass audience responsible for a significant degree of cultural literacy? The corporation established the duration and the tone of the addresses, but their format remained unmistakably that of the lecture. The medium was not quite the message yet. Thereafter, the relation capsized. For France, Régis Debray traced the turnaround to May 1968. During that upheaval of social values, a permutation of significance took place. From that moment, novelty became authority setting, and the news, as the formal expression of novelty, imposed itself as normative criteria of intellectual value.

In his study of intellectual power in France, Debray recycled the Western tradition of slicing history into three ages. He did not identify them, but Joaquim de Fiore's theological ages of the Father, the Son, and the Holy Spirit, the traditional division of European history into ancient, medieval, and modern, or Comte's law of three stages – the theological, the metaphysical, and the positive – were clear precedents. The threefold has a hold on the Western imagination. The following year, Alvin Toffler would follow up his immensely popular *Future Shock* with *The Third Wave*. In this work he divided history into three waves of civilization: the agricultural age, the industrial revolution, and the age of information flows. For Debray the three cultural stages spanned a much shorter time frame. He called them "the university cycle," "the publishing cycle," and "the media cycle," running respectively from 1880 to1930, from 1920 to 1960, and from 1968 to the present. Perhaps he would now add an extension of the third cycle to account for the Internet. In any case, the university had entered a stage of disorganization that was simultaneously the historical disorganization of the intelligentsia as a class. That disorganization was in effect "its reorganization under the aegis of the rival hegemonic interests" (59). When their traditional shrine began losing its social pre-eminence, intellectuals abandoned academic criteria of selection and espoused the media's commercial logic. Henceforth social success was to be measured by repercussion in the media, by the waves a person or a cultural event made.

Between these two regimes of legitimacy, the university's and the media's, Debray placed the cycle of the publishers, asserting that in France the university first lost its social authority to the publishing houses in the 1920s. Through this power shift the profit motive became the effective arbiter of cultural selection, a court without appeal on the life or death of authors. For a time, though, the relation between literature and business rested on a fruitful ambiguity. The publishing house not only promoted its authors to make them profitable, but also furnished them with an intellectual community defined by the values associated with the publisher's logo. The values represented by Editions Gallimard, for example, were proclaimed in the second issue of *La Nouvelle Revue française* (*NRF*) in 1909, one year before the authors of this group, Gide among them, founded the publishing house. In that issue the group declared their "intention of fighting against journalism, Americanism, mercantilism, and the self-complacency of the times" (cit. Debray 78). We can leave aside anti-Americanism as a French *lieu commun*, or if you will, as proof that Europeans were fretting about the ongoing shift in social legitimation. Most striking in that statement is the declaration of war on journalism, perceived as a threat to high culture at the very moment when this culture, in the guise of literature, had become autonomous. For the first time writers were able to define their activity apart from criteria emanating from the Académie and the aristocratic salons. The paradox was that writers purchased their independence by submitting to the very mercantilism that the *NRF* blasted in the name of *bon goût*. Recourse to good taste as a gauge of value entailed the question of who arbitrated taste and what social institution was entitled to settle the competing claims.

This competence had once belonged to the Church as patron of the arts and purveyor of its themes. With the birth of republicanism and the rise of the post-revolutionary religion of the state, culture became a state apparatus and was thereby shielded from social opinion. The professorial class was the new priesthood of this secular sphere. As the bourgeois logic of privatization developed, however, a literary elite outside the walls of the university arrogated the power to adjudicate in matters of taste. This new elite, lacking institutional support and compelled to rely on the bourgeois virtue of individualism, propped itself up on its subjective refinement. But in the absence of authoritative institutions, it was a matter of time before taste became democratized and the criterion of number abetted the commercialism that the *NRF* deplored.

Matters were different in Spain. Republicanism had failed to assert itself and the state continued beholden to the Church. Universities did not become the new temples of positivism and lay speculation they were in France. At the height of the rule of the *clercs* in the neighbouring country, Spanish universities were dismal institutions, reflecting derivative knowledge at a second, third, or fourth remove. In his autobiographical *The Gray Notebook*, Pla presented a grim picture of the formation of the intellectual and professional elites in the early twentieth century (1:552–86). Nor was the publishing industry strong enough to sustain an alternative elite that could play the role that an extensive body of independent writers played in France. So, in Spain generally and in Barcelona in particular, the press became early on the one and only alternative to the university chair, displacing the latter in its mission of educating the community, guiding it in matters of taste, telling it what and how to think, and providing it with values. Out of school and with a law degree he never intended to put to use, Pla joined one of the local newspapers and learned the trade from the ground up. Conditions were austere. He became a hired pen and remained so for most of his life. Having accepted the necessity in order to pursue a writing career, he resolved to do his job "according to all the rules of the art" (5:9). Focusing on well-defined, limited projects could yield excellent results, as much as if not more so than pursuing the will-o'-the-wisp of unlimited, poorly defined ambitions. "There is no need to add the frustration of sterility, the resentment for not finding oneself, to a line of work that is unhappy enough in itself" (5:9). In the end, what counts artistically and professionally is not what one intends but what one achieves. "What is important is not gratuitous imagination but real justification" (5:9).

Writing reports as a foreign correspondent, he carved a niche for himself in Barcelona's literary scene, resolving from the start some of the questions that plague, or at least ought to plague, the self-conscious writer. Who does one write for? In the 1920s Spain's cultural establishment was prone to answer along the lines of Juan Ramón Jiménez's dedication of his poetry "to the immense minority." Ortega y Gasset was busy asking for elites to hold back the pesky masses and his collaborators at *Revista de Occidente* were following the master's injunctions and developing a "dehumanized art." In Catalonia the *noucentistes*, though on a different theory, were nonetheless writing poetry for the few. Exquisitely turned out, as in Josep Carner's or Guerau de Liost's, but without connection to people's lives or problems. To that question, Pla replied: for as many readers as possible, for everyone. There simply weren't enough minorities, because the Catalan literary market was too small to support the literary coteries that prevailed in France, England, Germany, and other countries, where, as he pointed out, the respective minorities outnumbered the Catalan majority.

It was not only a question of demography but also of politics. Since 1715 Catalan had been proscribed from public life, with brief, intermittent periods during which the proscription was relaxed. At the time he was writing, Catalan was still excluded from public instruction, most media, and from the press, with a deleterious effect on people's ability to read or write in their own language. In these circumstances, he concluded that Catalan writers had an obligation "to create a literature for everyone, for the minority and the majority, with the highest dignity, underscoring the simplicity with which it is always possible to write a language, to go near the people" (26:195).

Pla knew that to reach the broadest audience he needed to write in a clear, comprehensible manner, in a tone familiar to the average person, as if he were conversing with them, and that he had to write about topics of immediate interest, practising the virtues of finitude and relevance for the present. All of these conditions could be fulfilled by journalism, and perhaps only in it. In *L'emprise*, Debray has written: "journalism has the providential talent of optimizing the resource by changing the defects of the reader into qualities of writing, and its own constraints (both internal and external, professional and commercial) into creative stimuli" (53). This is as close a description of Pla's achievement as is likely ever to be made. No matter that Debray did not know Pla or that Pla would hardly have appreciated an accolade from a Marxist writer. But there you are: unintended and yet a perfect assessment of Pla's goal. Since Catalan was banned from the press between 1939 and 1976, he resorted to writing in Spanish for the weekly *Destino* and for the dailies *El Correo Catalán* and *El Diario de Barcelona*, while he wrote books and prepared his Collected Works in Catalan, optimizing "the resource" by navigating around the Spanish government's language policies. In this way, by the end of his life he had become the most read Catalan author.

His betting on a reader-oriented literature of great simplicity at a time when the literary front was dominated by an aristocratic disposition to separate "real literature" from conversational language accessible to all proved prescient. Recently the distance between journalism and literature has been retrenching with the emergence of a rougher, more pressing fictional realism set by the media paradigm. Literature responds to the media's pressure the way painting did to photography. Challenged by the camera's unmatchable precision, painting veered towards the abstract or towards a photographically inspired hyperreality. Likewise, literary creation dug itself deeper in self-referentiality, wallowing in what Roland Barthes called "writerly texts" (10); or else adopted a journalistic style, mimicking the reporter's standpoint and even exploiting the periodical room to create the novel's reality effect. Where this effect was once predicated on psychological perceptiveness, it now hinges on the illusion that information is reality.

Journalism's reportorial style and directness penetrated American literature early on. And this literature influenced pre- and post-war French literature profoundly. Witness the Sartre of *Nausea*. Pla read Hemingway, but his models lay elsewhere: the Stendhal of the *Memoirs d'un tourist*, Boswell's *Life of Johnson*, and in general works devoted to the anecdotal and the commonplace: the stuff of life. Pla's partiality for the trivia that flesh out the structure of the present amounted to a choice of society. His ideal readership was modelled on the social gatherings he attended in cafés throughout the world and in Barcelona's Ateneu. The reciprocal influence between his books and his newspaper chronicles, the objective manner of the former and the carefully crafted style of the latter merit the term "literary journalism." Journalism is socially successful because it mediates between extraordinarily diverse and no longer synthesizable sources of significance and a readership that has no adequate understanding of most of those sources, be they science, politics, culture, or simply historical developments. Journalism casts a very broad net and fits the events it gets hold of into micro-narratives to create a sense of world available to all. Such reduction of complexity is eminently community forming, and this might explain the strange status of Pla's work as that which, more than any other, produces the illusion of being a complete account of a country. Indeed, it is impossible to obtain a general image of Catalonia's multifarious reality in language without having recourse to Pla's oeuvre.

Something like a "journalistic attitude" may well exist outside journalism, as Joseph Bensman and Robert Lilienfeld proposed in "Phenomenology of Journalism" (107). But it may just be that journalism is the triumphant expression of a passion best described as the desire for presence. Walter Benjamin characterized it as "the desire of contemporary masses to bring things 'closer' spatially and humanly, which is just as ardent as their bent towards overcoming the uniqueness of every reality by accepting its reproduction" (223). To replicate an object or experience is to detach it from its immediate circumstances and make it virtually omnipresent. Indeed, the media's highest achievement is to have generalized the willingness to accept abstractions as if they were experiences. But Pla's genius lay in overcoming the tendency to run after inflated words that contain nothing. He tried hard and often succeeded in recreating an object, a conversation, an event, a situation along with its circumstances, knowing that it was the circumstances that gave the quality of "presentness" to the object.

People's aspiration to be everywhere and experience everything used to be served by the journalist's pledge of having been where the action was. Commitment to truthful reporting was not only the press's point of honour but good business too, and the impression of truthfulness hinged on a newspaper's ability to guarantee first-hand reporting. This "compact" between a newspaper and its readership, broken today through the mediation of the news agencies, permitted Pla to begin his career as press correspondent in Paris. He was one among the last great generation of journalists who did not separate literature and journalism into different compartments, producing that rare flower in the readers' market: the literary chronicle. This rare plant was native to societies where cosmopolitanism coexisted with strong national

Figure 1. Members of the *penya* (discussion group) at Barcelona's Ateneu. Barcelona, 1921.

Photographer unknown. Courtesy of Fundació Josep Pla, coll. Col·legi de Periodistes.

Standing, from left to right: Vicenç Solé de Sojo, Antoni López Llausàs, Joaquim Muntaner, Joaquim Borralleras, Màrius Anglada. Seated: Josep Pla, Salvador Tayà, Josep Barbey

and local traditions and where journalists moved in and out of literary circles, measuring themselves and being measured by the standards of literary achievement in the national language. This was certainly the case in Paris, Vienna, or Berlin, as it was the case in Barcelona. At present the worldwide expansion of coverage in response to demand for around-the-clock news puts producers at the same distance from reality as their audiences. Today's pressroom is connected to online news agencies, which supply the materials that reporters will hammer into shape before they are distributed through news outlets. A few media groups can afford foreign correspondents to provide the pictures and the sound background necessary for the feel of authenticity in the global sensorama. These bites of visual and audio information are added to the comments or themselves commented on by experts after the digital editors have performed the necessary selecting, mixing, and cropping for maximal effect. In most cases the news is delivered by people who are as remote from the source as their audiences are. Today a journalist is no more than a ring in the media corporation's chain of transmission. The foreign correspondent who used to decide what was newsworthy, gathered information, and analysed it in situ, before wiring or telephoning the report to the office, is a figure of the past. It is probably disappearance of the foreign correspondent that affords us the necessary perspective to appreciate the craftsmanship and aesthetic significance of that kind of work considered as signature writing.

The anonymous feel of today's journalism, even when signed by the reporter or news analyst, is responsible for the somewhat nostalgic appeal to reclaim the aesthetic aspects of journalism in a critical mode, not just of the depersonalized journalism for mass consumption but of the world view it encourages. Alfredo Cramerotti's notion of aesthetic journalism is a plea for the role of artists not so much in delivering information as in penetrating the surface of appearance that journalism allegedly skims. His proposal rests on modern art's anti-mimetic development and is, ultimately, a critique of realist art, of which he considers journalism a distant relative. The affinity is undeniable. Thomas Connery has studied the genetic connection between journalism and realism in the rise of illustrated magazines (chapter 5 of *Journalism and Realism*). Cramerotti believes that traditional journalism is in crisis and aesthetic journalism, led by art, comes to the rescue by casting doubt on the world presented by the media and laying bare its status as a representation. His recipe is a version of the postmodern predilection for "the use of imagination, open-ended meaning and the individual interpretation of documents" (114).

Although this formula may resonate with some readers, it may fail to satisfy a mass audience's craving for easily digestible stories based on someone's ascertainable, i.e., falsifiable experience. The newspaper readers or evening news watchers who obtain their sense of reality in small capsules expect the media to honour the tacit covenant that news should not be open-ended but airtight. Twentieth-century journalists of the golden era of journalism knew how to combine a personal, that is, subjective approach with the impression of genuine experience that being on the scene contributed to their pledge to truthfulness. Pla was a master at blending a sceptical, self-effacing, relativistic attitude towards the truth with the techniques of *presencing*, giving a sense of reality to meetings that never took place or to events that he learned from other sources.

Cramerotti's plea for the fusion of information and imagination, of creativity and reporting, was fulfilled by some of the great journalists who stepped boldly outside of the strictures of witnessing and documenting, and have been criticized for it. By itself, though, the critical function of his "aesthetic journalism" could only have damaging consequences – for journalism, that is – unless corrected by a renewed pledge for objective mediation. It is not enough to point out that the mediated world is a representation; one must provide convincing reasons why a particular representation is inadequate and then try to replace it with a better one. But adequacy depends on the purpose for which something is put to use. And it seems that the purpose of the representations presented by the media is not to invite news consumers to let their private imaginations run wild but to momentarily stabilize a picture of the world for the convenience of societal decision making. That a representation can be checked and if necessary corrected through another representation is the reason freedom of the press is indispensable to a functioning democracy. Unhampered creativity in reporting through open-ended meaning, that is, the potential for semantic inflation, all too easily turns into propaganda. One might reply that this is the case only where a representation is presented as objectified truth, and that propaganda ceases to exist where reporting calls attention to its own perspectivalism. This would be right, of course, but then information is not all that newspaper readers and news channel watchers look for. The public seeks reassurance that a practical meaning is not only possible but is in fact dispensed daily by reliable agents. It seeks reassurance that the world is fundamentally comprehensible and that a specialized body of mediators discerns, encompasses, and makes sense of its upheavals.

Aesthetic journalism need not give up traditional journalism's realistic approximation to events or its contribution to a history of the present. These have always been journalism's defining attributes. Classic journalism differs from literature in not claiming the latter's licence to imagine, borrow, or transfer the data from which its creations emerge. Hemingway thought that the objective stance of newspaper reporting distorted human actions by refusing to go beyond their appearance. His remedy for this deficiency was "to use the creative imagination and the latitude allowed in art to present a picture that he believed penetrated more fully into the texture of life and probed more meaningfully into the psychology of human beings than anything that journalism's methods of picturing reality could attain" (Underwood 126–7). But recourse to the imagination to add psychological depth to his subjects is what distinguishes the fiction writer from the reporter. In the event, Hemingway was sparing of imagination and of psychological depth in his novels. His sharp, objective style, his refusal to peer into his characters' thoughts or feelings, and his preference for a sober description of their behaviour captured as if on camera; all these narrative traits that revolutionized literature in the 1930s were associated with the American style of writing (and rejected by European coteries, such as the *NRF*), but in fact they stemmed from journalism. Quick, confident strokes of the pen to sketch a situation through its essential aspects. A reality governed by an external viewpoint, by unuttered feelings, by abridged musings and vastly scaled-down or absent lyricism. By irony and sarcasm when applicable.

But the imagination may not be a relevant criterion to discriminate between these two kinds of writing. No less than poets or artists, journalists bring imagination into play. How could they ever render a scene vivid and convincing, if they did not flesh out an image and transmitted only the bare bones of the event? The difference lies in how they use the imagination. The journalist relies on it to select the facts that best fit his story among all the available ones. He condenses the story out of a nebula of details capable of cohering in any number of constellations. Typically, the plot is motivated by existing strictures of relevance. And these are defined by generic conventions: what counts as objectivity, impartiality, realism, or truth. The masters of journalism come face to face with the realities they report and painstakingly trace the historical and psychological relations that are to the event what cause is to effect in science. These journalists tread in the no-man's-land of aesthetic journalism, just as artists begin to report on reality as soon as they start dealing with facts that resist the prevailing formal arrangements. Writers like Ryszard Kapuscinski, Norman Mailer, and George Orwell – and, of course, Pla – were capable of laxity with the facts in exchange for poetic effect, but there is no question that they contributed a great deal to a history of the present. Sometimes labelled "literary journalists," they differed from other writers in rejecting the dilemma between interpreting the world and changing it.

These writers were committed to the here and now. Describing the present was for them a form of acting upon their times. As Richard Rorty said of Orwell, "[his] best novels will be widely read only as long as we describe the politics of the twentieth century as Orwell did" (169).

Rorty anticipated the fate not just of Orwell but of all literary journalism. Writing that is so univocally committed to the present trades survival for efficacy, and the choice is at once its burden and its glory. If critics give up the idea of timelessness as the ruling criterion of literary value and trade the yardstick of lasting fame for that of practical influence, if they renounce the prejudice which isolates books that elicit aesthetic pleasure from those that seek a moral reaction, there will be no longer any reason to exclude audience-dependent authors such as Pla from the literary canon.

I am not suggesting that style is unimportant or proposing to collapse all genres into *discourse*. Doug Underwood's hesitation to assign the category of "literary" to journalistic texts merits consideration. Could it be, asks Underwood, that we have lowered the standards for what counts as "literary" (189)? Or could it be that institutional changes in the study of literature and criticism have created the conditions for the acceptance of literary journalism as a line of study serving yet another special interest (Underwood 189)? This is certainly possible. The "high and low" strife of the 1980s in academic criticism, an extended form of the class struggle of the 1960s, was a conscious redrawing of the lines of literary merit, often with criteria that subverted the very notion of merit. Another possibility, though, is that the postmodern severance of text and meaning and the rejection of the idea of the self-enclosed text spelled the end of the categorical separation between literature and reporting that goes back, in the English language, to the middle decades of the nineteenth century (Hartsock 212).

Yet, despite their historical divergence, literary reportage does not differ substantially from literary narrative. In 1937, Edwin H. Ford pointed out: "The literary journalist sees news in relation to its human quality, its possibilities of showing people in the midst of life, a life that may seem comic, tragic, pathetic, farcical" (311). In the same period, Joseph North, editor of the *New Masses*, championed the artistic status of literary reportage, asserting that it could become durable literature. Reportage, he said, is three-dimensional reporting. "The writer not only condenses reality, he helps the reader feel the fact" (cit. Hartsock 241). That brief moment of convergence between journalism and literature (a moment that has its parallels in France in the journalistic background of Simenon's novels, in Joseph Roth's articles in Viennese and Berlin newspapers, in Dino Buzzati or in Giovannino Guareschi's in Italy, and in Pla's reporting from various places in Europe) was brought to an end by the dominance of the New Criticism and various types of formalism at the universities. But it continued to exist through the vigour and persistence with which, after that time and in extremely adverse circumstances, an exceptional writer like Pla continued to work towards completion of his literary ambition. In 1946, in the preface to the second edition of *Viatge a Catalunya,* he wrote: "The edition of this book pleases me because it could be, and I hope that it will be allowed to be, the beginning of the publication in Catalan of all my books" (*Viatge* 7). To be understood in the full strength of its ambition, this desideratum must be placed against its historical background. In 1946, after the defeat of the Axis powers in Europe and in the context of a new policy of rapprochement to the victorious democracies, the Spanish government was parsimoniously beginning to lift the ban on Catalan publishing. It did so as a token of liberality towards the hegemonic powers. This expedient benefitted only a meagre number of selectively chosen titles, mostly reprints of classics or, as in this case, travel books devoid of ideological implications. *Viatge a Catalunya* was Pla's first book to be printed in Catalan after the Spanish Civil War. At once he takes the opportunity to call readers' attention to the fact that all his works, even those published in Spanish, were originally written in Catalan and should therefore appear in this language. Unthinkable in the 1940s, but to express such programmatic desire must have exercised the censor's tolerance. At the time a preface like this was as good as a manifesto.

Underwood's concern that literary journalism could become yet another special interest within the fragmented literary disciplines should not be taken lightly. If it were to become a subfield of literary studies, journalism might contribute to levelling the field of judgment by putting the special interest before questions of literary merit. But there is no reason to fear this outcome if literary scholars subject literary journalism, or journalism *tout court,* to the same analytical standards they apply to other works. This would require evaluating the effectiveness of journalistic texts as texts, as renditions in language of whatever circumstances prompted their composition. In time, the circumstances melt away and are forgotten, while the texts remain. They alone are the cause and the object of the literary experience. Journalistic texts should certainly be studied in relation to their generic constraints but also to their capacity to move new readers in ways different from how they moved contemporaneous ones. This capacity for reasserting meaning in altered contexts is the time-tested guarantee of literary worth. It is a test that Pla's work has passed with flying colours, achieving recognition as the towering prose writer in the twentieth-century Catalan canon and pre-eminence in the various Iberian literatures. In English he remains largely undiscovered, due to the marginality of the Catalan language in Spain and the corresponding invisibility of its literature. A relative invisibility, however, in that the number of translations from this literature has been on the increase over the last two decades. Once the excavation of literary riches began, it was only a matter of time before Pla's oeuvre intrigued publishers and inspired translators. Publication of *The Gray Notebook* and *La vida amarga* (*Life Embitters*) and Peter Bush's intention to go on translating Pla bodes well for his induction into the ranks of world literature. An implicit criterion for the consolidation of a writer as a modern classic is the existence of critical support, the secondary underbrush that provides literary giants with the environment of reflection and ongoing attention that creates and maintains their relevance. Critical works are the equivalent of those ephemeral books that Pla considered necessary to fill the spaces between permanent works. "The binding of the works by great artists is accomplished by these ordinary books, these efforts that seem useless and lacking in importance" (5:470). He was referring to his own work in a book ostensibly motivated by actuality. Poets, on the other hand, consort with nobler themes. "Poets work only with lasting materials" (5:470). The irony is unmistakable, and yet Pla was earnestly self-effacing with regard to his own merits. He knew, however, that the journalism-versus-literature division was a false dilemma and a poor critical yardstick.

This book, the first on Pla to appear in English, aims to lay the groundwork for the reflective attention that binds the salient themes of an oeuvre as vast as Pla's. Its subject is unquestionably deserving of this attention on strictly literary terms, but beyond the wealth of experiences and the pleasures derived from acquaintance with a keen observer of various societies, an intelligent analyst of broad social movements, a superb describer of environments, and an ironic commentator of contemporary mores, Pla's work is significant as a paradigm of the epochal shift towards a re-evaluation of journalism as literature and as one of the most compelling instances of the literary construction of a country through detailed observation, searching memory, and stirring depiction.

2 Journalism on the High End

In the entry for 15 November 1919 that concludes *The Gray Notebook,* Josep Pla tersely announces that he is buying a suitcase that evening. Three days earlier he had been offered a position as foreign correspondent in Paris for the daily *La Publicidad*. The Catalan press had been reporting news from Paris for a long time, but in 1919 few Catalan newspapers could afford a special correspondent and often resorted to someone already in place to send reports from the City of Light. Some careers in journalism started this way. Agustí Calvet, managing editor of *La Vanguardia* until the Spanish Civil War, entered the newspaper business when, as a graduate student of philosophy in Paris, he wrote a handful of articles for *La Veu de Catalunya* before returning to Barcelona in December 1914 (*Tots els camins* 461). These articles prompted Miquel dels Sants Oliver, then editor of *La Vanguardia,* to commission Calvet to write a series of articles on his Parisian experience in the weeks following the declaration of hostilities. These articles were published as *Diario de un estudiante en París* (Diary of a student in Paris), one of the most brilliant accounts of Parisian life during mobilization and a work that, republished in book form in 1915, became one of the sharpest reflections on the splintering of European society in 1914. In his prologue to Calvet's book, Oliver observed that, with the war, "nothing from before was left standing, and as if to confirm the general upheaval, even the newspaper chronicle has undergone the most profound transformation" (*París, 1914* 13). Oliver describes the new policy of limiting the access of reporters to the theatre of war and, as a consequence, their need to fall back on the social repercussions of the conflict, or in other words, "on the human background against which the war unfolds" (*París, 1914* 14). The new attention to the "spiritual" (Oliver's adjective) aspects of the event –

attention to themes and features that journalists neglected in their more focused attention to the drama of war – announced a new style of journalism with a broader social scope and higher literary ambition.

Oliver not only published Calvet's *Diary* but sent him back to France as war correspondent for the duration of the conflict. It was a rare opportunity. In his history of *La Vanguardia*, Calvet, who early on adopted the pen name Gaziel, explained that, before the years of the Second Spanish Republic, the newspaper lacked "a network of well chosen correspondents residing in the main centers of world life – as free and authentic informers should be and in fact are – but was supplied with news by the mercenary and necessarily informal service of the largest agencies, which are called international although in truth they are all more or less controlled by the governments of the important countries that support them" (Gaziel, *Història de "La Vanguardia"* 57).

While not exceptional, an extended sojourn in Paris was a grand opportunity for a young Catalan of relatively modest background. Leaving aside the inaccuracy of the dates in his fictional diary – elsewhere Pla declares that he arrived in France on 26 April 1920, aged twenty-two (4:327) – Paris must have been as alluring to the young Pla as it was to the thousands of Americans who flocked there seeking to escape from the stifling atmosphere of Prohibition. By 1927 there were thirty-five thousand Americans in Paris, according to the police (Wickes 150). They constituted a colony. Undoubtedly, Paris acted as a magnet for writers and artists from many countries, but the American landing added a nuance to the colourful mix of artists, poets, long-term tourists, and bohemians. It brought a throng of real and improvised journalists, for whom, in the words of the managing editor of a Paris-American newspaper, a job in the press "was a passport to all the pleasures of Paris, an identification, however ephemeral for most, with a new generation of writers and artists" (cit. Weber 12). For most of these young people journalism was not an end in itself but a pretext to live in Paris and with some luck a passport to the higher call of a literary career. They saw themselves, in Ronald Weber's words, as "writers-in-waiting," enjoying life "in the setting of a magnificent city until the literary breakthrough came" (Weber 10). While they waited for it, they spent their time clustered in American circles. In his book on the American literary community in Paris, George Wickes says of its denizens: "Their contacts with the French were restricted mainly to waiters and shopkeepers. Since European life was not easy to penetrate, they generally

Figure 2. Josep Pla on the terrace of Barcelona's Ateneu shortly before his commission as press correspondent in Paris. Barcelona, 1919.

Photographer unknown. Courtesy of Fundació Josep Pla, coll. Josep Vergés.

stayed on the surface. Montparnasse, where the greatest number of them congregated, became an American village" (Wickes 150).

Along the Boulevard du Montparnasse, the Americans led a displaced national life, congregating in the sidewalk cafés, "where they read their American newspapers, received letters from home, and met other Americans who like themselves had little to occupy them besides an occasional trip to the Morgan Bank or American Express to cash a check" (Wickes 151). Their unofficial embassy was the Café Dôme, a "cathedral of American sophistication," in Sinclair Lewis's gibe ("Self-Conscious," qtd. Wickes 152). Shortly after arriving in Paris, Pla moved to Montparnasse in order, he says, to be closer to his Catalan friends (4:238). Although the number of Catalans in Paris was nowhere near that of Americans, there had been a floating Catalan community there since the turn of the century. It included artists like Picasso, Miró, and Dalí. In the pos-twar period, the traffic between Barcelona and Paris intensified. Pla begins the short story "Un home fatal" (A fatal man) with the assertion: "At the time I am speaking of – after the war of 1914 – there was a tendency among the well-to-do of this country to sojourn in Paris" (6:227). This indefinite sojourn was the counterstroke of the wartime influx of French refugees to Barcelona. As the French repatriated, pleasure-seeking Catalans followed in their train. Paris now looming larger on the horizon of the Catalan middle class, newspapers stepped up reporting from the Ville Lumière.

Pla does not seem to have much noticed the Americans, or the other way around. Such unawareness despite the physical and professional proximity is intriguing. He lodged on Rue Delambre, probably in the same hotel to which Harold Stearns retreated shortly before he began working for the *Herald* (Weber 28). Nor can an encounter with Hemingway at Lipp's, Pla's favourite brasserie, be ruled out (Hemingway 72–3). But if the two journalists exchanged casual glances there, they had no recollection of it when they met a decade later at the Madrid home of Rex Smith, the director of the Associated Press. By then Hemingway was already famous and displayed the signs of financial success. Thickset, tanned, and condescending, he embodied the role of the great writer. Not only was he indifferent to Pla's literature but seemed to ignore the fact that he was a writer at all. Hemingway was only concerned with Pla's opinion about his novels. Already in possession of the few ideas about Spain that he would entertain for the rest of his life, Hemingway could not understand Pla's apathy towards bullfighting or accept his opinion about Baroja's limited ability to construct novelistic plots. Pla must have felt slighted, since his recollection is steeped in polite irony ("Hemingway"). Earlier, when they might have met on more equal terms, their paths had veered away from each other not only on account of their national identities, but more importantly, of their different outlooks.

The Americans, self-enclosed and with their lives pivoting around New York, Chicago, and London, did not take notice of a young Catalan writing for an obscure Barcelona newspaper. For his part, Pla did not yet grasp the significance of the American presence at the heart of Europe or the changes in the local American press (Weber 32), a harbinger of the worldwide transformation of the media. But although unmindful of the Americans around him, Pla did notice their influence on the environment of Montparnasse. Comparing the two most popular cafés, he judged the Rotonde more cosmopolitan, its patronage subdivided into different national groups with the Russian-Polish element dominating. In contrast, the Dôme was "newer, more spruced up, with tiny corners – shall we say – more intimate, with more ambitious ladies whose looks were less from a department store, more Americanized" (4:241). And it did not escape him that the mixture of disillusion and nostalgia perceptible in these cafés attracted a wealthy clientele (4:240), adding a layer of self-conscious bohemianism.

Whether or not Paris was "the center of the American literary world" in the twenties (Wickes 160), it certainly was "the center of American journalism in Europe," as Vincent Sheean, one of the aspiring young journalists of that period, called it (Weber 5). But even with venues like the *Paris Times*, the European edition of the *Chicago Tribune*, and the European edition of the *New York Herald* abetting the "exodus of the young American writing class to Paris," in Ford Madox Ford's expression (cit. Weber 13), getting literary credit was hardly guaranteed. Only a small fraction of aspirants achieved literary success during or after their Paris years. Like Jake Barnes, the character in Hemingway's novel *The Sun Also Rises*, most remained stuck in newspaper work. Still, Paris was reputed to be the shortest route from journalism to literary glory. "In that city, in those days," writes Weber, "the pathway from journalism to literature seemed obvious and accessible, as perhaps it never would again with quite the same compelling clarity" (Weber 12). Barnes, whose real-life model Stearns is supposed to have been, embodied the fate Hemingway was determined to avoid. For a short time, it did not seem a bad fate. The debased franc made living in Paris attractive, as Hemingway reported in the *Toronto Star*: "Paris in the winter is rainy, cold, beautiful and cheap. It is also noisy, jostling, crowded and cheap. It is anything you want – and cheap" (cit. Weber 5).

Pla, who was Hemingway's senior by two years, also basked in the interim affluence brought by the post-war depression of the French currency. Later he would trace his lifelong dependence on journalism to the favourable exchange rate in those years: "In this sense, I am somehow a product of the value of our currency between the first general war and our civil war" (6:7–8). Like Hemingway, he nursed literary hopes, but the exiguous opportunities for gain in the Catalan literary market made it hard to renounce the paltry security of a journalism job. In the preface to *La vida amarga*, a collection of short stories compiled in later years, he confessed:

> This is a book of narrative literature, which is the literature I would have liked to cultivate if I had not devoted myself to journalism. In other words, if the anguishing dispersion of journalism had allowed it. But it was not possible. The problem of knowing if I would have had any skill for narrative is, of course, moot. The interest, the taste for this kind of literature, I felt them. But this means so little! I count myself among those who believe that every position, let us say literary, originates in a personal capacity for intuition of external reality aided by a long, permanent, unending experience of observation, memory, and work. What I lacked was the time that people consider unproductive. (6:7)

Pla's lack of unproductive time was inextricable from the urgencies of the daily article. Even so, he managed to publish a number of books, which it would be wrong to consider mere by-products of his journalistic practice. Above all, he took the newspaper article to a new level of virtuosity. Combining information with reflection, Pla resolved the dichotomy between journalism and literature and produced a hybrid of the article and the essay. In the process he developed a characteristic style as influential on the future of Catalan prose as Hemingway's was for the American. Comparing the two writers may seem fanciful to readers who have never heard of Pla. Where is the sense of weighing on the same scale a Nobel Prize winner and a seldom translated columnist, bookkeeper of the quintessentially fleeting event? And yet, Pla's writing endures beyond the momentary contingency, while so much of Hemingway has aged along with the adolescent values once associated with his crusty, mannish repartee.

When the patina of juvenile blustering falls off, what remains of Hemingway's literary accomplishment is intellectually thin. He was a writer of attitude rather than observation, and when the attitude lost its freshness and appeal, the fictional world he had created became two-dimensional and flat. *A Moveable Feast*, his account of his time in Paris, shows him skimming French life, reading English books borrowed from Sylvia Beach or bought from used-book stalls, noticing little beyond the circle of American émigrés, and showing no curiosity for the social, political, and literary wealth of a city that Paul Valéry, a rising star at the time, described in *Monsieur Teste* as a "cloud of words," in which "a thousand titles of works *per second* appeared and perished indistinctly" (Valéry 81). Pla, on the other hand, from the moment he obtained his accreditation from the Maison de la Presse, plunged into Parisian life, making the city come alive for his readers in a prodigious display of observation and intelligent evaluation. As a member of a society that looked to Paris for intellectual and artistic cues, he had brought a cultural baggage that included a good deal of French literature and political history. But it was above all his privileging "the intuition of external reality" that allowed him to write articles on French contemporary life with extraordinary crispness and perspicuity. No American journalist was able to write on French culture with such intimacy before Herbert R. Lottman's *The Left Bank*, a book that nonetheless falls short of the breadth, entertainment quality, and wit of Pla's *Sobre París i França*.

Pla's oeuvre poses insistently the question about the relation between journalism and literature – a relation that in the 1920s was formulated in terms of means to end, or more precisely, of indulgence versus sublimation. It is the question about the management of a tension between modalities of writing that were considered not just different but incompatible. It is thus the question of genres with very distinct, even mutually exclusive categories of decorum. From its inception in the eighteenth century, journalism was considered a careless sort of writing, mass produced for quick consumption and instant forgetting. Who would, under those conditions, devote time and intellectual energy to the production of style? If the goal is to crank out "readerly" texts (in Roland Barthes's structuralist terminology) for immediate use and to renew a constantly depleted actuality, then Pla's concern with the *mot juste*, or more precisely the *adjectif juste*, was a waste of time, and his criterion of descriptive "adjustment" incongruent with the medium's demand for transparency.

Pla's uncompromising search for intelligibility and his defence of the classic as a remedy for, as he saw it, the frivolity of interwar experimentation would seem to run up against Barthes's notion of the "writerly." But Pla's conception of the writer's unending struggle for the right adjective turns him into a partisan of the "writerly." Of a "writerly" mode that is far from the structuralist activation of analytical codes or the post-structuralist dance of the signifiers but is nonetheless engaged with the fluidity of the world as it manifests itself in the lifelong "accumulation of pages of a vast intimate diary" (6:8). A personal "diary," furthermore, that Pla refused to consider accomplished or finished. Nothing could be farther from a "product" than this work in progress, which he regarded as a necessary by-product of the unsystematic business of living. In Pla's self-diagnosed "devilish mania of writing," a compulsion to which no sacrifice was too big or too costly (1:451), Barthes would have recognized the "we in the process of writing" of the writerly text (Barthes 11). And we should note that in Catalan the term "diari" means both "diary" and "newspaper." Pla was in effect describing his writing as a personal notation indistinguishable from an intimate appropriation of the newspaper.

It is remarkable how quickly structuralism, which once held the promise of systematic literary criticism, has aged while Pla's texts, which belong to the typology of the personally observational, retain their freshness. Furthermore, if Barthes's scholastic language can be invoked in this regard, it is through Pla's ironic treatment of the "readerly" quality commonly attributed to his texts. Pla's programmatic clarity is deceptively consumable or digestible, rendering inoperative the structural opposition whereby Barthes claimed that linguistics hierarchized literary texts through the dominance of denotation over connotation in the sign (Barthes 13). The fact is worth pointing out, for, in spite of enormous differences in background and temperament, these two magicians of language were equally impatient with the closure of discourse, equally detested the reflex assembling of words, the commonplace dictated by the routines of thinking. Pla's oeuvre is about Pla reflecting on the act of writing, on the social forces that pushed him along the path of *écriture* and limited his professional elbow room, on the personal and collective limitations, and on the reflective "we in the process of writing," which in Pla is never majestic but deceptively unassuming. "I have never been anything but a vulgar journalist. Do not think that I have made an unheard of, extraordinary effort. I have always worked because I believed that this was the only way to kill time and fight the tedium and boredom that has overtaken us all" ("La meva literatura" 44:287). And yet this disarming disclaimer implies a concept of literature as *jouissance,* as play to capture the attention of the public that was available to him in his language. This intrinsic limitation led him to produce a form of writing that mimicked everyday communication and to affirm a seemingly naive metaphysics of representation.

Obviously, the conventions of journalism – reporting objective facts or events in univocal language, the precedence of denotation over connotation, the generalization and availability of the communicative codes – had a great deal to do with Pla's choice of style. We may doubt the accuracy of the statement, "I had to do the literature that goes with my temperament and I have done no other" (44:286), wondering if he came to believe it long after this form of writing had become second nature to him. We have reason to suspect his exaggerated modesty, his repeated claim that "all I have written is vulgar, mundane, insignificant" (44:286), without necessarily dismissing his self-evaluation as "a conscious, convinced realist" (44:286). We may accept his declaration of intentionality, as when he asserts: "I owe this tendency not to spontaneity of let us say physical character, but because I have pondered it" (44:286). This is not an avowal of his adherence to an outdated naturalism but a function of his revolt against the rhetoric of the blatantly literary. It is his way of resolving the divorce between reader and writer in the traditional economy of the literary institution. But instead of challenging the "inactive" reader to complete the text's potentially infinite semantic curve, Pla opts to provide a painless "readerly" experience. Yet deference towards the *referendum* does not imply opting for a facile construction of the text: "I have tried to do something that people could read without real, excessive pain. I have never been part of any coterie devoted to verbal facility" (44:287).

Pla's connotative parsimony, far from emanating from a subjectivity that precedes the text, concerns a subject that is engaged in the interminable exercise of translating a hyperconnoted reality into the stability of a signifying system. This reductive effort, like any phenomenological description, grounds the subject in the endeavour to isolate the essence of experience. He believed that literature had fallen under the empire of the verbal and oratorical and tried to erase the mark of "literariness" from his texts in the name of a conversational style that, for lack of a better term, he called "realism." But this style was realistic only in the sense of linking language to a world of presences, of things, whose existence stimulated the production of discourse. "This realism, which I have always defended and practised, has been very contested. People have argued that realism cannot be realized in its rawness but must be poetized. I will not be the one to oppose it. But in fact, personally, I have been unable to poetize. Had I known how to do it, I would have been a tolerable writer. Now I am an insignificant writer" (44:286–7). He vindicates realism without *poiesis*, a type of text without the imprimatur of the literary institution. The insignificance of his stake in the republic of letters is ironic only in part. There is no false modesty in his self-description. Rather, it fits his deflation of the idea of literature as a structure of meaning that replaces experience.

As ongoing addition of pages of a vast intimate diary, writing is not a galaxy of signifiers (Barthes 12), which would still procure an illusion of permanence through fixed stars, but dust from a spent meteorite. He calls the accumulation of pages in his oeuvre, "some reminiscences of life's cinders" (6:8). Not even a residue but a trace of what remains of a spent life. As a trace of experience evoked by an "I" that is constituted in and by the act of writing, literature is as unsubstantial as an image. Writing is a vain attempt to stem the flow of life, fixing it in the imagination as it was seen at a precise point in time. It is a relation of language to the phenomenon, of consciousness to the unconscious. From their incommensurability arises the oft-repeated warning about the futility of representation. Pla had only disdain for the avant-garde's iconoclasm. Having pledged to communicate information, journalism can engage either naively or self-consciously in this task. In the former case, it will look at the world as an object and at language as a vehicle that faithfully conveys the form the world takes at any given time, calling the language/object correlation "information." In the latter case, it produces second-degree observations, by which I mean observations that take into account not only the things observed but also the act and conditions of the observation.

Pla belongs to this second species of journalists who are aware of the instability of things and the caducity of representations: "By reason of chronology and coherence, that is to say, in deference to the modifications that time impresses on things, it is especially necessary to clarify one thing. These writings are from a specific epoch and the landscapes, especially the urban landscapes, which constitute the background of some of these stories, have changed considerably" (6:9). The point is not that every representation needs to consider the situation of the subject, but that it has to question the permanence of the object. "Realism" is not for Pla naive positivism. His idea of the landscape is not inducted from an incomplete collection of "facts"; rather, it gathers significations in an assembly that is itself significant, that is, points to other realities: human, economic, historical. Realism is for him life that is conscious of itself and links up with the world through this self-consciousness. Heidegger thought that human reality (Dasein) and world are inextricable. Pla believed that a conscious being is necessarily intentional. Its existential awareness consists in being projected onto the world. Only then can an authentic representation arise: "For an artist, for a man who aspires to accomplish something in this world, consciousness of this fact [of being alive] is of the essence. If one does not have it, deviations are inevitable, because literature, in the worst sense of the word, changes the real world into a cardboard world" (14:90).

It is unlikely that Pla read much professional philosophy. In *The Gray Notebook,* in the entry for 6 May 1918, he praises an essay on Kierkegaard published by Joan Estelrich in *La Revista* as a novelty in the climate of superannuated Thomism on the right and positivism on the left. The reference to Kierkegaard as surveyor of a "vast and mysterious terra incognita" (1:159) serves to validate his own "existentialist" enterprise by means of a prestigious precedent. Many years later, in a literary portrait of Estelrich, Pla confessed that at the time he did not know who Kierkegaard was (11:483). It would be pure speculation to assert that this essay prompted Pla to read the Danish philosopher. He might have waited until the Kierkegaard renaissance of the post-war period to become directly acquainted with the existentialist thinker. It was then, as he says, "that the Danish existentialist obtained universal fame" (11:483). In any case, long before he redacted *The Gray Notebook.*

What interests Pla in Kierkegaard is, fundamentally, the personal nature of his thought, best represented in his *Journal,* which is, not coincidentally, the genre Pla adopts at the pretended start of his career. "In philosophy wordplay produces a progressive general dissatisfaction. The only way to bring philosophy back to its authenticity is to make it sojourn for some time in the purgatory of the personal confession, the subjective note, the private diary" (1:59). In this undertaking, the ultimate referent is Montaigne, whose scepticism towards the philosophical schools and concern with everyday experience caused him to be ignored by professional philosophers after 1650. Montaigne's *Essais* carried on the scepticism of Sextus Empiricus, who set forth the classic ideas of the sceptics, according to which nothing can be known with absolute certainty, and to claim doctrinal superiority amounts to foolhardy arrogance. Readers of Pla will recognize these insights in his blunt dismissal of abstract universality and his frequent disclaimer of intellectual self-confidence. Pla in fact belongs in the rare group of twentieth century writers who, in a considered and deliberate manner, articulate in their work a critique of the foundationalist line of thinking that, beginning with Descartes, has been responsible for the dominance of theory at the expense of sensory experience, of what Stephen Toulmin calls "the World of

Where and When, a world in which everything we say refers to a particular time and place, without claiming any abstract, universal validity" (192).

As a citizen of that world, Pla sought to correct the imbalance that caused European thought to favour the generalizing, logocentric, and theoretical over the practical, situated, and experiential. As a writer, he knew that the latter posed the highest challenge, causing him "to run against the limits of language," in Wittgenstein's phrase (Toulmin 196). Pla implemented in a practical, non-theoretical way Husserl's task for twentieth-century philosophy: "to go back to things themselves" (168). Although Pla does not seem aware of the existence of Husserl and never resorts to technical language, but, on the contrary, professes "incapacity to understand metaphysics" (11:508–9), his sustained reflection on the relation between writing and the objects he writes about justifies our recourse to academic shorthand. A phenomenological approach is appropriate to describe his abiding emphasis on perception, if for no other reason than because this philosophical method was contemporaneous with his career and its radiation could have reached him through more popular channels. Rightly or wrongly, phenomenology was considered relevant to the writing of authors like Hemingway or Camus, who also started out as journalists, because they reduced the profuse worlds of naturalism to a laconic description of appearances (Hemingway) or the stark impression of the external world upon a consciousness (Camus in *L'étranger*). Pla would have nothing to do with the postmodern waltz of signifiers, a distortion of phenomenology's distinction between facts and phenomena that semiotics translated into the dichotomy of signifier and signified. In the nuclear splitting of the sign, the signifier is the side that looks towards consciousness, while the signified points to the elusive *referendum*, the impossible to intuit thing-in-itself. For Pla the thing is never an essence, but a synthesis of impressions that can be inspected through a self-conscious act. Phenomenology performs its famous reduction in order to isolate the essence of phenomena through eidetic intuition. It is through the essence that the primary observer identifies and organizes empirical facts. Obviously, the eidetic reduction is not a spontaneous operation of the mind, and at the limit it is impossible. But neither is writing spontaneous, much less writing that becomes aware of itself by meeting with resistance in the transaction between the repertory of available words and

Figure 3. Josep Pla at his farmhouse. Llofriu, 1972.

Photographer: Lluís Maimí. Courtesy of Fundació Josep Pla, coll. Alsius and Juriol Family

the objects from which consciousness abstracts in order to identify their essences.

On his own account, writing did not come easily to Pla. This is doubtful in view of his manuscripts, in which tight rows of regular handwriting run on the page virtually free of corrections. Pla blamed language's parsimony for his smoking habit. He would roll a cigarette whenever he needed time to turn over the words in his mind. To this ritual he added a great consumption of matches expended to relight cigarettes that had gone out while he was searching for the right adjective (35:313). He believed that the adjective was the key to good writing and its elusiveness constituted a text's "writerly" quality:

> In literature there is a basic, extremely difficult problem: finding the adjective. To qualify the nouns, to place after the noun the adjective that corresponds to it cannot be done casually, haphazardly, frivolously. One must first observe and ponder […] The adjective must be, first of all, intelligible and clear, and then, if possible, precise. Is it possible to do this without previously observing things? Sometimes the adjective appears right away; sometimes more slowly, sometimes never. In the things of life I have always been quite tolerant; with the adjectives I would never be. […] In my opinion this is the great problem of literature: the adjective. (35:53)

Accurate description was the greatest challenge: "It is almost certain that the hardest task in the writing profession is to choose the adjective" ("L'adjectivació" 44:291). The reason for this exertion is that the adjective is not intuitive. Since it is not available to empirical scrutiny, finding it requires the reduction of spontaneous perception (as such still non-significant) to reflected thought. Consciousness acts through various operations (intentionality, recollection, recourse to a stock of images, delay) that redirect attention from the external object to the object of consciousness. After this reduction is performed, the essence of the thing is distilled into the adjective. "The adjective in a phrase is immutable: the masculine, the feminine, the neutral. The noun perhaps even more so. But then, if the idea is to formulate some literary paper, the phrase must have its adjectives. To choose the adjective is very difficult. It implies many things: observation, memory, knowledge, patience … if the aim is to fight gibberish" ("L'adjectivació" 44:291).

He insists: there is nothing spontaneous about finding the adjective. On the contrary, the right adjective, the one that reveals the essence of the thing, only appears – if at all – at the end of an *époché*. The reduction starts by suspending the extemporaneous adjective of unreflected perception and then waiting for the emergence of the reflected description of the thing:

> The reader sometimes thinks that an acceptable adjective comes from speed, from the mental flash. I said it a moment ago: I drop the intuitive adjective, which sometimes, not often, turns up. I believe instead that it comes slowly, through observation and patience, through what some friends call a waste of time. (44:294)

The right adjective can be slow in coming and may never turn up. "One can produce books of great volume, well written, clear, fast, and not find any adjective perfectly suited to a given noun. Problem! This work, no matter how big it may be, will soon be forgotten" (35:308–9). A writer does not always succeed, and his adjectives may fall short of the object they are meant to present to the reader's intuition. Apropos a poem about fish by the Baroque poet Francesc Vicent Garcia i Torres, better known as Rector de Vallfogona, Pla observes that the poem's fish inventory contains three types of adjectives: "the totally gratuitous, the loose, the precise" (2:33). Pla is interested only in the third type. The honest writer does not hold reality hostage to the imagination. He must not think deductively but should only describe, and what he describes are the syntheses resulting from a sober observation. "To write means to describe, with the utmost possible intelligibility. I think that this way is the most difficult and complicated" (44:295). His aim is to make things intelligible to the senses, graspable in their qualitative presence.

Kant ascribed to the concept the role of assisting the synthesis of the data of intuition. But a concept may not correspond a priori to the features of the object, and without some correspondence it remains uselessly abstract or false. For the synthesis to occur something must mediate between consciousness and the sense data. And for the mediation to succeed, it must share equally in the incongruent faculties of the understanding and intuition. In the *Critique of Pure Reason* Kant says that this third element must be something like a "sensible" concept of an object and that it "must be homogeneous with the category, on the one hand, and with the appearance, on the other hand" (Lohmar 99). He calls this mediating element a schema. At the boundary between the concept and the phenomenon, the schemata bridge the gap between the purely discursive concept of a thing and its sensible features. If we turn from perception to description, we find that what mediates between the discursive concept of a thing and its appearance is attribution. Insofar as attribution emanates from the thing *and* from the observer, it either validates or refutes the correspondence between the category and the senses. And this is the reason why, without being a Kantian, Pla thinks of the adjective as the correspondence between an otherwise abstract discourse and a mediated representation of the external world. By eschewing routine associations, the surprising adjective refreshes the senses with clues to a relevance that is both of language and transcends it. Adjectives such as "[air] the colour of the wing of a fly" (3:450), "the bleary, slimy light of Barcelona's moon" (3:334), "vowels that resemble moist moss" (6:422), "a half-baked face" (17:185), "vice looked bloodless and white like the wall" (4:620) wrap the objects through sensuous intuition that clings to the mind. Josep Maria Castellet has studied Pla's use of adjectives, emphasizing their chromatic wealth, but also his use of synaesthesia in "the winds have their own colour" (20:106) and various other rhetorical practices. There is no point in repeating his exhaustive analysis, but it is worth mentioning his understanding that by this means the author aims to produce not so much a literary as a cognitive effect. Pla describes by linguistically processing sensory data in order to discover the world. "Without the category of discovery or revelation of the world, the importance of Pla's prose, despite the high level of its style, would not have the value we credit it with" (Castellet, "Aspectes estilístics de Josep Pla" 464 and *Josep Pla o la raó narrativa* 134).

But the attribution of qualities has nothing to do with regressing to an analogical understanding of reality. The world is not held together with ideal glue, and, rigorously speaking, things are not resemblances of other things. When Pla says that the phonology of certain vowels has the tactile properties of wet moss, he is merely evoking a sensory memory. The sensual concept "wet moss" mediates between an internal state of awareness and the intuition of an object of perception that in this case happens to be an audible event. For Pla to describe is not simply to compare: "Some writers choose the adjective by analogy. It is a facile method. They say that this man is shrill and early like a rooster, and that young lady a nymph from a Greek fountain. It is all bogus" (44:295). He not only eschews the trite description anticipated by semi-learned usage; he also rejects imagination as the criterion for choosing the adjective. The arbiter of style can only be a rigorous description of perception uncluttered of mental additives. "What one sees with one's own eyes must be established. Not all writers think so. They believe that they will have many more readers if they engage in a crazy use of adjectives and in madness" (44:295). An arbitrary adjective, not originating in the correspondence between the noumenon and the phenomenon, between the mental synthesis and the transcendent thing, will not serve to discover reality. Nor will the metonymic transference of a property help to establish the essence, which for Pla, as for phenomenology, consists in the appearance of a thing. "Thinking about the sinister adjective 'black,' which we apply to a specific kind of wine in our country, it is almost certain that the adjective comes from the darkness of the bottle in which this wine is kept. Thus, the application of the adjective must originate in our ancestral mental drowsiness" (22:454).

The search for the revealing adjective has little to do with poetic intent. It stems from a passion for objectivity that can be traced to Pla's lifelong acculturation to the newspaper medium. His insistence on the objective conditions of writing dispels any notion of lyricism. Even when the style sparkles with the rare or unexpected adjective, it would be misleading to present his prose as a synthesis of poetry and materialism (Carbonell 23). The word "synthesis" indeed accounts for what is going on in Pla's choice of descriptors, but it is not essentially a function of style. It has deeper philosophical motivations. His style emerges from his determination to produce a record of the world as he experienced it. At the most one could say, taking him at his own word, that he saw the world in the form of newspaper articles (8:20). Literature is not a pleasing and ultimately gratuitous aesthetic activity but a means to produce reminiscences of experiences – "memories of feelings or of objective things" (35:309). It does not produce the things or the feelings themselves, which are inaccessible to a differently situated observer, but processed impressions of those things. This is how the term "reminiscence" ought to be understood. The reminiscence of a thing or a feeling is its internalized form, its schema, and it is this cognitive, rather than aesthetic or emotive function that Pla's "reporting" strives to satisfy. We can only define this approach as journalistic, but journalism that is self-conscious and rigorous to an eminent degree.

For a journalist self-consciousness should not mean self-neutralization in pursuit of a factitious objectivity, but acknowledging one's situation as the medium through which the world is apprehended and reported. "A writer's first obligation is to observe, narrate, manifest the epoch in which he finds himself. This is infinitely more important than the useless and barren attempts to attain a savage and primordial originality. Literature is the reflection of a specific society at a specific time" (6:8). Reflection theory has had a bad press since the decline of Marxist aesthetics. It was Lenin's basic concept in support of materialistic epistemology. In *Materialism and Empirio-Criticism*, Lenin claimed that "all matter possesses a property, essentially related to sensation, the property of reflection" (Katvan 88). Lenin needed to explain the emergence of consciousness from a purely materialistic conception and so he endowed matter with the attribute of reflection, which is the equivalent of a God in the machine. Soviet philosophy, for the most part, followed him dogmatically.

Pla, whose reference is not Lenin but the nineteenth-century literary historian Francesco De Sanctis, merely adopts social reflection theory in the sense that one aspect of society, in this case the production of literary works, broadly corresponds to the entire form of the society from which it arises. For a journalist this assumption is basic. How could "reporting" make sense otherwise? The discrete story is relevant because of the implicit assumption that it reveals something about the society in which it arises or the momentary condition of the world, that it is symptomatic of a trend or announces broad changes. News coverage is not about isolated occurrences but about the shaping of history in the present. Even so, Pla does not assume that literary production is determined by another social agency, be it an institution, a different profession, or a social class; nor does he assume the existence of a causal link between a privileged aspect of society (the base level) and a secondary one (the superstructure). He merely asserts his conviction that literature is an endless undertaking to capture the "image" of the entire historical moment as observed by a consciousness whose "reflection" is far from reflexive and whose precision cannot be taken for granted.

"My position in journalism led me to something that, if I could, I would recommend to the people of the same profession: I have not written anything for publication that is not intensely observed, thought, and meditated" (32:618). Observation and reflection prepare the synthesis of impressions that writing achieves. The synthesis takes place through a reduction of the perceptual complexity by means of the "sensible concept," that is, through the mediation between mind and world. Once the mediation has been tapped, writing flows unobstructed from the rock of intuition. "When you have long observed and thought about an object, a story, you write quickly: all that is superfluous and useless is completely discarded. The pen should not be able to follow your thought. This is the problem. It is difficult. But it is perhaps the only way" (35:89). Journalism turns this process into an everyday occupation, since its materials are precisely the everyday:

> Journalism is a profession that, when practised in good faith and normally, is overwhelmingly hard and exhausting. It is a profession tied to human life as it happens, daily, extremely vulgar and without style. It is the perennially flowing magma, a profession that admits of no pedantry or internal bragging. It is the stream of life offered in the form most ignored and always gropingly. (35:182)

The conditions under which a Catalan journalist laboured in the 1920s were denounced by Joan Puig i Ferreter in his novel *Servitud*. The title already expresses the demeaning conditions under which the fledgling journalist must work in the office of a fictitious, yet perfectly recognizable, Barcelona daily. In the passage just quoted, Pla seems to reflect on his profession's hostility to anything like stylistic or conceptual refinement. Journalism is brute life, captured at the source and without the possibility of formally elaborating it. Yet, by adopting a humble stance towards his profession, Pla turned Marcel Proust's low opinion of it on its head. In a famous passage in *Swann's Way,* Swann objects to his aunt's taking pleasure in the newspapers: "The fault I find with our journalism is that it forces us to take an interest in some fresh triviality or other every day, whereas only three or four books in a lifetime give us anything that is of real importance" (27). Things of real importance (the original says "essential things," as opposed to "insignificant things," 26) are here opposed to the passing flow of events, the micro changes that constitute the prose of the world.

Surely, this is Swann's opinion, and the narrator makes it clear that, in his effort not to appear pedantic, Swan is in fact being so (26). Nonetheless, as Michael Finn points out, journalism stands for unauthentic writing in *A la recherche du temps perdu* (Finn 119). This may be Proust's way of getting even with his own journalistic involvement as a writer of society notes, but granted the divergence of method and intent between those ad hoc writings and his masterpiece, nothing could be farther from Pascal's *Pensées* (Swann's example of essential reading) than the flood of trivia and everyday impressions making up *A la recherche du temps perdu.* Unlike Swann, Pla refused to associate inauthenticity to the everyday. On the contrary, he suggests that the flow of incident, observation, and recollection in his own "*chronique-fleuve*" is only possible through the writer's immanence in the world. "When one's spirit and body are bound inseparably with human life and with the life of things, it is very difficult to exit from this exceedingly vast, indescribable prose" (35:183).

In the passage referenced above, Swann distinguishes between information and publicity and speaks about the need to arrive at the right balance between the two (27). Josep Maria Casasús has spoken about the separation between "facts" and "commentary," or "facts" and "ideas," as the principle on which the new journalism of the twentieth century was beginning to operate when Pla was initiated into the profession. According to Casasús, Pla would have received this principle from his mentor Josep Miró i Folguera, chief editor of *Las Noticias,* and internalized it (124). Pla has in fact reported his mentor's advice: "The company is not interested in the shall we say transcendental significance of the news. It is interested in the raw, real, tangible, concrete, heavy, materialized and definitive fact. This can keep you quite busy, because it is a task from which you must deliberately exclude all gracefulness, all fantasy, all feeling. No feelings! Neither ideas nor feelings!" (11:565). But what stands out in this recollection, articulated in Pla's recognizable style – so that one could say he is ventriloquizing a phantom and projecting his current opinion back in time – is not so much the enthronement of absolute facts as the reduction of phenomena to their schemata, an operation that "requires quite a bit of work" because it involves the exclusion of everything that is not of the essence, the distillation of phenomena into "news."

Pla expresses negatively, as subtraction of the intellectual and sentimental surcharge of events, the journalist's role in transforming Swann's "insignificant things" into "essential things." Signification becomes a paradoxical function of language, proceeding by elimination through the double negative of removing "insignificance" from things. The removal takes place by means of signs, that is, vectors that redirect the non-significant episodes of raw life to their verbal essence through the mediation of the journalistic article. The present, as the quarry from which the journalist extracts his materials, is "insignificant" by definition. Pla speaks about "the obsession with the rowdy, insignificant present" (8:20). The journalist – unlike the speculative philosopher or the historian rummaging in the storeroom of the past – is fascinated by the rumblings of ongoing creation. The volatility of half-baked occurrences and uncertain trends engages his attention and challenges his ability to give the present a meaning that tallies with experience, not just his own but also that of his readers. Only, in removing sentiments and ideas from his report, the journalist takes care not to subtract the circumstances attending on the phenomenon. Quite the opposite, the circumstances are for him the essence of events.

This penchant for description, so intimately linked to the journalist's need to capture and retain the reader's attention, inspired what we might call Pla's "aesthetic theory." Ennui is, according to him, the prime motivation for reading; hence, writing is a form of entertainment, and excellent writing entertains best. If Catalan literature is weak, he says, it is because writers never tried to amuse their readers. "We must break the notion that authentic Catalan literature cannot reverberate outside very limited minority milieus" (35:171–2). Challenging the dominant elitism had momentous consequences for Catalan literature, helping promote a canon considerably different from the one in force when Pla came literarily of age. Near the end of his life he traced his genealogy to the prose writers who had practised reportage: "To write in prose is more difficult than having the talent of knowing how to make two words rhyme. As prose writers, I greatly admire Verdaguer, Maragall, and Mr Ruyra" (44:289). This meant, in effect, the articulation of a literary style that was influenced by journalism. Drawing on a much-abused concept, it is possible to see in Pla's style the emergence of a hybrid form of writing. But his prose is not so much an example of discursive promiscuity as a response to the requirements of his audience. He claims that he moulded his style to promote the readership necessary for cultural continuity. "I have done what seemed to me most urgent: an easy, clear, intelligible, everyday literature" (44:289). The goal was to facilitate the habituation of people to the use of Catalan. This was necessary because the language, and everything that hinged on it, had been stunted by repeated attempts to eradicate it, the last and most brutal of which had taken place during the Franco regime that spanned the greater part of Pla's professional life. "Continuation! This is the great problem. I say this in the bloodiest, most demented century of the Christian era, which is the twentieth century. Do not ever forget it" (44:289).

But the modesty that Pla cultivated in his public persona should not deceive us. He was aware of the difficulty of writing sentences that ring true. And he knew that under modern conditions, literature – all the more so a literature that is politically besieged and demographically constrained – cannot subsist as the pursuit of rarified minorities, but must furnish mundane reading to the masses whose literacy is moulded by the daily consumption of news. When he commends the poet Vicent Andrés Estellés, a journalist and chief editor of the daily *Las Provincias*, Pla hints at the new symbiosis between journalism and time-honoured literary convention, such as writing in verse: "Mr Estellés has imported his professional journalism into excellent literary forms, of a complex and poetic realism" (35:182). But beyond establishing his own criteria of excellence, with journalism as the substantial and versification the incidental parts of Estellés's formula – "He is a huge prose writer (journalist) who writes in verse" (35:182) – Pla discloses his own agenda in this passage: winning for journalism the recognition of literary excellence when it achieves a complex, self-aware realism whose poetic quality does not stem from lyricism but from the laboured transparency of the prose.

For Pla Paris was not the shortest route between journalism and literature. Or it was after all. Only, it did not amount to an overseas sojourn between the wars. Pla fell prey to journalism's demands for a lifetime of relentless devotion – "For more than thirty years I have been rowing in a galley from which holidays, fantasies, and foolishness are excluded" (8:20). But he avoided the dichotomy of journalism or literature to which the majority of aspiring American writers succumbed in their gilded Parisian exile. Instead, he elevated journalism to the level of literature. He was able to live by practising the first and to obtain glory by achieving in the second. And he managed it without accepting this dualism, learning how to serve both masters in the same text.

3 *The Gray Notebook*: Between Chronicle and Memoir

Although readers generally consider *The Gray Notebook* to be Josep Pla's masterpiece, they rarely substantiate their preference. Supported by universal consensus, the objectivity of that choice is taken for granted. And since this book, not being a collection of newspaper articles, can be ranged forthwith in the category of literature, people assume that its eminence is simply a matter of aesthetic judgment. This opinion is abetted by the fact that *The Gray Notebook* is the first volume of the series, its foundational stone so to speak. And programmatically so, because chronologically it was not Pla's first book. When it appeared in 1966, Pla had an extensive bibliography to his name. The fact that he chose this work to inaugurate and in a sense to frame his literary legacy contributes to its popular primacy, as if ordinal priority translated into stylistic superiority. The choice was even more paradoxical, since for a long time people believed that this book was the literal transcription of a youthful journal. From that viewpoint, Pla would have produced his mature prose at the start of his writing career, and thus the quality of his writing would have decreased as he learned the trade. Gabriel Ferrater seems to have been the first to cast doubt on that myth when he remarked in a lecture delivered on 8 May 1967, one year after the book's publication: "*The Gray Notebook* is a very curious work, because it presents itself as the diary of a twenty-one or twenty-two year old, but at that age one does not write eight hundred good pages" (119).

Xavier Pla, who edited the original notebook (which does exist), stressed that *The Gray Notebook* was a rearranged, expanded, and thoroughly rewritten version of the urtext. Critically distinguishing between the textual "I" and the author, he reflected intelligently about the generic ascription of this surprising work. The author himself encouraged its categorization as a memoir or testimonial work in line with his definition of his first book, *Coses vistes* (Seen things), in an interview with Carles Soldevila in December 1925. On that occasion he described this publication as "a book of memories ... of unimportant memories" (A:504). Later he will define his work as "a vast intimate diary" and "some reminiscences of life's cinders" (6:8). And even as a "very long [autobiography], which is nothing other than these Collected Works" (12:531). To this self-ascription one should add the term "chronicle," also used by the author in relation to his journalistic activity. For the purposes of self-representation, this activity begins at the end of *The Gray Notebook* when the Barcelona daily *La Publicitat* commissions the eighteen-year-old student to go to Paris as foreign correspondent. Read in the mode of anticipation, the journal would be the first instalment of the memoirs that so many journalists write at the end of their lives,[1] but Pla considered he had been writing all along. A Proust Questionnaire submitted by the weekly *Destino* in 1967 asked: "Do you think that a writer should publish his memoirs while still alive?" Pla replied: "A writer's memoirs are his books. To repeat them in the form of memoirs tends to result in duplication" (Valls, *Converses* 161).

In Pla's oeuvre journalism and literature are inextricable, as his friend Josep Martinell pointed out (*Josep Pla vist de prop* 21), but there is nonetheless a categorical difference between texts of an informative nature – in the genre of the chronicle or of small events expected of him as foreign or political correspondent – and the bulk of his Collected Works, distinguished not just by the quality and entertainment value of the prose but also, and more decisively, by the intention of conjuring the presence of a country, its towns and villages, its people, orography, climate, landscapes, and flavours. Many of these things were lost or disappearing, but were still close enough in time for readers to recognize their refraction in language. In Pla's uncanny ability to bring back large chunks of reality from the social pre-conscious lies much of his success. He anticipated the flourishing memory industry of the last quarter of the twentieth century, after the swift loss of referents through frantic modernization and demographic mobility turned memory into the last refuge of familiarity.

---

1 Examples of this tradition are the three volumes of Claudi Ametlla's *Memòries polítiques* and Eugeni Xammar's *Seixanta anys d'anar pel món*, although the latter was dictated rather than written by its author.

Martinell's opinion that journalism was inseparable from Pla's literature restated a theme advanced by the author. More than once Pla explained how journalism had determined his literary vocation through circumstantial necessity. And Martinell accepted the duality unquestioningly: "In this sense, the influence of journalism has been decisive. The brief, incisive chronicle of the present that he practiced so many years gave his prose the nimbleness we all know. Journalism was his school then, even if his vocation as writer was settled since adolescence" (21). As if literature were the transcendental essence of writing and journalism a secular and somewhat lowly embodiment of that vocation. If one places such weight on journalism's influence on Pla's writing, it is because one considers his work to be of an entirely different substance. According to this view, journalism would be an apprenticeship undergone by the writer in order to emerge from it into the higher sphere of his true vocation. This is also the opinion, however nuanced and elaborated, of Joan Fuster, who in the prologue to *The Gray Notebook* also identified journalism as the school where Pla learned the main features of his style ("Notes" 1:14). He asserts: "Only in the 'profession' could he find the stimulus and the stringent commitment capable of orienting his will to write" ("Notes" 1:15).

Such a view maps out an anabasis, an ascent through journalism up to the heights of his authentic literary persona, as the author himself proposed by means of what Xavier Pla called *The Gray Notebook*'s "autobiographical impulse" (*Josep Pla. Ficció autobiogràfica i veritat literària* 120). This plot would be convincing enough, were it not that Pla himself associated the violence of writing with the deformation of that same authenticity that critics, for some implicit reason, take for granted in the will to write. "I write since I was a child," he says, "but writing is for me a superimposed, artificial activity" (1:196). He often complained about this artificiality, about how difficult it is to write, to "find the adjective," but he was equally emphatic in his denial that journalism formed or deformed his writing. In the article "La meva literatura" (My literature), written towards the end of his life, he was explicit about the limiting role of the personality: "I had to do the literature that goes with my temperament and I have done no other" (44:286).

Perhaps the stress should be laid less on the authenticity, which is after all a dubious reification of the will, and more on the will itself. Pla was essentially a vitalist who found in writing a challenge adequate to his vital impulse. "Sitting pen in hand at the table in front of a white, immaculate sheet, I often think that hope is one of the most limited things in this world" (1:199). In *The Gray Notebook*, he mentions as the motivating impulse in his career the repeated failure of his youthful attempts to describe the landscape surrounding the Sant Sebastià shrine near Palafrugell (1:206). It would not be far-fetched to assume that impotence to capture the gist of reality in words set the young Pla on the path to a literature of the real, a form of writing to which journalism offered a convenient point of entry. Entry point or means of access, though, no matter how adventitious it may have been at the time, should not obscure the less contingent aims of his writing.

The autobiographic impulse is doubtless present in Pla's work, but it does not account for the ultimate goal of either the *Notebook* or the Collected Works. Pla is at the centre of his oeuvre the way his admired Montaigne is at the centre of the *Essais*: as focalizer of a slew of observations and reflections. Time and again critics bring up Pla's affinity for the French author, including the decision to withdraw from public life in order to become a sort of rural thinker on the family farm, but they neglect the decisive parallelism. The two writers shared not only indifference to official life and honours but also an anti-rhetorical attitude with which they revamped their respective literatures. In Montaigne we also find the autobiographical impulse referred to in the "I" of a private citizen capable of recalling his weaknesses and vulgar tics and reflexes, exactly as Pla does when he confesses his alcoholic binges (1:181) or his erotic fantasies (*La vida lenta* [Slow life] 219), stressing with suspicious frequency his own vulgarity and insignificance:

> The passing through life of an infinite number of generations of obscure peasants can produce as a result the presence of a man – myself in this case – who not only is good for nothing concrete but suffers all the pains in the world when he needs to write one of these absurd things called a news brief. The result is not very important, I should think. (1:185)

Such humble self-mistrust is a snare for naive readers, exactly like the snare Montaigne set up, both being fully aware of the novelty of their achievements within their respective cultural traditions. If by means of self-portrait Montaigne set himself the task of exploring human nature broadly, Pla – more self-effacing or more sceptical of big words – surveys the life of people in a small country subjected to a specific climate and to particular historical events. The parallelism goes even further, because Montaigne, indifferent to the eloquence that characterizes his century, broke with his immediate predecessors, rhetoricians of Ciceronian rootstock. He was an anti-didactic writer who showed no intention to dazzle, preach, edify, or convince anyone. Marc Fumaroli observes that the *Essais* do not bring into play any of the three objectives of oratory art: to please, move, and instruct (202). Pla also parted ways with the rhetoric that prevailed in Catalan letters at the beginning of the twentieth century, that of *Noucentisme*. The *noucentistes* aimed to produce the three objectives of oratory art, because they either had a role in the public administration or hoped to have it through their involvement in the cultural politics of the Mancomunitat, Catalonia's managerial bureau, the embryonic form of a regional government.

The stylistic break, in addition to altering the pragmatic aspects of discourse, impinged on language itself. Montaigne rejected rhetorical flourishes in favour of bare orality. The ordinary voice, rooted in the physiological apparatus, guaranteed the vitality and sincerity of the discourse. In turn Pla seems always to be chatting with a group of friends. Having adopted a conversational style at the opposite end from *noucentista* marquetry, he levels his acerbic critique against Eugeni d'Ors's neo-baroque. Not even Jacint Verdaguer escapes his criticism, at any rate not the author of the epic poems *L'Atlàntida* and *Canigó* – the Verdaguer of the travel chronicles commands his respect – of which Pla declared himself incapable of finishing one single canto: "The feeling of emptiness, the crash of verbalism, glorious, successful, but completely detached from authentic human life, the grandiose resonance of the stanzas, sterilizes in me all possibilities of attention or curiosity" (1:124).

Fumaroli, quoting a passage in which Montaigne asserts that conversation is the spirit's most natural exercise and the occupation that most pleases him, comments: "This Montaignean conversation is exactly the reverse of the scholastic *disputatio*, even of the humanistic one, a ritual governed by an objective rule. Whereas here the rule, inapprehensible, nimble, lively, is born of the harmony and even the spiritual complicity between two 'natures' and two 'souls' that help each other make their deeper resources flow" (210n48). Pla speaks about the artificiality of writing and how it deforms the self, whose production and exteriorization Montaigne associated with conversation (1:196). Conversation was a physical necessity for Pla, who became a virtuoso of the chat. Even so, in his mind the solitary individual had a stronger claim to authenticity than the gregarious one. Such preference for the loner, more typical of a taciturn and insufficiently articulate society such as the Catalan than of French loquacity and *sprit*, was embodied in Hermós, one of the few characters in *The Gray Notebook* whom Pla genuinely admired. He belongs to the class of antisocial individuals who manage to avoid the pressures of the collective "they." Pla observes that the most intelligent people in Palafrugell evince a tendency to self-limitation in order to avoid responsibilities. Such people have little in common. They are truly themselves. If there is spiritual complicity between them, it is in a negative sense only. The rule is not to get involved, to avoid creating bonds in pursuit of objectives that transcend the most immediate personal interests. Pla approves this attitude, although he realizes that such generalized individualism "has obviously a great drawback: the impossibility that people experience in consorting means that social life practically does not exist. What one misses most in the country is conversation, the hygienic volubility of social relation. If I had to choose, though, between conversation and freedom – the solitary freedom – I would always choose freedom" (1:438).

Coming back to the pre-eminence generally accorded to *The Gray Notebook*, we can now assert that any analysis of Pla's oeuvre that does not start with this volume may be more or less incisive but will miss the sense of the bid that Pla describes at the end of *Notes disperses* (Scattered notes) as working "to increase the will to be" (12:577). Pla, author of an ontology? Not quite. Relying on plain language in his work to describe things with hyperreal precision, he never mistakes the writer for a demiurge. He does not create, does not invent, does not imagine, if imagining means trafficking with the forms of fantasy, with phantoms. He knows that he cannot augment being, but he thinks that he can reveal it in what exists. Then the will to be increases in the form of pages of prose, engendering a Collected Works as a (doomed?) attempt to stabilize and make durable the transitory phenomena of life. A first inference: the writer is driven by the anguishing inconsistency of being. He is pushed to write by the softening and melting away of things. Pla shares this intuition with his contemporary fellow countryman Salvador Dalí, painter of melting watches on top of the rocky, enduring landscape of Port Lligat.

Pla is not, for all that, a metaphysical writer. His will to be is not a searching for absolutes or – as in Nietzsche's case – a will to power, which still presupposes a notion of biological puissance as absolute. Rejecting all metaphysical referents unceremoniously, Pla conceives being in and through time. He finds it in the beginning and ending of things that are subject to their own duration. To increase being through the will can only mean to increase the duration of things, to extend their existence, if not in time then at least in human consciousness, which is always consciousness of temporality and obtains in the tension between retention and forgetting. Indeed, if the goal in writing is to increase the will to be, the difficulty lies in curbing the natural tendency to forget. Hence: "The great problem for a writer rooted in the country is to contribute to the struggle against forgetting" (17:8). And this struggle takes us back to Pla's definition of his literary production as a work of memory, with *The Gray Notebook* as foundation stone.

We can now advance, then, a criterion to justify placing this book ahead of the rest, not only in the ordinal sense of inaugurating the Collected Works, but also in an aesthetic sense and on account of its ultimate intention. If, as Valentí Puig claims, "memory can supplant art, but art would not survive without memory" (11), then the value of Pla's work lies in the mnemonic energy with which the first volume empowers the will to write. Memory at the service of composition explains Pla's otherwise mystifying decision to alter the date of the closing of the University of Barcelona on acount of the influenza epidemic. He changed the date from 12 October to 8 March 1918 (Bonada, *"El quadern gris" de Josep Pla* 11). This manipulation was not a consequence of faulty memory but a strategy to inaugurate his entire oeuvre making the inception of the diary coincide with the birthday on which he came of age (1:87).

As Xavier Pla saw, the writer from Palafrugell begins his memoir quite differently from the majority of autobiographers. He transgresses the convention of starting this kind of text with a childhood narrative (*Josep Pla. Ficció autobiogràfica i veritat literària* 154), that is, with the *Ordo Naturalis* of the rhetorical treatises. This critic suggests that the reason for such alteration of the natural order of self-narration is that "childhood had not left strong enough traces in his memory" (155). The author himself says in *The Gray Notebook*: "About my childhood I remember absolutely nothing" (1:93). This may be true or may be yet one more justification of his decision to begin his diary with the official birth of the adult person. Nevertheless, Cornell University professor of psychology Qi Wang makes the same point when she notes that "very early memories […] become inaccessible later on because they are not linked to the newly established self-concept and therefore are not made autobiographical" (114). She cites a consensus among theorists that autobiographical memory requires a self-concept prior to the emergence of such memories. Without such self-concept events could not be organized and structured or made available for retrieval in association with the personality over a long time.

If childhood left no traces in a writer as well endowed with memory as Pla, the same could be expected from other autobiographical writers, who do in fact write extensively and in detail about their formative years. Did they fantasize their earlier selves? Pla thought so and discredited their reliability with this comment: "Nobody remembers anything – nothing. And if things that happened less than one year ago take the form of an impenetrable fog, what can we say about what happened ten, fifty, one hundred, eight hundred years ago?" (35:552).

This realist critique of conventional autobiography grounds his decision to adopt the *Ordo Artificialis* and begin his life story in medias res. The decision is consistent with Pla's conception of writing as an activity contrary to nature and a crutch for memory, whose devastation Plato associated with the advent of writing, and which the anti-Platonic Pla attributed to laziness and neglect. But the critique of conventional autobiographies, of their generic though unreliable recollection of childhood and even infancy, can also be seen as a by-product of Pla's fidelity not so much to the diary's veracity – *The Gray Notebook* is full of errors and marked by chronological imprecision – as to the question of memory, which he broaches from the standpoint of consciousness; in other words, reflectively. Before adulthood there occurs a rite of passage that the English language aptly calls "coming of age," suggesting that before this moment life had been ageless and that memory is unreflective, a somatic registering of impressions. The past consists of a few sketchy impressions and vague feelings of either well-being or discomfort, incapable by themselves of translating into an image of lost time. "Youth typically has little memory – other than sexual memory, which is unfocussed and interchangeable – although a child can occasionally repeat a page from a book or play the piano admirably. Moral memory – the only one that matters – is born at a certain stage in the organism's development" (1:366).

The distinction between moral memory, which I prefer to call reflexive memory, and agent memory (to be able to repeat a page or a music score) corresponds to the difference Bergson established in *Matière et mèmoire* between a memory generated through repetition and habituation on the one hand and on the other hand a memory-reminiscence, which would be an image or representation of an event or unrepeatable experience (227). Pla was acquainted with Bergson's philosophy.

In Paris, he had attended Bergson's lectures at the College de France (44:559). The *maître à penser* was then the country's most distinguished cultural personality (35:190). It was nearly impossible to ignore his challenge to the Kantian transcendental subject, straighjacketed by the a priori categories of time and space. In an article on the occasion of Bergson's retirement, Pla wrote: "Bergson has tried to ground metaphysics in experience and to constitute – appealing to science and consciousness and unfolding the faculty of intuition – a philosophy capable of producing not only some general theories but also concrete explanations of particular facts" (43:101). This last phrase is revealing of Pla's affinity with Bergsonism. He was much more interested in particular facts than in general theories, although he does on occasion rise to the formulation of general laws applicable to limited areas of geographic or social validity and always based on induction from experience.

Pla's reception of Bergson's philosophy transpired above all in his conception of time as personal substance. "Discovery of personal time, which has nothing to do with physical time (which is totally indifferent), is a phenomenon that occurs in adolescence and youth. It does not happen suddenly or by way of an illumination. Personal time is discovered through experience. Experience is acquired and is very sad" (31:421). This passage provides confirmation that, in a subjective sense, childhood remains off limits for the adult consciousness. While immersed in physical time, subject to external temporalization in the phase of organic growth, the child has no internal temporality and thus no memories.

In the same passage, personal time and physical time are transliterations of Bergson's chronological time and *durée*. But on the theme of memory, Pla was more influenced by applied Bergsonism, especially Proust's great novel. In his chronicle of literary Parisian life in the 1920s in the book *Sobre París i França*, he observed perceptively: "Marcel Proust is not a realist of raw, direct, and some times poeticized reality. He is a realist of the memories of reality – of time regained – which is something quite different and often more complicated" (4:230). We see here explicit recognition of a superior, subtler realism and an intuition that Proust's method – inspired by Bergson – was to isolate time as something experienced by an observer of memory. In other words, Pla found in Proust a literary fulfilment of the reflections with which Bergson anticipated a phenomenological examination of memory. Years later, on the occasion of the Proust Questionnaire submitted by *Destino*,

Pla said in conversation with a friend that Proust "started copying Bergson like a madman" (Valls, *Converses* 30).

The obligation of sending a spate of articles on current affairs to the newspaper office prevented Pla from embarking on a sustained reflection about memory and the absent past, but there is no doubt that his sense of reality was permanently affected by his acquaintance with Proust's great novel. Pla would never again be a naive memorialist. "Time regained" will become the leitmotif of his entire oeuvre, and his assimilation – direct or mediated – of Bergsonism will be responsible for the radicalism of his idea of duration and even the denial, at one point, of the objectivity of time. Time, for him, is nothing but a concept, a *flatus vocis*: "the reality is the human heart, which disintegrates continuously" (35:202). At other moments, it is the medium in which we move like fish in Heraclitus's river. Pla said to his friend Josep Valls that the Latin people used to define time as a *nunc fluens*, a runaway present, which at "every moment exists only in order to give way to another moment" (Valls, *Converses* 30). Even when he considers time from a classic perspective, he still has in mind the unrepeatability of the instant. And it is this consciousness of unrepeatability that shows the paradox of writing when understood as a tool to retrieve the past. Nonetheless the paradox is resolved through the distinction between reflexive memory and agent memory, the faculty that allows a child to play the piano and to regurgitate a lesson. The lesson is precisely the example chosen by Bergson to illustrate the repetitive memory that he associates with habits like walking or writing and situates within the horizon of the present, since the remembered action is realized (becomes real) at the moment of its repetition. The writer's habit, "the devilish mania of writing," as Pla called it (1:451), is a form of memory, as are the seasonal routines of sowing and reaping, which return at the appointed time without their cyclicity implying in the farmer the kind of memory based on the reminiscence-event (Proust's sudden and uniquely induced flashback). In *The Gray Notebook*, we are presented therefore with two different forms of memory, which Pla separates chronologically, although they evidently overlap before and after the parting date: Pla's twenty-first birthday, the date when he officially came of age. The beginning of the diary is both the beginning of a habit-forming activity and the inception of reflexive memory through writing in future perfect mode, that is to say in the form of entries that in time will become memories and that are composed under the law that makes inevitable the preterition of everything inscribed therein.

In his treatise "On Memory and Reminiscence," Aristotle states that memory pertains (is about) the past (449b 15). Paul Ricoeur translates "tou genomenou" (16) literally as "what has occurred, happened" (509n16). But Aristotle himself notes that it is in the soul that certainty of having heard or thought something before arises (449b 23). But a purely psychological theory of memory assumes that it functions without exercising knowledge or perception, that is, in the absence of the things remembered (449b 19) and "when time has elapsed" (449b 26). Aristotle's veering from the Platonic theory of memory consists in an intensification of the temporality of memory, insisting that time is its true object. He does not entirely abandon the Platonic notion of *eikon*, the impression left by the object in the soul, which awakens the recollection. In *De anima* 424a Aristotle defines the sensory apparatus as the faculty for receiving the sensible forms without the matter. To illustrate how it is possible for the soul to store the forms only, he turns to the classic metaphor of the wax keeping the impression of a signet ring or *tupos* without admitting the metal itself (424a, lines 19–21). Modern languages retain a trace of this theory in the word "impression" and its derivatives. For Aristotle the production of the *eikon* takes place at the moment of perception, that is, in the presence of the object, whereas memory operates in a vacuum, since what is recollected is precisely the form of an absence. This emptying out of reality, the constant disappearance of phenomena and their rebirth as mnemonic phantoms, underlies the experience of time. The physical impression at the origin of a reminiscence is what permits the distinction between a before and an after. When the impression becomes reflexive (is reflected upon), it causes the subjective experience of recollection.

This is exactly what happens at the beginning of *The Gray Notebook*. Pla is reborn as an author when he reflects on a recent event, a vulgar yet exceptional event: the closing of the university, which starts a period of productive leisure for the student, with the village life as background for his observations and musings, which he records in his journal after sifting his impressions through a newly found reflexive consciousness. If the present instituted by each impression changes unceasingly, it also recommences at every instant. And this passing away followed by retrieval in memory is effectively expressed in the form of the diary through the staccato succession of the daily entries.

Continual beginning and ending sets the rhythm of the discourse and shapes the movement of time, which above and beyond the anecdotes that it gives rise to, is the hub of Pla's reflection. The time alluded to is of course time experienced as a flux of instants that come on each other's heels. Pla declared himself a keen observer of this modality of "lived" time: "it is the passion that I have always felt for the hours, for time as successive durations in human life. Abstract, motionless, eternal time is one of the most unpleasant, most tragic things in our life" (44:370). Time is an integral component of his writing not only because the diary pertains to the category of temporal things, of objects that must be comprehended in their seriality, but above all because this immaterial substance plays a crucial role in the emergence and recognition of the forms that are the stuff of his depictions of reality. Time, or more exactly duration, is in effect the acknowledged source of his reflection:

> Clocks that try to measure merely sensorial time have created the painful obsession with Time. I have tried to live in a house in which clocks stopped years ago. Every day I am more fearful of the illusions of Time, of the future, of intellectual, philosophical, social, and political prophecies. The whole problem consists in knowing how to limit oneself in order not to mistake flies for eagles. (35:202)

Time is bound up with illusion and anguish, but also with more exalted things such as the philosophy of history and its political derivatives, which Pla counted among mankind's self-inflicted catastrophes. Between the mechanical time of clocks and the falsification of life there is a correlation to which Pla opposes a personal, intimate intuition of time that owes much to Bergson's *durée*. In the frequent use he made of a commonplace expression such as "in my time" lies concealed the insight of a temporality intimately and inextricably bound up with his own personal life. Opposed to the notion of absolute time, in effect a metaphysical variation on the idea of eternity, this relative temporality, which he associated with the experience of loss and the instability of human reality, is what makes it possible to measure the beginning and end of all things. And the yardstick, as Protagoras said twenty-six centuries ago, is human life itself. "Everything is mobile, plastic, unexpected, and unsuspected. Everything hangs from a thread and, in every aspect, life's insecurity is total, continuous, and absolute" (35:54). So much instability necessarily translates into a sharp feeling of absence and a keen intuition of time.

Knowing the past through absence entails significant epistemological problems. What is there to know when nothing of what one wishes to know is there? For the past is neither in actuality nor potentially as the future is. Philologists and historians – two of the branches of inquiry that claim to elucidate the past – use the tools of textual criticism and documentary research to approach it indirectly, by excavating its material ruins (which include dead languages and fragments of official and unofficial discourse) for meaning that is hypothetical at best and at worst fabulated. Pla goes about it stressing his all-encompassing scepticism, always favouring what is concrete and lies close to his sensory apparatus – in short, the kind of memory that Jan Assmann called "communicative memory" (50), that is to say, memory of things for which witnesses are still around, as distinguished from "cultural memory," which relies on the symbolic apparatus for its transmission and concentrates on emblematic anchor points (52). Pla calls this proximate kind of memory "the perceptible past" (35:291). His prioritizing of the senses, the classic windows of the soul, made him impatient with those who defect the tangible world for cosmopolitan abstractions. It explains his cautious, reluctant appeal to truth within the empirical limits of the individual. Insistence on material certainty grounded his regionalism. This programmatic regionalism had nothing to do with insularity or narrow-mindedness. It was coherent with his radical empiricism and consequent with his philosophical situationism. But it could be and often was self-critical. And it could manifest itself in the form of irony and wit, as when, in a café discussion, he proclaimed that one of the speakers was right, and upon being asked why he thought so, he replied "because this gentleman is from Palafrugell."

It is one of many ways of propping up the need for certainty. Pla, who was familiar with the philological critique with which Nietzsche destabilized the belief that language can recover the original object, tempers his scepticism by ironically affirming the importance of the origin, not metaphysical but decidedly physical, of every being. It may be worth considering the otherwise trivial opinion of Josep Martinell, according to which the importance of *The Gray Notebook* consists in introducing certain characters and references from Pla's formative milieu (*Josep Pla vist de prop* 32). The fact is that both the characters and the milieu go a long way towards illustrating the forces at work in the entire oeuvre. In this Pla behaved somewhat like Balzac introducing in *Le Père Goriot* characters whose reappearance in subsequent novels contributes to unify the world of the *Comédie Humaine*.

The concept of *aletheia,* as recognition of that presence in which the Greeks located the fullness of being, made possible the distinction between truth and error. Plato added the permanent traces of this presence in the soul, which would thus always already know the truth and need only remember it by climbing out of the world of appearances. Pla, needless to say, was not in the least Platonic, but of the doctrine of the *eikon* he retained the idea of the existence of some ineffaceable impressions to which the birth and life of memory were connected. These impressions had a disturbing effect on the subject – being something akin to the Lacanian invasion of the real. But contrary to what happens in Freudian psychoanalysis, where impressions that have not been neutralized take refuge in the dark chamber of the unconscious, in Pla the "traumatic" sensation is processed reflectively and objectified through the distance that memory inserts like a wedge between the ego and the impressions:

> Fear is, it seems to me, at the basis of the mechanism of memory. Memory seems especially designed to keep fear active – the moments of fear that the body refuses to digest and eliminate. What makes the human organism change, what operates the transition from adolescence to the definitive crystallization are these moments of panic that will never be erased. It is a force that lends character. It entails the appearance in the organism of an element that keeps the memory alive, in permanent, anguishing tension. […] Fear of losing what one has or of not obtaining what one hankers after is what stings, what moulds life. Fear is born of biological injustice, that is, of the possible or real infringement of the notion of justice that every organism possesses by the mere fact of living. (1:365–6)

Fear of losing what one has or not receiving what one imagines is due one. The first of these fears is an anticipation of the destructive passage of time. The second is fear of non-materialization, the fear that time will end up discrediting the expected availability of an object that represents an "increase of the will to be." The first relates to previous experiences of loss – without which fear would not have any basis to arise – and thus engages memory. The second is based on the non-appearance of an object of which there is nonetheless an anticipatory imprint in the mind, like an upturned memory so to speak. In Pla memory is often at work not so much out of a desire to remain locked in the past (as expected of an avowed conservative) as from fear that an oblivious present becomes vapourous, de-realized, and plunges the subject into an illusory future. The realism with which the mature subject accepts the ruin of expectations marks the end of childish omnipotence and the exhaustion of the Panglossian attitude that Pla observed around him, especially among fellow journalists. "Generally, journalism is Panglossian. It rarely delves deeply. This is why in a country at peace and public quiet, with outer order assured and a government with staying power, the correspondent has little to do" (4:297).

The journalist digs deeper provided that things are uncertain, that there is fear, that events are possible. When the journalist is content to mirror the flatness of the present, he betrays the profession's vocation to in-form, to excavate the form of the present by means of memory. The critical journalist relates the event to its precedents showing that something has come out of something else. This is, after all, the meaning of "event," from Latin *eventus*, from "ex" (out of) and "venire" (to come). And this "something else," this unknown X out of which today's news emerges, the true journalist reveals it by delving beneath the surface of the present moment. Although the chronicle, a generic term for the journalism of current events, bears no apparent relation to the historical chronicle, a term derived from the Greek *kronika biblios* (books arranged in temporal or diachronic order), it is possible for the journalistic chronicler to rise to the condition of historian of the present. Both meanings of the term "chronicle" merge in the three volumes that Pla published under the title *Cròniques parlamentàries* (Parliamentary chronicles) (vols. 40, 41, and 42 of the Collected Works). These chronicles were daily reports about the debates in the Spanish *Cortes*, and they have exceptional value in reconstructing the day-to-day political climate of the country between the advent of the Second Republic and the start of the Spanish Civil War.

The temporal ordering of the newspaper chronicle ordinarily does not extend beyond the medium's periodicity. The timing is set by the random incidence of potential interest stories. Otherwise, the medium's frequency of publication (daily, weekly, monthly) provides whatever sequencing there is in the press. So everything and anything could be the subject of news. But an authentic chronicle requires the existence of events, an event being the kind of impression the reflexive memory privileges. A journal is a selection of the things considered worth remembering among the myriad experiences of the day. The fact that they are salvaged for memory constitutes them as events. But although we speak of reflexive memory, and thus of consciousness, there is no reason for the event to be a private experience of the journal keeper. It can very well be something of general character, a collective occurrence, a development memorable for an entire group of people, which thus becomes paradigmatic. Paul Ricoeur notes that memorable encounters are recalled less on the grounds of their unrepeatable singularity than on account of their typical or emblematic character (28). This is in fact the guiding principle behind many entries in *The Gray Notebook*. For instance, the event that sets Pla's diary going: the flu pandemic of the year 1918, subject of the entry for 14 March, where the writer refers to this broadly shared experience in order to refer ironically to one of the moments of greatest disunion in modern Catalan society. "Now finally living in Catalonia is a pleasure. Unanimity is complete. We all have had, have, or will ineluctably have the flu" (1:104). Or else the entry for 6 June, seemingly unmotivated yet ironically allusive to Eugeni d'Ors's aphorism "L'arranjament de les muntanyes" (Fixing the mountains) (15 May 1907; *Glosari 1906–1907*, 492), contains in a nutshell a revolt against *Noucentisme*'s aesthetic and social principles. "It can't be denied, I think, that mountains are well made. If someone holds a different opinion and disagrees ... he gets the cigar. Some are never happy" (1:184). That *The Gray Notebook* was conceived as a recollection-event dating the overcoming of *Noucentisme*, Catalonia's dominant aesthetic in the second decade of the twentieth century, is shown by the entry of 23 June, dedicated to Eugeni d'Ors, *Noucentisme*'s founder and spokesman:

> It is true, though, that this man is not fit to be a contemporary – he is only potable at a distance, in the suggestion of distance. Between his life, his social presentation, and what he has proposed as the goal of his mastery there is a huge illogicality. However, youth rarely understands illogicalities. (1:693)

The gist of this entry is the consignment of d'Ors and hence of *Noucentisme* to the past, an anachronism unfit to guide the present culture. Taking d'Ors's personality as his criterion of contemporaneousness, Pla asserts that *Noucentisme*, in 1918, amounts to confusion between memory and perception, between a past cultural event and its uncritical reiteration by youth, the way a child plays a melody on the piano or repeats a lesson. The distinction between *Noucentisme* being "potable" at a distance and its illogical claim to present mastery is of the same order as that between Bergson's memory-as-habit and memory-as-representation. Like a lesson uncritically memorized, *Noucentisme*'s institutionalization was the mechanical repetition of a few formulas, meaningful perhaps in the context of certain experiences that no longer defined the cultural moment. The young were *noucentistes* heedlessly, unthinkingly oblivious to the origins of the doctrine. If, on the contrary, the subject recalls the phases of learning, in this case the process through which it adopted a particular aesthetic, if one – we would say today – historicizes one's habits, then, according to Bergson, this person "reascends the slope of the past" in search of the image of that foregone moment which constitutes the memory-as-representation (*Matière* 227, cit. Ricoeur 25). And once the image has been found, once this modern version of the Platonic *eikon* becomes a part of memory, then, says Bergson, the world of human interests and activities is suspended and the detached subject becomes a reflexive observer, a second-order observer who contemplates the world in the form of images. More precisely, this subject contemplates the image of a world that changes into the past, or better yet, contemplates the past becoming world by virtue of the image. "To call up the past in the form of an image, we must be able to withdraw ourselves from the action of the moment, we must have the power to value the useless, we must have the will to dream" (*Matière* 228, cit. Ricoeur 25). To admire the useless, to go gaping through the world like a "lucid looker-on," in Martinell's felicitous expression (*Josep Pla vist de prop* 47), is what Pla did throughout his life. Looking on in assumed naiveté, which he emphasized ever more in his self-presentation, should not be confused with a passive disposition towards the images that come off the world and find their way into the pages of his diary.

The Gray Notebook thematizes the suspension of activity from the start, consigning to its pages the unexpected vacation occasioned by the closing of the university on account of the flu. This historical fact becomes, in the textual memory, the occasion that permits Pla to become a detached observer and consign his observations to the notebook, nourishing it with reflections drawn from his idling in the village, his existence as a barfly and inveterate chatterbox among the habitués at the local café, and as friend of scruffy, footloose characters like Hermós, the image of freedom for the young Pla.

But his looking on has nothing to do with the automatism of perception and the spontaneity of automatic memory. It does not matter if the endeavour is concealed by apparent effortlessness (a date, an entry), *The Gray Notebook* is an achievement of voluntary memory that penetrates through layers of consciousness. Obviously it can be read in the same way, lingering on the trivial and more transparent or venturing into the more opaque. In *Notes del capvesprol* (Notes of the eventide breeze, 1979), a notebook written in old age, he will insist: "Literature must produce memories of feelings or objectivities. If it does not produce them, forgetting is instantaneous and complete"

(35:309). Of course, the feelings and the objects are not literature; the memory of these things is – a memory assembled artificially with exertion and pain.

If in Pla's oeuvre we separate the part consisting of journalistic reporting, the part that fits the genre of the chronicle, we recognize in it the purpose of recovering experiences or events preferably from the standpoint of everyday life. At the beginning of "Notes sobre política francesa" (Notes on French politics), a popularizing text in which Pla has conspicuously transcribed portions of his own readings, he warns: "My intention in speaking about these things is purely informative" (4:475). And yet it is not exactly true, as he claims immediately after, that he writes without the intention of convincing anyone. In Pla there is a recognizable world view and an implicit effort at persuasion. It could hardly be otherwise, if we accept – albeit with reservations – the opinion of his friend Joan Fuster that "all philosophy is propaganda" and "behind the fashionable weighty concepts, from the *ens* to the *noümen* [*sic*], from *existence* to *spirit*, flow intentions and snares set up to fascinate the customer and lead him to one or other enclosure no longer properly philosophical" (*Viure per viure*, 92). Ostensibly more anti-intellectual than his friend from Sueca, who still held a class vision of history, Pla believed that politics had to adapt to the character of nations, and preferred the Socratic to the Marxist dialectic, privileging the chat and the debate with a view to reaching a certain agreement or at least a temporary climate of opinion (4:476).

In reality Pla does nothing else. Even his reports, stylistically the quintessence of the chronicle, reveal an eagerness to promote a perspective akin to that of a cosmopolitan who has discovered the value of proximity, of someone sufficiently sceptical to be unreservedly liberal, of an autarkic loner with the instincts of someone deeply socialized. This is perhaps the key to his success during the years when all of these traits were unmistakable marks of civilization in a country devastated by a brutal, uncouth dictatorship. He impressed on *Destino*, a weekly that represented the conservative *juste milieu* in the post-war era, the dominant opinion of the Catalan middle class. It was not only, or at least not primarily, a commercial calculation. Pla associated dominant opinion with the politics of the French minister Guizot between 1816 and 1848, whom he credited for the creation of a middle class capable of working but also of enjoying leisure, in other words, of balancing activity with the freedom to think, and with enough money to avoid the dangers of subservience and revolt (4:484). After the enormous setbacks of the revolution and the dictatorship, Pla remembered and applied what he had learned in France during the 1920s and, in his view, needed to be rebuilt in Catalonia if liberalism was to become viable again. Although he protests the strict objectivity of his chronicles and denies having an ulterior motive, the fact is that, as early as his first post as correspondent in France, he uses comparative strategies to stimulate the desire for emulation. "There is perhaps one country that could have attained, in small scale but appreciably, this considerable well-being, and that is our country" (4:479).

From the pages of *Destino*, Pla will strive to create a climate of opinion capable of generating a middle-class equivalent to that of the Western European countries, and he will do so starting from the "general public, which is the one I have always tried to satisfy with my poor writings" (44:272). A general public is not necessarily a class descriptor, but from this public Pla tried to obtain a reasonably liberal, and reasonably educated, class, in the sense of familiar with their own country, and he entrusted this class with the task of lifting Catalonia out of the misery into which class fanaticism had plunged it: "The middle-class man must direct society. If the class exists, it directs it de facto" (4:484). In the mid-1960s, when Pla published "Notes sobre política francesa," this class was as refractory to the dictatorship as it was to the brewing revolt; it was an accommodating class that, biding their time in apparent conformity, kept Catalan society alive and on the path of progress. In reality, Pla had in mind the middle class of the years when he started out as a journalist and that imploded with the Civil War. He hoped to call it back onto the stage of history through anamnessis, a return, rediscovery, or renewal. Against this feat of recovery oblivion is actively at work, with ignorance as its ally. Ignorance of the elemental things of life, disguised under the pretentious varnish of "an education" (9:159).

Pla anticipated the notion of historical memory, while refusing the political uses to which it has been harnessed:

> I have not tried to cultivate my memory in order to apply it to the demonstration of human indignity. On this point I think that the most forgetful are the ones who know how to live. On the other hand – since we are speaking of memory – I have a certain capacity to retain readings and books. Of the things that I read, what interest me most are the details, the insignificant, petty things. Dead and live people fascinate me equally. The historical memory is as real to me as the present itself. (1:192)

Incidentally, the appearance of the expression "historical memory" in *The Gray Notebook* should have alerted critics that this text could not be from the year 1918. The term "historical memory" began to circulate after Maurice Halbwachs used it in *The Collective Memory*, a work first published in 1950. This is hardly a trivial observation. When Pla asserts that the historical memory fascinates him as much as the present, he is not saying that he is attracted by the past that is definitively beyond memory-as-representation. He is fascinated by the recent past, the past that remains as an imprint in consciousness rather than in history books, which for the most part he considers unreliable. "I am a man of the immediate past, I mean of the relatively perceptible past – because the other, the distant past, is a picture card more or less painted" (35:291). A relatively perceptible past means nothing else than a past impressed in the memory and converted into a representation of the absent thing. It is not an imaginary construction – a painted picture card – but the bringing back, the recall, of something that has fallen behind. This double movement of the mind, the shuttling back and forth between the past perceived through its representation and the presentation itself, is called recognition, the miracle – to say it with Ricoeur – that is "to coat with presence the otherness of that which is over and gone" (39).

Recognition performs the miracle of introducing relative continuity in the human sphere. Continuity, the contrary of Adamism and primitiveness. Memory is more than a theme for Pla; it is a self-assumed obligation. "Memory is very important. It is scarce. It is civilization. Indifference covers everything, devours everything" (35:260). Pla's demonstrative regionalism was a way of resisting forgetfulness, a struggle against indifference. It was his way of confronting the individual adrift on the earth's surface like tumbleweed in a ghost town. "When one lives normally in the country in which one was born, the first obligation is to know the things that have notoriously happened there" (44:310). The journalist who has travelled through the world and reported on the major events of the twentieth century is the same person who says, with respect to a country landmark such as the Saint Sebastian shrine in Palafrugell: "These four white walls make me feel my roots: this is my country, here I was born; in the two or three cemeteries of the environs rest the family generations of which I am no more than the dream momentarily realized" (1:464). The consciousness of temporality, of the flash of subjectivity that will soon flicker out, is also consciousness of the beginning ("here I was born") that continuity presupposes, even the continuous chain of generations that can only be a memory for the living, just as he, Pla, could have been no more than a dream for his ancestors. Even so, this memory is all important, because it centres his life, thus providing it with a perspective. Such an existential centre of gravity is the foundation of a culture. To know is, for Pla, to know concretely, physically, coating with presence what was one moment, one year, one decade ago and now is no more.

"This is the essence of literature: details, observation, knowledge," he pronounces (35:266). Making knowledge depend on details imposes the discipline of circumscribing the radius of recognition. The circle traced by this radius of genuine acquaintance is what Pla calls "country" ("país"), the area in which representation of what has gone before is mediated by the impression made on a consciousness that connects to the world through the senses. Ricoeur, who never read Pla, provides phenomenological support for the latter's decision to limit mnemonically the space and time that the subject can hope to retain. Circumscribed time and space generate the illusion of familiarity, of being within grasp, although in fact time and space are constantly slipping away. Says Ricoeur: "It becomes legitimate to suppose that it is always in historically limited cultural forms that the capacity to remember (*faire mémoire*) can be apprehended" (392).

How does Pla administer, literarily, his capacity to make memory? Although the newspaper article is the predominant genre in much of his oeuvre, his is no ordinary journalism. Facts, for instance, are often presented in the form of memories and reflections about time. But then, reflection about time is the cradle of Western thought and one of its permanent themes. Does this mean that Pla was a budding philosophical spirit stunted by his circumstance? The question is meaningless if asked in the sense of projecting a different life trajectory in a different society at a different time. In actual life he rejected philosophy, as he did all imaginative literature, as empty loquacity, as rhetorical bombast, as "nothing at all" (35:50). He was "partial to the literature of observation of human life, of what is before us" (35:50). As a rule this kind of statement, frequent in the Collected Works, has been understood in the sense of a naively realist disposition, a myopic frame of mind. Pla certainly feels distaste for metaphysical temptations, but the naive positivist, like the country bumpkin image he cultivated, was an ironic construction, a form of mimetism with the environment intended to catch inattentive readers. In *The Gray Notebook*, that alleged urtext of Pla's literary career, he gives a clue about the purpose of his entire literature: the philosophy in low key of a village Socrates, in the spirit of what his admired Montaigne undertook on the other side of the Pyrenees a few centuries earlier: "In philosophy wordplay produces a progressive general dissatisfaction. The only way to bring philosophy back to its authenticity is to make it sojourn for some time in the purgatory of the personal confession, the subjective note, the private diary" (1:159). *The Gray Notebook* is or aims to be this philosophy in the homely purgatory. And just as the *Essais* inaugurated an anti-rhetorical mode of self-reflection, the *Notebook* inaugurates a long series of books centred on memory. Pla suggested as much when he referred to his very first book, *Coses vistes* (1925), as "a book of memories ... of memories without the slightest importance" (A:504).

The genre of the memoir goes back to the edition of Philippe de Commines's chronicle of the kingdoms of Louis XI and Charles VIII by Denis Sauvage in 1552. In his edition, Sauvage changed the medieval title of *Chronicle and History* to *Memoirs*. As Fumaroli explains, this change was motivated by the historiographical debates going on in French humanistic circles at this time (290). People argued about the relation between style and the fidelity to the facts. Medieval historiography and Ciceronism in general were accused of falsifying truth by their use of imagination, panegyric writing, and adulation. In 1531 Cornelius Agrippa published *De incertitudine et vanitate scientiarum*, plunging historiography into radical scepticism (Fumaroli 293). Generalization of the critique of historiographic Ciceronism provoked the emergence of an anti-rhetorical convention. In the prefaces to their books, authors formulaically apologized for a deliberately plain style, suggesting that truthful representation of the past depended on rhetorical austerity. In 1569, when René Du Bellay published *Memoirs of Messire Martin Du Bellay and his brother Guillaume*, he explains that his relative called his manuscript "mémoires" out of modesty, because the title of "history" presupposed a rhetorical affectation that he had not deployed (Fumaroli 297). But it was François Bodin who defined the criteria for the new historiography embodied in the memoirs. They boil down to the historian's independence, competence based on his experience with the themes he deals with, and separation of history from rhetoric and moral philosophy so as to avoid adulation or moral preaching (Fumaroli 303).

We have seen Pla asserting that he wrote with a purely informative purpose, not pretending to convince anyone. Time and again he eschews embroidering and academicism. He not only avoids them; he critiques them. His verdict on Spanish historians, apropos the sugar-coating of humanist Joan Lluís Vives, is as harsh as Vives's attack on ancient historiography in *De disciplinis libri XX*. Says Pla: "Scholars, in general, have been a bunch of lazybones and their true mission in life has been to adulate. Everything they have done has been in the employ of adulation; they have subjected truth to adulation" (28:92). Was this not also, speaking quite generally, the self-imposed mission of journalists? In a period of absolute muzzling of the press, Pla gave vent to the priority of intellectual independence in his personal axiology and literary ethics. Although his hostility to the Republican regime and his support of Franco's faction during the Civil War (an issue discussed in chapter 9) won him the rejection of the Catalan literary establishment long after the post-war period, he remained ostentatiously independent and often clashed with the censors on account of his opinions, never currying favour with the regime.

Pla inscribed himself in the memoirist current that led to the *Memòries de Saint Simon* and which, having begun with a defence of the driest verism, ended by incorporating a whole series of literary modalities, such as the short novel (*El carrer Estret* [The narrow street] or *L'herència* [The inheritance]); the portrait (his biographical sketches or his *Retrats de passaport* [Passport photos])); "character compositions" (*Homenots*); compilations of celebrated phrases (the anecdotes and citations that pepper Pla's works); the maxims and moral reflections that are its constitutive fabric; the genealogical treatises whose equivalent can be found in the family histories with which Pla endows the lives of his characters with a collective dimension; diplomatic letters (which compare with the chronicles of parliamentary sessions and the reports of the foreign correspondent); and the accounts of ceremonies, which in Pla occur in the form of stories about social and political gatherings of all sorts. Through the Collected Works parade the entire political, artistic, journalistic, and literary classes of his day, as so many tableaux vivants supplemented by splendid studies of the peasantry and the middle class. There are, in addition, lengthy travel reports, broad and astute perspectives on foreign countries, the guides to the Catalan-speaking lands, and the excursions at sea or on rural roads, expanding the reader's geographic consciousness while probing deeper in the historic dimension of the visual surfaces evoked.

Although he places his work under the advocacy of time as consciousness of the passing and vanishing of things, Pla does not admit the philosophy of history. He considers the sum of human actions something irreducible to the parameters of reason. "Human history is not incomprehensible: it is unthinkable. But this has been, is, and will be" (35:20).

Unthinkable, for Pla, is synonymous with inhuman (44:370). The aporia of considering history as both human (a determining adjective) and inhuman (a qualifying adjective) is not truly contradictory but a riposte to the reduction, by Wilhelm Dilthey among others, of human behaviour to a cultural phenomenon, to an activity, in other words, which because it originates in the human being must be governed by reason. But history relentlessly curtails the scope of reason, as does death. Ironically, the defensive denial of one's own death (and the defensive denial of history's receding and fading, which is the equivalent of death on a giant, collective scale) arouses amnesia. Forgetting our own death prevents us from radically rationalizing life (1:219–20). Given over to oblivion, reason sinks into any variation on the empty eloquence that French moralists castigated and Montaigne tried to overcome by centring discourse on the immediate experiences of the mortal I. Pla: "Human reason, abstracted from the presence of death, turns into what it actually is: a pure pedantic game. On the contrary, in everything that is inaccessible to death's projection – for instance, in the system of mathematical verification – reason plays a great role and its constructions seem sculpted in marble and definitive" (1:220).

These reflections, more becoming of an older person than a college student, put the origin of *The Gray Book* at a distance from a young man's diary and move it closer to the experiences of a man who, disappointed by politics and detached from journalism, as he had practised it before the Civil War, withdrew to the family's farmhouse to write hundreds of articles for *Destino*, some requiring extensive travel throughout the world, but above all with the purpose of ordering his work and turning it into a huge mnemonic exercise about an era – a time centred in and limited by his personal capacity for testimony. In this too he coincided with sixteenth-century memoirists, men of action fallen from favour and alienated from the court who found themselves forcibly disengaged and inactive, or else, as Fumaroli remarks, caught in this other misfortune that is old age and the proximity of death (316). The key to *The Gray Notebook* lies in its being a work of maturity fictively transposed to a youthful consciousness at the moment of its transition to reflection, that is, to the first glimmer of death's reality. This meeting between the inner self of the mature man and the young self he once was, as in Borges's tale "The Other," implied that a consciousness of representation presided over *The Gray Notebook*, in the sense of the memory of thoughts and reflections that really and demonstrably, if in a more elemental, less developed stage, existed in a journal of the years

1918–1919. A representation that also served the purpose of providing continuity for the self and attaching it to some form of permanence by "collaborating with these elementary necessities, the images, pleasures, and pains of past generations [that] have created a tradition, a law that governed our dead inexorably, that guides us, that will guide the future" (1:465). But if in the original notebook, the young Pla – enthusiastic reader of Maurice Barrès – still believed in the guidance of the dead and in tradition's future, the mature Pla is far more sceptical and no longer believes in any promise of permanence. "This pretence to immortality is one of so many of romanticism's absurdities. The only ones who believe in it are pedants and conceited people. Nothing" (35:314).

So, why would a writer who did not believe in the persistence of literature commit to a far-reaching memoir that absorbed the better part of his life? Pla, the cynical Pla, the intellectual who posed as a peasant and sought refuge in his farmhouse, believed that he had lived in the cruellest period of history. He considered that "freedom is vanishing before our eyes. Personal freedom – the only one that there is – is breathing its last" under the hegemony of socialist man and of the masses (35:553). As in Orwell's socialist utopia, no one remembers any longer how things had been in the past. "Everything is legendary and ungraspable" (35:552). Against this perception of the dissipation of the past, with a cyclopean strength of devotion, he lifted the weight of the forty-five volumes of his oeuvre and threw it against the wall of forgetfulness surrounding a world that had been annihilated and could no longer be retrieved but which, in the very fact of having been, passed judgment on the present. The resolve to bear intimate, genuine testimony, together with his contempt for abstraction and all the forms of fantasy, clinched his commitment to objective writing, to representing things as they are or were, in line with the *res ut res* (the thing as it is) of the memoirists.

4 Difficulty of the Novel

A book on Josep Pla will always be incomplete. His interests were so diverse, his curiosity so catholic in scope, and his oeuvre so extensive that no matter how comprehensive, the commentary will never be inclusive. This slender book does not aim for comprehensiveness or even representativeness with regard to the myriad themes and subthemes. It hopes, nonetheless, to identify the gist of Pla's writing with the assumption that it stands at a transitional moment not only with regard to the stylistic evolution of Catalan prose (as has been said often enough) but also to the seismic landslide away from an elaborate, ultimately aestheticist conception of literary production that we might loosely call modernist, and towards a more communicative, context-bound, orality-governed, and community-directed (Pla would have said "gossipy") form of writing.

In *The Life of the Mind*, Hannah Arendt discusses the Cartesian opposition between thought and reality in terms of the dislocation of the thinker, who, "moving among universals, among invisible essences, is, strictly speaking, nowhere; it is homeless in an emphatic sense – which may explain the early rise of a cosmopolitan spirit among the philosophers" (199). Josep Pla was no philosopher and had no truck with invisible essences or universals. Although he lived many years in boarding houses and cheap hotels all over Europe, crossing the oceans in oil tankers and cargo ships, he was always existentially at home, rooted in his *país*, the Empordanet or "little Empordà," a region within a region within a region of Spain. This local, some might say "parochial," ascription provided him with an angle for his perspective on a large part of the world and with a keen awareness of the inescapable embodiment of all thought. Although cosmopolitanism rests on the assumption that the immediate scope of one's existence can be ignored or neutralized, the fact is that one can transcend it as easily as one can leap over one's shadow. As Agnes Heller memorably wrote, "the terrain of a king's everyday life is not his country but his court" (6).

"Thinking always 'generalizes,'" wrote Arendt, "squeezes out of many particulars – which, thanks to the de-sensing process, it can pack together for swift manipulation – whatever meaning may inhere" (*The Life of the Mind* 199). Pla was mindful of the de-sensing produced by abstraction and the futility of manipulating thought from which the particulars have been squeezed out. Sensory experience precedes thought, which is not inevitable or defining in a Cartesian sense. The writer's task is to convey the world of appearances, not essences. Thus, coming home from a funeral in a crowded train, he observes the passengers immersed in dense silence:

> If one could imagine a train full of thinkers, it would look like this one. Every face shaded by the brim of the hat. What are we thinking? Perhaps nothing. The drama is that there are so many things in the presence of which one can think nothing – so many things in the presence of which the mental mechanism is barren. (1:379)

Facing the impenetrable silence of a crowd, Pla attests to the impossibility of thought when the shadow of death (for this seems to be the implication of the hats' shadows on the faces of mourners) falls across one's face. On this occasion his power of observation is heightened to the degree that his thinking apparatus stalls. But even in the midst of his non-thinking, which does not entail lack of awareness, Pla generalizes from his silence (replicated in his lack of mental articulation of thoughts) to that of the rest of the passengers, who resemble an assembly of thinkers gathered, who knows by what prank of destiny, in a railway carriage. Heller sees Arendt's opposition between the general and the particular in a dialectical fashion as co-determining of consciousness. "Only he who generalizes – she claims – can have self-awareness, awareness of his particularity [...] Where there is no generalization, where there is no promulgation of human species-essentiality, there is no human particularity" (9).

Pla's focus on particularity is, in point of fact, predicated on generalization, both small scale and large, encompassing all classes (for instance, his quasi-anthropological depiction of peasants, small shopkeepers, and urbanites), and national groups, generalizations that risk and often incur the cliché. What counts, however, is that all these generalizations are attempts at manipulating the world as perceived from a particular viewpoint. What centres the perspective is a historical individual who refuses to pose as a disembodied, floating intellect and insists on the essential identity between his self-awareness and world-awareness through his senses. His fierce scepticism towards abstraction and his insistence on the cognitive value of sensory impressions place him squarely in the empiricist tradition. Since this school of thought had penetrated nineteenth-century Catalonia through the Scottish common-sense philosophy, suiting its aversion to idealism and subjectivism, Pla could easily be considered a popular exponent of this line of thought. This is true only to a certain extent. In many of Pla's reflections about impermanence there is an echo of Hume's contention that all we know is a succession of states produced by experience. And without going as far as Berkeley in denying substance to the external world, he was nonetheless in agreement with Locke's assertion (in *An Essay Concerning Human Understanding*, Book II, Ch. XI §17) that "external and internal sensation are the only passages I can find of knowledge to the understanding. These alone, as far as I can discover, are the windows by which light is let into this *dark room*" (63).

Pla practised a literature of observation, a *theory* of things, in the etymological sense of *theorein* (to look at). But his observation did not imply a withdrawal, such as, according to Arendt, is implied in all mental activities. "Thinking," she said, "deals with absences and removes itself from what is present and close at hand" (*The Life of the Mind*, 199). Pla, on the contrary, is a writer of proximity, a man who deliberately embraces limits and writes from within the horizon of his senses. He rejects the "generally meaningful," which is for Arendt the intended object of thought. Since "essences cannot be localized" (199), Pla rejects such distillations, preferring the raw sensations in which he discerns the honest truth of experience. If sight is the speculative sense par excellence, Pla foregrounds taste as the innermost sense, the one that merges self and world in an osmotic relation and removes the fallacy of an ideal world made of essences or universals:

> Life is variety, nature very hard – in fact impossible – to unify and to read. And, since observation proves what we are saying, I do not think it necessary to add anything else to what we have already recounted. It is obvious that on this occasion the palate has been our criterion of reason – and that this criterion will be rejected by the votaries of systematic transcendence. (35:235)

Since his earliest narrative attempts, modified and collected in volume 2 of the Collected Works, Pla aimed to create a narrative of the object as humanly perceived, a *Gesamtkuntswerk* of the senses. In this festival of carnal intelligence, taste comes into its own in a rare literary vindication of the world materially consumed and spiritualized in moods that arise from the body's well-being or discomfort. Thus, under the pretext of recounting the memories of time spent in a small fishermen's hamlet in the Costa Brava, the text "Bodegó amb peixos" (Still life with fish) becomes a tract on the arts of fishing and the culinary qualities of the local species of fish. But it is in the story "Un viatge frustrat" (A frustrated voyage) that Pla rises to the challenge of subjecting the reader's imagination to the forward thrust of narrative teleology while anchoring each paragraph and each phrase in the phenomenology of the sea, through its visual, aural, tactile, olfactory, and gustatory presence to the narrator. In this story fish also feature prominently, but treated as the *punctum* (to use classic Barthes terminology from his book on photography) in a larger image encompassing the experience (geographic, cultural, social, even historical) of the northern coast of Catalonia, from Calella de Palafrugell to the first villages on the French side of the border. As readers of Barthes will recall, the *punctum* refers to the detail in an image that centres the view by a spontaneous, powerful appeal to the spectator. It is, so to speak, the spot on the image's surface that fascinates the viewer because, in some undefined way, it is the point towards which the semantic or emotional force of the image centripetally converges. A relatively long quotation will help clarify how the presence of fish, even as a meal, can concentrate in a few lines the corporeally experienced intuition of the sea:

> Hermós slices the bread and deposits a huge tray with fish on the hatch of the stern. He sprinkles them with abundant oil and vinegar. Since the light wind begins to abate, we fasten the rudder and start eating as if we were at a guesthouse. My travelling partner takes the fish by the head with the fingers of one hand and by the tail with the fingers of the other and eats the sardines as if he were playing an ocarina. He devours them by aspiration, sucking them. The fish bone comes out of this operation bare and clean. Displays of avidity suit quite well this ancient sea. There are places in this sea where one seems to smell the stench of Homeric hecatombs. I eat them – without false modesty – in a more academic fashion: on bread, but with my fingers.
>
> After eating the first twenty (each), accompanied by the corresponding wine, Hermós prepares a salad of green pepper and tomato. The sun

> gleams on the scales of the fish and on the oil drops of the food; it touches off tiny sparks on the flesh of the pepper and on the wine bottle. The morning is glorious. The sun is strong. The sky's dazzle, of a deep blue, seems a cushion of delights. The wind slowly dies down. (2:90)

In Pla the cognitive role of the senses is paramount. Life's material foundation underpins its diversity and provides the main objection to the universalization of experience, the "nowhere" of philosophical idealism. Depending on the salinity of the water, Pla remarks, a variety of fish changes to the point of becoming a different culinary species. The red mullet that lives on the muddy bottom of deep waters is tasteless. But the mullet that lives on sandy, rocky beds along the coast of Tossa, Torroella, or Begur makes a first-rate dish. Cooking reveals its quality by the colour the flesh takes on the grill. Fire draws a pinkish, pallid colour from the lower quality mullets. From the good mullet it brings out "a deep, sumptuous, cardinal red, the red that we all know and that so strongly resembles the immortal reds that Velasquez put on the portrait of Pope Innocent X of the Doria Gallery in Rome" (2:21). Material conditions determine everything that is actualized in any of the forms of human experience. Recalling Feuerbach's dictum that "man is what he eats," Pla claims that, with much better cause, this is true of the mullet. He does not specifically cite Feuerbach but refers to materialists of seventy years earlier. The reference is ironical. The point is not to vindicate an opinion that Feuerbach himself had retracted (Cherno 397), but rather to reject Hegelian idealism while endorsing a vague form of historical materialism. "In other places, the origin of many things can be spiritual. Here the cause of almost everything is the weight of matter" (2:115). For Pla, it is not the idea that materializes in world history, but human voraciousness that shapes culture by pursuing its prey. Hence, the bouillabaisse ignites the following reflection: "It seems to me that a dish only becomes popular when in one way or another it serves the instinct of human avidity. It is sad to have to say it: in every man, no matter how normal his appearance, lurks a gourmand of something: of something spiritual or material" (2:344).

The Rotation of the Senses

Taste – broadly understood – was for Pla the conscious reflection of a pragmatic need. The keener the need, the higher the degree of aesthetic appreciation. In *Viaje en autobús* (Travel by bus, 1942), he describes the awe produced on starved post-war travellers by the sight of a potato field. The Romantic sublime, associated with the contemplation of the landscape, is an effect of the outside referents on the volitional economy of the individual. "The idea of the landscape depends on how hungry one is" (9:71). Post-war famine, exacerbated by government-tolerated black marketeering, exasperates the senses, producing aesthetic delusions. In the historical conditions alluded to by Pla, resolving aesthetics into organic deprivation had political overtones. It raised the question, how much or in what way does the possibility of narrating one's experience as a facet of historical incident depend on the senses? And to what extent is history aesthetic in the fundamental, somatic sense of the term *aesthesis*? Pla, who often incorporates brief historical accounts into his descriptions of place, provides an inner history of society through everyday experience and fleshing out a culture of the senses.

The replication of cultural identity is embedded in material practices like those described in Pla's texts about fishing, cooking, or working on the land. Conversely, because identities are impervious to indoctrination, they dissipate at the same rate as those practices are dilapidated by standardizing behaviour, or when people move to cities and cast off their practical wisdom in exchange for what Pla calls derisively "el batxillerat dels nens" (the high school diploma for the children). Economic processes are paramount in his account of the demise of traditional culture. Those processes underlie cultural exchanges and enable or hinder, as the case might be, the perceptual appropriation of the environment. Handwork relies on the transmission of sensory experience, of a slow, disciplined mastery of its materials. It is the embodiment of memories of past generations transformed into objects of practical beauty. When the crafts are evacuated through the introduction of mechanized labour, the accumulated power of discrimination vanishes along with the sensory memories that constitute the local world as a system of exchanges with the environment. In the short story "Contraban" (Smuggling), Pla writes: "The crafts have created the most beautiful, most graceful, most elegant things in the world. What machines make is sad, horrible, depressing, of a funereal vulgarity" (2:313–14).

Nature, the most universal of concepts, is knowable only within the radius of rooted human life. The sea, the cliffs, the salty air, the light, in short the elemental world at the basis of our increasingly abstract worlds, is known to the senses as native presences long familiarized through multigenerational adaptation. This primitive, material attendance acts upon the human organism, which seeks relief in a man-made environment of duller objects that soothe the senses through their topical generality:

> The fierce air of indigenous things makes me appreciate the fading aspect of vague things. After the tang of the water and the reef, of the salt and the wind, the sun-drenched eyes, the windswept skin, the scattered thought – a bouquet of roses, the muted flicker of light on the backdrop of a mirror, the sheen of the old wood furniture, make a delightful sedative. (2:141)

The universal is for Pla a contraction and lessening of the efficient presence of the actual – a temporary refuge from the more rugged and fascinating play of the concretely real on the body's surface. All of the stories in *Aigua de mar* (Sea water) (a collection of previously published texts) support a view of the sea as a realm of freedom and adventure, as well as danger, where survival hinges on a sensory apparatus capable of intuitive prediction. The degree of humidity, the pressure of the air on the skin, the discrimination of the winds, their strength and duration, the gradation of the waves and the colour of the water, are the alphabet of sailing, easily read by professional sailors who trust their intuitions. Such people never forget that the sea is mysterious and uncertain. That is why they nurse utopian dreams of a tame, rationalized environment. In "Navegació d'estiu" (Summer sailing), Martinet wishes for a providential universe devoid of surprises and discontinuities. "He longed for a purely ideal, imaginary nature, like the nature the peasants dream about. An absolutely rational, mechanical nature, governed by a perfect yet hypothetical calendar" (2:533).

In her poignant study of the destruction of sensory geographies in Greece (a process that affected the Catalan coast ever more deeply since the 1950s), C. Nadia Semeretakis observes that the senses "are a social fact to the extent that they are a collective medium of communication that is both voluntary and involuntary, stylized and personal" (4). In Pla's stories, characters constantly exchange interpretations of their sensory experiences and in this way build the ideal scaffolding for their socialization. Extending their action over generations, the senses help separate a precipitate of material culture out of the haphazard fluid of experience. Recording the vestiges of this secular precipitate, Pla becomes, first inadvertently and later deliberately, a historian of the material existence of Catalans in the twentieth century. In this respect, more than in a superficial political sense, his self-description as a conservative shows concern that society may lose the glue of accumulated experience and come apart: "If we do not preserve what the society that we find ourselves in has to offer [...] everything will collapse. Everything will be lost" (35:225–6). In an article titled "Per què sóc conservador ?" (Why am I conservative?), he asks: "if everything, by the simple fact of its existence, is bound to destruction and ruin, if of so many good things hardly anything remains but a memory, and of the most beautiful not even a memory, if everything turns the corner of fleetingness and oblivion ... how could one even think that one might stop being conservative? Should we not set a limit to the madness of our phantasmagoria?" (24:293).

Pla's stories capture the sensory infrastructure of a culture or country, if by country we understand the circumscription of publicly typified exchange between the somatic power to register and appreciate and the significance deposited by human activity on the world's surface. Seremetakis speaks of the literality of sensory experience in the sense of rationalization and refunctionalization of the perceptual capacities embedded in a culture. These processes are undertaken with a view to commodifying sensory experiences for normative consumption. In this context, literality refers to the extrapolation of a limited aspect of experience, which is then made to pass for the whole experience. "Literality, as a cultural code, prescribes and insures norms of limited, functional and repetitious engagement with the disposable commodity unit" (10). Writing in the same vein, Pla declares: "Literary literature makes me throw up" (35:225).

Commoditized experiences replace each other in quick succession, obliterating the sensory investment each previous experience had elicited. Standardized sensory experience produces no accumulation and hence no learning. Since the last experience has no purchase on the current one, the latter invades and holds the attention for as long as it lasts; then, it falls away like cinder. When tradition does not hold, a void opens in formerly active and productive societies. This void is occupied by dust, in Seremetakis's terms, and by abstract, meaningless talk, in Pla's. "Dust," for Seremetakis, "is created by any perceptual stance that hastily traverses the object world, skims over its surface, treating it as a nullity that casts no meaning into our bodies, or recovers no stories from our past" (12). The opposite of dust is what Pla calls "an authentic reality" (35:225), for instance, the writing of authors whose work still rouses critical animosity centuries after their death. Lingering animosity proves, according to Pla, that those works have a temporal substance, an accumulated force of presence, which their insubstantial critics, scanning the surface of things, cannot hope to achieve. Pla criticizes people who live on the Earth's surface without caring about the realities that meet their senses. Distraction can afflict anybody, but he considers it intrinsic to intellectuals (professors, critics) and more generally to cosmopolitanism, which he defines, like Arendt, as the neutralization of place and the promotion of homelessness as a virtuous path to abstraction. Pla assigns cosmopolitanism the value of dust, which he sees not only as the waste and litter of a depleted world but also as the Midas touch that downgrades, dulls, and makes homogeneous everything it comes into contact with. "Dust," says Seremetakis, "is not deposited only on the object but also on the eye. Sensory numbing constructs not only the perceived but also the perceiving subject and the media of perception" (38). And each of these, she says, is a component of a historical process of eradication of ancestral experience.

In this respect, recovering stories from the past and preserving a memory of the senses is a *conservative* line of attack against the social and economic trends that deplete the possibilities of sensory experience by extinguishing their material conditions. This is no doubt the meaning of Pla's assertion that man is not rational but sensual (Pániker 2). Essential human sensuality is the reason why all dictatorships, beginning with Plato's Republic, are puritanical schemes of rationalization, whereas for Pla life is a heap of contradictions, and the achievement of some basic order, such as the appearance of a baguette every morning, a true mystery (Pániker 3). Pla's politics, which may be described as conservative liberalism, can be seen as an aspect of his poetics. His insistence on straightforward language, on simple sentence structure, on adjectival precision, and phenomenological description rather than artificial emplotment, correlates with his confession that "politics for me is very hard to understand" (35:230), a programmatic statement from someone who devoted years and hundreds of pages to reporting the sessions of the Spanish Parliament (from 1931 to 1936) and penned countless articles and even books on political matters. There is no paradox in this. What he meant in the sentence just cited is that politics, like language, becomes comprehensible only at the level of everyday experience, of the things one sees and grasps without mystification. Seremetakis goes further in relating Aristotle's definition of man as a political form of life, the *zóon politikón*, to a poetics, that is, a *making* of community through the sensory modulation of experience, which she calls "a politics of everyday life" (14).

It would be wrong to look at Pla's narrations about fishing villages and shipwrecks as the expression of nostalgia for a romanticized way of life that modernity was grinding to dust. Pla has no truck with modernist writers like W.B. Yeats, D.H. Lawrence, Wyndham Lewis, or E.M. Forster, who revered the peasant as the humble antithesis to the conceited bourgeois and the even more execrable petty bourgeois. Pla's book on the peasants (*Els pagesos*), written in proximity to the subject matter, is far from the fanciful modernist glorying in the "purity and beauty of the peasant vision," in Wyndham Lewis's words (Carey 206). Such panegyrics from afar were the product of the intellectuals' reaction to the triumph of the middle class and the industrial economy based on science and the liberal bourgeois values that made it possible. The modernists revered the peasant as the representative of a residual culture whose lack of political pertinence allowed it to be ascribed to the archaic and used as an expedient to attack the forms of sensibility (or insensibility, as they would have it) that characterized their dismal view of contemporary society. Pla despised this intellectual pose and blasted the modernist writers' cultivation of formal obscurantism with a view to excluding the hated masses from the audience. To Eliot's claim that "Poets in our civilization, as it exists at present, must be difficult" (Carey 17), Pla replied with a call for absolute clarity, the writer's challenge and true merit being, in his view, to attain the quality of crystalline expression under the pressure of referentiality. It is the external, objective world known to everyone, and not a coterie of supercilious intellectuals, that passes the ultimate judgment of whether he's pulled it off. Thus, he considered it a duty to write for everyone, "for the minority and the majority, with the highest dignity, underscoring the simplicity with which it is always possible to write a language to approach people" (26:195).

Pla exhibited none of the modernist writers' hatred of the bourgeoisie. Thanks to this class, he says, contemporary society offers the best conditions that ever existed, despite the tragedy of the recent wars (35:225–6). Notwithstanding his horror of anarchy, he shared none of the twentieth-century intellectuals' fondness for dictatorships of the right or the left, not because of greater or lesser affinity with one or the other ideology, or because he was, as he put it, "an instinctive, fierce, incorruptible individualist" (3:469), but because of a deep-seated respect for reality. For him, this was the touchstone of socially effective thought. Thus, he considered Sartre's espousal of Marxism incidental to a personal aversion to existing human nature and a puritanical ambition to replace it with a different one. "Jean-Paul Sartre is a utopian thinker of considerable ambition and very long range. To say that he is a communist, with or without a card, a Marxist, is to say very little ... He is a utopian of the deep and grandiose kind, as Rousseau was in his oeuvre" (33:495).

Pla's politics is best described as "commensality," which Seremetakis defines "as the exchange of sensory memories and emotions, and of substances and objects incarnating remembrance and feeling" (37). Although a self-described shy type, Pla observed that from time to time he loved to submerge himself in thick, extremely dense human settings (3:470). Paradox: the Llofriu recluse was one of the great conversationalists of his time, the architect of a vast verbal edifice built on the real or fictionalized exchanges with countless persons from all walks of life and a great variety of countries. Pla's oeuvre can only be compared to Dante's in the patient reconstruction of a cosmos through the dialogic fleshing out of reminiscences, sympathies, attitudes, sensory information, and emotions, amounting to a moral universe revealed through the pitiless accuracy of human memory. "When I was still very young, I grasped the liveliness of human memory in relation to the evil one has perpetrated and the good one has failed to do owing to carelessness, neglect, or pure chance" (3:470). If Dante's circuit through the spiritual realms of the medieval cosmos was a kind of spiritual bread-breaking with the souls of the dead through intensified acts of memory, Pla's moral assessment of his age was decanted through figural and often literal commensality, that is, through the exchange of memories and emotions ultimately rooted in sensory impressions, from which there was no honest escape or transcendence to metaphysical realms of experience. "What do we know about life, about the people around us, the friends who we constantly meet, with whom we speak and whom we love? Do we know anything about them? Do we have any precise idea about them? Do we know anything situated behind or to the side of their physical presence?" (26:552).

It was this physical presence that Pla endeavoured to capture with phenomenological accuracy, bracketing the metaphysical vagueness and romantic pretensions of human oratory. Sensory inspection rather than intellectual persuasion (which is always a form of self- and mutual deceptiveness) sets the limits of the knowable through social exchange. "The eyes are our most decisive dialectical instrument – they are perhaps the dialectic itself" (3:550). Only Pla could have given an account of an ex-cathedra lecture by prestigious Spanish philosopher José Ortega y Gasset without the slightest mention of the lecture's content. The entire allocution is reduced to a phenomenological description of the professor's voice and its incantatory power. "I found myself, then, not in front of a theme, of a question that, had I known its heading, could have interested me more or less, but in front of a human voice, of a man who speaks" (3:551). He compares the voice to an old piece of furniture, solid and with shiny surfaces attractive to the touch (3:552). There is evident irony in the assertion that "the professor's voice reaches the acme of beauty when one realizes that everything he says – whatever it might be – is lost in the desert" (3:552). And yet, the gratuity of the spectacle is not without a certain splendour, like the architectural mass of El Escorial, isolated in the barren uplands of a decaying empire. Pla succeeds in presenting the most influential Spanish philosopher of the twentieth century as a sophist who can dispense with rhetorical tricks, because he has mastered the melodic inflection of nineteenth-century parliamentary orators. But beyond the irony, he is concerned with the bounds of human expression and the confinement of knowledge claims to the experience certified by the senses.

Situated Literature

Nature cannot be unified through universal laws, which are man-made instruments designed to manipulate and exploit it. Efforts to read nature as a book mistake phenomena for signs organized by an invisible grammar. What cannot be explained in those terms is often ascribed to supernatural causes. Pla, who sees flux and uncertainty everywhere, attributes chance to a let-up in nature's mechanical predictability. He defines miracles as nature's inattentiveness ("A miracle is an oversight of nature," cit. Valls, *Josep Pla oral* 119). Life's irregularities and inconsistencies tear the conceptual yarns spun by abstract thought. Concretely situated life is the "truth" to which a human observer can aspire. If "essences cannot be localized" (Arendt, *The Life of the Mind* 199), it is because truth is not essential but existential, a term Pla does not adopt, however, because he wants no truck with formalized thought. But if the everywhere of abstract thought is a *nowhere*, and thought replaces the paratactic relation between sensory experiences with a *succession* of soundless words, de-sensing and de-spatializing experience (Arendt, *The Life of the Mind* 200), then Pla reacts to both negations by insisting on the inexorable localization of genuine experience and adopting a form of writing that conveys its sensory, efficient presence:

> In literature I have always been in favour of texts displaying geographic precision, of their having an explicit temporal frame. [...] Some people assert that on this point vagueness, imprecision, not ever knowing if we are in Poland or in Matadepera, amounts to being universal! It's idiocy pure and simple. In literature only concrete things are interesting. Concretion implies providing the situation – at the very least. At the very least ... Difficulty consists in describing the facts, the people, in presenting the atmosphere of the times. (12:272)

If literature is to convey presence, its linguistic expression must reproduce not merely the phonetics of colloquial discourse but also its syntactical and semantic aspects. Josep Valls, who saw Pla almost daily during his final years, corroborates what readers have always sensed and his clean manuscripts attest, namely, that he wrote a conversational vernacular. "The Josep Pla I knew wrote as he talked and talked as he wrote" (Valls, *Josep Pla oral* 11). Pla himself endorsed this practice axiomatically: "One must write as one speaks, as if one were writing for one's spinster aunt" (cit. Valls, *Josep Pla oral* 67). Adopting the colloquial tone of the *penyes* or conversation societies, which governed the transmission of opinion in Barcelona, he restored a semblance of orality to script. We must be mindful of this communicational concern when considering the vexed question of Pla's narrative. At sixty-eight, when asked if he read novels, he replied:

> I consider that a man who, after forty, still reads novels is a pure cretin. Which does not mean that there exist in the world eight or ten magnificent novels. Stendhal; two or three things by Balzac; *War and Peace*, by Tolstoy; some narratives by this English lad, Dickens; excellent. And finally, this story of Proust's, which is not bad at all. (Pániker 3)

This statement was bound to infuriate other writers. But Pla was serious in his relative disdain of fiction. By 1979, at the age of eighty-two, his admiration for Stendhal's fiction had declined drastically:

> When I was young, I was very partial to Stendhal. Now I am less so. Stendhal's novels and his notes on Italian painting make me yawn. The novels are theatrical and contrived, taking advantage of all that is hyperbolic and exaggerated in literature. Rightly observed and reflected upon, they make one yawn." (35:27)

If Stendhal's *The Red and the Black* and *The Charterhouse of Parma* could lose their appeal over time, the pulp fiction (and the fiction barely above pulp) that flooded the literary market could hardly elicit respect from someone who despised formulaic chatter and admired the ability to make or communicate explicit and irrefutable entities. Earlier, Pla had admired the fiction of Simenon, whose appeal, he claimed, did not lie in imaginative plots or tautly argued deductions but in his powers of observation. In one of several articles on the Belgian author published in the weekly *Destino* in the 1940s, he wrote: "I do not think his strength rests on a form or other of rich and inextricable imagination, like most writers of novels of this genre, but in a supersensitive receptiveness to grasp what is in front of him" ("Georges Simenon y la técnica de la novela" 5). As Xavier Pla points out in his study of the reception of Simenon in Catalonia, in the 1930s and 1940s Pla developed "an obsession" with this writer (*Simenon i la connexió catalana* 79). In the article just cited, he declared that Simenon had helped him reflect about the novel. Whether Pla drew his ideas about the novel from Simenon or discovered an affinity between this popular writer and his own literary inclinations is a moot question. It is certain at any rate that Simenon served him as an established mirror for his own literary persona. In the interview he conducted with the creator of Inspector Maigret on the isle of Porquerolles, off the coast of the Côte d'Azur in March 1937, the Belgian writer uses terms so similar to the later Pla's that Xavier Pla rightly remarks that in some of his answers, Simenon speaks somewhat like Pla (*Simenon i la connexió catalana* 73). What is certain is that Pla projected his own literary predilections on Simenon, magnifying his own narrative style in the mirror of a popular writer who had succeeded in transitioning from the kiosk to the catalogue of the *NRF* and had received accolades from the French critical establishment:

> A novelist's first quality must be a certain mental and imaginative passivity with regard to the environments, a notary's position so to speak in front of the life of his characters – which is perfectly compatible with the highest literary qualities – or technical qualities, to say it more clearly. ("Georges Simenon y la técnica de la novela" 5)

Counter-intuitively, Pla did not consider the psychological kernel of Simenon's novels their main attraction, but the faithful, notarial transcription of the settings and the people observed in real life. In an article on Conrad, also from the early 1940s, Pla had already combined deflation of novelistic thrill with unstinting admiration for the Polish writer's descriptions of the sea. "The kind of novel that Conrad cultivated is hugely dangerous. The adventure novel is, generally, a childish and insignificant sophistry based on the interest that melodramas produce against a background of exotic remoteness" (33:79). The dramas, he said elsewhere, are never part of reality. They are constructs; we fabricate them when we apply dialectic to the things or events and subject the external world to a preconceived idea, in short, when we take sides (2:399). Real are, for Pla, the things and events that we experience before they vanish, indifferent to the plots with which people strive to retain them in rhetorical constructions of greater or lesser sophistication. Storylines and narrative scenarios are for him clumsy attempts to fill the gaps between experiences with childish logic. Speaking of Pío Baroja, he wrote: "When his works are seen for what they really are, namely, a sequence of landscapes, figures, and milieus, they have a superb, unique, insuperable, fabulous quality. But it is hard – and tiresome – to eliminate from these books what they have of useless tripe, fictitious intrigue, added ploy, novelistic coiffure" (33:627). That is why, when all is said and done, Pla refuses to be judged by the genre he did not believe in or, in any case, did not practise: "I am not a novelist and I do not believe that novels exist in real life. There is nothing but a stream of disconnected, disordered, haphazard facts that take place, lapse, and evaporate. Novelists must believe that memory is man's strongest faculty, or else they would not have room to play. In reality, man's strongest faculty is forgetfulness" (2:398).

It is this observation that memory is an illusory strength, an unstable source of stability and identity, that led Pla to record the fleeting aspect of the world as it passes away, having touched the writer's sensitivity. This fleetingness of the world, the inherent instability of the concepts we create by adding sensations, is at the basis of his poetics, a realism that values the detail, the precise observation, and the permanent struggle to lend it the dubious permanence of linguistic expression. Pla settled on this poetics early on. In December 1925, just after the publication of his first book, *Coses vistes*, he was interviewed by Carles Soldevila for the journal *D'Ací i d'Allà*. Soldevila asked what genre the book belonged to, and Pla, understanding that he was being asked to write a novel, replied: "Novels can be written, must be written, if you will, by novelists. I have other work. My genre is inferior? You'll see that later. Everybody is good for one thing. I probably have a vague disposition to write the things I have seen" (A:506). Two years later, in another, possibly simulated interview, Pla stated: "I would have to write novels with a beginning, a crisis and a denouement, that is, I would have to cultivate the lowest literary genre, and insensibly my disposition leads me, regrettably, to save what I can of this profession. Thus sometimes I devote myself to pure realism and at other times, shamefacedly, to the noblest form that literature can attain, which is dialogue and polemic" (X.X.).

Nevertheless, in the preface to *Aigua de mar* (1966), a volume of stories written years earlier, Pla regretted not having had enough leisure to persist with the narrative work undertaken in his youth: "I would have liked enormously to be able to devote myself to narrative literature in a systematic way. I cultivated it with some vitality until the age of twenty-five. Thereafter, the necessities of life inserted me in the journalistic mechanism and its unavoidable dispersion" (2:7). In face of the previous disclaimers, it is not entirely clear that Pla had a narrative vocation, which more pressing constraints – his bondage to journalism – prevented him from developing. It seems more likely that what he called his disposition to pure realism blocked his dramatic imagination, his capacity to believe in and mentally transfer himself to the complications of a novelistic scheme in an invented or manipulated scenario.

This limitation is so evident in the large corpus of his works that one could flatly deny that Pla ever wrote fiction, let alone novels. But then, where would one place generically books such as *El carrer Estret*, *L'herència*, or *Nocturn de primavera* (Spring nocturne), and the stories contained in the volumes *La vida amarga* and *Aigua de mar*? Tantalizingly, Josep Maria Castellet titled one of the first monographs ever devoted to Pla, *Josep Pla o la raó narrativa* (Josep Pla or narrative reason), suggesting that narrative is the hidden spring of the twenty-six first volumes of the Collected Works that had appeared when this critical summary came out in 1977. However, the "narrative reason" identified axiomatically with Pla in the title was not justified in the body of the text or in the conclusion, where the book's title reverberates again in the title of this section: "La vida quotidiana o la 'raó narrativa'" (Everyday life or "narrative reason"). Only in an appendix did Castellet devote a little over two pages to the novel in Pla. This belated attention can be summarized in the opinion that "Pla's formal carelessness with regard to the novel, the story or the short narration is practically absolute," because he avoided "the inevitable formal, structural, or theoretical reflection required by the practise of these genres" (*Josep Pla o la raó narrativa* 232). Castellet's judgment evinces a conception of the novel that may be slanted towards narrative forms that simply did not tally with Pla's poetics of prose. In the early fifties, under the influence of Georg Lukács, Castellet had sponsored social realism. In 1957, he inaugurated the reception of the nouveau roman in Spain in an essay with the explicit title "De la objetividad al objeto" (From objectivity to the object) and in the book *La hora del lector* (The time of the reader). A few years later, as literary adviser for publisher Seix-Barral, he sponsored some Latin American writers, launching the boom of the Latin American novel (Santana). With this background, it seems likely that when Castellet laid formal carelessness at Pla's door, he had in mind types of novels that were strongly theorized or relied on non-mimetic construction of fictional worlds. Pla certainly did not set great store by traditional narrative structure, but instead of holding him accountable to an ideal definition of genre, it seems more productive to accept his view of nature's inexhaustible variability and proceed inductively. Then, from a consideration of the fictional prose that he produced in close proximity to his subjects and within the circle of his personal experience, it may be possible to reach some conclusions about the genre he cultivated and the merits or liabilities incurred therein.

Early on, in an interview for the daily *La Publicitat* that took place shortly after the publication of *Relacions* (1927), Pla declared: "A novel, if one wishes to respect reality, must be a succession of chaotic elements. My opinion is that reality is sufficiently important and complicated in itself to clutter it with compositions, cardboard arches, and garlands of artificial flowers. This is the reason why I think that Stendhal was right when he said that the interest of a novel is in the details, never in the composition. This will not be admitted, I know. The public admires illiterate writers to a very high degree" (X.X.).

He was aware that his "theory of the novel" clashed with the ordinary understanding of the genre. In the same interview he went on to say: "Critics ask me for a novel, a well-constructed thing, something well rounded that keeps up the interest of the middle class and the idiotic aristocracy in striped pants. Critics ask me for, that is, something absolutely bad. I make extraordinary efforts to please them and it seems that step by step I come closer to doing so" (X.X.). Although patently he did not hold literary critics in high regard, he found in Francesco De Sanctis's *Storia della letteratura italiana* a congenial authority to back his own stylistic choices. This work confirmed him in the validity of the realism to which he was partial, whether spontaneously or out of necessity. From De Sanctis, Pla drew theoretical justification for the kind of reportorial writing he had always engaged in: "One must always keep in mind the principle defended by De Sanctis: the writer, by the fact of being one, has a duty toward his time, namely, writing what he sees and hears around him" (Valls, *Josep Pla oral* 66). Writing about that which one experiences limits the fictional dimension considerably. Observation, if rigorously understood, compromises the imagination. Pla's strict notion of realism encouraged him to dispense with the construction of elaborate plots. Everyday life, full of complications and excitement, offers enough incentives without the need to adulterate them with artificial or fantastic structures.

Castellet considered Pla's attention to the everyday a salient feature of his prose. I would add that it is a constitutive principle. This statement should not be understood in the platitudinous sense that realism deals with objects of daily experience or with ordinary feelings and sentiments, but in a primordial sense, referring to something at once banal and elemental. Focusing on the everyday at the expense of fictional emplotment removes the novel from its origins in fantasy and illusion and secularizes it. Through a *reductio* of the grand themes of transcendent action, Pla pours significance on the petty gestures of a desublimated everyday.

He identifies the novel – or narrative in the broader sense – as the discursive frame for the display of prosaic and for the most part dull situations, conversations, and petty passions, in which the truth of our lives is revealed after idealism and romanticism have been bracketed. In an article on James Joyce, published in February of 1927, shortly before the interview in which he laid out his "theory of the novel," Pla praised Joyce's "lack of stylization" in terms suggestive of his own manner: "To place human material in a milieu, without caring to idealize or denigrate. At most a little humour, that which emerges naturally from a situation and from real people" ("James Joyce" 1). These are, of course, all features of Pla's prose, which casts a detached, often unemotional, at times sarcastic look on the situations and environments that he appropriates. He defended himself against allegations of cynicism by pointing out that his veristic writing shunned the snares of anthropocentric euphemism. If this entailed a cynical point of view, it was in the classical sense of cultivating lucidity and clarity of expression:

> I have been a writer from the school of life. My literature has been called cynical. It could well be. I have not been a crude, spontaneous cynic. I got there by reasoning. The contrast between the limitation of the human species and the literature built upon this species – rhetorical, triumphalist, and false – has caused me to see things from a cynical point of view – in the ancient sense of the word. (26:552)

Pla's dispassionate approach objectivizes the world, denuding it of imaginative flights or the bird's-eye view of abstract speculation. Hence his narratives, rich in the presentation of human types in situations that permit us to study them as specimens in a fish tank, are essentially anthropological. They contain an anthropology of the human condition, assembled from psychological, sociological, and almost folkloric portrayals of manners, reflexes, and traditions, in short, what Lionel Trilling called "a culture's hum and buzz of implication" (12). Yet, the *anthropos* involved is not the generic human being or the archetypal representative of the species, but the person encountered within and in the terms of everyday life, and in the first place the person who describes the everyday from inside. Internal perspective places the narrator on the same plane of cognizance as the people who turn up as characters in the story. Such levelling of the ground of awareness has nothing to do with the modernist relativizing of the focalizer, as practised by, say, Henry James. In Pla's narratives we cannot be sure what the other characters feel, except for what they communicate (and they are rarely completely sincere), but this does not mean that their motives are inscrutable. Communal pressures and implicit circuits of communication hinder the understanding for the outsider. Comprehension is compromised by the fact that meaning arises from the actions and reactions in daily exchanges, eliciting a gradual consensus of expectation in a slow learning process that integrates individuals into the shared horizon of a cultural community.

The Gossipy Novel

Everyday consensus as the outcome of intensive, face-to-face communication among individuals presupposes strategies of adaptation and survival leading to the discovery and integration of the value structure of the society in question. This is why *The Gray Notebook*, an autobiographical journal with fictional modifications, could be classified as a narrative of the anthropocentric everyday. I am aware that classifying Pla's journal as narrative could seem counter-intuitive, but it may appear less so if, instead of the nineteenth-century novel based on action, we recall earlier forms based on private communication, such as the epistolary novel of the eighteenth century, which relied on the juxtaposition of letters written by various persons representing different points of view. The notations in the private journal can be seen as a collection of letters that the author sends to a future self who is thereby invested with a reader's privileges.

Philip Lejeune considers the journal a site where the past negotiates with the future (*Écrire sa vie* 89). A place not of transcription but of elaboration of an identity that, since it overarches past and future, must be a narrative identity. In this more recent book, Lejeune appears to be revising his earlier opinion that the journal prevents the evolution of the personal past (*Signes de vie* 65). The problem of a non-evolving past seems less a matter of the particular form of the journal, which pins events permanently to a date but on the other hand elicits progress of the self-image from date to date, than of memory itself. Indeed, the status of memory in the journal, the question of whether the text can be considered an accumulation of traces from the past, is crucial to its understanding as the record of a self's formation. Only then can the paratactic regularity of diary entries be understood as progress towards a point from which the personal past will be apprehended as a destiny. The author of a diary writes blindly into the future, pushing forward as one lives life, but obtains the sense of his writing only by reading at a later time, in retrospect, as life is remembered and recognized for what it was only after it has happened. And because the future self for whom the diarist writes his daily impressions and thoughts is imagined as the mature, wiser prolongation of the self whose evolution is exposed in the journal, *The Gray Notebook* might be looked upon as a particular instance of the Bildungsroman. In his dissertation *Literatur und Organisation von Lebenserfahrung*, Peter Sloterdijk brings all autobiographical writing under the canopy of identity formation and socialization (18). Sloterdijk's assumption of a pre-social human being whose socialization is resolved in the course of autobiographical self-narrative refers in effect to a being as yet deprived of memory. And whereas few would dispute that autobiographies trace their subject's identity formation, the consensus may not include awareness that self-writing is performative, that it is, in other words, the occasion for and the means to elicit memories that might otherwise remain inaccessible.

The Gray Notebook is a memory artefact and also a text about the growth of a writer's vocation. It is an account of Pla's coming of age both legally and professionally. And yet, it is not an autobiographical novel in the sense Philippe Lejeune has given to this generic subcategory as "the fictional texts in which the reader has reason to suspect, from the perceived similarities, the identity between the author and the character, whereas the author has chosen to deny this identity or at least no to assert it" (*Le pacte autobiographique* 25). On the contrary, Pla wishes the reader to believe in the identity not only between the author of the text and the character who evolves through multiple acts of self-analysis, but also in the identity between the text given to the press and the annotations set down in a journal forty-nine years earlier. Although Pla was able to maintain the illusion for years, today we know that the published *Gray Notebook* greatly elaborates the original one, using it as a source or mnemonic device for a thoroughly composed literary masterpiece. The elaboration goes so far as to alter the dates of the original entries in order to configure the book as a Bildungsroman, belying the author's alleged unconcern with structure. Whereas 13 October 1918 was the original notebook's inaugural date, *The Gray Notebook* begins seven months earlier, on 8 March, making the journal's overture, Pla's baptism of ink, coincide with his twenty-first birthday, the legal age in Spain at the time. Furthermore, for the depiction of the family meal on his anniversary, he uses materials intended for the entry for 13 June in the original journal (*El primer quadern gris* 282). This date corresponds to St Anthony in the Catholic calendar and was his father's onomastic holiday.

Although *The Gray Notebook* complies with Lejeune's pivotal criterion of autobiographical texts, namely, the "mark" of the proper name, which refers to a lived reality outside of the text and a real person who claims ultimate responsibility for the enunciation of the entire text (*Le pacte autobiographique* 23), it is skewed by the insertion of a fictional structure, which inevitably impinges on the status of the proper name as a character within the text. In fact, the proper name as placeholder for an identity that the reader assumes to be ontologically grounded is a questionable criterion of veracity. As Micaela Maftei contends, the so-called autobiographical pact between author and reader is predicated on the assumption that these are stable identities. Such stability is a necessary fiction, not just because, as she points out, the author must be removed from the experience in order to write about it, wearing various masks to create the illusion of being both protagonist and recorder of the story (59), but also because what the self-imaging process shows is the transformation of a self that comes into being and expands by resisting crystallization. Furthermore, *The Gray Notebook,* inaugurating what seems to be a chronological publication of Pla's works, mimics the very situation that, according to Lejeune, makes for an infelicitous autobiographical pact with the reader. If, as Lejeune says, the previous production of non-autobiographical texts by the same author is indispensable for the emergence of "autobiographical space" (*Le pacte autobiographique* 23), then an aspiring author's autobiography would never succeed in creating "autobiographical space," because it would fail to enlist the readers' complicity. However, by the time *The Gray Notebook* appeared in 1966 as the incipit of the Collected Works starting to be published by Destino, Pla was already a famous journalist and the author of many books, including a previous, incomplete edition of his Collected Works, which had been appearing under the imprint of Editorial Selecta.

The Gray Notebook confronts us with a fictionalization of the problematic autobiographical situation described by Lejeune, but this time from the position of an author who could rely on his fame to draw readers into the "autobiographical space" of not just this one book but of an already substantial oeuvre. That Pla considered his Collected Works a macro-autobiography is attested by his friend Josep Valls, who, at a time when memoirs of all stripes proliferated, recorded Pla as saying: "Why write one's memoirs? A writer's memoirs are his books. To repeat them in the form of memoirs is usually redundant" (*Josep Pla oral* 66).

The diary format of *The Gray Notebook* masks the presence of fictional elements that converge on the sentimental education of a budding writer. The fictional diary, built with materials from an earlier and more limited journal, directs us to a privileged modality of communication that Pla had made the conscious focus of his attention. I refer to the café badinage, townspeople's chit-chat, or coterie repartee, in short, the social infrastructure of gossip. Joan Fuster, with customary sharpness, pointed out the prevalence of this form of sociability in Pla's works. "Pla is a character in a permanent after-dinner conversation, a powerful *causeur*, and his literature is also, ultimately, an inexhaustible table talk in which he leads and pricks up his ears" ("Notes per a una introducció" 30). Fuster calls *The Gray Notebook* "a lavish summa of Palafrugell gossip" (30). And truly, more than anyone else, with the possible exception of Proust, Pla made gossip the cognitive building block of his literature. In 1944 he explicitly linked gossip and the novel, claiming that the production of good novels depends on the vitality of gossip in a given society. The so-called crisis of the novel was due to the writers' incompetence in writing anecdotes. All the great novels, from the works of Balzac and Tolstoy to those of Manzoni and Dickens, are "a string of anecdotes intelligibly expressed" (31:151). Hence, gossip is the lifeblood of the novel, and characters in *The Gray Notebook* and elsewhere are temporary aggregates, momentary blobs in the fluid mass of circulating gossip that constitutes society.

It has been said that Pla's primary technique of composition was to insert discontinuous descriptive fragments and anecdotes into a narrative structure (Coromina 230). In other words, to motivate the scraps of gossip salvaged from social intercourse. The technique involved is the opposite of the collage. But if *The Gray Notebook* is formally a succession of independent anecdotes and reflections unified by the "mark of the proper name" (Lejeune, *Le pacte autobiographique* 23), *El carrer Estret* (The narrow street, 1951) succeeds in motivating its gossipy construction through a basic narrative form. In the introduction, Pla espouses the "mimetic" type of realism, citing Stendhal's dictum that "A novel is a mirror carried along a high road" (557). Only, Pla changes the Stendhalian high road for a narrow street. "I am so tired of finding that behind the 'great things' there is nothing at all, that I incline almost unconsciously to judge things with a criterion inverse to their external dimensions" (8:470). His mirror reflects humble, unpretentious images, the images of provincial life. "'Thus, I passed a mirror—my modest mirror!—through a small municipality of this country, a town named Torrelles, of about four thousand residents'" (8:439). The adoption of mimetic realism may in fact be disingenuous, as the qualification of his mirror as "modest" would imply. Xavier Pla warns that "Josep Pla's mirror does not reflect reality, does not reproduce it. If anything, it acts 'as if' it did. But in fact it invents, constructs, creates a world of fiction" ("La prehistòria" 20–1). The modesty of the mirror corresponds to Pla's own programmatic adoption of rhetorical modesty throughout his career; it is a giveaway sign of the subjectivity of the choices of locale, subject matter, and scope. As objectified consciousness, the aesthetics of realism allows the author to repudiate anything that in conventional representation can be dissociated from the spontaneous appearance of things. Stendhal used the mirror as a disclaimer for his novel's indifference to the prevailing morality – "His mirror shows the mire, and you accuse the mirror!" (557). And Pla resorts to the same metaphor to decline responsibility for the lack of a plot in his novel:

> The looking glass – beautiful word! – gave me, then, a series of images, but I was forced to realize that it did not reflect any consistent argument, any comprehensive architecture. A mirror is a passive force that lacks organizing faculties. If the mirror does not reflect any plot, it is because none passes in front of it. However, since this fact confirmed me in the suspicion that in life plots happen only by rare chance – and, consequently, that novels with a plot, rather than reflecting life, arbitrate a form of

> simulation – I did not consider myself authorized to be holier than the Pope or to modify ever so slightly the reflections in the mirror. (8:439)

Pla believed that readers demanded plots out of fatigue with the chaotic variation of life. Their longing for order and coherence prompted their consumption of fanciful, improbable plots. "Life's character is marked by an inflexible variety. That is why we always speak about unity as a paradise lost at a distance so great that it disheartens us" (8:440). Unity is, at best, an ideal tendency, never an a priori condition of experience; thus, narrative that is true to life does not presuppose unity as a stylistic convention, any more than it selects its themes and images for their beauty. There is no need, Pla suggests, for any magical realism, because reality itself is "prodigious and inexhaustible, crude and magical" (8:440). Even, he would add, when it appears vulgar, trivial, and lacking in transcendence. Apropos Stendhal, he recalled that a contemporary of the writer, Victor Jacquemont, declared his novels worthless because the author wrote like a concierge. Pla reacts by transvaluating the offence: "It is the highest tribute a writer can get. In literary prose, one must replicate human conversation intelligibly, like, let us say, when one writes to one's own family" (35:88). In 1950, Pla wrote that "we are all children of Stendhal, a fact we discovered between 1919 and 1920," that is, the year Pla began his writing career (31:274). The reason for this filiation is that Stendhal "materialized human psychology. He materialized as much as possible. […] Whatever results in the materialization of things is great. Otherwise we will never understand anything" (31:274). Materializing, producing presence, this was Pla's touchtone for literary honesty. Today there is a great deal of intellectual talk about the body, presence, and materialism, revealing tremendous nostalgia for immediacy, even as these discourses continue to excavate the hollow abstraction of "theory." Pla could have subscribed to Archibald MacLeish's famous lines that "a poem should not mean but be," with the qualification that it is prose, not poetry, that offers the greatest potential for invoking experience.

Torrelles, the fictional town of *El carrer Estret*, is, like Fontclara in the novels *L'herència* and *Nocturn de primavera*, the prototypical provincial municipality. "For its size," says Pla, "the town is absolutely standard" (8:460). The panoramic view that follows has been traced to the description of Verrières at the beginning of Stendhal's *Le rouge et le noir* (Bonada, "Una lectura del carrer Estret" 57); it was in fact inspired by Zola's depiction of Plassans in chapter 2 of *La fortune des*

Rougon. Pla's overview of the historical development of Torrelles is a masterly synopsis of the urban expansion of Catalan cities in the twentieth century. With the bird's-eye view of the provincial town, Pla maps the social and economic evolution of the country since the nineteeth century and the appearance of the new classes. With new ideas, ambitions, and lifestyles, the bourgeoisie and the working class burst upon a scene traditionally dominated by peasants and a rural aristocracy.

In the map of Torrelles Pla traces the history of modern Catalonia with its basic class structure. This short novel thus became a précis of his larger project to write a "human comedy," which he planned, on Dante's model, as a conceptual triptych. However, the cosmic spaces of metaphysical fate were to be the social classes. This tripartite structure consisted of books dealing with the peasantry, the shopkeepers, and the bourgeoisie, respectively. In the prologue to *Àlbum de Fontclara* (1971), the volume devoted to the shopkeepers, Pla confessed that he had not been able to sketch the book on the bourgeoisie yet. The difficulty in depicting this class, which had a "great, decisive transcendence [...] in the modern history of this country" (23:7), was to write about it "without recourse to convention or preconceptions" (23:8). To do this, he said, is quite difficult, as opposed to writing a sociological treatise with a prejudiced attitude either for or against the class. Sociological studies do not depict the environment created by the class, its ordinary habitat. Sociology fails to describe its way of being, the gestures of its members, their behaviour in concrete situations. "These books," he asserts, "have contributed to the tendency to posit all problems on the level of the universal, on the international level, and to consider all countries interchangeable, not to say identical. This tendency is grotesque because it is false, absolutely inconsistent, of an evidently laughable fantasy" (23:9). Instead he proposed the method of making the generalization contained in the idea of class compatible with the particulars of direct observation, a technique that, as Pla could not help being aware, had been perfected by Balzac and the other great nineteenth-century novelists. Of Balzac, specifically, he affirmed that his best novel was *La vieille fille*, and this for a reason that chimes with Pla's ideas about the novel as narrative devoid of fabulation. "It is a novel without a plot, that is to say with a purely moral plot, but with a prodigious accumulation of details" (35:266).

In its attention to detail, the great nineteenth-century novel pointed to the emergence of the "phenomenological novel" in the twentieth century. Pla attributed this formal modification to the maturing of a readership that could do without the mythic aspects of the traditional story, or, at least, was capable of an ironic relation to them. A "prodigious accumulation of details" presupposed running a thicker lens over a smaller surface. For Pla this precondition meant privileging bounded localities and intensifying the significance of what ordinarily passes under the threshold of narrative awareness. If the nineteenth-century novel could use the description of a provincial town (Saumur, Verrières, Plassans) as synecdoche of national life, there was no reason for Pla not to reduce the scale even further to a single street, and a narrow one at that. His opening gambit in *El carrer Estret* obeys his anti-romantic stance and his aversion to infinities. "Limitation, the details – this is the entire purpose of writing in our time" (23:9). And it is his insistence on the techniques of reportorial writing that led many critics to assume that Pla was stuck in an obsolete aesthetic of mimetic representation. Jordi Castellanos, for instance, doubted Pla's receptiveness to Joyce's innovations in *Ulysses* (59), although Pla wrote an early review of the book in February of 1927. Since Pla's knowledge of English was limited, it is possible that he did not follow Joyce's abstruse prose in every detail, but there is no reason to think that he missed the main thrust of the novel. Summarizing it as a painstaking description of the conscious and unconscious activity of a Dublin Jew in the space of nineteen hours is certainly compressing a great deal but is not fundamentally wrong or inadequate.

Pla's evaluation of Joyce's feat is interesting because, as is often the case with his appraisals of other novelists, it reveals his own hierarchy of narrative values. "This is a historical record in curiosity. Eight hundred pages situated between eight in the morning and three a.m. of the same day [*sic*] – of a completely vulgar day, of course, because otherwise the thing would lack interest – represent a first-rate immersion in reality" ("James Joyce" 1). In the 1960s he reread the book in the French translation of the *NRF*, which, incidentally, was published in 1942 under the German occupation. Again he was enthusiastic: "one of the most hallucinating documents of apparently fantastic realism in the history of literature. It is not only important – it seems to me – for its truculence, for the unstoppable draught of truth it contains, but for its subtleness and because technically it is a wondrous achievement" (26:230–1).

Castellanos pointed out the presence of Joycean features in Pla's first narrative book, *Relacions* (1927), which in his opinion betrays the influence of *Ulysses*. I fail to detect any parallelisms, either stylistic or thematic, with that work, but Pla, whose acquaintance with Joyce probably predated his reading of *Ulysses*, could have read one of the stories of *Dubliners* in Catalan, since a translation of *Eveline* appeared in the journal *D'Ací i D'Allà* in February of 1926. And in fact, *Relacions* seems closer to *Dubliners* than to *Ulysses*. The tone is recognizable in some of the chapters, which are, in fact, independent narratives unified by the narrator's function. Pla never claimed to have written a novel. In the preface to the book, he wrote: "This book which I have titled *Relacions*, I do not know exactly what it is. […] Perhaps the admiration I feel for the Dutch character painters has led me to put on paper, staggered, a series of scenes of human life; very diverse scenes in which misery and beauty mix, alternating vice with virtue, crying, mask, and grace. It would not be surprising if the book were this. But I cannot be sure" (10). Many years later, he was at least sure that the book did not add up to a novel. He did not include it in his Collected Works, but instead broke it up into its constitutive parts, rewriting and recombining some of the chapters, discarding others, and incorporating them as individual narratives in *La vida amarga*. Echoes from "The Boarding House" are discernible in "Pensió barcelonina cèntrica" (Centrally located Barcelona boarding house) and, especially, "Un mort a Barcelona" ("A death in Barcelona"), featured in this volume.

More intriguing is Teresa Iribarren's thesis that *El carrer Estret* reveals Joyce's lasting hold on the Catalan writer (49). This critic finds identical "thematic nuclei" in *El carrer Estret* and in *Dubliners*, but also some formal features, such as recourse to humour and the polarization of narrative materials around an epiphany, a moment of heightened understanding triggered by a trivial phrase or otherwise meaningless gesture. More decisive, she insists, are the use of the concept of paralysis in a broad moral as well as physical sense, and the presence of death (49). I am not entirely convinced about the attribution of some of these features to Joyce's enduring influence. Humour and an irrepressible will to sarcasm are permanent features in Pla, and the concentration of meaning around trivial moments follows from Pla's decision to focus on the everyday in a provincial small town. Nor is the presence of death sufficient to affiliate the novel to a particular aesthetic, although the allusions to a town in the grip of death noted by Iribarren are numerous. Regardless of whether Pla had *Dubliners* in mind when he wrote *El carrer Estret*, in 1951 the suspension of life and the deep somnolence of Torrelles comprised a criticism embedded in the town's potential generalization as the paradigm of a deeply provincial Spain. This was, in any case, the author's explicit intention in a letter to his publisher, Josep Maria Cruzet, dated 9 June 1951. To Cruzet's concern with the government's censorship, Pla replies that there is no reason to worry, because the censor will not grasp that this book "is the photograph of the sordid village life *in these times*" (my emphasis; Pla and Cruzet 154).

If *El carrer Estret* reveals traits of any personal poetics, this poetics is surely Pla's. Upon reading the manuscript, Cruzet congratulated him on "the good choice of a theme so clearly yours, suitable to be converted into a novel" (letter of 5 June 1951) (Pla and Cruzet 152). More recently, Maria Josepa Gallofré observed that the inception of the story is characteristic of his writings both before and after the Spanish Civil War (40). The main character, a recently appointed veterinarian, arrives by bus and takes lodgings at the inn, where the innkeeper is an example of the shiftless businessperson or employee who takes no interest in his occupation. The story is loosely structured around two points of view, that of the disinterested and somewhat naive outsider who observes at times uncomprehendingly the reality unfolding before his eyes, and that of his female cook, a villager who is passionately involved in the weft of rumour and hearsay that constitutes the social life of the village. Both are the author's alter egos. The external point of view, excluded from the perception of events that occur under his threshold of attention, is balanced with the participatory point of view of the cook, to whom Pla transfers the nosiness and prying that were personal and professional traits of his as journalist and irrepressible tattler. At the beginning of chapter 17, the narrator declares, "I am not nosey or curious. This is doubtless the reason why I will never be happy. The little merriment that hovers over this world consists, probably, in savouring the small details, the miniscule, amoebic anecdotes of microscopic gossip" (8:519). This self-appraisal represents only one half of the author's personality. The other half is Francisqueta, the cook who gloats when she can pry into other people's lives. "To my cook, ferreting out the lives of others is sheer delight" (8:489).

In *El carrer Estret*, Pla deployed a poetics of banality, the magnifying glass that turns the droning of a fly into a reportable event:

> In the room one can hear a fly. It must be only one. If there are two, the concentrated summer feeling produced by the winged insect makes one frankly uneasy. The aerial bug must still glide in sleepwalking fashion, as if it were crossing an extremely dense medium, a sugary atmosphere. Sitting at the table, pen in hand, in front of a white sheet of paper, I write these lines. The silence makes one hear obsessively the calligraphic nervousness

> on the paper. When the pen stops, one can hear the remote, dreamlike vagueness of the gnat's flight. (8:515)

This passage produces a heightened impression of boredom, of the futility of all endeavours, of the directionless life in the Spanish province of the early 1950s. The vacuity in a dense medium provides a clue for the remarkable amplification of local scandal and the anxious magnitude of the latest buzz in the midst of social paralysis. Merely by adjusting his lens to the scale of provincial reality, Pla is able to compare the passion of a village cook with the existential agonies of French intellectuals in the Left Bank.

> Intermittingly I read, in books and newspapers, that the trendy philosophers, the prized authors of the moment, ask themselves – with an anguishing tremolo of the pen that may be fake – what is the sense of their lives. What a strange question, my God! Francisqueta, who is located in life, perfectly rooted in life, who exists in life, knows perfectly its sense. We all know exactly the sense of our own life. […] Only, what happens is that the sense of our own life, when not a pure trifle, is so miniscule, so insignificant, so immeasurably laughable, that it cannot be revealed even to one's closest friends. (8:490)

Phenomenologically, the fly that interferes with the movement of the pen and imposes itself on the writer's attention is as important as the most refined dialectic. Its buzz becomes the immediate truth of existence. And if anyone does not consider a fly a lofty enough subject, then, as Pla would say, so much the worse for him. It is not through abstract reflection but through the shrewdness of the senses and the passionate exchange of opinion that knowledge is acquired. Thus, the veterinarian admits that everything he knows about his neighbours and the village, he knows through his cook. "Francisqueta has imposed on me her way of looking at things with an inexplicable ease" (8:519). Francisqueta's viewpoint is banal, but for Pla life happens for the most part on the level of banality. Most conversations are, he says, *flatus vocis*. An analysis of their contents would throw a mediocre result. "If every night, when we go to bed we had the strength and the courage to remember what we have said during the day, we would be astonished to realize how many useless, gratuitous, generally malevolent and often malign stupidities we have produced during the previous hours" (8:525).

This dust of words is the unreflective product of socialization, the matter-of-fact logic of the everyday collective self that Heidegger calls the "they-self" (167). We talk automatically, led on by the existence of ready-made phrases that we string together without a previous intention or a guiding object. It's talking for talk's sake. A phrase leads predictably to another phrase, and so on. Situations emerge whose representation requires putting aside the dramatic conventions of the novel, whose characters speak in conformity with the author's need to move the plot forward. "Only the characters of novels know exactly what they say to each other, they speak in a deliberate, conscious manner" (8:628). But real-life situations do not move forward purposefully; often they do not progress at all. Hence, Pla's text – a novel of sorts – must turn away from the novelistic convention of meaningful dialogue and opt for the hyperrealism of discretion. "In that coterie of shopkeepers the colloquial automatism was enormous. Sometimes they talked for half an hour by means of stock phrases – by means of phrases whose occurrence could be predicted with perfect confidence. [...] I did not record any conversation of this sort, but it would not be hard to reproduce them. I decided not to do it in order not to overdo the realism of these papers" (8:629). And this is the appropriate thing to do. How much banality can readers digest? Seemingly a lot, if one judges by the consumption of newspapers in the earlier part of the twentieth century and of television in the second half. But Pla's experiment with the novel called for a dialectic between this genre and the trivia that supplied the realism of newspapers and, even more, of non-fiction television programs. The new protagonists in the mass society of the twentieth century were the ordinary people whose unspectacular lives literature, "the noble, grandiloquent literature" (8:669), was not qualified to reflect. And these protagonists, the average man and woman, made necessary a new form of writing adapted to the cyclical pattern of life. They forced upon writers the modest realization that stories pre-exist the events. Stories are mythical patterns, which, like the change of seasons, provide structure to otherwise fragmentary anecdotes and variations on the subjective disposition of the characters. Anna Aguiló observes that "the change of the seasons and the climate variations alter the moods and activities of the villagers of Torrelles" (9). Pla, in other words, resorts to elementary referents of change and transformation to bestow a semblance of progress and variation on a life that, by and large, remains immutable except at the level of paltry and insignificant detail:

> Nothing particular, new, or important ever happens to the gray, opaque, commonplace persons who populate the earth's surface. Life begins,

> goes on, ends in more or less analogous circumstances, with more or less money, more or less sensibility, more or less lucidity. In reality, nothing more happens. The novels ...? Where are the novels? The novels can be found only in the imagination of the novelists; their characters are pure illusions of their spirit, which readers out of pure modesty mistake for themselves. (8:669)

Nothing happens in Torrelles, and the veterinarian concludes that he is in imminent danger of sinking into the village pre-established order, engulfed by the relative comfort of being definitively classified. This realization of the danger suggests Pla's awareness that life is not reducible to surface phenomena and that the apparent stillness of a given society presupposes a blind spot to social processes. Pla's blind spot was the reality of industrial work. Industry was the engine of Catalonia's growth since the nineteenth century and drove social transformation throughout the twentieth century. The main source of the material reality of his day did not feature in his project for a Catalan human comedy, where work, as distinguished from trade, was to be represented only by the peasantry, that is, by a form of production that went into accelerated decline during Pla's life. The relation of the peasant with the land or the fisherman with the sea seemed to Pla a more authentic and longer lasting influence on the physical constitution of the country and on the moral aspects of its history than the urban concentration of deracinated industrial workers. He certainly cannot be accused of idealism or of ignoring the labour base of consumption. Unlike writers who devote long paragraphs to describing meals in their novels, he never mystifies the origin of primary material consumption. But since he favours the kinds of labour that seem to guarantee the individual's self-sufficiency, he nowhere illustrates the conditions of production of the wares that the shopkeepers sell to the peasants, their victims on the immediately lower level of the social food chain. This is so much the case that Orwell's objections to Dickens also apply to Pla, notwithstanding the vast difference between both writers. "Much that he wrote is extremely factual, and in the power of evoking visual images he has probably never been equaled. [...] But in a way the concreteness of his vision is a sign of what he is missing. [...] Wonderfully as he can describe an appearance, Dickens does not often describe a process" ("Charles Dickens," *A World Like This* 443). The characters in *El carrer Estret*, like the caricatures in *The Pickwick Papers*, are sketches; they are so definitively marred by provincial indolence that they will go on forever behaving like the stunted creatures they are at any one moment. Of course, the one-dimensional characterization was meant subversively, and this intent can be intellectually retrieved by recalling that in 1950, when Pla began the novel, Spain was just beginning to come out of its political and economic isolation, its decade-long autarky. In that light, the veterinarian's reflection that he must gather all his willpower in order to leave Torrelles takes unexpected political significance. But this kind of gesture, repeated throughout his work of the period, coexists with moments of passive compliance, when Pla accepts the immutability of things and even warns against any attempt to change them. Radicalism for him amounts to obscenity. He is adept at tracing human action to traditional motives such as malevolence, ambition, avarice, sensuality, revenge, but misses the desire for freedom when, beyond the individual's self-determination, it is made extensive to the conditions in which the individual must exercise that essential right. In other words, he does not understand or endorse collective political struggle unless it is mediated by a superior personality. His admiration for a self-made liberal like Francesc Cambó and his aversion to the encroachments of government in ever-larger spheres of life must be judged in light of his fierce individualism.

A Hybrid Genre

It may be that novels – the paramount fictional genre – do not exist outside the imagination; but then the imagination has a central place in social life, in business as in politics, in science as in love. Eroticism is largely based on the imagination, as are religion, education, and advertising. Northrop Frye made this last point eloquently in a series of broadcast lectures in the mid-1960s. In the last lecture, "The Vocation of Eloquence," Frye said that advertising is one example of the programmed creation of illusion, and then remarked that "[o]ur reaction to advertising is really a form of literary criticism" (138). This is an insightful remark that can be extended to other reactions, for instance, to scepticism with regard to the notion that journalism is in the business of producing objective information, that is, information free from presuppositions. Journalism does present information but it does so in the shape of a story, a narrative of something that happened or is reputed to have happened. And when the journalist is not a novelist, or he is but acts as if he wasn't, segregating his creative approach from his objective attitude, then he must reach for the toolbox of news storytelling and choose one of the readily available plots.

As Jack Lule writes, "[j]ournalists approach events with stories already in mind. They employ common understandings. They borrow from shared narratives" (29). It is not hard to see that reporting on celebrities calls for an elevated tone, as if the journalist instinctively understood the ancient law of decorum. The assassination of a head of state, a great tragedy, a catastrophe – such events automatically shape the story and the language used to report it. In the case of the human-interest story, a journalistic subgenre introduced by the penny press, the focus is on the everyday, and the narrative forms available are based on different expectations from those governing stories about power and force. The human-interest story is the product of an individualistic society, interested in confirming the importance of personal acts without delving into the institutional and political causes of the situations described. James Curran, Angus Douglas, and Garry Whannel argued that human-interest stories consolidate "a community that shares common universal experiences: birth, love, death, accident, illness, and crucially, the experience of consuming" and that "this community is further given focus by the stock of commonsense assumptions about the world implicit in human-interest stories" (cit. Lule 120).

Many of Pla's articles share formal aspects with the human-interest story, with the further twist that he is always conscious of producing literature. By that I mean that he is at all moments conscious of writing with a view to enhancing the powers of imagination of his readers, even if he engages the imagination in the anti-romantic direction of destroying social illusions. Paradoxically, his sceptical, often sarcastic attack on those illusions contributes to giving a focus to the community implicit in his writings, a community of varying geographic dimensions referred to with the vague substantive of "this country." This is the case because Pla's insistence on common sense and tangible, sensually ascertainable, experience exerted subversive force in an environment corrupted by official lies and idealistic pieties. Conversely, his call for the locally circumscribed truths of sober experience had a constructive potential, manifest in the undeniable fact that it is impossible to conceive of Catalonia without the aide-memoire of Pla's oeuvre, even if, as has often been pointed out, his vision of Catalonia no longer corresponds to the reality, if it ever did. But this amounts to saying that Pla's work, for all its reportorial dimension and journalistic ballast, exists in the imagination, is in fact a work of imagination and survives the alleged demise of its referents, like all great literature does. There is in fact no other proof of literary greatness.

Pla's works could be styled aesthetic journalism, to use Alfredo Cramerotti's term. This qualification does not imply that non-literary journalism lacks aesthetic sense. But the aesthetics that shaped journalism since its inception in the eighteenth century has succeeded so broadly that reportage has been able to pass its conventions for objectivity itself. So naturalized are in fact the journalistic conventions that the impression of objectivity remains in effect even when we are aware of the distortion the reporter imposes on the subject of news. Being an alternative to aesthetically unconscious journalism, aesthetic journalism builds critical knowledge by raising doubts about the truth value of traditional reporting (Cramerotti 22). Of course, it matters what notion of "aesthetic" we bring to bear. The adjectival use of "aesthetic" in relation to the substantive "journalism" precludes a purely formalistic conception, as in art for art's sake. In this use, "aesthetic" is clearly associated with information, understood as the conveyance of someone's concrete relation to actual objects, circumstances, or events. Cramerotti's definition of "aesthetic" as "the capacity of an art form to put our sensibility in motion, and convert what we feel about nature and the human race into a concrete (visual, oral, bodily) experience" (21), is broad enough and yet circumscribed enough to hold the two terms together. But whereas he is concerned with the emergence of reporting in art, film (the explosion of documentary), advertising, and the Internet, rather than with the aesthetic modulation of "media journalism," his definition can be extended to cover the renovation of traditional, that is, media-based journalism through adoption of artistic forms of expression. It certainly fits Pla's exaction of literary demands on the journalistic prose of his time, and his matchless ability to set the reader's sensibility in motion through the conversion of previously vague or ideal notions about nature, the human condition, or society into concrete, sensory experience. By means of keen observation and a canny use of metaphor based on adjectival incantation, Pla was able to marshal the memory of the senses to produce a powerful illusion of presence.

In fact, Pla was keenly aware of the existence of aesthetic journalism in the 1920s and 1930s. He called it "poetic journalism," the term he used to classify Simenon's intersection between journalism and literature. The conceptually more restrictive term "poetic" should not hide the fact that, in the pre-television age, literary journalism was the most immediate form of realism responsible both to personal observation and to the highest standards of expression. The documentary film and photojournalism were emerging as new forces in the shaping of public opinion, forces with compositional complexity an indubitable aesthetic appeal. But they were not yet as widely available and as accessible as the journal, the magazine, or the cheap paperback that could be obtained at the nearest kiosk or news stand. In the technologically backward and economically ruined Spain of the 1940s, Pla saw the need for a newly defined form of writing, a hybrid between the stilted forms of, as he saw it, a dated literary elitism and the conventional, and thus spurious, objectivity of the press, which in Spain was state-managed misinformation. In this context, praising Simenon's "poetic journalism" as "an infinitely better school than any that has been organized in recent years" ("Georges Simenon y la técnica de la novela" 5) entailed a challenge to the status quo. But beyond the momentary conditions and urgency of a freer poetics of fact, Pla was using Simenon as a screen for his own long-term aesthetic choices.

It is possible to argue historically that poetic journalism, that is literary non-fiction or semi-fictional prose based on real events has been a staple of prose writing since the rise of journalism, and that literary history, including the history of the novel, owes much to the work of writers who learned the trade in journalism. Doug Underwood reflects that "[f]rom the beginning of the novel in English, writers who had experience in the world of journalism have been at the center of a movement that has repeatedly returned to journalistic methodology as the basis for developing realistic plots and journalistic research to provide the material for the construction of literature that draws upon actual events as the inspiration for dramatic narrative" (3). Undeniably, the transition from romance to novel represented a shift from mythological and legendary convention to stories inspired in real people and actual events. But as Lule has argued in the wake of critics like Frye, myth may be the foundation of all storytelling, and so every attempt to secularize narrative ends up re-establishing myth. In this regard, it is surely significant that Joyce's realistic feat, which Pla so admired, was structured on an ironic yet devoted updating of Homeric myth in twentieth-century Irish garb. If the history of the novel can be seen as an ongoing effort to precipitate a core of truth ordinarily dissolved in narrative convention, then each local attempt responds to local convention and to a local horizon of expectations.

Only with a bias for the modernist experiment with altered syntax, chronology, sequentiality, and point of view, can Pla's revolt against the melodramatic novel be considered formally conservative. Or, if we agree that he conserves the communicational aspects of traditional fiction, we must add that he does so while rejecting the fascination of the fanciful incident and the pleasures of the logical subterfuge. He is formally conservative – like Simenon, Camus, or Truman Capote for that matter – for the same reason that he is conservative in outlook. In a world full of confusion and semantic anomie, why should the writer contribute to the universal pandemonium? Pla referred on different occasions to the twentieth century as the most savage of all centuries in history. He also spoke of the general tendency to confuse things and of the need for clarity. In this sense, one can accept Jordi Castellanos's assessment that Pla's literary revolution was limited, and that he did not challenge narrative form, because to do so would have reduced his readership. This is partly true. Pla had nothing of the romantic genius about him; he was persuaded that the writer subscribed a contract with his audience. And yet, is it actually the case that he did not challenge narrative form, as the literary establishment understood it? If this had been the case, no one would have doubted the novelistic status of texts like *The Gray Notebook* or *El carrer Estret*. But the former is never considered part of the genre and the latter only conditionally so.

Having asserted that Pla's innovation of the novel was limited, Castellanos then asks in what might the break with its traditional form consist. He answers: in the dilution of the novelistic convention in a journalistic perspective, and follows this observation with an interesting remark. "It seems that Pla has transferred the 'formal perfection' to a space that is not the genre but the narrative voice; that is to say, a space in which he does not need to leap out of himself, invent other realities, or act like a literary 'author-God'" (63). The remark forces on us the question, what might the narrative voice be if not a genre-establishing gesture? The epic poet does not act as a literary demiurge either. At the beginning of the *Odyssey*, Homer asks the muse to tell "of the man of many ways, who was driven to far journeys" (*Odyssey* 1.1). Virgil likewise calls on the muse to tell "the causes" (*Aeneid* 1.13) and thereby establishes the genre of his poem. Paradoxically, Castellanos, who imputes formal conservatism to Pla, seems to think of the novel strictly in terms of the classic convention of the omniscient narrator who blows a world with his creative breath, like a bubble smoothly sealed with the colours of the imagination. Only if we accept the conventional association of literature with illusion can we agree with Castellanos that Pla's purpose was to "de-literaturize" the novel" (63). But if we, like Pla, reject that traditional definition, then we cannot accept the thesis that Pla's "great problem with regard to the genre [of the novel] was to merge literature (that is to say, novel, fiction) and a narrative voice that seeks credibility in transparency" (63). Castellanos believes that Pla's solution to this alleged problem was to recycle journalism's "neutral point of view" (63), in other words, to import journalism into literature. But rather than a journalist smuggling his viewpoint across the boundary of genre, Pla sets up the formal conditions of his writing and takes care to define them again and again. What his narrative voice summons is neither the epic muse nor the disembodied narrator of the classic novel, but a character who resembles Josep Pla and also goes by that name. This is to say that the genre actuated by the voice is neither the journalistic article nor the "timeless" novel but the "poetic journalism" that Pla described under the pretence of explaining Simenon.

The significance of this hybrid method is that, while it purports to reflect reality as on the surface of a mirror, its goal is to produce an efficient narrative, not in the sense of telling a better story but of acting on the world. Pla achieves this goal by providing the outline and the sensory elements to construct a reality. His oeuvre has the ambiguity of all great works of art. It produces an invincible feeling of presence, of a world objectivized under his scrutiny, whose very intensity and power of persuasion imbues his readers with the illusion of actuality. It is a literature that operates in a regime of truth, while warning us, sometimes explicitly, about the unreliability of journalistic representations. In the story "Una anàlisi" (An analysis), Pla judges journalism through a narrative alter ego: "Journalism, with its hollow and necessary prattle, industrializes your intuition, catalogues the world for you in schematic fashion and gives you at any moment the right word to suggest that you're at the top" (6:215). But it is also "poetic" in the sense that it holds traditional journalism and traditional fiction at arm's length, making it clear that what is presented is neither an image of what the world looks like at any given time (the ideological task of journalism) nor the image of an alternative reality but the specific, relative, and motivated vision of the author regarding a particular scenery and always in relation to the reader as an equal who may agree or disagree, but who in every case carries the burden of the decision, just as the author carries that of his choices.

5 Rural Roots of Catalan Modernity

To be a peasant does not mean only knowing how to plough, turn over the ground, rake, sow, beat, prune, dig over, thin the forest, or harvest. It means, above all, to know how to mix the furrows of the ground with the clouds, to live between earth and sky.

– Josep Pla, *El pagès i el seu món*

Regardless of his reputation for conservatism, which he cultivated and many literary critics have endorsed, Pla is not a facile, reassuring writer for a sparsely educated bourgeoisie. He is steadily focused on the relation between consciousness and the phenomena it registers, a writer whose attitude towards existence is often as bewildered and absorbed by the untamable being there of things as Antoine Roquentin's is before the tumultuous roots of the chestnut tree in Jean-Paul Sartre's *Nausea*. The comparison is not erratic. Although never expressed in the form of Northern angst but rather of Mediterranean melancholy, Pla shared existentialism's sense that nature is alien to reason and tragically indifferent to human purpose. "Tragically" may be too strong a term to describe Pla's homely stoicism. But it captures his permanent awareness of the cross-purposes between nature's blind mechanisms and a human consciousness caught in the turmoil but looking at it as if from the outside.

As time passes, the commonsensical, quotidian, homely Pla starts looking more and more like a visionary. In the meantime the country he described in hyperreal detail has become a fictional country, even if in this case the fiction is supported by memory. I believe that this gradual derealization offers a clue to the author's intention at the start of his rural phase in the early 1950s, that is, at the moment he decided to change his image of cosmopolitan traveller who lived for a quarter of a century in hotels and boarding houses throughout Europe to that of a villager secluded in his family's farmhouse. He stated his purpose unambiguously: "The most urgent issue is to create a generation that avoids the enormous errors of the past: I mean a generation that is not stranger, that is profoundly acquainted with the country" (8:19). This phrase will probably puzzle readers unfamiliar with the modern history of Catalonia. The 1930s and 1940s had been disastrous for the country. The enormous errors of the past included the revolutionary destruction of tradition, epitomized by the indiscriminate burning of churches and artwork throughout Catalonia, the Spanish Civil War, and the thoroughgoing liquidation of its history, language, and culture by the military and police state that emerged from the war, aiming unequivocally and systematically at the destruction of Catalonia and the eradication of its collective memory. The denaturalization of Catalan society was faster and deeper in the larger cities, especially in Barcelona, where the forces of occupation concentrated and the new authorities set up their command centres. Soon after the war, Barcelona and nearby industrial towns became the preferred destination of migratory waves of rural people encouraged to resettle there by the government's firing of Catalan workers and functionaries and their replacement through non-Catalan ones. Those waves intensified in the fifties and accelerated in the 1960s, as industrial activity picked up and large population surpluses from southern and central Spain moved to Catalonia. Because that transfer took place during decades when the Catalan culture and language were politically suppressed, the net, calculated effect was to flood Catalonia with people who had no relation to or interest in its history, traditions, or character. Even the post-war generations of autochthonous Catalans were growing up in blissful ignorance of their history and traditions. Cultural replacement was under way. The ever-larger weight of Barcelona's conurbation in the demographic and economic structure of Catalonia profoundly modified the consciousness of its population, so much so that Pla felt compelled to affirm the primacy of the rural in the social and economic make-up of Catalonia. "This country's social structure emanates from, is fed by our country houses. Out of these farms came, comes, and will come the country's best blood, its basic human force, forever active, positive, and ascendant in every way" (8:14). This remark, indisputable for the nineteenth century and even the first decades of the twentieth, no longer held true in the second half of the century. By the time of the 1992 summer Olympics, Barcelona's mid-century provincialization had developed into a factitious decoupling from its hinterland whereby a self-effacing Catalan upper class, represented politically in City Hall governments, oscillated between a servile rivalry with Madrid (as the ever-present term of comparison) and dislocation into an abstract, global world space that excluded something as insular, small-town, and parochial as Catalonia's language, character, and history. The 1990s saw the institutional flowering of the dehistoricized "socialism" that Pla had combated in its Francoist and left-wing avatars. Both formats promoted an ideology of modernity for deracinated functionaries who disparaged Catalan culture, associating it with rurality, conservatism, and backwardness.

Pla did not idealize village life. He depicted its narrow-mindedness, petty jealousies, and limited world view on many occasions. This is by no means an isolated sentence: "I sincerely assert that life in rural villages is suffocating and unbearable" (8:17–18). Defining himself as "a defector from the plough, the hoe, and the rake" (8:10), he claimed to be the first member of an ancient peasant family who stopped working the land. He saw himself as an instance of the great demographic shift that took place when Catalonia's rural population abandoned the prevailing form of life of the previous millennium. Although this shift entailed a gradual relocation from Catalonia's interior to the ever denser coastal strip, the change was, above all, sociological, economic, and cultural. To put it very simply, it was above all a displacement of the point of view. The earthbound peasant, with his back tracing the figure of a Romanesque arch, mutated into the urbanite who holds up the office wall. The latter's wider angle of vision opened the perspective required to observe and objectivize the peasant. Knowing himself to be of peasant background, feeling himself a peasant at heart, rather than simply being one, allowed Pla to build up his work as one of the most solid and convincing proofs of his country's existence. Not because Pla was a historian, a chronicler, or an antiquarian, but because he was capable of raising the immediate relation to the land, the villages, and the towns to a representation whose authenticity is open to dispute, but not its methodic quality or the tenacity with which he carved in language the mental correlate of impressions and experiences hitherto unavailable on the cultural plane. This is at any rate his persuasion: "At the time of writing this book, I tried to obtain whatever was written about the peasants in general, but I was surprised to find out that there was nothing at all, that it was virgin territory" (8:9). The book in question is *El pagès i el seu món* (The peasant and his world), a masterpiece of rural psychology. Pla would most definitely have scorned its description as a work of cultural anthropology, which it is, and of the highest quality, provided it is also understood that the anthropologist is in this case a virtual insider who sneers at anyone putting on academic airs and graces.

In the peasantry Pla discerned the bountiful quarry of Catalan society. Today that quarry is exhausted and the society renewed through foreign contributions, the vast majority of which swell the cities and spill over into the adjacent sprawl. Barcelona's metropolitan area is now a large head atop a puny body, a tail wagging its dog. In the 1950s Pla witnessed the dawn of this development, but it was still possible for him to consider peasants as the sedentary population par excellence, and as such the prime subsystem of Catalan society. Historically speaking, he was experiencing the sweet moment before the ideological fissure between socialist metropolitanism and an allegedly rural, conservative Catalan identity. This rift, exacerbated by the socialists' subservience to state politics, veiled a sociological conflict of a quite different nature. Barcelona had been profoundly ruralized through successive waves of migrants stemming from Spain's backward regions. Much of its post–Civil War working class consisted of unskilled workers concentrated in Barcelona and its surrounding industrial districts. Beginning in the 1960s these areas had morphed into a mirror image of provincial Spain, with the result that those districts, socially speaking, were less modern and culturally advanced than smaller towns of the Catalan hinterland. As Marx had warned, ideology projects an inverted image of reality. Such inverted image was for decades the ideology of Barcelona's City Hall. Its programmatic decoupling of Barcelona from Catalonia amounted to the beheading of a country.

Pla (and, ironically, the socialists too) were right, nonetheless, in stressing the small-town substance of Catalan society. They differed in its valuation. But it was that traditional core of the Catalan country that prevented the heavy resettling of Spanish people (sometimes entire villages) from turning Barcelona into an Andalusian, Extremenian, or Aragonese town. That same core, retaining a proximate or distant attachment to the Catalan farmhouse, ensured Barcelona's difference, its entrepreneurial pre-eminence, cosmopolitanism, and visible modernity within the Iberian Peninsula. Its industrial predominance and ostensible modernity long preceded the demographic avalanche of the 1960s, as nineteenth- and early twentieth-century foreign travellers routinely observed. It was not and could never have been the effect of transplanting several millions of unskilled and scantily educated day labourers from the southern provinces of Spain but of a social and cultural continuity strong enough to resist the clash of cultures during a time when the Catalan institutions were wrecked and Catalan culture submerged by the Spanish dictatorship. What preserved Barcelona's economic and cultural eminence was the memory of a prior reality; a social memory crystalized in behavioural patterns, forms of expression, attitudes, and, notwithstanding the prohibition, the presence of the Catalan language in the nooks and crannies of everyday life. That prior reality is no mystical essence or theoretical daydream, but an age-old organization of the exploitation of the land and the transmission of property. Modern Barcelona was built by the enterprising siblings of the landlords in a legal tradition that preserved the integrity of landed property by conveying it entirely to the first male child, the *hereu* (heir) or female child, the *pubilla* (from Latin *puella*), depriving the younger children of independent livelihood. This system, going back to the Roman colonization of Catalonia, was responsible for the countryside's conservatism. Property, having been real or landed property for a very long time, was the greatest determinant of the social distribution of power. Which is why Pla claimed that in Catalonia revolutions always took place in the offices of public notaries, where property changed hands.

Today, the intense exploitation of Barcelona's urban space and Catalonia's coast by the tourist industry – which has triggered another round of immigration in response to demand for unskilled, low-paid labour – strains to the limit the balance between cultural identity and multicultural dispersion. Since the end of the dictatorship the attempts to restore Barcelona as the cultural capital of Catalonia have revealed the existence of a wound in the Catalan social body. This legacy of the Civil War and Francoism is geographically visible in the dislocation of an economically powerful and demographically dominant metropolitan area and the more sparsely populated *comarques*, regional seats of Catalan memory and identity. This hard-to-suture dislocation between territorial realities of different magnitude and significance intensified the reciprocal scrutiny between segments of the population identified with either category: the Catalan and the Barcelonan, the latter identity being a construct conceived during the dictatorship to contain and defuse the politics of Catalanism in a toothless, ineffectual, and circumscribed Barcelonism.

Critical self-scrutiny made Catalonia an object of observation and analysis, producing, by dialectical recoil, a refocusing of attention on observation itself. To observe is to remain in a state of heightened alertness with respect to an object that opposes us, an object that is categorically different, hence absolutely distant from the observing agent, the subject, that which is thrown under, submitted, or proposed. In other words, the assumed or presumed entity that submits to or is forcibly brought under the state of observation by the irruption of the object in its perceptual field.

Observation can be a spontaneous relation to the observed as an object of pragmatic interest; or it may step out of the circle of pragmatic reaction, deviate from the object, and observe itself through the self-splitting characteristic of consciousness. Niklas Luhmann called the latter mode of attention second-order observation. This form of self-reflection in which the subject captures its intentional relation to the world is obviously related to the phenomenological reduction or *epoché* whereby Husserl claimed to be able to suspend or bracket the external data of perception, retaining only the content of consciousness in the intentional act.

Luhmann's notion of second-order observation may help us understand the idea of country circumventing, on the one hand, ontological definitions (often described in non-pilosophical, primarily derogatory terms as "essentialist"), and on the other, constructivist postulates that abusively reduce nations to strategic falsifications and manipulations of collective life by economic elites. The ideologically neutral notion of the second-order observer makes it possible to pass beyond the straits without being wrecked on the Scylla of primordialism or the Charybdis of intentionalism. Neither creationism nor superstructuralism provides a reasonable account of long-term symbiosis between human groups and their territories. Second-order observations are neither natural (although they seem native to the human species) nor contrived. They exert violence on spontaneous intentional acts, forcing an acrobatic performance on them. Not being instinctive, second-order observation is improbable. Reflexivity may well be a distinctive trait of the human species, the one irreducible exception in the biosphere. It is present in humanity's earliest recorded life, associated with its predatory activity. The cave artists at Altamira and Lascaux represented their groups while hunting; more accurately, they represented the hunt in a mental exercise of abstraction from the pragmatic moment of execution. Consider also the many paintings depicting a human figure contemplating a landscape or someone looking out of a window, for instance, Salvador Dalí's *Figure at a Window*, whose conscious precedents are Rembrandt's *Girl at a Window*, and, especially, Vermeer's *Girl Reading a Letter at an Open Window*. In all of these works the artist assumes a reflexive aesthetics. The represented figure is a pretext for representing the previously unrepresentable. The true theme of these paintings is the viewer's contemplation captured *en abîme*. The picture's frame defines the window, the opening of consciousness to the world, inducing a reversal of the gaze and the switching of inside and outside through the interplay of subjective and objectivized attention.

Observation singularizes. Every intentional act presupposes a distinction between that which is observed and the rest of the world. The distinction constitutes the object, which stands out from a mass of stimuli peripheral to the focus of attention. The nature of the distinction depends on the observer's intentionality. If I have a sweet tooth, candy shops will stand out from the background of my perceptual horizon; my environment will tend to materialize according to the binary sweet/unsweet. The distinctions that structure our observation organize the world as a space marked by the presence or absence of candy shops – or farms, if we adopt Pla's viewpoint – while revealing the observer's intentionality.

The second-order observer is always already a first-order observer. Pla looks at the countryside as any peasant would, but his way of looking takes in the peasant's observation, his mode of being in the world. Much of his book on peasants is devoted to mediated first-order observations, which should be distinguished from second-order observations proper. An oblique way of seeing comes to the fore when he mentions his habit of looking at things in the form of newspaper articles (8:20). Writing modifies the impression of reality, as the inveterate habit of sublimating perception into words is mediated by readers' anticipated recognition of things taking shape in the shadow play of language. In a variation on this indirect approach to reality, Pla adopts another observer's viewpoint, frequently that of the landscape painter, to show the difficulty of grasping the world through a virginal sensorium. First-order observation does not refer to pristine, unlearned perception but to attention directed to the things that present themselves, to the collection of entities Heidegger defined by their presentness, those things that constitute the realm of the *Vorhandensein* or "presence-at-hand."

Many pages of Pla's peasant book deal with the landscape, animals, or people, including himself, but these things are nearly always refracted by the peasants' world view. Theirs is an instrumental relation, a privileging of the realm of the *Zuhandesein*, the ready-to-hand. "If a peasant contemplates the landscape, do me a small favour: do not think that his mind throbs with a whim of pantheism, with a version or other of the love of nature. The landscape is beautiful or simply lovely insofar as it is a pretext to fantasize or close a sale contract" (8:34). In this passage something peculiar has occurred. A hypothetical peasant looks at the landscape as a means of exchange. The author, strictly speaking, is not looking at the landscape but at the peasant's gaze, which assesses the scenery in terms of profit, of its potential to minister to his greed. Interest for the gaze of others incorporates the writer to the peasant's observation in the role of second-order observer. In this displacement of the phenomenology of attention there appears a hint, not realized, of a third-order observation. Pla feels himself observed in his role as observer, classified as stranger to the "natural," pragmatic relation to the land:

> "You won't make much money going up and down the roads" ... After this remark, they give you a third once-over, after which you feel definitively classified: classified in the farthest and most decisive horizons of modesty and insignificance. (8:33–4)

Observing is not the activity of a transcendent subject. It does not happen outside the world, as a purely intellectual exercise. The second-order observer also entertains a pragmatic relation to things; he cannot avoid dealing with them through a collection of intentional acts. First-order observation is implicit in the second order. Feeling himself observed by the peasant, Pla intuits the valuation of his persona not through mystical empathy but from having grown up in a family of relatively prosperous landowners. In truth the criterion with which the peasant establishes his judgment remains inaccessible. Luhmann asserts that every observation relies on a blind spot. Although we can observe others in the act of observing, we cannot observe the observation itself (*Art as a Social System* 57). And just as Pla has no access to the peasant's observation and must guess it, he cannot, despite the ambitious title of his book, take in the peasant's world in its totality. To do that he would need to stand on the surface of a larger sphere that contained that world and afforded a comprehensive perspective on it. Yet, Pla proposes such paradoxical overlap of immanence and transcendence: "Peasants constitute another world, but they constitute a world that is indivisible from the world we all live in" (8:193). The paradox lies in positing an outside and negating it, in defining otherness and reducing it to identity. Pla resolves the paradox by styling himself a defector from the peasantry, hence a subject both immanent and transcendent to a world that is precisely located and circumscribed. The peasants' is a world in the full sense of the word, inasmuch as it can be described in empirical detail with the reflexive detachment of someone who discerns its limits and appreciates its contrasts.

Bracketing the paradox is fundamental to grasping the meaning of the term "country" as deployed by Pla, often preceded by the demonstrative "this." Sometimes he uses the word in a political sense, meaning "nation." On those rare occasions it refers to Spain. More often it refers to Catalonia, a politically subdued "nation" with a well-defined personality, whose outline Pla traces in its climate, geography, history, culture, language, manners, and social and economic disposition. More often yet, he wields the term to name a particular district. Then it adopts the limiting sense of the Italian *paese* or the French *pays*, terms derived from the Latin *pagus*, a district or even a village. In the Middle Ages it was a close-knit territorial unit under the jurisdiction of a feudal lord. Originally a loose confederation of counties struggling for hegemony, Catalonia preserved its original subdivision and internal differentiation into modern times, while its language retained the time-honoured denomination for traditional circumscriptions inhabited by *pagenses*, the Catalan *pagesos* or peasants. The possibility of bracketing the paradox arises when this class comes into crisis in modern times and segregates an internal consciousness, so to speak, as some of its members lift their eyes from the soil and look at the world around them. Still a peasant and yet no longer one, the inhabitant of the country can now trace the web of relations in which he and his ancestors exist and takes stock of the phenomena that constitute their reality: the quality of the light; the strength and direction of the winds; the trees, paths, farms, and fields; his neighbours and the domestic animals who assist him ad provide him with food. But also the towns where he sells his produce and buys his necessities and scanty luxuries, the means of transportation, the meagre intellectual life, reduced to political discussions in cafés and clubhouses and to solitary enquiry by the obscure heroes of local erudition. When someone has the strength to push aside the weight of dead generations and rise from the languor of a millennial past, that person gains a birds-eye view of the passions and wretchedness of his own milieu. In the life of communities this is the moment when tradition snaps and modernity crawls in through the crevices.

A peasant who no longer tills the soil, a freed serf who remains attached to the memory of the land, is the living paradox of second-order observation; it is in effect the paradox of modernity itself. I do not mean this in a periodizing sense but in the sense of a functional transformation in the evolution of a social system. Commenting on the literary topos of "Beatus ille ...," Joan Fuster points out that Horace expressed nostalgia for the rural life in the voice of Alfi, an urban usurer. The Horacian commonplace, Fuster asserts, was a satire of those who claim to miss the simplicity of rural life yet never put their idealization to the test of reality (*Causar-se d'esperar* 37). If literature idealized the peasant's life, this is because it was never written by peasants (41). In the nineteenth century Ralph Waldo Emerson made a similar point when, walking in the fields of Concord, Massachusetts, he considered that only the leisured eye can take possession of the landscape. "I leave the village politics and personalities, yes, and the world of villages and personalities, behind, and pass into a delicate realm of sunset and moonlight, too bright almost for spotted man to enter without novitiate and probation" (*Nature* 172–3). Pla agrees: "Peasants do not have this sense of beauty. It is as if they had been excluded from it, cast out, as if they lacked a sense that other people have, as if they were born without this kind of sensibility" (8:131). But he is more radical than the New England transcendentalist when he asserts: "The peasant is the only human species who does not love the countryside and never looks at it" (45:115). Far from Emerson's pantheism, Pla incorporates the viewpoint of *homo economicus* in the aesthetics of landscape. He finds beauty in well-tended fields and in groves of trees planted at the right interval to maximize profit (9:175). Beauty, in other words, is not the kantian "purporless purpose" that lifts it out of the world of human affairs. It often is the unintentional result of some unrelated purpose, seen with the eye of a removed, reflective observer. From this Pla derives the axiom "convenience begets beauty" (8:131). This is far from Emerson's romantic apotheosis of the poet, but both the New England transcendentalist and the Empordà sceptic share an understanding of the categorical difference between mediated and immediate relation to nature, between observing the world expeditiously in order to eke out a livelihood or squeeze profits and observing this utilitarian relation in a detached attitude, as if exempted from need, habit, and custom.

Deluded by Pla's miscellaneous writings, humility of subject matter, offhand judgmentalism, and eventually by his rustic persona, scholars have failed to discern in his work the foundations of modern Catalan thought. This statement will be found bewildering and in need of justification. But perhaps it will be conceded that Pla constantly formulates observations intended to hold general or permanent validity, which he reaches by reflecting on immediate certainties, the way great philosophers do. That his repeated attempts to draw general conclusions, disavowed by excessive humility and disowned or recanted by expressions of relativism and self-doubt, have been ignored or dismissed as rhetoric is strange. Although Pla was not the first Catalan author to adopt second-order observation, he certainly was the most deliberate and arguably most successful at grasping the relations between the various strata of Catalan society and between the latter and its milieu. As this society becomes intelligible through description, the microcosm that stands in for the world arises out of the bevy of relations, which Pla traces inexhaustibly in web-like intricacy. Such intricacy owes to the iterations and recurrence of motifs in apparently unrelated places, the piling up and thickening of impressions conveyed through precise, communicative language, which ensures epistemological efficiency. Pla confirms in practice Luhmann's assertion that observations are never about singular, isolated facts (*Art as a Social System* 59). A single fact may be detected but not recognized. It glides past like a nameless asteroid and vanishes into the black hole where the universe's historical energy spirals down as in a drain. In order for observation to be possible, differentiation, i.e., the force out of which energy arises, must be grounded in recurring connections, whether it be to earlier observations that endow the new differentiation with volume and reality, or to forecasts of the role played by the new distinction, anticipating its cultural effects (59). Decisive, from the standpoint of cultural evolution, is the mutation of the current system of communication. Such systemic change is in evidence in Pla's work, in the transit from the description of the peasant's behavioural disposition as a factor of his relation to the land, to the description of a system built with the author's observations, which rely on memory as much as on perception, but also in the evaluative conclusions he draws from what he observes. The sum of those conclusions could be called sceptical possibilism, that is, a form of relativized modal realism, neither affirming nor denying that whatever is possible exists.

Integrating the distinction constitutive of peasantry into the act of observing, Pla advances a specific view of the *país*. From this conjunction further distinctions derive, for instance, those supporting an inside and an outside with respect to the *world* of the peasant. In this regard, it is hardly irrelevant that the title of Pla's book is *El pagès* i *el seu món* (my emphasis). Pla is convinced that the individual's and the social classes' scope of awareness is limited; hence the peasant (like everyone else) is immersed in an order and contributes to its maintenance without being conscious of all the consequences of his actions. For instance, the peasant ignores the aesthetic effect of his quest for material benefit:

> Over the land there is perfect order. This order is the product of calculation, it follows a plan of material yield. But this order – and this might seem a miracle – coincides with an order of beauty and harmony in the landscape that the peasant may not suspect yet obeys faithfully. (9:180)

Circumscribed by a particular range of observations, the peasant world is constituted as a system of internal communication, in this case one governed by the logic of gain. But it can also be conceived as the essential core of a surrounding space or outer world, one more complex yet still limited through another distinction and another outside: the world of beauty as referred to the landscape, historical product of the rise of a different class (as discussed in the next chapter). Ultimately, and through yet another distinction, or several, it would be subsumed under a larger, more encompassing outside: the Catalan world. Thus Pla's peasant book stands in the same relation to his oeuvre as the world of the peasant does to the *país* in the increasingly broader semantic range of this word.

That Pla's oeuvre can be considered a ground for Catalan thought, that is, for thought wearing the red cap made famous by Miró in his 1925 painting *Head of a Catalan Peasant* and worn defiantly by Pla's fellow countryman Salvador Dalí, will be decried by those who object to thinking chronotopically, people for whom thought is not respectable unless it is utopian, as if the second-order observer were not also, inescapably, a first-order observer. Refusal to think the *país* and to think from the *país*, a prejudice that plagued Pla's reputation among the vocationally progressive Catalan intelligentsia for a long time, was and remains a provincial affection. Pla was fully cognizant of the roots of such prejudice. He wrote: "The provincial spirit implies loss of one's personal discernment" (8:194). One stops thinking for oneself and submits to opinion that appears enhanced by the glitter of some prestige or other. Mutatis mutandis, this definition of provincialism coincides with Kant's definition of the unillustrated mind. Not to think for oneself is the clearest proof of dependence. It manifests itself in superstition and all forms of cargo cults.

Yet Pla was no reactionary. Nature was not for him the repository and guarantor of authenticity. It was no ontological fortress of Being. It was simply the realm of the "present-at-hand," the permanent confirmation of the existence of raw behavioural patterns and of physical processes that take their course with absolute indifference to human will. "In itself," Pla said, "nature is atonic, it gives nothing for free. Nature intends quite simply to reach death passing almost always through very narrow doors" (8:250). Here Pla came very close to Freud's idea that death is the true aim of nature and life a more or less convoluted detour that matter takes in order to reach the state of inorganic repose. Pla does not stake anything on final causes, unless death is considered one. But death is no essence and cannot *act* on anything. As the goal towards which life races, it does not explain what is but how the biologically existing behaves.

Preference for the *how* rather than the *what* conforms to the second-order observer. The first-order observer focuses on an object, fact, or experience that emerges within his radius of action, while the second-order observer trains his attention on how others observe. This observer takes in the limit of the first-order observer's range of attention and traces its outline. Beyond it other realms of action, sustained by other forms of attention, exist. Surrounding the peasant's world there is another world peopled by businessmen, traders, shopkeepers, fishermen, journalists, and functionaries. The peasant suffers from chronic information deficit and this lack colours his reactions. Little complexity, for lack of mental stimulation, produces behavioural monotony to the point that the peasant's attitudes seem anthropological. Paucity of information conforms his dull, undemonstrative outlook and the resigned mood that meets the frustration of his hopes. This temperament, shaped by the regularities of climate and geography in the course of centuries, has crystallized in language.

A writer of customs and manners would not fail to exploit the rich palette of Catalan proverbs, many of which stem from the peasantry. But Pla does not fall for cheap tricks and refuses to turn the peasant's "occupational dialect" into a myth of authenticity. Proverbs do not contain a rural "philosophy." They do not represent the age-old distillation of experience or reveal an innate capacity to process information efficiently. Rather, they are proof of the contradictions with which the first-order observer disposes of information. "Opposite to ten locutions with a given meaning – which, emphatically pronounced, seem the essence of truth – there are ten other locutions with an antithetical tone, which, pronounced with similar emphasis, produce the same effect" (8:318). Proverbs are generally considered the collective wisdom of cultures that have not taken the leap to second-order observation and rely on knowledge that is useful only in concrete situations. Systematization is alien to the archive of proverbial wisdom. Users of proverbs make no effort to eliminate contradiction and overcome paradox. This is so, says Luhmann, because the wise person – in this case the peasant who turns to popular prudence – applies this wisdom to the situation in which he is immersed, without taking other perspectives (other worlds) into consideration (Luhmann, *Observations* 37). In face of the profusion of natural contexts, the individual who subscribes to popular wisdom is unconcerned with the coherence of the repertoire of sayings. This person can overlook their incoherence because the world does not appear in the light of reduced complexity that systematization promotes. In itself contradiction between proverbial generalization and pragmatic restriction of the proverb's relevance does not make traditional wisdom futile and dispensable. Symbolic systems tolerate contradiction. But contradiction is lethal to operational systems, for instance, when the peasant knows that a pest is destroying the crop but instead of fumigating applies the axiom: "We found it thus and thus we'll leave it."

The first-order observer considers the world he lives in irrefutable; to him other worlds seem improbable. He does not observe them with the intentional implication he invests in his own world. To the second-order observer, on the contrary, it is first-order observation that often looks improbable, since every action and every gesture, no matter how routine and ordinary, appear against a background of other equally possible actions (Luhmann, *Art as a Social System* 62). From this divergent sense of plausibility stems the feeling of absurdity and arbitrariness that peasant gestures and decisions often produce in Pla. Many more possibilities exist than those actualized by first-order observers. The peasant could react differently to weather or market contingencies, but his "peasantness" limits the range of his reactions to a relatively restricted assortment of options. Second-order observation is tied to the perceptual amplification and broadening of contingency. The very concreteness of the peasant's focus reduces complexity, not through the articulation of the laws governing regularities, as in systematic thinking, but through ejection of possibilities that fall outside the scope of received wisdom. This reduction contrasts with the second-order observer's awareness of this self-limitation. For this reason Luhmann calls him the inventor of the world of possibility (62).

Pla's contribution to a theory of modernization after 1920 lies in his capacity to offer a vision against the grain of then dominant *noucentista* theory, a full-fledged cultural program based on Eugeni d'Ors's theory of the metaphysical opposition between nature and culture, instinct and will. Making of reflexivity not an affair of the will or the basis for a brutal intervention in the environment but an observation of observations, Pla broke out of the binarism that crystallized in *Noucentisme*'s famous dichotomies of rural/urban, country/capital, local/cosmopolitan. Whereas *Noucentisme* promoted full urbanization of the territory by proposing a Catalonia-city (Catalunya-ciutat), Pla associated modernity with second-order observation, which entailed a courageous departure from the dominant viewpoint, the latter corresponding generally to the pragmatic intentionality of the first-order observer. "The fascination that cities elicit is a phenomenon so general, vulgar, and provincial that resisting this commonplace requires a great personality" (226).

Contempt of rural society, which Pla was keen enough to trace to a long-standing conflict of interests, played out in his time as a cultural politics built on stereotypes that eventually impinged on the perception of Pla's oeuvre. He was one of very few, and the only writer of great distinction, to challenge Catalan literature's trend since the turn of the twentieth century, when leading writers Raimon Casellas and Caterina Albert wrote influential anti-rural novels such as *Els sots feréstecs* (*Dark Vales*) (1901) and *Solitud* (*Solitude*) (1905), setting off a modernistic trend with long-lasting consequences. In *El pagès i el seu món Pla* described the constitution of society as a complex system based, ultimately, on the extraction of value from a way of life tied to place and to long-term social structures. The appearance of uprooted populations who were ignorant of the history and culture associated with the land aggravated the condition of the peasantry, no longer considered a repository of tradition but the waste product of progress. Almost twenty years before Eric R. Wolf's *Europe and the People without History*, Pla had called peasants "history's absent ones" (9:306). And now, these people who were the very foundation on which history was erected and the floor on which every historical figure or movement trampled, these necessary absent ones were placed on an extinction course, as modernization altered the millennial balance between town and country.

Freed from their age-old overlord – the landed aristocracy – peasants now faced a harsher, more unrelenting taskmaster in the anonymous market. The new hegemony of the city's rising classes, the bourgeoisie and petty bourgeoisie, definitively tipped the demographic balance. In mid-century Pla could remember how "until a few decades earlier, significant Catalan towns were settlements living off the land" and that the grandparents of half a million Barcelona residents had worked the land. A couple of decades later, he could have added another half million, because from the 1960s onward Barcelona's metropolitan area received a large surplus of Spain's rural population.

Pla believed that the rural origins of Barcelona's artisans, middle classes, and patricians had shaped Catalonia's character. Projected on "the harshness of modern life" and displaced to "more complex milieus," the aboriginal, undeveloped traits of the peasantry occasionally crystallized in a fuller personality with distinct contours. In Pla's awareness of the hidden synchronicity of urban and rural in modern life it is possible to discern the link between modernity and complexity corresponding to the emergence of the second-order observer. The peasant's incompleteness is consistent with his intense, exclusive dedication to first-order observation, a form of attention that makes out things and events while losing sight of the ensemble. A world can only be observed from outside. In order to observe something immanent the world must be invisible. On the other hand, in making observation an intentional object, the second-order observer traces a relational horizon that is also a form of differentiation and the condition of increasing complexity. By reflecting on the conditions of traditional society and tracing its limits, that is, by turning attention on the mode society is constituted and making it aware of the relations between all its elements, modernity can be defined as an instance of such complexification.

The depth of field resulting from the altered perspective reveals the contingency of everything that appeared necessary to the first-order observer. Second-order observation discloses new relations and the possibility of working purposefully on the immediate data of perception. It makes it possible to plan the future. In Pla's words: "every basic form of being can be improved on condition of not losing entirely its positive primitive traits and balancing the defects with a staunch, cohesive, efficient counterweight" (8:194). This is Pla's way of saying that no second-order observation is possible without the simultaneous presence of a first-order observer. Pla was the ablest, most compelling corrective to the phenomenological shortcoming on which Catalonia's modernity was predicated by the *noucentistes* and later by ideologues of supermodernity. Marc Augé called "supermodernity" the displacement of observation that, following Luhmann, we have been calling second-order observation. Augé, however, emphasized the draining of the landscape and of the look that appropriates it, which becomes in turn the object of a secondary look that cannot be attributed to anyone in particular. With the term "supermodernity" Augé refers to this draining of consciousness, particularly to the general and systematic evacuation of concrete, time-hallowed references that used to anchor human life before it came under the aegis of the global economy.

Classic modernity projected itself on the future by cancelling the social links with the past. The future was conceived as the resolution of the present, that is, of the mode of consciousness moderns experienced as contradiction. The light that always came from the north, according to Joan Maragall, was the Catalan version of futurism, a rejection of the dead hand of the past and of Spain's Oriental fatalism. In this *modernist* mood, the North was nothing more than the aestheticization of the Enlightenment's conceptual system, marked by the emergence of the self-determined individual. For the *noucentista* (and anti-Maragall) writer Eugeni d'Ors, the ideal Catalonia-city was a speculative notion locked inside its own potential. The individual was no longer justified in seeking autonomy. Civility, the highest value in *noucentista* axiology, was achieved through the self's sacrifice of the primary impulses to normative organization from above; "above" designating some Platonic constellation of ideas, socially mediated through the principle of authority. The peasant's contribution lay in his remaining within the regime of first-order observation, trapped in the mindless repetition of received custom, unaware of other worlds and possibilities. In d'Ors's cynical classicism, modernity was the prerogative of the elite, the distinction that enclosed the first-order observations of the peasants in a space of recurrence that, the moment it became the object of second-order observation, rose to the status of a world: the world of tradition.

Since modernity could define itself only with respect to the past from which it differed, it lacked a stable identity. Constantly breaking away from the immediate past, modern society could not configure its identity around tradition, the way all previous societies had. Its defining characteristic was not a stable content but the permanent generation of difference (Luhmann, *Observations* 3). And this meant inducing the emergence of a new sense of time to which history was immolated. Modernity could not become cumulative without relapsing into some form of tradition. Were it to do so and give up the perspective gained from second-order observation, it would revert to blind repetition and lose its differentiating perspective in the pragmatic objectivation of its objects. Culture responds to this quandary by creating forms that aim to resolve symbolically the paradox that distinctions propelling society to ever higher levels of complexity end up re-entering the observations (Luhmann, *Observations* 102). Pla finds himself halfway through this process. His scepticism with regard to culture as symbolic resolution of life's quandaries comes from his practice of reintegrating distinctions into the observation without letting the distinction lapse. "Peasantness" is the distinguishing boundary of a "world" that can be grasped by observing the countless first-order observations that make up its environment and objectivized by describing its internal relations, that is, by tracing its outline and separating it from the adjacent worlds. But Pla reintroduces the distinction itself into the peasant world by describing his own observation in the form of ironic self-awareness. He knows that his gaze is connate with that of the people he encounters therein, that the gathering quality of his view is kindred to the dispersion of the looks and purposes of the other characters.

Pla lacks the superstition of culture. He is intensely aware of modern society's indifference to memory and tradition, yet he does not believe that culture prevents the reversion of distinctions to the status of observable things. Culture generates complex social systems by excluding the primary system of natural sensations. But this system cannot be truly eliminated, and so it is replaced by a synthetic, ahistorical one. Pla combats this development. His peasant book is an intellectual move against the grain to bring to light a part of society that by then had become the underlying social unconscious, a labouring class unacknowledged by the hegemonic Marxist intelligentsia and in the process of being eradicated throughout the planet. He does not expel from consciousness time, the landscape, the small things that appear – the "present at hand" – or the tools – the "ready-to-hand" – which mediate the peasant's relations to his world. For him the first-order observer remains active and enjoys primacy. Pla describes this sinking continent more as a psychoanalyst than an anthropologist, in the sense that by observing the observations that define the peasant's psychosocial environment, he is speaking of a set of relations that do not really vanish from the face of the earth with advancing modernity but withdraw to the dark areas of our collective repressions. This is doubtless the meaning of his idea that the peasantry is the permanent foundation of society and everyone is a peasant at heart. He knows that the distinction – the boundary between heaven and earth, between mud and sky – collapses as soon as reflexivity is turned on the second-order observer, an interminable process that culture can neither steady nor prevent.

6 The Catalan Landscape Seen as a Painting

In the first chapter of his book *Landscape and Power*, W.J.T. Mitchell proposed nine theses on landscape. The first, "landscape is not a genre but a medium" (5), is by far the most suggestive. According to this thesis, landscape is not a recognizable theme of artistic expression but the means through which expression is actualized. This includes, of course, self-expression. Reflecting the spirit of the times, Mitchell advocated for a shift from landscape as object of contemplation to landscape as *process*. And what could landscape process if not "social and subjective identities" (1), "identity" being the other great catchword of the period? This programmatic statement at the beginning of a book on landscape not only advertises its membership in the great current of postmodern academic literature; it also reveals postmodernism's addiction to breaking down, dissolving, extracting, mingling, blending, compounding, tampering with, modifying, and transforming all that used to be solid, exactly as the food industry processes the prime materials of human nutrition out of recognition into newly identifiable products. But precisely because "identities" are, for postmoderns, always being processed and negotiated, they cannot be concrete and actual. Nothing can be an identity if it does not remain equal to itself, which is the meaning of *identitas*. As soon as something tries to firm up its definition and ensure a modicum of semantic permanence, essentialism, the postmodern sin par excellence, is brought down on the unsophisticated.

Mitchell's thesis perfectly illustrates the postmodern marriage of social constructionism with semiology in that it reverses the traditional, intuitive correlation of the subject/object phenomenon in the perception of landscape. In his account, it is not identity (subjective or collective) that brings the landscape into being through an intentional act, but the other way around: landscape becomes *the* process in and through which identities are determined and recognized. Choice of landscape for bringing to consciousness the social determinants of "identity" allows Mitchell to deploy matter-of-factly the counter-ideological concept of "naturalization." What could be more natural, in the age of reality-bending, synthetic experience, than treating the landscape as the great naturalizer and supreme example of "ideological" nature, as a "process," that is, which "effaces its own readability and naturalizes itself" (2)?

Seen from this point of view, Josep Pla's studied descriptions of landscapes could be exposed as "naturalizing" and accused of rendering traditional relations of ownership and exploitation of the land unassailable. This allegation would be trivial if it weren't false. Time and again, Pla stresses the relation between exploitation of the land and its aesthetic effect on the landscape. And he knows that landscape is always a *process*, partly semiological projection, partly social manipulation of the environment. "In a landscape there is the lucubration one puts on top, and then, underneath, the possible usefulness" (8:225). One could easily translate this intuition into Marxist jargon about superstructure and infrastructure and miss the point. But Pla traces the idea to the ancient Greeks, contrasting it with the modern "verbal noises," that is, aesthetic theories, which are good for nothing (43:643).

For him physical transformation of the landscape is crucial, but the observer's collaboration, what he calls here "lucubration," is constitutive. And vice versa, landscape constitutes the observer, enclosing him in the awareness of his perception: "The process of light – in slow declination – leaves on all things – or perhaps draws out from things – the spirit of this landscape, a spirit that projects on the person contemplating it a feeling of isolation, of distant remoteness" (2:283). He would have scoffed at Mitchell's post-colonial sixth thesis that "landscape is a particular historical formation associated with European imperialism," incongruously trailing another thesis, the fifth, which asserts that "landscape is a medium found in all cultures," and followed by a hardly reassuring seventh thesis, which denies any contradiction between the previous two (5). And he would doubtless have sneered at thesis eight, which claims that "landscape is an exhausted medium, no longer viable as a mode of artistic expression," even if this claim needs to be supported by a ninth and final thesis asserting that the landscape in question is that of thesis six, thus rendering the latter thesis invalid for non-European cultures. Mitchell proposes, in short, the equivalent of a historical law with pseudo-analytical premises attempting to do the work of historical investigation.

Mitchell does make a valid point when he distinguishes two different approaches to landscape: a contemplative one, linked to the history of painting, which he associates with *modernism*, and a postmodern approach that treats landscape as "an allegory of psychological or ideological themes" (1). He then claims to transcend both methods in favour of a third, Foucauldian one, which considers landscape an instrument of power, perhaps "even an agent of power" (2). This is far from Pla's attitude to landscape, but it is useful nonetheless as a starting point. Pla was perfectly aware of the relation between landscape and power when he asserted that "politics must be taken away from the salons and the committees and projected on the landscape" (8:18). And he combined, rather than choose between the two approaches, the pictorial and the psychological, in an attempt to render landscape both perceptible and comprehensible.

In his extensive travel accounts and his books on regional history, Pla treats landscape as a medium that reveals historical action, but he incorporates the pictorial education of sight into the detailing of his visual descriptions. The formation of a pictorial perception is thereby historicized, with the reference to a given artist or school supplying a visual quality that the writer cannot otherwise put into words. He renders the ambient light around Bellver Castle, in Mallorca, by comparing it to the aura (in effect, the glimmer of the fire) that Lucas Cranach the Elder painted around the distant buildings in *Lot and His Daughters*, which Pla had seen at the Alte Pinakothek in Munich in the 1920s: "Munich of my memory, probably arbitrary: beer and nudes by Lucas Cranach" (5:169):

> From outside, from the breakwater of Palma's harbour, for instance, the castle seems an ancient thing without tension, a figure full and sweet like the filigreed, linear buildings surrounded by a golden halo that Lucas Cranach the Elder used to paint. (15:97)

Landscape becomes for Pla a medium through which he invokes a contemplative relation to the world in order to elicit a second, interpretive moment in which the "signs" give way to reflective, second-order discourse.

The word *landscape* derives from Middle Dutch *landscap*, or region. Likewise, the Catalan word for landscape, *paisatge*, includes the term *país*, country or region, as its radical. Both derive from the Latin *pagus*, a rural district. Hence, the landscape is the *countryness* or *regionness* of a part of the earth. Joan Nogué calls it "the face of the territory" (56), meaning that landscape receives and retains human values and feelings and can be conceived of as a dynamic symbolic code that transmits cultural investments. The fact that a section of the earth is marked off through human presence settles a priori the false issue of the landscape's naturalness or artificiality. The region, the *país*, is a territory composed of interrelated places without solution of continuity in space and time, which means that all these places are contemporary to each other, that together they constitute the stage of a history. Official narrative, that is, historiography and the related discourse of political science has displaced the term "country" from its original meaning and applied it to abstract space defined from above, from the state, which may have its reasons but never its landscapes. The distinction is important, because Pla used the word *país* in the traditional sense. He deployed it flexibly to denote larger or smaller spaces, but always spaces individualized as the meaningful product of the activity and experience of their dwellers.

There is no question that spatial or geographic continuity arises from observation, that *regionness* is a function of the presence of a mind that models its perceptions according to certain referents that are meaningful insofar as they coalesce in the model. But it would be as odd to describe the effect of human observation as a *construction* of the region as to challenge the naturalness of solar storms because they are recorded in an observatory. Furthermore, Pla is aware of the composite nature of reality. By this I mean that his operative model is no longer of a piece, but a superposition of overlapping models, which permit him to move intellectually from one area of experience to the next without giving up the sense of a general reality. Transitioning between different areas explains his flexible use of the term *país* to denote realities of different scales inside which certain statements are valid and certain observations possible. In spite of their internal differentiation, these areas are compatible with a cohesive description. Notwithstanding the global scope of his travels and the motley landscapes described in his numerous books, Pla was always careful to delimit the area of observation so as to represent totalities that fell within the range and power of his senses. That is why in his works the term *país* often refers to an area that lacks administrative identity but is objectively defined by geographic, climatic, and social traits. "I have always had a weakness for small, limited, and manageable things.

Empordà as a whole exceeds my means of perception. The Small Empordà goes well with my way of being, with my short-range flight, with the pleasure I take in concrete, specific things" (7:463). He had no qualms declaring the discretionary nature of such an entity, the fact that framing the space of the canvas is more for the artist's convenience than because nature comes pre-divided into so-called natural regions and ready-made landscapes. "The existence of the Small Empordà is a mere convenience – a requirement of my working method. We are all equal: the neighbours on the hither side and those on the yonder side" (7:468).

It was the *longue durée* of human action, therefore history, that created territorial units held together by shared semantic fields, entrenched social dispositions, broadly acknowledged institutions, and a common world view; units that subsist after being fragmented by political fiat and challenge the forces of fragmentation – the superstructure of the European nation states – with a unity surpassing individual decisions, because founded on deeper continuities of life. This is, on a larger scale, another application of *país* as a pre-political entity:

> I am one of those who believe – and my European experience justifies my assertion – that the Catalan-speaking lands (Old and New Catalonia, Mallorca, Valencia, and the Roussillon) form one of the most unified European complexes. Men and women from these lands are united not through superficial, anecdotal, or folkloric reasons: we are united by a common conception of life, by the identical meaning of our words when referring to basic things. One and the same law unites us, as does a juridical system, and the idea that our relation with people is based on a contract. This is our unifying general trait. (7:468)

In the above paragraph, Pla describes a European region that is politically fragmented but existentially unified. This unofficial, indeed counter-official mapping of a cultural unity fits the definition of "region" offered above: a territory composed of interrelated places without solution of continuity in space and time. In the region, time individualizes space through the encounter between cosmic forces that create the setting for history and human action (or passion), which moulds the experience undergone by the region's inhabitants. The name for such historically shared experience is tradition.

Pla is arguably the best landscape writer in contemporary Iberian literature. He claimed that he discovered his writing vocation when attempting to describe the landscape he saw during his afternoon walks to the Sant Sebastià hermitage near his hometown of Palafrugell. "One day, without knowing how it happened, I found myself with a pencil and a notebook in my hand. I started placing adjectives after each pine grove, each field, each piece of sea" (7:475). Nothing in Pla's writing resembles any of the approaches to landscape described or narrated in Simon Schama's *Landscape and Memory*. Pla had no taste for either the Romantic sublime or the neoclassical manipulations of nature studied in such profusion in that book. The following description of the Collsacabra valley is an example of his attitude towards the sublime:

> The mountains surrounding it are not tall, nor do they have the obsessive verticality often present in Alpine or Pyreneean valleys. One is protected but not smothered by them. I have never experienced the temptation to climb mountains or to dominate these huge warts on the scab of the earth, and this explains the fact that the mountains have annoyed me much less than they permanently envisage. In any case, I wish to testify to my gratitude to the mountains of Collsacabra for their discrete height. (9:352)

Nothing could be further from the ecstatic look of a Caspar David Friedrich overwhelmed by geology's power. Pla flees from any hint of pantheism and reacts by desublimating any pretence of mystical communion with nature. "Catalonia is a mountainous country. One would wish, by blowing, to reduce the height of these warts of the planet by half" (9:403). His preference for civilized, reliable landscapes has something of the ancient Greek warning about the virtues of limits and moderation. "To be of human measure, a landscape needs some gentleness" (2:255). Measured by human standards, a landscape must incorporate the average of human perception without inducing awe through its magnitude or inaccessibility. To be livable, a landscape must be prosaic:

> The landscape of Empordà has the good sense of presenting itself in anti-literary fashion. This land is neither majestic nor noble like the Camp de Tarragona, nor does it have Mallorca's grandiose exaltation or the polished gothic that other nooks of Girona have. Empordà is a normal, human landscape, adequate for its inhabitants, all of us, rich or poor, of middle class. It is a reliable landscape. To pay tribute to the pedantry surrounding us we will say that in this landscape comes to pass the miracle of the contraction of the sublime to this imponderable thing that is the happy medium, to this tragic, profound, and most painful of all things. (*Coses vistes* 37)

The calm, non-dramatic landscapes Pla cherished are alien to the landscape cultures studied by Schama. And yet, the landscapes he described meticulously and with evident relish are indeed about memory. They are, or so he claims, soberly realistic, but there is no question that he retained aspects of the idealization promoted by the *noucentistes*. This generation of artists, intellectuals, and politicians based their territorial policy on the transformation of landscape according to a nationalized Mediterranean aesthetic that pitted austere, well-defined contours against northern wildness and profusion. They associated the lush, shady forests of Germanic myth with instinctual disorder and rebellion against civilized norms. Thus Eugeni d'Ors, *Noucentisme*'s chief theoretician and guiding light, placed a story of romantic passion leading to incest, the collapse of civilization's primary taboo, in the mountain village of Gualba, on the woody slopes of the Montseny. He famously called for an ordering of the mountains, and for "subjecting [the mountain] to architectural law" ("L'arranjament de les muntanyes," 15 May 1907, *Glosari 1906–1907*, 492).

Pla also favoured nature that was austere and preferably tame. But rather than the result of deliberate political intervention, he saw in the order and elegance of Catalan landscapes the accumulated effect of gradual modifications over long periods of time. "I still feel the liveliness of this landscape. Looking at it, I notice that the order infused in it by innumerable generations suggests an idea of ample, natural elegance" (7:475). Yet, the elements of this landscape remind us strongly of *noucentista* paintings such as those of Joaquim Sunyer:

> I look at Boet, now in autumn. It is the piece of land that I like best among all I have ever seen. It is a spot with crops, vineyards, and olive trees, which would be nothing especial if it wasn't crowned with the sweetest, most delicate, liveliest, most sensitive curves one can ever dream. People harvest grapes and the vines gradually dry up and become golden. The early rains have polished the green of the alfalfa and the sainfoin. The tillage has primitive, brutal colours. The birds fly close together over the exhausted figures. The dominant tone is clayish, but put on top of the coals and embers of the vines, the thousand colours of the apple green of the fields, the ancient, smooth light of the olive tree. It is an earthly tapestry, calm and clear, framed by pine trees, of an ideal polychrome rusticity. In every tract of land there is a whitewashed house, a well, a cistern for the sulfate. There may be one hundred of them ... Above, in

> this fine, charmed hour of the evening – suspended joy – a white cloud navigates, leaving a flush, roving shadow. (7:475–6)

Considered as the representation of qualitative space, the landscape and the region it defines are the maximal categories within which the natural world is offered to our experience. And because art is the medium that aspires to create qualitative space, landscape painting has always been regional. Aulic painting represented the elements of power: portraits of monarchs and statesmen, military commanders and battle scenes, high bureaucrats and dignitaries; while religious painting reproduced biblical scenes, popular saints, and members of the Church hierarchy. In short, the foundations of the state's legitimacy and its stylization in awe-evoking artistic works. Landscape painting, on the other hand, is eminently secular and specific. Its primary clientele has been the bourgeoisie and its space of choice the private collection. It produces a different form of satisfaction by representing familiar spaces and, after the eclosion of the romantic cult of the fatherland, spaces thought to preserve the formative elements of the nation in pristine form. Romanticism has been blamed for using landscape as a vehicle for myths in an effort to consolidate the relation between people and territory in the rising national imagination. It must be noted, however, that the association between land and history was achieved by suppressing closer associations between landscape and people in the narrower and more natural, i.e., more concretely lived, scope of the region. Consolidating national space and creating national imaginaries by means of landscape necessitated dislocating previous identities based on the coexistence of the places that made up the region. On the other hand, romanticism remains the source of attitudes and values that resist modernity's turning places into mere locations. More precisely, landscape art is the act of aesthetic consciousness that documents the evacuating of places, the painting being the place's posthumous image, at the moment it is absorbed by national space before the latter atomizes into the global. One of today's most innovative landscape artists, Perejaume writes:

> In this sense, the painter who goes to the place acts as a kind of blotting paper capable of lifting it away. The landscape painter must know how to pull the image from the soil, preserving its integrity as much as its luxuriance. Thus, the layer of place must be as capable of being lifted as possible, superficial enough to be detached and transported. As if the landscape had existence independent from the land. (18)

Catalanism, which in its origin was not a form of nationalism but a regional vindication, owed its inspiration to the romantic search for the remnants of popular culture that played such a strong role in the German cultural renaissance of the late eighteenth century. In this case, however, the remnants of a formerly robust culture were submerged, not by French neoclassic universalism as in Germany, but by another form of romanticism: the Spanish cult of the nation. And this was a nation whose art continued to be dominated by courtly values and ecclesiastical omnipotence, as could be seen in Goya's paintings and sketch work before the shocked and almost desperate *Disasters of War* series. Landscape painting remained strange to the *castiza* tradition of Spain. It emerged in Catalonia during the transition from romantic historicism to everyday themes and natural surroundings in which city folks re-encountered their family's origins. Interest in landscape art arose at the very moment when people were migrating to the cities in great numbers to feed the newly established factories or to start a new life in commerce.

In Narcís Oller's *L'escanyapobres* (The miser, 1884), one of the characters gives voice to this phenomenon: "What is growing today? The large cities ... The new civilization tends to concentrate. You've seen it already: of your friends, those who are not in heaven are now in Barcelona" (*L'escanyapobres* 217–18). Migration meant uprooting. And with the growing imbalance between urban and rural, the conditions were building up for a revalorization of the country in its particular, concrete aspects, precisely those that could not be reduced to the ever more abstract conditions of the big city. One of the defining aspects of the Renaixença was precisely this revalorization, found not just among painters but also among the so-called river poets: lo Gaiter del Llobregat (the Bagpiper of the Llobregat), pseudonym of Joaquim Rubió i Ors; lo tamboriner del Fluvià (the drummer of the Fluvià River), pseudonym of Pau Estroch; lo Gaiter de la Muga (the Bagpiper of the Muga River), pseudonym of Carles Fages de Climent. And in the greatest poet of the period, Jacint Verdaguer, author of the epic mountain poem *Canigó*.

Ironically, the wake-up call to the value of the homeland landscape came from a man who had left it for the capital city. Bonaventura Aribau's *Oda a la Pàtria* (Ode to the fatherland), the poem credited with starting off the renaissance of literary Catalan, begins with the verse: "Adieu, mountains, forever adieu." This farewell was surely an expression of nostalgia by a Catalan away from home, but it had the unexpected effect of triggering enthusiasm for the land, especially the mountain areas, among the very people who had fled those areas, flocking to Catalonia's industrial cities in search of a better life. It was those urban classes that, from the mid-nineteenth century onward, supported landscape painting as the pre-eminent genre in Barcelona's art market.

The Renaixença fostered hiking as rediscovery of the land, and this physical acquaintance with places that may have been forgotten but were never truly unknown stimulated interest in pictorial representations of nature. Pla's tireless travels throughout Catalonia to get acquainted with its landscapes, local customs, and histories were a reminiscence of that earlier enthusiasm for exploring the folds, bends, and heights of the hinterland. The new trend did not entail a form of nativism or proclaim a return to the home ground. It revealed a cultural, perhaps even a political interest, in the sense that the land, in its physical accidents and natural characteristics, was increasingly considered the cradle of the identity Catalans were starting to vindicate. Critics of Catalan nationalism claim that identification with a distant rurality was nothing but bad conscience for the industrial city that the new rural poets and painters had before their eyes (Fradera 161). However that may be, it is also possible to see that trend as compensatory for the price paid for progress. We only see things truly after we have lost them. Then their form comes to life again in us as an image.

In Catalonia, landscape painting was established when Ramon Martí Alsina (1826–94) transitioned from depicting medieval ruins in the style of Lluís Rigalt to realist natural scenery somewhat influenced by Courbet. According to art historian Francesc Fontbona, Martí Alsina turned to nature painting as a consequence of his aesthetic ideas (51). He considered pictorial representation of landscape a direct, detailed approximation to reality. Constancy in representing the landscape was a way to affirm the region's singularity, whose essence the artist sought to capture in the canvas. This form of realism presupposed, besides passion for truthfulness in art, knowledge of geography. This science was useful, for instance, to obtain a perfect orientation of the masses with respect to the sun. He also considered detailed knowledge of trees necessary. The artist got it by practising analytic drawing, beginning with the structure of the branches and going on to minimal details that would not even be included in the picture, but knowledge of which he considered indispensable for an honest representation. Echoing Martí Alsina, Pla will later assert:

> In reality the condition for painting a landscape is botany. Corot, who is one of the greatest landscape painters in history, is unimaginable in Normandy; unimaginable in Italy. The oak is a dense, strong tree, with perennial leaves and elegant solidity. (9:121)

He means that the landscape artist, insofar as he hopes to capture the essence of a region, studies the relation between it and the forms of life it contains. Pla looks at the landscape with technical concerns in mind that are very similar to those of painters. For instance, the quality of light, which can be elusive. Speaking with Josep Valls, Pla said about the light in his region: "Sometimes over the Empordà hovers a small and mysterious light, a light that is serene but never sublime. Dalí is perhaps the one who comes nearest to doing this light" (Valls, *Converses* 134). Elsewhere, describing the colour of the autumnal sunset, he draws pictorial resources from some still life. Light is "the colour of the flesh of a peach, a tasty, dense, slow clarity of juicy morbidity" (8:23). Inside the rooms of the rural houses, this light, "slightly yellow, of foamy, dense brush stroke, we saw it before in Vermeer de Delft, descending on an inclined plane from a window, grazing the mauve silk of a lady's dress, a head of hair of old gold, transfiguring a wall, a water puddle, the tops of some trees seen in a reverie" (8:24).

With exaggerated modesty, he casually comments: "In the course of my insignificant literary activity, I have sometimes tried to formulate a landscape, to establish the colours of a precise landscape, to draw its forms, to capture its spirit" (9:520). Whenever he looks at a landscape, pictorial references spring up. In *The Gray Notebook*, Pla compares the colours the rain brings out in things with the strong coloration of primitive art: "The colours are strong and glossy and the contours present a deep incision, a precise crease. The landscape makes me think of the paintings of primitive artists that I see occasionally reproduced in illustrated magazines" (1:162). Correlating perception of the landscape with the way it has been represented on canvas is neither remarkable nor even surprising. Art theorists have shown persuasively how art has educated our vision, how cultural our spontaneous acts of perception are. But one thing is to evoke pictorial references to help the reader visualize the hues and shades of a given landscape and quite another to attempt to capture its spirit. How does one convey the spirit of a natural thing? Isn't this a risky enterprise for an objectivist writer? Is there such thing as a spirit of the landscape? What is meant by it? Verdaguer described the history of Canigó as a struggle between the original fairies and the monks that expelled them from the mountain, an allegory of the Christianization of formerly pagan lands. Lamenting the decadence of Catalan traditions in the Cerdagne and the Roussillon, he decried in "La barretina" (The Phrygian cap) the disappearance of the age-old culture from these Catalan regions assimilated by France:

> Catalan is this land,
> the villages Catalan,
> Catalan the plain and the mountain,
> but of France the inhabitants.
> Canigó, robed in white,
> says: – I do not understand this parlance. (237)

All the tension between history and politics, tradition and law, is packed in these few verses. Village structure and architecture, customs, the traditional language, patronymics are all from an older, autochthonous culture, but that older identity is being replaced with a new one supplied by the state. What does it mean for Canigó, old Catalonia's central mountain, to claim, personified, that it does not understand the language of the state? Verdaguer practises a kind of historical naturalism, pitting it against the state's arbitrary rationalism. For centuries France had coveted these regions in the name of an allegedly natural geometry: the Hexagon. It is no coincidence that precisely in the mid-seventeenth century, when mathematics and geometry had become the ruling science, France was able to advance its borders to the southern Pyrenees. Baruch Spinoza published *Renati Descartes Principia Philosophiae, More Geometrico Demonstrata* only four years after France and Spain signed the Treaty of the Pyrenees, by which France acquired the northern Catalan regions. Verdaguer, in the nineteenth century, witnessed the reacculturation of Catalans under a new political dispensation. Pla, in turn, complained: "All traditions have been lost, each day we distance ourselves more from the things of the land; everything turns into smoke and nothing: photography and papers" (9:96).

On several occasions, Pla mentioned Canigó, its significance for the Rousillon's economy (9:585) or its influence on the entire region through its distribution of the winds, the mountain being nothing short of a ruler of people's moods and habits (7:253–4). Verdaguer asserted nature's permanence in the famous last stanza of "Los dos campanars" (The two bell towers):

> What one century built up, another brings down,
> but God's monument remains;
> and storm, gale, hatred and War
> will not bring down Canigó,
> will not dismember the haughty Pyrenee. (*Antologia* 245)

Similarly Pla, in his matter-of-fact way, speaks about the mountains', i.e., Old Catalonia's, permanence: "One of the most agreeable things in Empordà is the earth's stillness, its lack of surprises, to know that we have found it thus and thus we shall leave it" (7:200). By contrast, the coastline, he says, must have changed considerably since ancient times (7:201). Like Verdaguer in the poem just cited, Pla is speaking here in tectonic terms, and unlike his predecessor admitting a relative sort of permanence even on these terms. He is gratified with the low contingency of the Empordà's orography. Other regions are less fortunate. And he is otherwise quite aware that landscape can be transformed radically in a very short time. The Empordà furnished him with an impressive, relatively recent transfiguration when in 1879 the phylloxera plague, leaping over the Pyrenees, devastated the extensive vineyards of Empordà, plunging the region into poverty. Then, says Pla, in addition to the economic disaster, "before the eyes of people a change of landscape manifested itself" (44:24).

Let us ask again: if landscape changes, sometimes swiftly and unexpectedly, how does one capture its spirit? The answer can only be that the observer stands before the landscape with an open mind and open senses, hoping to grasp an intimate reaction, a stirring of one's own spirit by the impressions of the world's visual surface. Carles Riba discerned in Pla's landscape visions "a continuous oscillation between two moments: the moment I would call pictorial, when things concentrate, opposing to him their profile, their masses, their colour, and he fixes them with a sharp, precise eye; and the authentically poetic moment, when, already filtered, they bring out their human values and associate with his sentimental world" (211). Pla's ambition was to evoke a lived space. And so tenacious was his purpose that, between representation and spatial feeling, he chose the second. "I like painted landscapes. I like more the contemplation of real landscapes. And even more do I like to become an element of the landscape, a small thing the landscape contains" (24:376).

It was probably the difficulty of describing the landscape that led Pla to rate Joaquim Ruyra, author of *Marines i boscatges*, higher than more canonical writers. A minor author, Ruyra achieved linguistic mastery in naturalist description, a feature that Pla always appreciated. But the main reason for his admiration was that in his sketches of nature Ruyra managed to raise the places described to a superior level, where they take on the representation of a larger space that endows them with consistency and significance. Pla knew that one single look or perspective such as painting provides does not suffice to convey a landscape, not to speak of a region. Hence, on occasion he inverts the natural order and tries to explain the region through landscape. Apropos the poplars along the Tordera River, he writes:

> These groves offer perhaps the botanical spectacle that is closest to our way of being. It is a permanently shifting spectacle with a variety that sometimes seems hard to explain. Perhaps the light – as I see it – is one of the most decisive elements of its spirit. There are lights that lend the groves – especially those in the morning – a happy, radiant, and optimistic spirit. With the afternoon light they sometimes take on a sad, depressed, and solitary aspect. When, in the evening, this solitude becomes more acute and the spot is deserted, they even produce a hint of fear. As a result, if someone goes through them, that person quickens the pace. It's a purely imaginary fear, due perhaps to the fact that a geometric vision is scarier than a disordered vision. (9:175)

The landscape may be immutable, or certain landscapes at any rate, but the aspect it presents to human apprehension is not. Pla stresses the variability of the landscape's appearance and therewith the alternation of its "spirit," of the mood it induces in the observer depending on time of day and atmospheric conditions such as the quality and intensity of the light. But these are precisely the phenomenal variations *plein air* painters have always taken into account. And he never denies the confluence of nature and history in the landscape. Thus, speaking about *noucentista* painter Joaquim Sunyer, he writes: "Sunyer is the painter of a cultivated, ordered nature onto which Roman Law has been projected, of a permanent composition, if one knows how to see it – of the nature that peasants fashion each year on the country, tilling and sowing the land, pruning the vineyard, snipping the olives, defending the fruit trees, irrigating the terraces" (21:295). These activities are not mechanical routines but adaptive behaviour manifesting a will, a system of preferences, a way of relating to the environment tested over the centuries; in short, the spirit that Pla thought he could discern in a landscape. A painter can just depict its surface, its appearance, or he can "paint a given physical surface trying to include the very especial heartbeat that informs it by the fact of serving as substratum of a given spirit" (21:301). The phrase is somewhat abstruse and rather untypical of Pla in its mystifying recourse to conjectural entities – "heartbeat," "substratum," "spirit." But Pla had no truck with the territorial mystique. For him landscapes do not symbolize a transcendent reality; they are not instances supporting generalizations but the concrete boundaries of human action within the range of the actor. And they can be minimalist, as in this description strongly reminiscent of Joan Miró's *Hort amb ase* (*The Vegetable Garden with Donkey*):

> In these spring twilights one of the few things that structure me [...] is contemplating a vegetable garden, such as those one finds outside the village. Admirably cultivated, they are pure, exquisite delicacies of labour. I hear the steady walk of an old animal turning a badly greased water wheel that creaks. It is the poor music of poverty excited by the hope of tender vegetables. (1:151)

In this humble arrangement of nature with a view to human sustenance, Pla experiences something that structures him internally in the act of contemplating the age-old organization of space practised by modest villagers and mediated by the expectation of the seasonal yield. He does not claim that the physical medium is a modality of spirit, as an idealist would, or a record of spirit, the way a tablet preserves the encoded motions of the mind. In this conception of "life painting," landscape is neither a local articulation of *res extensa* nor a modality of Spinoza's single substance. It is rather, as Antoni Marí observes, a synthesis of perception and reflection, a meeting of aesthetics and the understanding (120).

The spirit Pla perceives in the landscape is the synthesis of the passions, ambitions, fears, and natural limitations of the generations that left their seal on the natural surroundings and were in turn moulded by them in their ancestral memory, customs, and language. "These mountains with an archaic profile, with an elephant-like outline, are so blended with our life, with the life of our ancestors, with our ancient reminiscences, that we wear them engraved in our hearts and our spirit. They encouraged us to have a home, a fatherland, and gave meaning to our life" (9:491). Considering again the poplar groves in the Tordera River basin, the variation in the spectator's mood produced by the change of light in the course of the day needs to be balanced with the intimations of the *longue durée,* in which permanent geographic features stabilize historical change. Variation within finite possibilities of transformative experience constitutes the region, making possible the emergence of landscape as visual poetry of the places.

The prominence of landscape art in Catalonia, Pla seems to be saying, is ultimately related to the country's visual diverseness, an effect of its climatic heterogeneity and its exposure to an assortment of winds:

> Catalonia, an extremely diverse country, with a geographic variety that is literally fascinating and surprising, has a clear meteorology of a complexity parallel to its varied geography. When our country falls within a clear meteorology of extensive range, then the phenomenon completely overwhelms the area on which it appears. But besides this fact, the importance and weight of local phenomena is indisputable. Local diversity turns our climate into a rigmarole. (7:230)

Pla is almost certainly repeating notions set forth by geographer Pau Vila, who observed: "The conditions of the plots, the climate, local needs and the interests of the economy create a nuanced mosaic that characterizes the country through a diversity of landscapes that surprises the observer" (cit. Pujals 108). Such variety exceeds the ability of one single artist or school. It requires the nuances of a multiple approach to landscape painting. The poplar groves along the Tordera River show orderliness and regularity because the trees were planted at the precise distance required for maximizing profit. Economic calculation lies at the base of their elegance and charm. Pla is reported to have said: "A landscape is beautiful if it provokes transfer of deeds of ownership at the title company" (cit. Valls *Converses* 159). Economic ambition could also ravage the landscape, as Pla lamented in his elegiac comments on the impact of tourism on the coast of Empordà. What he had in mind when tracing back the elegance of certain landscapes to economic motive was the traditional exploitation of the land. He admired the peasants' patient modification of the land in their struggle to eek out a meagre sustenance, finding the ensuing balance between human need and natural conditions eminently beautiful: "My heroes from real life are the peasants of poor lands, the authentic creators of landscape" (Valls, *Josep Pla oral* 43). Uncultivated landscapes, through their chaotic inconsistency and changeableness, resist artistic definition. Thus, the north coast of the island of Mallorca misleads the artist into a wrong use of aesthetics to defeat the understanding:

> These coves and having had the opportunity recently to see many metres of painting on the themes they propose lead me to speak about this landscape's pictoriality. I am convinced that the landscape of the north coast of Mallorca is unpictorial, and if I had to advise an artist to seek his own ineluctable destruction, I would recommend him this region. Everything here is unpictorial: the sea, the rocks, and the plant world; but above all the sea, whether it is in a state of grandiose agitation or in the days of dry calm, when the water seems ironed, fixed, and dead. [...] The environment disposes of human reason and prudence so easily that the painter is smothered by nature. The artist turns into a form of vegetable outgrowth of these inconsistent rocks affected by the sea's chemistry, softened by the marine magma's plasticity. – We are pantheists! – say the painters established in this region, and with this phrase they formulate the most unpictorial assertion a painter can make. Indeed, it was always agreed that drawing, the basis of all possible painting, was a corrective to man's dispersive tendency, an incision over the world's chaotic nature, over pantheism, of some concrete, habitual, and difficult forms. (15:121–2)

The idea of unpictoriality is intriguing. Why would Pla advise against painting these Mallorcan cliffs? His criteria of pictoriality can strike one as arbitrary. "Eivissa is," he says, "a piece of candy: it will always be pictorial and paintable." On the other hand, Menorca, the next island in the archipelago, inspires only bad painting. "The climate is unfavourable" (15:51). Pla compares the cloudy, vaporous skies of Eivissa to the bright, empty sky of Menorca and concludes that drawing rather than painting suits its luminosity. Elsewhere, speaking of Cadaqués, a favourite subject for painters, he asserts: "Many artists have drawn Cadaqués, but no one has painted it yet" (Valls, *Josep Pla oral* 105). Since this was empirically inaccurate, Pla must have meant something less literal. In the same statement he critiques the use of white and blue and the avoidance of brown in the stereotypical *noucentista* views of Cadaqués. He critiques, in other words, the reduction of the view of this fisherman's cove to the quaint stockpile of whitewashed houses contrasting with the marine blue of the bay and abstracting it from the setting dominated by miles of slate drywall work encircling the village to form man-made terraces of various elevations along the orography of the coast. But this is not all. If we extrapolate from the previous comments about pantheism and the difficulty of form in relation to Mallorca's north coast, we will see Pla projecting the Nietzschean dyad of Apollo versus Dionysus onto the landscape. Some landscapes are given over to rapture and frenzy – and thus can destroy the artist the way the maenads tore apart the god of mystery and intoxication – while other landscapes are luminous and easily contained within the painter's lines.

Despite this implicit mythological pedestal, Pla is in fact groping towards a naturalist theory of landscape, in which art depends less on the skill of the artist than on the natural conditions of the object. Pine trees, for instance, generate sadness and melancholy by inflecting the light through their monotone foliage. "The pine is a poor, sad tree typical of the land of cicadas. It contributes unquestionably to the clear, luminous sadness of the Mediterranean. The light that hovers inside the pine forests has an irremediable melancholy" (7:498). But artistic prejudice also plays a part in his verdict of unpictoriality for Mallorca's northern coast. In the event, he appears to use its cliffs as an opportunity to combat romanticism's projection of subjective states of mind onto the natural scenery:

> Twisted botanic forms, the sea's corrosion, a massive pine tree, sea, sky, and rock play in face of the scenery, of unbounded dispersion, of permanent exceptionality. However: is it possible to paint the infinite? Should one paint the exceptional? I don't think so. Neither the infinite ode, nor the infinite melody, nor the infinite sea can be painted. When this disquieting thing, empty of meaning like an empty eggshell, when the infinite gets mixed with our things and is naturalized in an act of aberration, then in the best of cases one enters into sheer balderdash, and in the worst of cases into the exploitation of the sublime, which is bad faith. (15:121)

Pla was attacking romanticism in the person of its foremost poet, Joan Maragall, author of an "Infinite Ode," whose initial verse announces the poem's endlessness: "I have started an ode, which I can never finish" (35). And it could not be finished because the poet was hostage to a nameless force hidden in the wind and in space, an ungraspable entity that of necessity must appear suspect to an empiricist like Pla, who, to the cosmic scope of romantic poetry and painting, opposed the discipline of the senses in the representation of concrete things (15:120).

But there was something else. Pla not only objected to the exceptionality of the pictorial or poetic theme. He also derided the romantic inflation of the artist. All his life he insisted on the writer's debt to other writers, denying the possibility of originality – "I have never known exactly what the thing people call originality might be, nor do I think that anyone knows" (9:412) – and carried this attitude to the extreme of justifying plagiarism. Speaking of Stendhal's *Mémoires d'un touriste*, he wrote that "he could do what every cultured person does when finding himself pen in hand: to continue, to progress, to leave a small contribution to their social group's fund of certain, ancient, and verified sensibility. He did what authors that scratch eternity call, disparagingly, plagiarism" (9:412).

Imitation, continuity, improvement, these were terms associated with tradition and with the artistic concept of "school." And in Catalonia, where landscape painting had great prestige, the most illustrious and influential school was the Olot school. It was founded by Joaquim Vayreda (1843–94), to whom, incidentally, Verdaguer had dedicated his poem "La barretina." In his book on Olot in the arts, Ramon Grabolosa says of Vayreda that, by the time he was twenty-two, he had painted the wildest nooks, the darkest forests, the enclosed valleys and rocky places of the region, mastering the chromatic realism that came, through Martí Alsina, ultimately from Delacroix and Courbet (90). Other members were Joaquim's brother, Marià (1853–1903), Josep Berga i Boix (1837–1914), and a group of younger painters, among whom Enric Galwey (1864–1931) stood out. Although not from Olot, Galwey synthesized the school's orientations (Fontbona 75). The group's reputation attracted other painters to Olot, whose work showed the school's influence. Eliseu Meifrèn, Modest Urgell, Santiago Rusiñol, Sebastià Junyent, Laureà Barrau, and Joaquim Mir were among them. The influence of realist landscape painting reached the *modernistes* at the turn of the century, a generation that would soon receive a new impulse from the impressionist art that triumphed in Paris.

Surprisingly, Pla denied the existence of the school: "I have met many painters from here and elsewhere who have painted these valleys: I have never perceived any concern for a school among them. Each marches to a different drummer" (9:521). Pla seems to be echoing an opinion expressed by Berga i Boix, who in a letter dated 1914, asserted that the Olot school did not exist, or rather it consisted of Joaquim Vayreda alone (cit. Pla 43:425). Elsewhere Pla had written about the Olot school of painting and described its members and activities in some detail

(43:420–6). The reason he denied the existence of the school despite the reality of an Olot Artistic Centre founded by Vayreda in 1869 and an Olot Public School of Drawing operating since 1877 under Berga's directorship may have been Pla's scepticism towards generic concepts and institutional determinations. He was ironical about academicism in art: "I admire academicism. I enjoy academicism when it has a flicker of life. Generally, though, it is insignificant, dead. Man rarely attains the living harmony – Milà i Fontanals's definition of the highest beauty, of academicism, that is. If we poor mortals do not reach it, I mean if we do not attain harmony, we have no other recourse than to be satisfied with life. Even then, to infuse life into a work of art is exceedingly difficult" (15:176–7).

Pla was extremely individualistic, also with regard to aesthetics. His refusal to admit an established school of painting may relate to his rejection of the literary style that had dominated Barcelona's literary establishment during his formative period. Even so, the assertion that the Olot school was non-existent is remarkable. After all, he recognized in Vayreda the origin of a painting style characterized by spatial identity but over time came to be recognized through an identity of pictorial influences. "Just as in France all modern painting starts with the school of Barbizon, here everything begins with Vayreda" (9:524). Pla traces all Catalan pictorial realism back to Vayreda. Coming from him, the assertion is significant since, as a realist himself, he shared with the painter certain assumptions about the representation of reality. But mostly it is significant because, as a landscape writer, he detected in Vayreda the dimension that made the difference between art with a "flicker of life" and academicism devoid of it. The dimension in question was time, always present in Pla's depictions of the scenery.

> All landscapes are a matter of moments, of time, of transience. Vayreda understood that on this point the Olot landscape attains indescribable ephemerality. No Olot landscape is motionless and static. There are diverse landscapes, diverse times and moments. Sometimes they are worth painting, at other times less so, at still others not at all. In some sense, it is a landscape in permanent becoming. In this country perhaps no other is more plastic, changing, of more visible ephemerality. To capture it in these crucial moments one needs great knowledge and the corresponding shrewdness. These were the virtues of Vayreda, the most lucid artist of his time. (9:522)

If the word *landscape* injects idealization into the concept of region or country, if it stylizes and flattens it to fit the canvas's two-dimensionality, Pla knows nevertheless that perspective is transient and that realism requires taking stock of the evolution of visual surfaces, these being generally the most frequent and popular means of access to a region's specificity. No landscape is truthful unless presented in the perspective of a temporal vanishing point, under the impression of its near demise and transformation. This is what Pla meant by "a flicker of life," a radically situated apprehension of the aesthetic object in which the original reception is not necessarily unrepeatable but its communication depends on the grasp of circumstances that make it a genuine experience:

> The Olot landscape starts being really interesting when the sky is overcast and in the softer, denser, and nuanced light the colours of the landscape appear. The monotone dark green of the unfurnished summer skies, which produces a sterile, unproductive chromatism, becomes richer, transforms itself, obtains a completely different aspect. There is a supreme moment in this landscape: it is in the spring, when a fine, slow, intermittent rain falls on the earth. Then a red, a yellow, a white appear – the colours that the earth delivers with perfect precision. This is then the landscape that must be seen at a specific moment and a specific time. It is somewhat uncomfortable to say: the Olot landscape appears in all its normal, modest personality when looked at from under an umbrella or at least with a trench coat on one's shoulders. (9: 520–1)

The landscape, says Pla, does not exist independently of the subject who looks at it. Its finest qualities cannot be abstracted from specific conditions of atmosphere, humidity, and light. For the Olot landscape, which was a staple of realist landscape painting in Catalonia, the harsher summer light depleted its specificity making it "monotonous," more habitual and commonplace, whereas the filtered light of spring brought out its nuances, showing it to be an integral site of the Garrotxa, thereby revealing its "regionness." This landscape reveals "all its normal, modest personality," says Pla, to the observer capable of going to the root of its variability, of taking visual stock of its temporality and cyclicality. To the spectator, in short, capable of negotiating the mixture of familiarity and revelation constitutive of the experience of the *país*.

Vayreda had written: "From the intimate and loving consortium of the artist with nature the artwork is born, whether you call it painting, poem, statue, architectural complex or musical harmony. And the purer and more legitimate the fecundation is, the easier and more natural the childbirth" (cit. Fontbona 65–7). Here it is not the case of a romantic claim about the work's naturalness, rather of artistic production giving nature its due. Sensory intimacy with the natural object allows the artist to turn it into an object of representation. Pla would have approved. Vayreda belonged to the category of artists known as métier artists. Hostile to the romantic cult of genius, these vocational artists rejected the inversion of the traditional relation between frame and object. They suspected speculative, mental art of leading to the dissolution of the profession.

Pla had no truck with metaphysics. When facing a landscape he resists being carried away by the late romantic symbolism of nature. "At Sils-Maria, in the Engadine, Nietzsche wrote: 'I am at three thousand five hundred feet above sea level. I see everything clearly. I have formulated the doctrine of eternal return.' I have never been so lucky. I see everything dark. I do not see anything and least of all do I see the eternal return" (9:403). Since the landscape is the cumulative work of men in their millennial adaptation to nature, the reasonable attitude is not to search for inaccessible sublimity but to wish for a landscape that accommodates both need and convenience. A "lazy," "bourgeois" appetite for domesticated landscape is the antithesis of nature mysticism: "Decidedly, the landscapes I like best are softly rounded, with cafés, restaurants, banks, and gracious, pleasant girls" (9:404).

Landscape challenges Pla's linguistic mastery. His struggle to find the words to adequately transcribe natural form and qualities resembles a painter's effort to find the true colour and the right perspective. Speaking of the difficulty to convey the right shade of colour, he said to Josep Valls: "The hard-to-concretize colour of Rome has always intrigued me. Perhaps it has the colour of the caramel that in the Empordà people add to the stew stuffing. Girona, on the other hand, has rheumatic colour" (*Jose Pla oral* 112). Mountains, the sea, rivers, forests, fields, roads and villages ... whenever Pla has something to recount, he places the narrative – often a simple one – within a rich descriptive background, calling up a convincing, sometimes arresting image in the reader. The technique is so deliberate that often the description moves to the foreground. The following excerpt from a narrated history of the Empordà shows him privileging the morose description of an evening summer dance under the awning of the yearly fair by the port of Palamós:

> In Palamós the sea, the bay, the small port in front of its urban encastling form a wonderful complex with a fine vivacity of forms and colours, which in calm days attains a suspended and ecstatic sweetness. [...] At night, the port, silent and drowsy, with the titillation of the green and red lanterns on the water and the vague oscillation of the lights on the ships created, right next to the dancing, a recess of mystery and solitude apt, however underused, for the things of love or to drift with fluctuating, frazzled, and misanthropic thoughts. The wind had been blowing for a long time; the awning was beginning to sag and the orchestra was drooping, and everything was coming to a languid, wistful end in the early hours. (7:382)

Whether he owed his visual education to the Olot school, to Impressionism, or to the Fauves, there is no doubt that in all his descriptions of place there is, as Marina Gustà pointed out, "a tendency to the painting, to make static whatever comes into the visual angle at every moment" ("Plasticitat i visualització" 111). As well as to adopt unusual perspectives and to present the landscape from unpredictable angles at unexpected times. One instance is the above description of late-night dancing under an awning made flabby by the wind, with the focus on the lonely harbour, where a misanthropic figure – possibly the writer himself – rambles steeped in melancholy thoughts while the party dies down in the wee hours. Such moments are part of the writer's deployment of the region; they are experiences committed to memory and preserved through the force of the image.

"To know a region is also to be able to *remember* it," writes Edward Casey, adding: "More important still is the fact that *only through memory is knowledge of an entire region sustained*" (76; emphasis in the original). The point is not that the extension, spatial breadth, and temporal depth of a region require the landscape painter to remember countless experiences of it in order to do justice to its diversity (Casey 76), but more profoundly, that memory is the material on which the painter works from the moment that the artist transforms a purely perceptive, phenomenological look into an intuition of the whole of the region through its landscape. This is the reason why Pla's works combine large swathes of landscape description with frequent reflections on memory. If large tracts of his oeuvre archive the experiences of the *país*, it is because he strove to preserve its visual memory through descriptions of its landscapes. Pla's conservatism can be understood in relation to his passion for retaining a memory of "regionness" in the temporal as well as the spatial dimension. This is why the self-avowed conservative Pla deplored the dearth of conservancy among his countrymen:

> In our country, rare are the men and even rarer the women who preserve the old papers, the recollections, who cultivate their memory filling it with the tremulous shadows from the past. Women especially are truly obsessed with destroying papers. They are arsonists. They do not even keep the old love letters. The cultivation of memory does not go beyond the pure mental mechanism. A new start. To start all over again every day. All is nothing. This is why the country often remains in a state of stupefied childishness. (9:53)

As perceptual frame of everyday experience, landscape was for Pla the unheeded glue of the community. The need for landscape is universal, for the simple reason that the landscape we inhabit provides us with the most immediate context of our self-awareness. As members of a group, we know who we are by the landscapes with which our memories are entangled, those we identify as extensions of ourselves. Landscape is beyond class, although access to it is class dependent. Pla once remarked: "Those who do not have a great deal of money go to the movies and watch landscapes pass before their eyes. Those who have it buy a car and pass before the landscapes" (Valls, *Josep Pla oral* 42).

Unlike some of the other great writers on landscape, he did not write about landscape with the reactive nostalgia of the lost paradise. He was closer perhaps to those German writers who strove to generate a sense of *Heimat* out of aesthetic worship of a selective landscape, that of the German primordial forest. Only, his version of *Heimat*, the *país*, was vague enough and at the same time specific enough to sidestep the requirements of political nationalism, a passion that Pla overcame early in life and castigated ever after. In his oeuvre, *país* is a modest, local, neo-Latin concept, a dwelling area in which certain customs prevail, ranging from the sounds of a language to the flavours of the popular cuisine. Pla's *país* could perhaps be understood in terms of nineteenth-century German sociologist Wilhelm Heinrich Riehl's conception of the *Heimat*, if instead of saying that it is "much more than a patriotic sentiment" (Schama 113), one says that it was all of that minus the patriotic sentiment. *País* was for Pla something concrete, "a physical topography with specific customs and idioms, in short the memories particular to [those who inhabit it], embedded in its soil" (Schama 113). More than embedded in the soil – a word with particular resonance in German culture – Pla would have said, "inscribed in the landscape." Which is why, despite the "unpatriotic" sarcasm he often levelled at his fellow countrymen, including the brave old peasants – who were the etymologically grounded inhabitants of the *país* – and despite the harsh irony he directed against their superficiality, stupidity, and obliviousness, in the end everything was made up for and redeemed by the landscape. As he put it in his narrative *El carrer Estret*: "But the landscape is the only thing in this country that never fails" (8:446).

Pla's oeuvre is a huge canvas unfolding before the inner eye of the reader, as well as a prodigious archive of Catalan life vividly depicted for the reader's imagination. Its excellence comes to the fore the moment the reader accepts that Pla was not a writer of ideas but of appearances, not of depths but of surfaces, not a metaphysical writer but an empirical one. If appearance, in good post-Kantian currency, is the meeting of time and space in the existential crossroads of a perceiving subject, it follows that appearances become conscious in representation. To put it more graphically: Pla is a Kantian in a trench coat, a sceptic who clutches at his impressions and promotes them to the level of landscape, that is, to a section of space cut out and framed through intentional perception and presented by artistic means to reflective contemplation.

7 Remembering the Region

Pla's entire work is the machination of a vengeance against time, the extolling of memory.

– Valentí Puig, *L'home de l'abric*

Since antiquity, civilization has been associated with the foundation and growth of cities. With the needs and possibilities created by the concentration of human settlement, politics appeared on the scene in the form of a long-term struggle between the city and the countryside, leading much of the time to the subjugation of the peasants. Modernity was, in essence, the acceleration of this process, and globalization the qualitative leap from the devastation of the landscape to the irreversible damage of the environment. Modern history can perhaps be best understood in terms of this *longue durée*. In Spain the civil wars of the nineteenth century, the Carlist Wars, were struggles between the rural landed property in regions that had retained the memory of seigniorial autonomy, and a bourgeoisie that was dependent on a court-based aristocracy in charge of the state machinery. In 1931 the monarchy fell in the aftermath of municipal elections after the scrutiny showed that it had lost the support of the larger cities. In 1936 the absolutist forces sought their revenge. Falange and the right-wing Catholics of the CEDA, representing the rural bourgeoisie and the large landholders, struck against the Republic that threatened the traditional distribution of the land. The defeat of the Republic was not only the defeat of the rural proletariat but also of the urban Basque and Catalan bourgeoisies at the hands of the southern and central Spanish elites.

Due to inherent contradictions, the Falange's experiment in autarchic economy during the 1940s failed miserably and was soon overtaken by the dependent capitalism that characterized Spain from the 1950s onward. An unstable truce between city and countryside took place in the middle years of the twentieth century, when industrial production resumed while Spain remained largely rural. But this balance soon tipped in favour of the city. The 1960s was an era of unprecedented internal migrations with some rural areas becoming depopulated through the urban resettlement of entire villages. This phenomenon could not have taken place without profound cultural upheavals.

Change often took place at breakneck speed. Its many facets cannot be summarized for the occasion. But they can be generally described as a desire to surmount the memory of the rural background of Spanish culture, which was amply perceived as abject and treated as an object of repression from the 1960s on. Catalonia had anticipated this process by over half a century, as can be seen from the literary tug of war between *ruralistes* and *modernistes* at the turn of the twentieth century. *Noucentisme* was the hard-nosed, Byzantine stylization of the urban devotion evidenced by the *modernistes*. It marked the apex in a cult of the city that would only attain similar proportions during the period leading to the 1992 Summer Olympic Games.

Since then the literary myth of the city has run its course and, although continuing to produce works of comparative value, it now faces competition from a new type of rural narrative that explores modern themes but is also grounded in local memory, a value that modernism had no use for. Novels like Maria Barbal's *Pedra de Tartera*, Jesús Moncada's Mequinensa cycle, or Jaume Cabré's *Les veus del Pamano* are compelling vindications of the regional through the excavation of Catalonia's collective memory. In no way can these or similar works be labelled as provincial literature (*literatura de comarques*). On the contrary, as worthy examples of the post-urban novel, they have re-centred the canon of contemporary Catalan literature balancing modern history with general human concerns.

The sociological reasons for this development are doubtless a complex set of determinants that need to be patiently laid out. On this occasion I merely want to point out a literary source for the new regionalism. I will argue that consciousness of the region as a coherent realm of experience owes much to its legitimation as mnemonic space. In a literary scene dominated by *noucentista* values first and then by the local emulators of international modernism, Josep Pla, one of the most travelled authors during the 1920s and 1930s, rediscovered a disregarded truth about intellectual production: that the best ideas often sprout, like seeds, in the obscurity of provincial retirement. Like Kant in Konigsberg, Heidegger in the Black Forest, and Michel de Montaigne in his manor house near Bordeaux, Pla spent long years reading and writing during his retirement at his family's country house in Llofriu, a hamlet in the

Figure 4. Josep Pla before his farmhouse, Llofriu, 1957.

Photographer: Ramon Dimas. Courtesy of Fundació Josep Pla.

Empordà, in the north of Catalonia. The city was the place where universal homelessness – the homelessness of the student and then the correspondent who lodged in countless boarding houses throughout Europe – revealed the basic, existential plight that Heidegger identified as the inescapable need of learning to dwell (161). For Pla Madrid was "a city of aristocrats (for the most part Andalusian), functionaries, and shopkeepers" that longed to emulate Barcelona (*Madrid* 26:61), and Barcelona, in turn, was a display of "demented architecture" (*Barcelona* 3:260). The arbitrary, anarchic architecture of the Eixample, as he saw it, failed as a spatial organizer of the cumulative intellectual work with which the city should have matched the measured, necessary form of the rural landscape:

> The architecture of Barcelona's expansion has contributed powerfully to prevent the necessary ripening of minds that in a developed "environment"

> could have achieved human fullness. In our country, to achieve a certain fullness of intelligence is very difficult, because the environment, excepting the landscape that the peasants build every year, is disturbing, chaotic, unpleasant. (3:260)

Strictly speaking, Pla is not against the city; rather, as a sensualist, he believes that intellectual composure is contingent on the degree of irritation or soothing of the senses that the milieu provides. To the idea that the city heightens intellectual life through the intensification of stimuli, to Eugeni d'Ors's "small fever" produced by the thousand lights, the traffic, and the cries of the newspaper salesmen (*Oceanografia del tedi* 82), Pla opposed a sceptical reflection on the inconveniences of urban life:

> If it were possible, one could say the following: writers who live permanently in big cities do so because they cannot do otherwise; adding to professional difficulties the inconveniences of a large city is a total mistake. The environment of a large city onto which a given political regime projects itself generates a marginal obsession and the environment becomes barren. Then there is the gratuitous, picturesque amenity. The assertion that in these centres one finds more ways of educating children – some writers have them – and much more society, more contacts, more life, more celebrities, more interesting ladies ... The notion that books can only be written in close proximity to others is one of this country's most archaic, provincial pieces of local wisdom. (9:8)

Although Pla is always impersonating a humble, down-to-earth peasant and advocating a naturalistic language, the previous passage contains certain tensions, places where the language grinds and the humdrum meaning is caught in a "snag." Let us examine the conditional, "if it were possible, one could say the following." Why foreground a doubt about the statement's possibility if the latter is articulated at once? What is the meaning of "possible" here, and what happens to the rhetorical deferral implied by the conditional form of the verb *poder* (can, be able to)? Does this phrase not contain a rhetorical implication that the thought might not, indeed cannot, be uttered? And yet, it is hard to see what would prevent the utterance. And if something could prevent it, why would it, and why does it not in the end? There is no trace here of a taboo or prohibition. Pla appears to be equivocating, "playing the peasant" ("fent el pagès"), which is idiomatic Catalan for faking bewilderment, but also for dithering and being indecisive, like a peasant at the marketplace. Although it cannot be ruled out that he is teasing the reader about the limited freedom of the press at this time (hence the reference to "a certain political regime"), the hesitancy appears to be governed by a gesture towards self-censorship triggered by self-doubt. Ramon Alcoberro denies that Pla is an Empordanès writer; in fact, he denies that such a thing exists, because a writer needs an environment with a reasonable amount of pedantry, libraries, publishing houses, universities, and other such conveniences in which the Empordà is utterly deficient. In fact, Alcoberro adds, during the years of the tourist boom, the Empordà has lacked the figure of the local historian, which was always the quarry from which regional (*comarcal*) writers emerged (137). And then: "Literarily and biographically speaking, Pla is a Barcelona writer" (139).

Entering into a discussion about the local identity of Pla's literature would be foolish. I have stated at the outset that he was not a regional writer. There is no question that after he retired to Llofriu he remained dependent on the Barcelona cultural industry, starting with Josep Vergès, the owner of the weekly *Destino*, who would become years later the publisher of his Collected Works. Alcoberro has an axe (or several) to grind when he blames Pla for launching the myth of the Empordà as the last reservation of Catalan native culture. According to Alcoberro, this myth triggered the region's invasion by droves of Barcelona weekenders and legions of foreigners who turned the stage of Catalan authenticity into a jungle of apartments and swarming villas. Alcoberro overstates the social influence of Pla's literature, but more importantly, he neglects to mention that in the nineteenth century Barcelona was the destination of thousands of Empordanesos displaced by the annihilation of the region's economy when a tiny insect called *Phylloxera vitifoliae* struck the vineyards. Others followed the same route throughout the century, expelled by the very conditions of land tenancy Alcoberro describes in his book. Three quarters of a century later, those migrants, converted into city folks, returned to their ancient family haunts as vacationers. They were attracted by a mythical promotion of the landscape, but some of them were hoping to rediscover the past through lingering associations of peasant culture with the local idiom. It is just possible that for some of these weekenders Pla represented the ideal combination of intellectual refinement and the capacity to relate aesthetically to the land. It is possible, in short, that for these people Pla represented the bourgeois point of view that hostile critics have often identified with modern Catalan culture. In the event, Pla would be guilty of bourgeois melancholy towards a rural culture that was long overtaken by tourism and industrial agribusiness (Alcoberro 140–1).

In the last analysis, his hesitant "if it were possible" implied that conditions were not ripe for his statement on writing to be understood. Pla often writes as if a barren space intervened between the writer and the audience, muffling his utterances. He associated this barrenness with the urban. Whether through pointless amusements or through political obsessions, the city distracts. It is an unproductive *environment* (Pla writes this word in English). The passage quoted above is from the preface to his book *Viatge a la Catalunya Vella* (Travel to Old Catalonia), a compendium of his itineraries through the northern part of Catalonia. It is a programmatic statement. In 1942, when Pla wrote this text, he had already left Barcelona to live in his native Empordà. In the volume *Notes disperses* he explains that in 1939 he moved to l'Escala in search of cafés that stayed open through the night. The Franco government had ordered cafés to close at midnight. L'Escala, a fishing town, was exempted from this injunction to accommodate the fishermen's working hours. Unfriendly critics offer a different explanation for Pla's departure. According to this version, Pla, who had been interim director of *La Vanguardia*, was miffed when Franco did not confirm him at the helm of the newspaper, appointing instead Falangist journalist Luis Martínez de Galinsoga (Alcoberro 139). Pla must have realized that a Catalan writer, even a conservative one, had little to look forward to in the new political circumstances.

In the past Pla had resolved his personal and political crises by escaping from Barcelona or staying away from it. In 1924 he was tried in absentia by a military court for an article criticizing the army's actions in Spanish Morocco. He did not return until 1927, and changed his allegiance from the liberal newspaper *La Publicitat* to the conservative *La Veu de Catalunya*, a daily at the service of the Lliga Catalana party. From this moment until the end of the Civil War, he collaborated with the Lliga's leader and patron of the arts Francesc Cambó, whose political biography he published in three volumes between 1928 and 1930. In 1930 the relation between the journalist and his sponsor was clinched when Pla sought Cambó's assistance and got it (Riquer 164–5). But in 1939 the Lliga was defunct and Cambó in exile. The new rulers of Spain were fiercely anti-Catalan and anyone vaguely associated with Catalanism was suspect. Pla made an initial effort to adapt to the new ideological circumstance, publishing a *History of the Second Spanish Republic* that legitimized the nationalist coup d'état. Very soon, however, he took distance from the new authorities, and his resounding defection from the newly reoriented *La Vanguardia*, highlighted by his departure from Barcelona, carried unmistakable political connotations at a time when blunt criticism of the regime had dire consequences. By refusing to remain in a city no longer worthy of the title of Paul Morand's novel *Open All Night*, Pla expressed his rejection of a totalitarian authority that impinged on every aspect of public life.

Although this explanation for his retreat to the country cannot be dismissed, it is possible that his decision also had to do with personal discomfort. The vibrant Barcelona he had known before the war no longer existed. In its place there was now a provincial town inhabited by an alien spirit. But for a few years it was still possible to entertain the illusion that the countryside remained unchanged. Catalonia had taken refuge in the villages and small towns, where the state machinery was less obtrusive and tradition endured. In these communities life was cheaper than in Barcelona, and this relative economic freedom suited Pla's independence.

To isolate resentment as the cause for his withdrawal from the journalistic limelight is to ignore the importance of habit, of the specific mode of inhabiting, of being at home in a location. And Pla, in much of his work, was a bookkeeper of habit. A propensity to record customs, sometimes fondly, at other times acerbically, spread over the entire spectrum of his social life. This scrutiny of manners was not apolitical. In his post-war texts he intercalated sarcasm against the ruling political ideology. One instance from the years of economic autarky after the Civil War is this comment about the quality of the tobacco from the state monopoly, verified by the nose of a bus traveller: "And so through my nostrils pass, in the form of smoke, all the products of the Arrendataria Tobacco Company, so diverse and scarcely unitary: leaf smoke, pipe smoke, cut tobacco smoke. And everything is of mid-fine, pre-fine, sub-fine, and extra-fine quality. Still, some will say that this country is dull! Such variety!" (9:17). Criticism of national production contrasted with official propaganda, but in this passage the sharpest irony is reserved for the youth who travel up and down the road on Sunday afternoon, always headed for the dancing in next town over. Whirling like flies inside a bottle or atoms in a rare medium, these youths, who come on and off the bus, provoke the question of whether the music or the female stock is any better in the yonder town. Like city youths spinning inside the suffocating tedium of weekend "entertainment," these country youths have lost the ability to inhabit, to remain in the space of habit, to stay put in life's purpose. A subtle irony against the myth of a self-denying, history-redeeming youth promoted at this time by fascist ideologues.

In his own, down-to-earth style, Pla was raising the issue of dwelling as developed by Heidegger in "Building, Dwelling, Thinking." When the German philosopher, describing a two-hundred-year-old farmhouse in the Black Forest, asserts, "Dwelling … is the basic character of Being in keeping with which mortals exist" (160), he has in mind the cosmic integration of the human. Pla had no use for Heidegger's tampering with divinities, but most of his post-war literature is an effort to oppose a Nietzschean intensification of life to human mortality. His vitalism stemmed, in the first place, from a culture of the senses, from perception bonded to the earth, sea, and sky; and then from preoccupation with memory, that is, with human resistance to universal decay and oblivion.[2]

Pla understood his life's work in these very terms. "The great problem for a writer who is rooted in a country is how to contribute to the struggle against forgetting" (17:8). The keywords here are "rooted" and "country." "Rooted" implies an existence plunged in the darkness of *habit* and fed from the humus of a culture. "Country" correlates the idea of an earthy abode. For "country" (*país*), Pla retains the Latin meaning of *pagus*, a rural district. Only, in the *pagus* the life of the *pagès*, the *cultor*, the inhabitant of habit, reaches deep into the past and resists forgetting through repetition. Habit is *immemorial*, reaches beyond memory, and that is the reason it can defeat forgetting. Pla saw in the peasantry society's rock-bottom foundation and the source of whatever stability there is. "The unshakeable permanence of the peasants has, to my mind, great advantages. The fact that society has a granite bottom incapable of being influenced by ephemeral things, by a flash in the pan, by the blurry, changeable fleetingness of the surface, is, I believe, a great blessing" (8:33). Habit and tradition anchor. When these attachments snap, people become uprooted. Rambling on the surface of the earth

---

2 For Pla's debt to Nietzsche, see Casajuana. On Pla's materialism and his tendency to trace elevated notions back to prosaic physical causes, pp. 38–9.

like tumbleweed, the individual is blown here and there by the slightest fad, wafted away without sojourn, stay, or residence. "Over our country there is also a huge historical precipitation, but, with rare exceptions, the people who live on it don't know the first thing about it" (35:426).

People who live *on* rather than *in* the *pagus* lead ahistorical lives. They circulate on a multilayered terrain without discerning anything but its outer, more abstract aspects. "I ask myself if our material culture has surpassed the stage of mere spectacular appearance" (9:82). Pla is unsatisfied with flat representations of the world. He requires a certain detachment, the perspective discussed in chapter 5 as second-order observation, the sort of look that corrects the squinting of first-order, pragmatic observation of things that do not add up to a world. "To recover from the sickness of proximity, from the distortion of proximity we are infected with, nothing is better than taking a little distance" (9:221). Pla's reticence about proximity has nothing to do with prejudice against the local. He had no patience with the intellectual arrogance of the self-styled cosmopolitan: "There is a certain 'Wagon-lit' or 'Concorde' flight cosmopolitanism, which tries to impose the notion that 'all countries are the same, identical and interchangeable, that all people and all psychologies are equivalent and the same'" (38:420). Pla recommends travel as a surrogate for history. The spatial perspective opened by travel does not abolish nearness, but it brackets proximity. When travelling, one exchanges the objects one is near to without preserving their closeness. Propinquity is not immediacy. Ultimately, travel is essential to the intensification of value. We come back from travel with a new hierarchy of preferences and a new system of permanences, as if we had lived long enough to experience time's natural decanting of things. "One must travel to realize that a passion, an idea, a man are important only if they withstand being projected on time and space" (9:221).

What counts, then, is the capacity to endure through, to move axially up and down, the arrow of time and to fulfil the movement initiated in space. Such ability is rare in the economy of decay and of "passing away" that Pla detects everywhere. That rarity feeds his conservatism. Given the cosmic law of universal ruin, conservatism, the attitude of the curator, of the *curor* or cultivator, is the only reasonable disposition. Pla was conservative because, as Valentí Puig points out, he was obsessed with Catalonia's vocation for self-destruction (15). He believed in personal effort and economic rationalism and feared utopias of all stripes. He could trust politicians that operated realistically within the realm of the possible and never lost sight of the material conditions of opportunity. Given inherent human anarchy and the ease with which societies disaggregate (he witnessed the early days of the Soviet Union, Mussolini's March on Rome, German hyperinflation, the collapse of the Spanish monarchy, the anarchist revolution in Barcelona, and Falangist neo-imperialism), Pla favoured small, unadventurous countries and mistrusted history. "I am delighted to have been born in a country that has produced no saviour, collector of rare sensations, or boisterous preacher. This gives me a feeling of lightness and freedom" (1:154). Lightness and freedom, that is, in the sense in which the Nietzsche of the *Untimely Reflections* spoke of a life-enhancing release from the weight of the past. History is for Pla "a herd of blind people led by madmen" (35:20). Better to accept life at its elemental, unadorned manifestations than to be the victim of universal convulsion.

Abstract, mystical ambitions arise in countries that, on account of their overblown dimensions, overrun the basic human pulsations. The Russian steppe appeared to him not as a region (a zone of experience whose atmosphere is the precipitation of active human quality) but as empty geography. In such unlimited reaches Pla discerned the physical grounds for the reduction of human life to quantitative equivalence. "It is hard to understand what the centre of spiritual gravitation might be for the habitual dweller of such a vast land. This loneliness explains internationalism, communism, and moral illusionism. This landscape must necessarily force people to live without vanity" (5:477). The contrast with his vision of Catalonia is apparent. As Carles Riba observes, "especially this last phrase gives us, in contrast, the key to his interpretation of our landscape and of our people as a function of each other" (212).

Small countries offer respite from idealism. Their empirical nature and immediacy of experience permits their denizens to withstand the temptation of abstraction. "Small countries are the only ones that fit inside people's brains" (34:709). By countries that fit inside people's heads, Pla did not mean figurative countries but countries that one can experience in their entire dimension. Not idealized countries, which are often diffuse and expansive (as in nationalism), but countries that are portable in memory. Not in a bland, collective memory but a concrete, personal memory.

Far from a representational reduction that places everything outside itself and inside the mind, he affirmed the possibility of what Heidegger called "presencing." This is possible when the topos, the site of the *habitus*, is commensurable with individual experience. Hence the privileging of the *pagus*, the region, understood not as a political demarcation but as the maximal unit of the human experience of nature that can be rendered from the point of view of representation. Pla had no use for "imagined communities" (Anderson). There is nothing imagined about countries that "fit" inside people's brains. But then, what does it mean that countries fit in the brain? Certainly not that they are contained, seized in subjectivity. The emphasis is not on the braininess but on the fit. Small countries can be experienced from top to bottom, their outlines can be known as well as their tiniest recesses. Gossip and anecdotes supplement records and chronicles to establish their history. Rather than setting in the mind as an ideal representation, the region leaves an imprint on life; it is the groundless ground of whatever can be experienced. Groundless, because in its supporting relation to everything that it contains, it cannot be referred to a prior, higher entity. As the primordial support of events experienced in the course of generations, the region is the basis of whatever permanence there is. Not only did it shape the ancient history of the country; it also projects that history into the present through each contemporary event.

The region is neither a storehouse for accidental contents nor the object of a representation that can be opposed to a subject. It is the original dwelling, the source of memories through which the past works its way to us. It allows us to set up residence by revealing the lines of the narrative in which our lives partake. The human will cannot break the region without it perishing in turn. The region shapes human character rather than the other way around. Thus, when the city-mind revolts against the region and vows to tame it, it merely creates the conditions for its own alienation.

I have already pointed out that in the entry for 6 June 1918 in *The Gray Notebook*, Pla countered Eugeni d'Ors's Neoplatonic attack on nature when he wrote: "It cannot be denied, I think, that mountains are well made" (1:184). D'Ors had written: "The mountain, as fatality leaves it, can be an instrument of evil," and called for the taming of mountains through architecture ("L'arranjament de les muntanyes," *Glosari 1906–1907* 492). Promoting subjectivity to a position of dominance strikes Pla as arrogant disregard of nature. From that point of view, countries are the work of great individuals rather than the accumulation of infinite responses to the challenge of nature. The regularities produced by such responses over time are what people call culture. "Don Eugeni's latest theory is that he does not owe anything to his country, that his birth within a given landscape is an absolutely accidental event – and that it is the country that owes him something. [...] This is simply the exacerbation of everything we have written so far: it is the most vulgar form of personalism, of romantic exceptionalism taken to its last consequences" (1:695).

There is probably a veiled reference to d'Ors in Pla's confession, "of this country I could not be a denatured renegade, only a melancholy one: this is the drama" (12:140). Why the drama? Because remaining *natured*, retaining his allegiance to place, the renegade would not be able to share in the external power whose will he fulfils. To do so without feeling the pain of betrayal the renegade must *ab-errare*, go astray from the path appointed to him by membership in a natural community. An *aberrant*, melancholy defector, a pining turncoat is a contradiction in terms. More than a fugitive or runaway slave (*fugitivus*), a *trans-fugax* is someone who flees across a boundary and loses himself on the other side – someone always ready to flee, someone forever fleeing, a fleeting entity. Pla asserts that he is incapable of giving in to the temptation of flight from his natural circumstances. But the fact that he thinks about the possibility suggests that he knows the temptation. His drama, he avows, is anticipating nostalgia in the wake of existential disloyalty. Could it be that his sensuous, somatic reintegration in the region after years of professional drifting was a categorical rejoinder to d'Ors's path of cultural treason?

Pla's commitment to the region, to the country that fits in the brain, whether it be Catalonia, the Empordà, or even the subsection that he calls "Empordanet" or "smaller Empordà," was inextricable from his keen sense of location, of the intersection of physical and psychological coordinates in the rendering of human phenomena. Among countless examples, let this sight of the fair at Sant Feliu de Guíxols suffice:

> A huge tent, flaccid and bloodless on the beach, touched by the light of dawn, looked like the side of a stuffed elephant. To the east the sky was purple. Over Sant Elm an angelic green was emerging; the light had a prodigious softness; the sea, curled by the wind that blew from the land, fresh and lively, was suspended in the twilight, uncertain. The bitter, exquisite melancholy of the spent sparkler, of the extinguished holiday floated in the air. (9:25)

This image is cosmic. It not only unites the four elements in a single snapshot, but also Heidegger's fourfold of earth and sky, mortals and divinities. It is an image of completion and of passing away. It captures the achievement and extinction of a cycle of life, suggesting its renewal from the cinders of what was mortal in the cycle. In this passage,

Heidegger's divinities stand forth as the epiphanic aura over the chapel of Sant Elm, a place consecrated to the mediating emanations from the Godhead. Nearer the earth, traces of the celebration are in the air and in the melancholy satisfaction of desire. *Animal triste*, the human being knows that fulfilment is death. But blowing from the earth, the wind, cool and lively, curls the surface of the sea, which hangs on the balance between night and day.

There is no question that this is a lyrical passage, one of many in Pla's extensive work. It is not poetic, however, in the sense of something made rather than discovered. Of something fabled instead of contemplated. Much less in the sense of something self-productive, of language speaking through grammatical building blocks that happen to get attached to meanings, as if language were a giant spider web in which the speaker is caught like a helpless insect. Here the lyricism stems from the objective situation as captured by a subject that knows how to dwell. The time and place are given: Sant Feliu de Guíxols, Costa Brava, in the early hours of an August day in 1942. The lyrical quality arises from perfected naturalism, called forth by Pla's effort to say what he sees or, at other times, what he learns through intermediaries. Always a marvelled witness of the world's unfolding, Pla remained supremely aware of locality, of the *locatedness* of everything. "Some people assert that vagueness, imprecision on this matter, the fact of not knowing if we are in Poland or Matadepera makes one universal! It's plain stupidity!" (12:272). Pla's reader knows, down to the minutest detail, the locality where the world stands revealed. This reader shares the impression that the phenomena conjured up by means of words could not happen anywhere else in precisely those terms. This is what "phenomenon" means: what appears, what reveals itself and in revealing itself to the witness, reveals the witness to himself.

Pla is modern Catalonia's supreme witness. Given the scope and density of his view, it does not greatly matter if he lost sight of certain things or left them out of the picture deliberately. His region may be an idealization, a hopeless attempt to retain a world that is passing, but it surely is not the lie that an extravagantly partial critic like Alcoberro would make it out to be. Alcoberro sums up Pla's work by declaring it a vindication of Arcadias for the use of Barcelonans (144). As an Empordanès, Alcoberro complains about the burden of having to symbolize authentic Catalonia (138) and blames Pla for his contribution to the myth. Alcoberro has every right to refuse to wear peasant clothes and a red Catalan cap, but quarrelling with Pla's representation of the region is misguided. Pla was the record keeper and popular historian of all Catalonia and the intelligent observer of a significant part of the world. If he was also the keenest and most inspired painter of the Empordà, thereby bearing some responsibility for the development of this region, the lament should be rather that other Catalan regions lacked the equivalent of a Josep Pla. The truth is, however, not so much that Pla endowed the Empordà with the burden of representing an ur-Catalonia or a primordial Catalan *Heimat*, as that in time he grew into something like an elemental Catalan: shrewd, cynical, chary of collective deceptions, and capable of looking at the country and its inhabitants without illusions.

By using the term "country" (*país*) interchangeably for concentric tracts of the Catalan geography, he suggests that the relation between those parts is metonymic rather than symbolic. Pla certainly adjudicates moral value at the same time that he describes a world moved by material interests on the grand or, more often, the petty scale. These interests notwithstanding, the world of his descriptions is governed by a fatality that reduces human drama to frantic and doomed attempts to escape natural law. At the end of the day, to unmask Pla as anti-revolutionary, as a writer with a horizon limited by pragmatic convenience, is no critical breakthrough. On these terms one would expect radical natives from Bordeaux or the Charente to denounce the "lie" that the monarchical, "Parisian" Balzac foisted on unsuspecting provincials. Pla was hostile to every form of planned economy. Blaming the unbridled development of the Empordà on his fond, albeit unsentimental, depiction of its coast and villages is to gravely confuse Marxist categories. Pla's intimacy with the region took shape in long intercourse with people, things, landscapes, and customs. From intense association with those things he obtained the yardstick by which he judged them in aching awareness of their transience. Pla did not describe a mythological, essential region but a disappearing one, as in this observation about the fading of the soundscape:

> The popular song, so lovely, so delightful, so elegant, has disappeared almost completely from the face of our country. Some of these songs, harmonized, of course, remain in the repertoire of some choirs as cabinet ornaments deprived of vital beat, like stuffed birds. Since musical internationalism rules, nothing is sung in public but exotic songs, silly zarzuela pieces, domestic service exhalations, secretions of jail and brothel. (9:35)

Ultimately, the region, the *país*, was the sum total of its disappearance, and far from an Arcadia for the use of city folk, it became the record of its own mutations. This was hardly a soothing, let alone a simple, proposition. For Pla the region and its manifestations were neither one and the same thing nor two different things adjoining each other in space. They interpenetrated one another and met for an instant before coming apart again. Their fortuitous encounter filled the ephemeral interval of the present with fleeting contents, giving rise to phenomena. In this relation, the elementary human remains constant, as does the spatial support of consciousness, while that which endows them with character passes into memory. There it lingers awhile, afloat among the historical wreckage, before sinking. Eddies on the surface testify to a writer's struggle against time. "These taverns do not change. Earlier, people sang the Marseillaise and the 'Over the Waves' waltz by turns. Now they sing the International and variety songs. People are always the same. It is the songs that pass" (1:154).

8 Shipwrecks with Monsters

In freto viximos; moriamur in portu.
– Lucius Annaeus Seneca, *Ad Lucilium epistulae morales*

In the summer of 1941, having failed to win the Battle for Britain, Germany turned east and invaded the Soviet Union. It was at this time that Carl Schmitt wrote *Land und Meer*, a small book of huge intellectual ambition and strategic importance. Although he dedicated the book to his daughter, as a legacy to the future of his nation, his immediate intention was to convince the German government to change its traditional emphasis on continental warfare. Germany – the message was – could alter world history by destroying Britain's hegemony in the oceans and conquering the new theatre of war. Decisively moving into and dominating the unfolding space of air power could lead to an unprecedented hegemony dictated by the new *nomos* of the earth that was emerging through the chaos and destruction of the war. The book begins with the banal statement that humans are land animals who move on firm ground. Having established this obvious fact, Schmitt brings up ancient myths and fables that place our origin in the water, going on to claim that the proto- and early history of mankind reveal its oceanic origins. With unruffled self-assurance he goes on to assert that in the mid-twentieth century there exist peoples, such as the South Seas islanders, to whom our conceptions of space and time are as foreign as those of pure sea people are to the rest of mankind. Finally, he raises the question whether we are indeed land creatures or rather sea creatures, answering that it is not possible to give a simple reply (11). The rest of the book is, of course, the elaborate reply to this question.

Very distant from Schmitt's pseudo-historical ruminations about the original element of mankind, Pla spent a great deal of time sailing and travelling by sea. He even played a small role in thwarting the German attempt to wrest control of the seas from the British. Throughout the Second World War he was an Anglophile, and with a small group of friends he organized a network to help smuggle fugitives from the German occupied zone and to supply information to the Allies. At some point, they may have spied the movement of ships along the northern coast of Catalonia. In the early 1940s Barcelona was a base for German U-boats operating in the Mediterranean. While the observation of ship movements by Pla and his friends is speculative, this sort of activity turns up in the short narrative "Un de Begur" (A man from Begur), one of the stories in *Aigua de mar*. Although Pla wrote the original of this story before the Second World War and the action takes place during the previous world war, the possibility that it features autobiographical elements cannot be dismissed. Not only did he rewrite the story at a later date, but in the prologue to the volume he confided to readers that all the stories in the book were testimonials to different moments and situations in his life (2:8).

"Un de Begur" tells the story of "the Miner," an unsavoury character who lives from illegal fishing and tobacco smuggling, and happens to be the man best acquainted with the coast from the Garraf cliffs south of Barcelona to Portvendres in France. One night German secret agents approach and offer him an enticing compensation in exchange for help in guiding their submarines on a secret operation. The Miner accepts the offer and boards the submarine. This simple plot gives Pla an opportunity to describe the interior of a U-boat in detail, exhibiting connoisseurship of the bowels of the ship, the effect of the closed atmosphere on an unaccustomed passenger, and the quality of the air inside the vessel: "It wasn't a foul or putrid air from some decomposing matter. On the contrary, everything was rigorously clean, ordered, sterilized. But it was an air that I had never breathed. It was an air loaded with effluviums of fuel oil, of lubricants, of mineral oils, of greasy fibres, of engine fumes or the tartness of the rusting metal" (2:203).

When the U-boat commander asks the Miner what vessels can be discerned from the coast, the reply suggests that Pla may have engaged in precisely this kind of observation. If so, he would have placed the information at the disposal of the Allies rather than the Germans. "Afterwards he asked a lot of questions related to the navigation one could observe from the coast. I told him what I had seen, that is, the truth: that there was a lot of traffic of small coastal shipping going to France. That these ships came very close to the shore. That large volume navigation was scarce, since a steamer navigating alone was a rare sight. 'On the other hand – I added – considerable convoys of ships pass this way'" (2:205–6). After days of navigating at minimal speed, the Miner begins to feel depressed by the monotony and the bad food. Above all, he misses conversation. With the crew, he communicates with signs. The commander can speak Spanish, but he is too busy to pay attention to his guest, who is not allowed to see him unless summoned and for days on end is unable to talk with anyone. When the urge to speak becomes pressing, he whistles or hums a song. Pla was probably describing his own impressions – olfactory, culinary, and communicative – during his trips on oil tankers, where, as a single passenger, he had no one to talk to except the ship's captain, who must have been too busy to do the honours to a talkative guest.

One day, the Miner notices the commander at the turret looking through the binoculars more intently than usual. In the cloudless sky, he can see a faint brushstroke of grey floating on the sea in the direction the commander is looking. Half an hour later, that tenuous brushstroke becomes the smoke from one or more steamers. It is the advance party of a large convoy sailing towards Marseilles. The submarine dives and gets ready to attack but is thwarted by the superiority of the convoy's escort. The mission seems forfeited. However, some hours after the main of the convoy has passed, the submarine sights an American tramp ship, an eight-thousand-tons, four-mast vessel that had fallen behind the group. The submarine approaches and torpedoes the straggler. Almost immediately the ship leans on its side and starts sinking. While the people on board run for the lifeboats, a huge yowl arises from the ship's belly. "In the majesty of the sea rose a frenzied, nervous, distressing neighing of three-hundred, four-hundred, five-hundred horses – perhaps more – inexorably trapped in the dying vessel" (2:212). The Miner starts crying and then, through misty eyes, he has the nightmarish vision of wraith-like, frantic horses jumping into the sea through the craters opened in the ship's hull by the torpedoes. The ship is already sinking and soon the water covers the holes. The last horse to escape, he remarks, seems to emerge from the bottom of the sea.

Although the hair-raising vision of a sinking ship with horses emerging from the hull and jumping into the sea is worthy of a horror tale, the episode has a historical basis. In 1916 the German U-72 commanded by Ernst Krafft sank the *Palermo*, an Italian ship transporting horses of the Italian Army, in front of the Catalan coast (Antón). Pla could have learned about this event from the fishermen he used to mingle with in his youth, or he might have read about it at a later time. Be that as it may, the incident provides a dramatic anchor for exquisite descriptions of the sea as backdrop to a breathtaking shoreline. Pla rendered these marine lanscapes with the same attention to their luminiscence as did Salvador Dalí, his co-native from Empordà. "That afternoon, at the time we went on board, there was a dim, crepuscular light. The sky was grey and low. The horizon, touched by a light fog – white, grey, matt – seemed to have come nearer. The air was heavy and humid and a feeble south-west wind passed, monotonous and in shreds, above a sea the colour of dirty tin. The small wind – which induced a headache – rose miniscule, choppy waves, which died on the beach making a dull sound" (2:195).

Regardless of his strategic intentions, Schmitt raises an interesting question at the beginning of *Land und Meer*, that of the limits of evolution and the leap forward of humanity. "If the human being were nothing but a living form completely determined by its environment, then it would be, depending on the environment, a land animal, or a fish, or a bird, or a fantastic mixture of these elemental determinations" (13). If that were the case, he concluded, there would be no human history as human action and human decision (12). His purpose was to substantiate the claim that the conquest and domination of the ocean by humans had opened new spaces to world history. Preceding the actual expansion of human horizons and making it possible, there had been a change of the image of space. In turn, this had come about through the liberation of new energies and forces. When new energies enter the consciousness of humans, said Schmitt, they change the spaces of historical existence (56).

Pla was never interested in historical speculation of this sort, but he would have agreed that human beings are not determined by their environment as essentially as other beings are; they have a dangerous margin of decision that for the most part lands them in trouble but is, nonetheless, the very thing that makes their life interesting. This margin of freedom adds a layer of indeterminacy to the simple and often predictable struggle for life. The aging Pla increasingly claimed to be a peasant and adopted external tokens of that identity. Having worn a bowler hat as a young man, from the 1950s on he increasingly donned the flat beret customary in the Catalan countryside. It was a sign of his identification with the land. This adopted and consciously cultivated persona should not make us forget that a large part of Pla's literature is devoted to the sea. The sea was present in his life since childhood, when his family, residing in Palafrugell, was among the privileged that owned a summer house in the nearby beach of Calella. From those summers before the invention of the Costa Brava and mass tourism, Pla retained a love of the sea, collecting stories to revisit in the future, and a maritime savvy he picked up while hanging out with the fishermen. The recurrence of nautical episodes, fishermen's customs, cooking, weather observations, and detailed knowledge of the orography and topography of the coast would justify calling his literature "amphibian."

In addition, a great deal of Pla's extensive travel was done by ship, especially in later life, when he undertook long voyages to write reports for the weekly *Destino.* Josep Vergés, the journal's owner, used his contacts to book Pla as a single passenger aboard oil tankers to economize on travel expenses. Pla complained about the long periods of abstinence from smoking these arrangements imposed on him. But he enjoyed talking with the ships' captains, whom he fascinated with his conversational skills. The sea, at any rate, claims a large portion of his Collected Works. He titled one of his books *Aigua de mar* (Sea water), another *Les escales de Llevant* (*Ports of call in the Levant*), a third *Les illes* (The isles), yet another *En mar* (At sea). This last volume includes five books: *Cabotatge mediterrani (1956)*(Mediterranean coastal shipping [1956]), *Viatge a l'Amèrica del Sud (1957)* (Travel to South America [1957]), *Un llarg viatge entre Kuwait, al Golf Pèrsic, i Valparaíso, a Chile (1959–1960)* (A long journey between Kuwait, in the Persian Gulf, and Valparaíso, in Chile [1959–1960]), *De Buenos Aires a Rotterdam (Gener-Febrer 1967)* (From Buenos Aires to Rotterdam [January–February 1967]), and *Intermezzo Fluvial. Viatge al Rin: De Rotterdam a Basilea (Primavera del 1966)* (Fluvial intermezzo. Journey to the Rhine: From Rotterdam to Basel [Spring 1966]). Still another volume bears the title *Itàlia i el Mediterrani* (Italy and the Mediterranean). Beyond these seafaring books, the sea appears in many of his other books, either seen from land or vice versa, looking at the land from the sea. For instance, in his book on Portugal he describes the arrival to Lisbon from the portside as having "a certain magnificence" (28:518), and the entry to the estuary of the Tejo River as "majestic" (28:523). The sea, for Pla, is never a spatial category – as it is for Schmitt – but a medium of human action and a space of dramatic struggle between human will and natural resistance. It is also a condition of perception and of beauty that defeats the raw philosophical dualism of subject and object. As a field of visibility, the sea sets the scope of human perception, merging the observer with the observed as inextricably as the waves and the shoreline at dusk, when the glow of the lighthouse seems to hover above nothingness: "The lighthouse of the Meda island burned like a glow-worm dangling in the air" (2:199).

An exhaustive examination of Pla's literature on the sea cannot be undertaken in a few pages. And to select just one aspect of his voluminous output on what, in Schmittian terms, we might call Pla's modification of the image of space from his more familiar land-based itineraries could seem exceedingly reductive. Still, necessity sways. I will therefore look at Pla's creation of an image of the sea as a distinct space for human action in the short narratives collected in *Aigua de mar*. To illustrate his realist aesthetic, Pla used to say that if someone wished to paint the sea, he must put the fish in it. And indeed, the first narrative in the book, "Bodegó amb peixos" (Still life with fish), is, as the title announces, a programmatic demonstration of Pla's conception of literary realism. In this autobiographical story, the fish are described in their local, concrete, particular specificity, just as in other books he describes peasants in their idiosyncrasy and singularity of customs, diet, or character as shaped and modified by their natural medium and regional history.

For Pla it will not do to place the fish as a class or genus in the water. He removes them from the scientific classifications and from the abstract, semantic fog of everyday language and relates them to the people whose physical perceptions and dispositions are inextricably attuned to the fish's singularity, to their habitat and survival skills, as well as to their uses and sensual specificities for purposes of consumption. He writes about fish, that is, from the viewpoint of fishermen. And he does so with the anti-romantic attitude that he deploys elsewhere in his descriptions of landscapes, relating the sumptuous or simply attractive natural setting to the human exploitation of its resources. "Sometimes," he says, "it seems that nature and capitalism have signed a friendship compact of eternal validity" (2:19). He writes this apropos of nature's falsification of its own products, an interesting debunking of the binary logic whereby nature correlates with authenticity, and capitalism, or more generally, man-made reality with artifice and deceit. Many fish, says Pla, have their own replicas, their substitutes. Some of these imitations are inferior, others superior. Whereas biological taxonomies know only one species of red mullet, Pla asserts that five types of this species exist. It is the same species, he explains, but entirely different fish depending on the medium where it lives and the food it ingests. The proof of the fish is in the cooking: on the coals, the good mullet extrudes "an intense, sumptuous, cardinal-like red, that red we all know and that so extraordinarily resembles the immortal reds that Velázquez used in his portrait of Pope Innocent X of the Doria Gallery in Rome" (2:21).

Things do not exist for themselves, and their being-in-themselves is irrelevant or, more precisely, unknowable. The red mullet acquires its qualities for humans when these provide the necessary conditions for it to reveal its essential colour and flavour. The qualitative hierarchy that Pla presents, echoing the fishermen's estimation, is objective insofar as it relies on long-settled, collectively certified experience, yet it is true only within the culinary system of these men, themselves adapted to local conditions of taste. Given the sensitive nature of this experience, how can one encapsulate it in words the way Velázquez conveyed the Church's solemnity in the red of the papal vestment and its worldliness in the pope's reddish, carnal face? This is the writer's challenge, one that Rilke famously expressed in the thirteenth sonnet to Orpheus:

> Dare to say what you call apple.
> This sweetness that condenses itself at first
> And then, quietly rising in taste,
> Becomes clear, awake and transparent,
> Equivocal, sunny, earthy, local –:
> Oh experience, feeling, joy –, immense! (1:739)

More prosaically, Pla writes about rockfish: "These pastures make them rockish: they give them an unmistakable flavour, a certain tartness, a flavour that could only be described if the palate had a clear literary percussion" (2:31–2).

In this piece Pla writes not only about the culinary advantages of certain Mediterranean species of fish; he also writes about the various ways of catching them, about the angler's sensuous pleasure, the skill of the spear fisher, and the methods of catching with a line, with multiple hooks, with a trawl net. He provides a whole inventory of the fishing arts, as if to underscore not just the ingenuity of the human predator but, above all, the infinite specialization of human modes of relating to nature. In the end, the equivocal taste (*Doppeldeutigkeit*) of the apple in Rilke's sonnet recurs in the fishers' preference when, after lengthy discussions about the qualities of the fish and the best ways of cooking it, one of them always ends up stating that, after all, the best fish of the sea will always be meat. And that is, says Pla, perfectly in

Figure 5. Josep Pla at the beach of l'Escala on turning seventy, March 1967.

Photographer: Eugeni Forcano. Courtesy of Casa museu Lluís Domènech i Montaner / Ajuntament de Canet de Mar.

harmony with human nature. We always want what we lack, and so while people from inland hunger for fish, sea people prefer meat (2:62).

Built on a tenuous narrative line, this initial story was Pla's homage to the men with whom he spent many a happy hour in his youth and then again in later life, when he took refuge from the unpleasant political environment that had enveloped post-war Barcelona by withdrawing first to the small harbour of Fornells and then to L'Escala in search of the elementary life of an earlier period. Immersion in the relatively unchanged conditions of these traditional societies furnished Pla the occasion to collect, interpret, and recount the practical knowledge, customs, and mental reflexes of their members.

Such attention to detail on multiple levels of behaviour makes of his work an application *avant la lettre* of certain approaches of cultural anthropology. Eliseu Carbonell suggests that the last part of the book *El meu poble* (My village), included in volume 7 of the Collected Works, anticipates Clifford Geertz's precept for cultural anthropologists to practise the "craft of observing general principles in local facts" (Carbonell 108–9). While I fail to find such anticipation or any allusion to the craft of observing in this part of Pla's work, it is true that in many of his books he seems uncannily close to Geertz's claim, in *The Interpretation of Cultures*, that culture "is a context, something within which [social events, behaviours, institutions, or processes] can be intelligibly – that is, thickly – described" (14). Geertz's "thick description" is a felicitous phrase for precisely the kind of "fieldwork" that Pla undertook in extraordinarily dense, detailed descriptions of village life, peasant behaviour, and psychology, the reflexes of small-town residents, or the social action of people who depend on the sea for their livelihood. Unsuspecting of future academic validation, Pla adhered to Geertz's injunction to the cultural analyst that "behavior must be attended to, and with some exactness, because it is through the flow of behavior – or, more precisely, social action – that cultural forms find articulation. They find it as well, of course, in various sorts of artifacts and various states of consciousness; but these draw their meaning from the role they play (Wittgenstein would say from their 'use') in an ongoing pattern of life, not from any intrinsic relationships they bear to one another" (17).

When he published *Aigua de mar* in the mid-1960s, bringing together stories written much earlier, Pla was not aware of anthropologists' efforts to reduce human behaviour to psychologically transcendent, that is, socially structured, symbolic patterns. Had he known about this way of approaching human reality, he would have dismissed it as a way of painting the sea and leaving out the fish. Yet, he clearly met Geertz's principle of thick description by observing the flow of behaviour without attempting to arrest it in pre-existing categories of thought, but moving instead along the unfolding pattern of life and drawing from events and human reactions to them pragmatic inferences about the relations that make this or that society what it is, rather than proceeding from axiomatic definitions of society to the abstract, deductive description of what those relations must be.

If there is one general postulate, an underlying connection, an encompassing theme in the stories of this book, it would be the struggle between the blind, indifferent cosmic forces and human will. Peculiar to Pla's character, though, is anti-romanticism, and so he largely avoids the sentimentality of the romantic sublime. Humans are persistent, hard-headed, light-headed, calculating, cunning, or stupid. But they are never titanic or heroic. These mythological projections have no place in Pla's essential view of the cosmos as supremely indifferent to human affairs, and of humans as beings floating on the surface of an unstable element and subject to the disastrous contingencies of chance. To be sure, Pla is not a thesis writer. He does not have a "message" to convey through allegory of any kind. Much less is he poetically beholden to the expressive power of metaphor. The sea is, for him, the expanse of water that meets the land at a precise spatial and temporal line of contact. The endless negotiation of this line has traced and continues to trace the shape of continents, the patterns of human settlement, and the economies, happiness, and dramas of real people. In Pla the sea not only contains fish but produces them in abundance, in a plethora of species that can be categorized according to their culinary qualities and described according to the methods for extracting their savoury values from the ocean and bringing them to the table.

Aigua de mar also includes several texts about shipwrecks in a curious departure from Pla's usual attention to the unexceptional flow of life. On the other hand, his focus on the everyday includes a heightened sense of the calamities besieging humanity and a stoic meditation on the groundlessness of illusions. It is in this matter-of-fact attitude and negative expectation concerning the "intentions" of nature that his stories about disaster at sea cohere with his sense of the precariousness of institutions, culture, and social utopias. These things, which mankind builds on land as if to convince itself of their permanence, are in constant movement, subject to all manner of social and historical agitation. Thus the shipwreck stories illustrate the contrast between human daring based on self-deceptive oblivion and the essential insecurity of existence. Physical insecurity is the basis of mankind's deepest cognitive insecurity. Pierre-Simon Laplace had asserted: "Given for one instant an intelligence which could comprehend all the forces by which nature is animated and the respective situation of the beings who compose it – an intelligence sufficiently vast to submit these data to analysis – it would embrace in the same formula the movements of the greatest bodies of the universe and those of the lightest atom; for it nothing would be uncertain and the future, as the past, would be present to its eyes" (4). Pla, who often seems to believe in natural determination and is keenly aware of the importance of one's situation, has no use for such speculation. Life is radically uncertain and probability just a pretentious name for plausibility. Events are not, for him, predictable through rational projection of the data at hand. At best they are likely, in the sense of fulfilling existing expectations and common narratives. At the start of "Un viatge frustrat," he tells of the free life everyone longs for in youth. This was, he explains, a common desire among many people in his native village and along the northern Catalan coast at that particular time. Thus, when rumours that Sebastià Puig, alias Hermós, a villager from Palafrugell, had left behind his ordinary life for an existence free of conventions and obligations in the rocky cove of Aigua Xellida, most people considered it "plausible" (2:67).

Plausibility does not commit to anything. It is the intellectual position closest to scepticism. It is scepticism positively stressed. The plausible leaves room for retraction if facts do not bear out the expectations. It suggests subjective agreement with the potential of a given situation – the notion that, since possibility sometimes correlates with realization, whatever is deemed plausible might be confirmed by a future event. Plausibility leaves plenty of room for contingency and hence cannot move beyond ambiguity. And "Un viatge frustrat" is the story of an ambiguity, of the undecidability whether the goal of the sea journey has been reached or not. Pla constructs the story with great subtlety. Although he presents it as an autobiographical memoir, the protagonist is Hermós, an illiterate jack-of-all-trades with a primitive – Pla says anthropoid-like (2:69) – appearance, but nonetheless someone who ranks high in Pla's estimation. Hermós knows how to do many things and does them well. Above all, he is useful and pleasant to have around (2: 70). Hermós is central to the story as an experienced mate for Pla on his journey along the coast in a small sailboat. Above all, he helps Pla set up narratively the opposition between dead, erudite knowledge and the practical reason in which Hermós is proficient. "Reflecting a great deal on my memories of my contact with this man, I have reached the conclusion that the essence of his personality was – despite his being illiterate – the solid culture that he possessed" (2:69).

Figure 6. Sebastià Puig "L'Hermós" and Josep Pla. Aigua Xelida, c.1925.

Photographer unknown. Courtesy Fundació Josep Pla, coll. Josep Vergés

The practical demonstration of this opposition arrives when Hermós proclaims at a tavern in L'Escala that the population of this town, located in the vicinity of the excavated Greek colony of Empúries, descends directly from the Greeks. "Assuming, of course, that those Greeks came with women and children, because women on board are more nuisance than help" (2:70–1). At this point, an archaeologist turns up and, hearing such theories, cannot restrain his laughter:

> "You assert," – said Hermós, "that these people of L'Escala are not the descendants of the Greeks ... but then, where would those Greeks have gone? Besides, where would they go to feel more comfortable than here? The anchovies and sardines from this area are extraordinary ... Do you understand? People are never as crazy as they seem at first. And those Greeks were not crazy at all. To live they chose a place of premium quality." (2:71)

Pla, who clearly enjoys Hermós's outlandish theories, gives vent to his suspicion of academicism. Between scholarly reconstruction of the past and Hermós's pedestrian theories formulated on the basis of personal experience, Pla opts for the latter:

> Like all people of his status, this excellent scholar believed that the Greeks were objects belonging in a museum cabinet and that their movements and way of being could only be explained with the nebulous, fantastic theories of archaeology. His idea was that the Greeks were and behaved exactly as archaeologists had ordered them two thousand five hundred years later. This seems a bit excessive. It is not. It is what often happens in archaeology. (2:71)

This is not an isolated example. In "Contraban," Pla takes his derision of intellectual reduction even further when another simple character says that he does not like France and the narrator comments: "The excessive generalization of his judgment showed that if this man had had an education and the necessary reading, he could have become a high-flying philosopher" (2:349). The frustrated voyage is in reality the occasion for Pla's description of a colourful character from real life, a sort of local Huck Finn to Pla's Tom Sawyer embarked on a spree of natural freedom. After ten days on board, though, Pla begins to feel fatigue and misses the milder impressions of interior life. This allows him to articulate another vitalist attack on culture:

> I think about the possibility that the immediate, unlimited outdoor life we now enjoy may not be quite compatible with the degree of silliness and stupidity produced by intensive culture. That is to say: the tragedy is that

in life a moment comes when one can only forbear bottled sun and the air described in books. Culture is a sickly form of life. (2:125)

Hermós's peroration in "Un viatge frustrat" is not merely the occasion for an anti-academic tirade. By siding, however ironically, with his outlandish theory about the biological continuity of the Greeks along the Catalan coast, Pla introduces the possibility that Hermós could be a fallen or degraded descendant of the ancient colonizers of Empordà. The coastal navigation in which the two of them engage is reminiscent of the *Odyssey*, as Carbonell observes (124). The fact that Hermós insists on a voyage with sail and oars supports the comparison. When he wrote this story Pla probably had in mind the central motif of *Ulysses*, choosing his Leopold Bloom among the real people of Palafrugell. The anthropoid-like traits of Hermós, who is nicknamed "handsome" by paronomasia, allude to the primitiveness of Bronze Age Greeks, or perhaps, anachronistically, to the degeneration of classical beauty through the centuries. And if Bloom was a pompous, poorly educated publicity peddler, Hermós is downright illiterate. His manual abilities, however, recall Homer's description of Ulysses as a man of many wiles. He is a good navigator and an excellent cook. His skill at eating sardines reminds Pla of Homeric slaughter: "Spectacles of avidity fit very well in this ancient sea. There are corners in this sea where I seem to scent the stench of Homeric hecatombs" (2:90).

Their plan had been to reach the coast of France and visit some acquaintances in the seaside villages of the Roussillon. Taking place in September 1918, with the First World War still raging, the journey, undertaken without documents or safe-conduct papers because Hermós insisted that it had always been done so (2:75–6), had a whiff of adventure. But as soon as the boat turns Cap de Creus and comes in sight of the Cervère roofs, he becomes anxious about the presence of a distant ship, which he takes to be either a warship or a coastguard vessel. Falling into a panic, he decides to turn back. For a gritty, experienced sailor it is a shameful decision, and Pla puts on his best face to mitigate his friend's embarrassment. Back in Calella, Hermós wastes no time going to the tavern to tell an incidental audience his adventures in the French villages of Banyuls, Portvendres, and Colliure. To avoid refuting the sailor's yarn, Pla leaves the tavern and goes back to the boat. The irony (and the gist of the story) is that Hermós is unsure whether they reached their destination or not. For him the pleasure of the trip (and its narrative essence) lies in boasting to his friends. Suddenly, though, doubts about their credulity assault him, and he asks Pla for support and reassurance. "Listen, what's the deal? Did we go or didn't we? – Of course we went, dear man!" answers Pla, newly reconciled with the indoor life of his writerly self (2:141). This is, then, a tale about a failed attempt at transgressing the border. Sailing without personal documents and permits, Hermós and Pla are infringing the coastal law. Their voyage is an expression of the rebellion against and the denial of the violence that established a border between adjacent Catalan regions. Turning around and failing to debark for fear of a virtual coastguard vessel or warship reveals the power of historical violence on the contemporary imagination. In the end, although the trip was cut, the fact that they were in French waters and had technically transgressed the border allowed for the final ambiguity, one, I submit, that replicates the ambiguous status of the villages concerned. They are culturally Catalan, but politically they are French. Pla makes this point explicitly in "Contraban," where he describes Cervère as a screen:

> Cervère is a stage curtain due to the wish to demonstrate that the border that goes through it is truly divisive, even for the people of the country. Between Catalonia and the Roussillon there is no real border. In view of this fact, a theatrical border was created. Planners tried to design a town for the purpose of marking a difference. Since nothing separated the dwellings, houses and roofs had to be built in a different style. (2:332)

"Derelictes" (Derelicts) is a rosary of shipwrecks. In this narrative, Pla strings up stories of navigation accidents in the rocky Catalonian coast. He reproduces the ships' descriptions, the cargo they carried, and the circumstances under which they foundered. The stories are entertaining and constitute a piece of local history. But their true interest lies in the use of these catastrophes as a basso continuo for life's inherent insecurity. What motivates people to leave behind the firmness of the land for the instability of the waters, the routines of a secure existence for the perils of moving over the abyss? The story about the *Phaedo*, an obsolete vessel refloated by a Greek trader who engineers its sinking in order to collect the insurance, furnishes the material for a description of *Homo economicus* in cultural context. "On the shores of the Mediterranean," says Pla, "poverty was always the origin of every possible knowledge, theoretical and practical, and in this sense the art of drawing out the life of these rickety contraptions is one of the great mysteries of the culture of this sea" (2:167).

In *Schiffbruch mit Zuschauer*, Hans Blumenberg recalls the ancient Mediterranean topos of greed as catalyst of the decision to embark. In the *Erga*, Hesiod regrets that his brother Perses has abandoned agriculture for the chance of acquiring wealth in coastal shipping. Hesiod mistrusts the sea because it is not subject to the regularities of the dominion of Zeus (11). The tradition of cursing the sea voyage prompted the Spanish military commander and historian Gonzalo Fernández de Oviedo to write that the fault did not lie with the sails but with "those persons who could live on land and yet go off to experience the tribulations of sea travel" (2). Still, he excused those who, like him, crossed the ocean in service to the Crown, and rebuffed critics who condemned seafaring without undertaking the experience themselves:

> Some persons brave these perils out of necessity to seek a better life; others do so to fulfil obligations such that good people must risk these and other dangers or bring shame upon themselves. And so I have learned to write and note down these things that cannot be so well explained by the chroniclers who do not voyage. (4)

Blumenberg remarks that it is from the ancient scruple against undergoing the risks of the sea that the connection of water and money in the concept of liquidity arises (11). Pla recuperates the idea when he explains that the derelicts themselves become objects of greed, either for the value of their cargo or, when this is irretrievable or decomposed, for the scrap metal that their skeletons yield. The *Phaedo* was in this situation; its cargo of beans, spoiled and unsellable by the time it was loaded and now swollen with seawater, serves as a regal meal for the fish. A diver's prospection allows Pla to present a scene of cosmic voracity: "The Phaedo transported the beans at bilge level and in abundance. The breach was teeming with fish. I have never seen a shoal of bream like the one I saw then. The fish ate the beans that the seawater had swollen considerably. The beans were twice as large as those on land. Fish eat everything and their avidity is literally indescribable" (2:176).

Sometimes an international conflict prevents the looting of a vessel. This was the case of the *Tregastel*, a French ship sunk in Spanish waters near the bay of Cadaqués. At a depth where the waves are no longer felt, the vessel lies in ghostly, spectral immobility in dimly lit waters. An uncanny corpse, whose shape the chemical reaction of the mineral incrustations and the slow action of the sea flora and fauna gradually abrade. "The big hull is no more than a shadow – on the bottom of the sea there are only shadows – in a medium of still, static waters, existing in a peace of death and silence" (2:181). Seen from the viewpoint of the reader who stands on solid ground, the spectacle of the decaying craft, a traditional metaphor for human daring and greed, illustrates Pla's scepticism with regard to human ambition and self-delusion. Recounting stories of vessels that lie at the bottom of local waters, he reminds us of the catastrophic end of human affairs and the shadowy existence in a murky hereafter, where, as in the Greek Hades, the greatest heroes seem suspended in disembodied, ahistorical existence without any other purpose than serving as warning posts for the living.

The sea voyage intensifies the perils that land people consign to oblivion. Speaking through a character in another story, "Anàlisis d'un naufragi" (Analysis of a shipwreck), Pla asserts: "All things considered, life is perhaps no more than a continued recklessness [...] People commit reckless acts on land and at sea, but the latter, due perhaps to the fact that there are fewer people at sea than on land, tend to be more spectacular and dramatic" (2:426). The sea is a multiplier of human temerity. Even if for no other reason than it turns foolhardiness into a spectacular, specular event, the shipwreck has its usefulness. Pla avoids the moral conclusions of the classic commentators. Remaining on land does not make people safer or wiser. It simply numbs consciousness to the fact of man's imprudence, disguising as routine the inherent recklessness of ordinary life. Such recklessness, rooted in life's deep-seated irrationality, cannot safeguard itself by appealing to judgment or foresight.

Everyday life is full of "terrible, obscure, unnoticed" tragedies, but they are not perceived as such unless one is sensitized by poverty and great adventurousness (2:368), the very conditions that, since ancient times, have induced people to face the perils of the sea. Properly speaking, "Contraban" is not a shipwreck story but comes close to becoming one. Pla and his two mates sail along the coast of the Roussillon and manoeuvre their boat into the bay of Salses, a virtual pond separated from the sea by a sandbank. That is where they expect to load the merchandise they plan to smuggle into Spain. But at the appointed time they are surprised by a gale. And what was meant to be a cruising adventure with some profit taken on the side turns into a confrontation with the same elemental forces that led Hesiod to regret that greed moves his brother to brave the hazards of Poseidon's realm. Pla describes the sudden change of weather as a throwback to the primeval showdown between man and the elements. Pure instability and vulnerability ensue. Out in the open, on a light boat shaken by the wind, he is as exposed and defenceless as on the day he engendered the gods out of his terror. "It was pure prehistory, raw nature, absolute chance, the transmutation of land and sea. There was nothing to do or say: only a yearning to remember static, comfortable things" (2:368).

The unchained force of nature cannot be opposed. Man must yield and his only chance to survive lies in obeying nature, riding its very force to escape its full blast. In the section of his book titled "Art of survival," Blumenberg discusses Goethe's use of the metaphor of the shipwreck through Werther, who recalls the efforts he had made "to escape the waves of death, just as later he had to rescue himself with difficulty from many a shipwreck and recovered arduously." Then he concludes in a surprising assignation of meaning: "And so are all the stories about sailors and fishermen" (54). Blumenberg remarks: "The identification of the genre of those 'stories' as a retrospective enhancement of the experience of danger can only apply to [his own story]" (55). Indeed, the permanent interest of stories about danger at sea is entwined with the human anxiety of living in an unstable universe, where sudden changes of circumstance threaten with personal catastrophe. Liquidity is in effect not only a common notion for water and money, sailing and fortune, but also for cosmic instability and permanent transformation: Heraclitus's fragment with the fluvial metaphor is the kernel of a potential story about losing one's foot in the current.

Smuggling is also the theme of "Pa i Raïm" (Bread and grapes), Pla's most skilful experiment with fiction and the closest he ever came to writing a thriller. "Pa i Raïm" is a murder tale. True to the genre, it introduces the clue early on, in a clever deployment of suspense. The story presents thematic continuity with "Contraban," since here again smuggling occurs against the background of a rugged coast swept by the powerful northwest wind. But the outcome is far more dramatic. As the story begins, a gale is blowing over the recessed village of Cadaqués. The *mestralada* or northwesterly wind has blown uninterruptedly for two whole days and has left a "clean, sharp sky of mineral hardness, with a faded blue and the fiery tips of the stars sparkling" (2:253). On Christmas Eve, a group of tipsy soldiers, unfamiliar with the treacherous moods of the sea, gets on a boat that was stranded on the beach and, disregarding the vehement warnings of bystanders, push it to the water with the intention of going for a fun ride around the bay. "To make those unfortunate men grasp that at twenty-five fathoms from the surface the sea was throbbing from ridge to ridge was a waste of time" (2:253). The outcome, as in a movie's opening sequence, sets the stage for what will happen next. "Needless to say, no one heard again of those unfortunate soldiers or find any trace of the boat; nor will it ever be found no matter how many years pass" (2:254).

Soon thereafter the appearance of an unfamiliar boat in a cove next to the bay of Cadaqués introduces an element of mystery, as does a shady character, eventually identified as Pa i Raïm, who emerges from the dark and asks the narrator for a small favour. In his daily walks to the cove, he is to observe any changes and report them to this enigmatic individual. From this moment, we are immersed in a spy story, although it soon transpires that, unlike in "Un de Begur," the motives are not political. Here the action turns on the rivalry between smugglers, on their struggle for control of the business in this segment of the Catalan coast. The narrative formula has great potential, and Pla manages it with unusual skill, settling the issue of his alleged narrative inability. The question of why his other stories lack narrative tension must therefore be posed outside the scope of his competence. This is not the place for it (the problem is discussed in chapter 4), but it is worth considering the possibility that Pla wrote this novella at the height of his admiration for Georges Simenon. "Pa i Raïm" appeared in 1951 and was probably written a few years earlier, perhaps in 1946, when Pla lived in Cadaqués, or 1947, the publication year of his book about this village. Or in 1949, when he published an article entitled "Georges Simenon y la técnica de la novela" (Simenon and the technique of the novel) in *Destino*. In this article, Pla praised the Belgian writer's sensitivity to the environment and his talent for reproducing the lives of ordinary people, but he also recognized his technical skill, in other words, his capacity to structure plots and generate expectations. Interestingly and perhaps conveniently, Pla considered that the more recent novels of Simenon, longer and more ambitious, lost in intensity, synthetic force, and fascination what they gained in extension (5). Simenon's better work was, for Pla, the period of his Commisioner Maigret novels: short mysteries that, with the pretext of investigating a crime, reproduced unique environments with the precision of a notary public (5).

"Pa i Raïm" manages to produce and maintain narrative tension, while doing what Pla praised in Simenon as perhaps an indirect way of commending his own superb ability to reproduce physical and social environments. As Miquel Pairolí observed, "the characters and their feelings are a human extension of this harsh, craggy geography" (185). Pairolí believes that the key to the story is the naturalistic mirroring by the characters of the rough, implacable features of the scenery. The plot can be summed up, he thinks, in the struggle for survival, "the first of nature's laws" (185).

Pla depicts, in fact, a scenario of merciless competition and unmotivated hatred, in which cunning and malice triumph. But his disillusioned view of human sympathy and altruism allows for a different inference. Pa i Raïm's decisive advantage over his enemies is due ultimately to his superior adaptation to the medium. If there is a moral to the story, it is Pla's bottom-line conviction that success hinges on realism, and that to be realistic is a matter of mastering the milieu. Local knowledge will always vanquish behaviour based on general assumptions. Pa i Raïm uses the features of the physical milieu as extensions of his self. He merges with the environment to the point that he makes it work for him, that he can, so to speak, bend it to his will.

"Pa i Raïm" is, as Pairolí suggests, a peculiar crime story. Not so much because the crime occurs at the end – there are precedents for such an inversion – as because the reader is thrown almost from the start into a state of expectation that something evil is bound to occur, without knowing the victim or how the violence will occur until the end. The murderer leaves it up to the sea to execute his dark intention, and since the wind is the weapon of choice, his is a perfect murder. The only person who suspects foul play cannot talk, because at the same time that he finds the evidence he realizes that he's been the accessory to the crime. In this cat-and-mouse tale, Pa i Raïm bides his time and uses the opportunity offered by a windstorm to cut the rope that moors the vessel in which his enemy is spending the night in an alcoholic slumber. Thus the plot circles back to the opening scene in which drunken soldiers embark for their death on another night of furious mistral. The earlier anecdote serves not only as premonition for the dramatic denouement; it also functions as the precedent that makes Pa i Raïm's commission of murder credible as a misfortune that can be chalked up to a stranger's imprudence.

Overall, Pla's book on the sea voyage yields a mournful wisdom. "En mar," a story about a simple transit from Sóller, a port in the isle of Mallorca, to Barcelona in a small yacht, a crossing that ought to have proceeded smoothly, turns into a near disaster and is aborted by the mistral. In good weather, the sea is a spectacle for contemplative spirits; its changeability and inconstancy are a permanent source of fascination, as if the spectator could discern the deepest truth of being therein. "For certain spirits, the sea's mere presence is enough to throw them into the lassitude of contemplative life. What do you contemplate there? In reality, nothing. Forms that come and go, take shape and dissolve, are gained and lost, change and mutate. In the sea everything is fleeting except the fascination of its permanent insecurity" (2:379). As this paragraph announces, the ecstatic contemplation of the quiescent sea of a homely, belated romanticism is about to be shaken. But Pla proceeds meticulously to ruin the platitude piece by piece. As the yacht leaves the port, it enters "a soapy, oily sea, white with calm, of the colour of melted silver" (2:379), and the travellers get a whiff of the scent of the island: "a delicious, warm gust of air from the soil of the island, the taste of toasted bread blended with an intense perfume of dry herbs" (2:379).

Soon Pla begins a conversation with the patron about the risks of going to sea. The boat is nice, he concedes, but it is a nutshell out of proportion with the immensity of the force the sea can muster. Because the weather is friendly and the sailing good, they do not take stock of the insignificance of the hull in which they navigate. "It would be a pity to be devoured by one of the monsters, big and small, that inhabit these waters" (2:391). Pla's comment elicits laughter from his companions. They do not grasp the gist of his thinking. The ancient imaginary of monsters expressed that element in nature that resisted culture, that which did not admit the order imposed with the violence of categorical thought and ritual structuring. The monster was the embodiment of the divine or natural force reacting to the overstepping of human boundaries. Jeffrey Cohen wrote that "this refusal to participate in the classificatory 'order of things' is true of monsters generally: they are disturbing hybrids whose externally incoherent bodies resist attempts to include them in any systematic structuration. And so the monster is dangerous, a form suspended between forms that threatens to smash distinctions" (6). Pla resorts to this venerable mythology to allude to an ever-present danger in the transgression of the distinction that makes humans land-based animals.

> The sea provides an exact idea, produces a physical feeling, of what primordial nature is, of the cosmos. From a given point of view, this colloidal thing in the sea, this pliable viscosity that envelops things in this medium, seems life's quintessence. But from the viewpoint of human life, grandeur has its limits, the feeling of smallness that we experience in front of it produces the same effect as a dispersion of molecules in space. Because of this, every reflection about the sea is like thinking of death, of the capital disintegration. (2:390)

But Pla does not engage in fantasy. Nature has no need for hybrids. Or rather, it is a commixture of all kinds of hybrids, since each living form grows and develops in gradations of biodiversity and survives by cannibalizing as many of the others as possible. There is no need to imagine composite beings occupying the interstitial spaces between the taxonomic forms. Nature itself is monstrous, and Pla shudders at the possibility of being devoured by the sea's ordinary denizens, the fish. Some species have a huge head and mouth. These eat by biting and tearing the flesh. Others have a tubular mouth and puny teeth. They must eat by sucking calmly, delicately, as if sipping through a straw. These, he says, are the ones that disgust him the most (2:390–1). He shudders at the thought of the tiny fish feeding on human intellect: "I am horrified when I think that the heart of many men, their brain matter, has been sucked by the cannulae in the shape of the mouth of a blunderbuss of these small fish" (2:391). Pla momentarily forgets the action of maggots on human flesh. For a materialist like him, such terror of the imagination must be very real. Like Blumenberg, he recalls the ancients' misgivings concerning navigation. Socrates, who is said to have displayed courage at the Battle of Plataea, was a complete coward when it came to adventure on the sea. His idea (already found in Hesiod, as we have seen) that it was inconceivable that men would embark unless tempted by the possibility of riches, has persisted until the invention of mechanical navigation (2:391). But this is, says Pla, the very same sea which all these illustrious thinkers looked on in fear and never trusted. Paul of Tarsus's defiance of seastorms and shipwrecks, he adds, was a symptom of the enormous revolution that this profound man caused in the spirits of the ancients (2:391–2).

The sea, he concludes, is a huge cemetery, but one that scatters the remains and swallows them to depths where they cannot be profaned. In the sea things cannot be retrieved, everything is lost forever. "The sea is sacred because it inspires terror, because it presents an invincible resistance, because its mystery is unfathomable" (2:392). And the mystery, he says to his interlocutor, begins two or three spans from the edge of the boat on which they are sailing (2:392). In this story, more than in any other in the volume, Pla uses the sea as a pretext to reiterate his philosophy of cosmic insignificance, an outlook more Pascalian than existentialist, although devoid of any religious correlate. At sea humans are utterly exposed and thus deprived of the illusions of tragic rebellion. For Pla, things are simpler: in the confrontation between natural powers of incomparable magnitudes, human bravado melts away and is exposed as bluffing:

> It is possible that the dry blow of the sea is harder, that its lesson annihilates human arrogance faster than any other obstacle. In the face of the sea, no braggart holds up. Everything leads one to think that life is a projection of obstacles to reveal to man, tangibly, his infinite smallness. If man does not use his vague, uncertain smallness to get a clear idea of his extreme insignificance, what is it good for? Ignorant yesterday, ignorant today and always. And the more ignorant we are, the more fatuous, the emptier, the more inconsistent we become. (2:393)

One could say that the sea is for Pla a school of classicism. "It is a school of supreme elegance, because it puts us in our own place with absolute precision" (2:393). As a hindrance, the sea is also a school of writing. "And I assure you that to write about the sea is difficult. Something really curious happens. The sea exerts a kind of fascination that is not conducive to self-splitting – I mean conducive to preserving, vis-à-vis the spectacle, enough lucidity to apply fitting adjectives to what one is contemplating" (2:398). The sea fascinates and thus robs the viewer of the self-presence necessary for the reflexivity that writing requires. On the other hand, the sea is a perfect metaphor for the kind of writing practised by Pla: the description of states of consciousness correlated with sensory perception. One might say that Pla is a phenomenologist who rejects the époché, a phenomenologist not of cognitive essences but of phenomena burdened with the ballast of sensory perception. The sea can be the setting for stories of shipwrecks and other adventures, but it is itself devoid of structure; it is the unstructured par excellence. Hence its dangers and its appeal. Pla claims to feel a pure interest for the sea:

> I find the sea interesting in itself. I am not a novelist and do not believe that novels exist in life. There is only a current of disconnected, disordered, fortuitous facts that happen, pass, and evaporate. Novelists must believe that the strongest faculty in man is memory, because otherwise they would not be in gear. In reality man's strongest faculty is forgetting. (2:398)

As a metaphor for inconstancy and flux, the sea holds aesthetic significance for Pla. It provides a model for a shapeless, free-flowing writing that moves hither and thither, "as the spirit bloweth." Contemplating the sea, "everything slides over the senses without leaving a trace. It's like a state of liquefaction of thought, in which the most solid things are light, colour, air, wind" (2:401). Inconstancy, antithetical to normativity, is the source of the endless diversification of phenomena. On land things appear fixed in their precise location – another way of expressing the regularity and normativity associated with its firmness. But the sea is variation itself. Pla does not speak about the oceans, mere geography for him, but about the Mediterranean, a sea he knows intimately from experience. The bounded nature of this sea amounts to a classic lesson on limits. "If the man of antiquity was characterized by limitation, I think I would have been an acceptable man of antiquity. Well, in the Mediterranean everything is local: meteorology, the cuisine, dialects, the people. Everything changes constantly" (2:400).

Insistence on limitation and refusal to project his vision onto the larger oceans suggest a rejection of universalism and its political dimension, imperialism. Such self-restraint with regard to the expansive fluidity of the seas amounts to the same girdling of experience that his preference for the *país*, understood as a unit of landscape, represents on land: namely, a challenge to the political abstractions of state and empire. Writing about early modern Iberia, Josiah Blackmore argues that "shipwreck narrative, though born of conquest/expansionist historiography, is, in reality, a type of counter-historiography that troubles the hegemonic vision of empire" (xxi–xxii). Perhaps it is not too farfetched to extrapolate this observation to Pla's narratives of peril at sea, in that the adventures of foundering ships take place along the Catalan littoral and often in front of the coast of Empordà. At home, so to speak. The corollary seems to be that adventure does not require political expansion or colonialism. On the contrary, Pla appears to be saying, the unexpected can happen as soon as the boat leaves harbour. Real monsters – all species of ravenous creatures – lurk under the surface and the winds decide man's fate. The pretext of the exotic to underpin colonial adventures is misguided, because diversity exists in direct proportion to the intimacy of acquaintance and the intensity of the gaze.

Appreciation of diversity and the limits within which it is best perceived is crucial to Pla's writing in general but key to the juxtaposition of shipwreck and near-shipwreck stories in this book. Each of these narratives reiterates the dangers of braving the potentially fatal confluence of water and wind. Each story is a pretext for splendid descriptions of seascapes and the application of "fitting adjectives" to the spectacle

(2:398). But there is no progression between the narratives, no overall development of concept or plot. This is in keeping with Pla's claim that the sea, like life, holds no plots but induces a state of liquefaction in the onlooker, whose mind oscillates between perceiving and forgetting, between the ebbing and flowing of consciousness. This narrative strategy is also in keeping with Paul Zweig's remark about the structure of adventure: "The condition of adventure is not development, but repetition, not coherence but illumination" (191).

Pla's stories about the sea contain dramatic moments that, if developed according to generic requirements, could have taken over the text and turned it into something of novelistic proportions. But, with the exception of "Pa i Raïm," Pla rejected this option in favour of iteration and illumination. "We, spectators of life, construct novels and dramas when we discuss the things that occur before our eyes, when we apply to them a dialectic, when we take sides. Facing the sea, what side would you take? You either contemplate it or you leave it alone. There's no other way" (2:399).

9 A *Sui Generis* Liberal

Towards the end of his life, Josep Pla denied having any intrinsic interest in politics. He considered the politician's life to be very uncomfortable and could not understand why anybody would choose that life (24:602). In another late book, *Escrits empordanesos* (Writings about Empordà), he denied ever having any political ambition and attributed his considerable texts of political analysis to his journalistic duty to inform: "I never had any political aspiration due to complete ignorance of this hard, bloody profession. If I have written about politics, it is simply because I have devoted myself to journalism for so many years" (38:164). The truth is, however, that he was deeply interested in politics and considered it one of the two most important things in life; the other was the value of the currency (38:373). Pla read Marx's *Capital* shortly after his return to Barcelona from a protracted stay in Germany as correspondent, during which he experienced the hyperinflation of the German mark. He found the volume on the accumulation of capital and the labour theory of value extremely interesting. He found the subsequent ones dry and confusing. Most impressive, however, was for him that Marx did not devote a single paragraph to inflation and to the problem of the currency, that is, to the value of money:

> How is it possible – I asked myself after reading this book – that Marx did not dedicate a single word to the problem of the currency, which is probably, if one is tangled in it, the greatest, perhaps even the greatest of life's problems? A book entitled *Capital* and integrally devoted to capital, which studies in the greatest detail all the forms that this commodity can take, does not allocate one single line to the currency. Where are we? Have we entered into fetishism and fanaticism, or into pure and simple madness? (34:298–9)

This assertion is of course misplaced, since Marx discusses money in chapter 3 of the first volume of *Capital*, and Pla could have found a more extensive reflection on the subject of money in the *Critique of Political Economy*, had he cared to look further into Marx's work.

Political interest marked key turning points in his career. He even had a brief stint as parliamentary deputy for the electoral district of La Bisbal-Torroella de Montgrí, in his home region of Baix Empordà. Soon after, during Miguel Primo de Rivera's dictatorship, he went into exile to avoid prison for publishing a critical article in the Mallorca newspaper *El Día*. In the early 1920s, and especially during his exile in France, Pla was one of the most radical political voices in the Catalan nationalist left. He went so far as to plot the assassination of Spain's King Alfonso XIII, but the scheme was never put into practice because he and fellow conspirator Eugeni Xammar reflected that neither of them was capable of killing him personally (Xammar 107). Next they offered their services to left nationalist leader Francesc Macià, a former army colonel who was also in exile, proposing to travel to Africa to convince the Moroccan leader Abd-el-Krim to start a rebellion in Spain's colony (Xammar 107–18). Between 1924 and 1926, during Primo de Rivera's dictatorship, Pla pinned his political hopes on the romantic figure of Macià, whom Pla considered at this time "the only man with a definite policy, our only hope" (cit. Gustà, *Els orígens ideològics* 246). But by the time Macià became Catalonia's first elected president in 1931, Pla had switched his allegiance to the conservative Lliga Regionalista, a coalition of business and land-owning interests, attaching himself to the party's leader, cultural Maecenas, and influential politician Francesc Cambó. A self-made man and successful lawyer, Cambó had become wealthy overnight through a historical piece of luck and his own ability. In 1914, electric power in Buenos Aires, the CATE (Compañía Alemana Transatlántica de Electricidad), was the property of German financiers. At the end of the First World War, the main stockholder, Deutsch Überseeische Elektrizitäts Gesellschaft, hit by the forced sale of its companies in Chile under British pressure, sought to avoid the same problem in Argentina by selling part of its shares to Spanish businessmen with most of the equity being held by the Belgian financial society SOFINA. Under the modified name of CHADE (Compañía Hispanoamericana de Electricidad), the company expanded to become a holding company with investments in electricity in South and Central America as well as in Europe (Vidal Oliverares 138). Cambó was the lawyer who facilitated the legal fiction that permitted the Germans to reorganize the company's management, and he became a stakeholder in the business and a millionaire in the process. Pla came to see in Cambó a politician capable of pragmatically dealing with reality, someone with the resources to lead Spanish politics out of the impasse of extremism into a period of stability and common sense.

Earlier, Pla had criticized Cambó rather harshly (Gustà, *Els orígens ideològics* 240–50), but now he made a political about-turn, distancing himself from not only politicians but also intellectuals of the left, whom he increasingly described as verbose and impractical. The reasons for this change are not clear. In a highly speculative book, Josep Guixà traces it to the wedding of Pla's brother Pere to the daughter of a local business leader, Joan Miquel, in October 1927. Like most Catalan businessmen, Miquel, who had helped Pla a few years earlier, supported the Lliga Regionalista. His daughter's becoming Pla's sister-in-law did not, Guixà admits, make any difference to the latter's precarious finances, but it raised the family's status in the village, and this, according to Guixà, brought Pla's deep conservatism to the surface (84). Needless to say, this is wild guesswork. More credible is the conjecture that he stopped collaborating with the leftist *La Publicitat* due to incompatibility with the editor, Antoni Rovira i Virgili, and the ideological environment of his new journalistic home, *La Veu de Catalunya*, gradually altered his political outlook. But the opposite process cannot be ruled out either. Growing disaffection from radical politics could have made the clash with Rovira inevitable and, once this happened, Pla's ideological fate would have been sealed. Gabriel Ferrater suggested that Pla had become fed up with the inconsequence of Spanish politics and disgusted with the routine assassinations in class-split Barcelona of the second decade of the twentieth century and craved for order (108). Be that as it may, after his political conversion Pla became a mordant critic of the left. To his former idol Macià, he now conceded one talent: having his clothes made at Barcelona's best tailor. Beyond that, "when he talked, I could never understand Mr Macià" (44:601).

Pla himself explained his political transition in terms of growing realism. In 1935, he wrote: "When I was thirty, I realized that the puerile, reckless position I had maintained until then did not suit a serious man like me. I went to *La Veu* because it seemed to me that the men of the Lliga were closer to reality that those of the left" (Bellmunt, *Homes de la terra* 110). Thirty. Jesus's age when his public ministry started. Dante's age when he realized he'd taken the wrong turn and went back to the straight path. As he would do again thirty years later when he started his autobiographical *Gray Notebook* on a symbolic date, Pla was tampering with the dates, depicting as sudden insight what must have been a gradual decantation. *The Gray Notebook* commemorated Pla's joining the staff of *La Veu de Catalunya* as a rite of passage on his coming of age. But in 1935, he anticipated that chronological resolution by interpreting his adherence to the conservative press as an existential threshold and a sign of political maturity.

Leaving the leftist newspaper *La Publicitat* for the Lliga's *La Veu de Catalunya* in 1928 was defining for Pla. He not only adopted the Lliga's liberal-conservative stance but began to work on its leader's biography. Cambó's political profile would appear in three volumes between 1928 and 1930.[3] It remains, despite its bias, the most interesting book on this key Catalan politician, spanning the history of Catalan nationalism from the turn of the century to the proclamation of the Republic. It was a long work executed at breakneck speed. Later, Pla would dovetail these volumes, with numerous modifications, into volume 25 of his Collected Works. For many readers then and some still today, it was a shamelessly partial book, a work of propaganda casting Catalonia's political life in the light of a glamorized Cambó. Pla had in fact written it under Cambó's supervision, but his view on this politician would not change substantially in his later books. The Lliga was compromised by its cooperation with Primo de Rivera's dictatorship and Cambó needed to vindicate his actions in preparation for the re-establishment of democracy and the corresponding onset of party politics and electoral campaigns.

The Lliga's role in the advent of the Primo de Rivera dictatorship remains disputed to this day, in part because there has been a tendency to narrowly identify the party with the interests of the captains of industry and to identify the latter with the conservative nationalists. Francesc Pujols, a member of Pla's intellectual coterie at Barcelona's Ateneu, claimed that Catalonia had given birth to the dictatorship as a paradoxical strategy for governing Spain (62). Pujols was a facetious polemicist, bent on expressing truths through irony. In this case, the kernel of truth was the support of members of the business class in the launching of a dictatorship, which the Lliga thought it could temper and perhaps arbitrate. Their intention was to put an end to the social violence in Catalonia, but once in power Primo de Rivera not only

---

3 Josep Pla, *Cambó. Materials per a una història d'aquests últims anys*. 3 vols. Barcelona: Edicions de la Nova Revista, 1928, 1929, and 1930.

repressed the anarchists; he also turned against the Lliga, banning it, persecuting Catalan culture, and eventually shutting down the Catalan government. In 1926 Pla wrote ironically against the wisdom of subscribing a compact with a military dictator: "A democratic man who knows from reading history how frequently these pacts are broken, is on guard and constantly tries to disable and counterbalance the shotgun's power" (*La Publicitat*, 27 January 1926).

By 1928 he had gone over to the Lliga and was understandably inclined to understate its involvement with the dictatorship. In *Cambó*, he no longer talked about civilian naiveté and the backfiring of a sinister compact. He just asserted that people had initially welcomed the military regime as a release from social violence that had become unendurable. Through incompetence, the liberal government had made a mockery of liberal principles, and the people had become cynical about those very principles (25:586). In his apology of Cambó, Pla went so far as to credit him with precipitating Primo de Rivera's fall. As evidence he mentioned certain critical letters, which the Lliga's leader had sent to the general towards the end of his regime (25:589). The argument is not just far-fetched; it contains a logical fallacy. If a few letters had such an effect on a military dictator, that could only mean that Cambó's support had been decisive all along and its withdrawal the clue to the regime's collapse. But even this assumption would be an exaggeration. Primo de Rivera fell because his regime ended in economic disaster and the general could not summon the support of the army or the king.

Two years later, in an article titled "El liberalisme fictici i el liberalisme real" (Fictitious liberalism and real liberalism), Pla insisted that the desire for dictatorship had been general in a context of a breakdown of the social contract. And indeed, violence had been rocking Barcelona for years. Assassinations were frequent and did not shake officialdom's passivity; worse yet, the state's representatives often fanned the flames. Military Governor Severiano Martínez Anido, infamous for his repression of the Cuban rebels, deployed terrorist methods against organized labour in a way that was unprecedented in Spain. Shooting prisoners on the pretence that they were trying to escape (the infamous *ley de fugas*), or abetting the "free unions," an anti-labour organization staffed with professional killers, were some of his innovations. After years of living with daily violence, Pla said, "the illusion of total change, the illusion of a dictatorship, built up in Catalonia through a process that involved all branches of society" (40:37). This desire, he claimed, was legitimate, since the first duty of the state is to secure the life of the citizens (40:38–9).

In 1930, Pla wanted to set the record straight regarding the necessity of the dictatorship. To counter the accusations of complicity levelled against the Lliga, he called on the distinction between reality and fiction, resorting to a rhetoric of stark contrasts and antithetical concepts that would become a permanent feature of his thought. "I ask myself, though, if it is not an unbearable travesty to describe a ministry as liberal while bonding it to a situation governed by the purest and most effective, real violence" (40:38). By simplifying human matters through starkly connoted oppositions, he produced a vigorous, opinionated writing that captivated some and repelled others. In this instance, pitting a real liberalism against a fictitious one, the former in reference to the Lliga, the latter to the regime that preceded the dictatorship, Pla seemed to be perpetrating an ideological legerdemain. He could appeal to his vocal opposition to the dictatorship, which he had paid for with years in exile, while accusing Santiago Alba, a member of Spains's Liberal Party and a former minister, of passivity and bad faith. After the fall of the dictator, Alba had denounced the complicity of some Catalan politicians with the coup d'état, unmistakably aiming at the Lliga's leadership. This anecdotal skirmish interests us insofar as it throws light on Pla's pivotal distinction between verbal politics (typically ascribed to the left) and efficient politics (to the moderate right), by which Pla understood one of gradual realization.

But the article is also significant in broaching the issue of truth and lying in politics. For Pla can hardly be considered a neutral observer. Hannah Arendt has written eloquently about the intrinsic relation between lying and politics, and her thought on this issue can help illuminate the reasons for Pla's striking one-sidedness in many of his political analyses. For action to occur, says Arendt, something must be removed or destroyed so as to change the previous state of things. Planning for action or even the mere disposition to act requires imagining how things might be. Action requires, that is, the deliberate rejection of the facts. Rejection of the facts in order to change them shares with denial of the facts a common source: imagination ("Lying in Politics" 5). Pla's lifelong insistence on his lack of imagination, on his narrow adherence to reality through concrete observation, was not only a defining factor of his aesthetics; it also had a political character as an aspect of his innate conservatism. It even had epistemological consequences in a lasting opposition of "academic truth" to "truth" without qualifiers, as the title of another article from 1930 proposed.

Over the years, Pla's scepticism of theoretical constructions at the expense of the facts precipitated a cosmic cynicism, a conviction that the human condition cannot be redeemed through political schemes. Paradoxically, this unyielding conservatism led him to respect only those politicians who tinkered with the social facts through realistic intervention in the field of political possibility. He called such considered intervention "action," "doing," "accomplishing." In the immediate post-dictatorship, as the political forces were once more vying for advantage, he used those same terms (grandiloquence versus humble, persistent doing) to oppose the Restoration liberals to the conservatives with whom he had identified in the final years of the dictatorship: "What results have these fiery men obtained? Very few, hardly any. Why? Simply: because they have acted in a vacuum, because they preferred having the cold, marble-like, funereal reason of the academy to transforming through tenacious, unseen work full of obstacles and disappointments, a piece of peninsular political reality" (40:33).

The Lliga was the great loser in the 1931 elections that led to Macià taking over the Spanish government's branch in Barcelona (the Diputación) and proclaiming a Catalan republic hours before Republicans in Madrid proclaimed the Spanish Republic, the second in little over a half century. That this republic was, at the outset, in the hands of the left liberals whom Pla had been criticizing could hardly elicit his enthusiasm. Henceforth he would never alter his view that the Lliga bore no responsibility for the coup d'état. On the contrary, he would blame the suppression of the regional government on hostility against Cambó (33:138), and would even suggest that the Republic had been tainted with anti-Cambonism from the outset, leading through a downward spiral to the Civil War (33:139).

From the dawn of the new regime until a few weeks before the start of the Civil War, Pla lived in Madrid, as parliamentary correspondent for *La Veu de Catalunya*. He reported the debates in the legislative chamber during the five-year democratic interregnum. His summaries of the sessions were published, apparently against his inclination (Vergés, "Unes notes explicatives" 8–9), in three long volumes shortly after his death. A strikingly different compilation of his testimony as a political correspondent was published in Spanish in four long volumes soon after the end of the Civil War. Commissioned by Cambó, the *Historia de la Segunda República Española* was an attempt to justify his patron's, and perhaps his own, support of the rebels during the Civil War. At this time, however, the book was not addressed to a no longer existing public opinion but to the new authorities, with whom Cambó had tried to curry favour by setting up a propaganda office in Paris during the war. But the new masters were proving singularly ungrateful to those Catalans who had contributed to their victory. In his journal entry for the last day of January of 1940, Joan Estelrich, Cambó's factotum and editor of the Francoist journal *Occident* between 1940 and 1942, confided: "One year ago, on liberation day, all Catalonia was unanimously for Franco and the Movement; it was the right time to initiate a politics of moral conciliation, of Spanish integration. Afterwards disappointment has sunk in; rightly or wrongly, all of Catalonia feels attacked" (Amat 116). Estelrich's claim about all Catalonia being for Franco was delusive. Hundreds of thousands had gone into exile and, apart from the pro-Franco groups that emerged from hiding, the bulk of the remaining population is more accurately described as, on the one hand, relieved that the war was over and, on the other hand, apprehensive about the retaliations that the conquerors would mete out. But he was right in his assessment that even those Catalans who had supported Franco's war effort were feeling antagonized by his regime. For all his trouble in favour of the rebel cause, Cambó himself would die in exile. This time, clearly, the fallout of the coup d'état was far more dramatic than it had been in the 1920s under Primo de Rivera, and Pla's post-hoc attempt to justify the military rebellion would damage his reputation among Catalan intellectuals without bringing him official reward. Later, he would always refuse to reissue this work and failed to incorporate it into his collected works.

Even so, the modus operandi was familiar. Whoever had read Pla's articles of 1930 denying the Lliga's responsibility in the Primo dictatorship would recognize the approach. The *Historia de la Segunda República Española* began with this assertion:

> The Second Spanish Republic has been a talking, verbal regime, which in reality was unable to go beyond the merely acoustic phase of the problems it tackled – of the old problems and of those that the new regime projected onto Spain through the fact of its implantation. In our country there was hardly ever a political figure that lived in a more persistent imbalance between "talking about things" and "doing things." Few will have roused and stirred more issues, problems, and passions. None, perhaps, presented a more innate inability to move from word to action. (*Historia de la Segunda República* 1:9)

A dichotomy between an ineffective Parliament that got bogged down in rhetoric while society sunk into a morass of violence, and a resolute regime that confronted the issues efficiently had been the formula Pla used to buoy up Cambó in 1930. There may be psychological truth in his attempt to exonerate the Catalan moderate liberals from the verdict of history. It is possible, even likely, that in 1936 Lliga members and sympathizers, faced with the outbreak of revolution in Catalonia, mistook this newest coup of the generals for a replay of the relatively innocuous and, in any case, short-lived dictatorship of Primo de Rivera. A matter of putting down a murderous revolution, restoring public order, and rebuilding a regime based on the rule of law. The *Historia*'s long, detailed account of the formation, consolidation, and decomposition of the regime follows this basic plot. From the start the Communists, under the cloak of a Popular Front campaign, manipulated the elections that led to the constitution of the Republic. In reality, he says, most people were not keen on changing the regime; they were merely casting a protest ballot against the recent dictatorship (*Historia de la Segunda República* 1:79). This account of the birth of the Republic is not only implausible; it does not concur with Pla's earlier version in *Madrid, l'adveniment de la república* (Madrid, the coming of the Republic). In this book, published in 1932, Pla had written that the monarchy collapsed because of the contrast between the relative prosperity of the central years of the dictatorship and the crisis of 1930. At this moment, he says, ordinarily conservative people embraced the movement of subversion and gave the masses not only ideological guarantees but also an object to blame as the obstacle to their well-being. This obstacle was the monarchy, which was struck dead the moment this opinion became general. Then Pla adds, with sarcasm that was not altogether off beam, that people at this point believed that "a Republic in the French style, bourgeois, with businesses and comfort, would make the country function admirably" (26:63).

Pla knew that the Popular Front had not come into electoral prominence in the 1931 elections, and that the communists had been a negligible factor at that time. In this book, he asserted that Azaña cast the Republic's politics in the mould of classic liberalism. Pla considered such politics neither good nor bad, merely utopian. In his view, democracy in Spain had never produced anything but paperwork (26:132). Why would he then, eight years later, affirm that the Republic had been established under communist supervision through the efforts of a Popular Front? Why twist the historical facts so brazenly? The answer lies, I think, in the new context. In 1940 the Spanish regime collaborated narrowly with the Third Reich. Barcelona was infested with Gestapo agents helping the new Spanish authorities with the repression. Pla was arrested in Madrid and forced to write two articles in praise of Mussolini (Vergés 45:38). The son of the editor and owner of *Destino*, Josep C. Vergés, claims that it was the Gestapo that forced Pla to publish those articles (Vergés Coma). Although this detail is undocumented, it has no bearing on the facts. The Falange-infested Spanish police collaborated closely with the German secret police in the early 1940s. It was through this collaboration, mediated by the Spanish embassy in Paris, that the Gestapo apprehended Catalan president-in-exile Lluís Companys i Jover in La Baule-les-Pins and, after briefly interning him at La Santé, handed him over to the Spanish authorities. Taken to the Dirección General de Seguridad in Madrid, Companys was tortured and humiliated before he was transferred to Barcelona to stand trial on charges of military rebellion. The trial, lasting for less than one hour, was the legal fiction to produce the predetermined death sentence. The president was executed in Montjuïc Castle on 15 October 1940. Forced to write in praise of the Italian regime, Pla managed to introduce a significant amount of irony into his articles: "Without this saving doctrine, without these methods of genius, one half of the continent would be balancing today between the liberal-democratic chaos and the communist revolution" (*Arriba*, 26 December 1940).

Pla was under no political constraint to write the history of the Second Spanish Republic. He probably did it for financial reasons, since he had been living on Cambó's munificence. But having accepted the commission, he could only write within the plot prescribed by the circumstances, that is, an apology of the military rebellion. The mandated storyline for years to come was the necessity of the coup d'état, legitimized by the need to re-establish the principles of government after the Republic became hostage to revolutionary parties, while civic life deteriorated and Spain plunged into anarchy. In this work, Pla meticulously records every instance of turmoil, every strike, criminal action, and clash of citizens with the police during those years, drawing up a picture of instability that, while not groundless, sensationalizes the events and dramatizes the historical juncture. Invariably and illogically, he attributes subversive intentions to the left-wing politicians, showing special aversion towards the president of the Parliamentary Council, Manuel Azaña. After a failed coup d'état led by General José Sanjurjo in 1932, Azaña informed Parliament of the actions, military and non-military, undertaken by the government to quell the rebellion in Seville. Pla comments: "With these phrases, he let it be understood that, for a specific length of time, the government would tolerate the most radical liberty in order to give the mob a chance to do the work it does when there is total impunity" (*Historia de la Segunda República* 2:126).

Pla's ostensible goal was to present the democratic regime as a dictatorship holding the country hostage to a politics of radicalization. He claimed that the Republican constitution had been designed to that effect:

> The foremost concern of the men who built the Republican constitutional system was to turn the moderating power not into a neutral force but into an innocuous institution. They created an essentially parliamentary republic, a true parliamentary dictatorship. One of its pivots was article 80 of the Constitution, which limited the right to dissolve Parliament to twice during the mandate of the President of the Republic. (*Historia de la Segunda República* 3:6)

A constitutional article intended to foster stability by limiting the presidential prerogative of dissolving the Parliament is presented as evidence of a dictatorship of Parliament. Even the conservative Alejandro Lerroux is accused of complicity with the constitutional system for accepting the role of prime minister and putting together a moderate government without socialists (*Historia de la Segunda República* 3:6). The retroactive condemnation of the parliamentary system as a whole, and the effort to present it, through an inversion of terms, as the true dictatorship of the political class are too redolent of the Francoist narrative, too subservient to the guiding principles of the official propaganda, and too divergent from Pla's independence of opinion before and after to leave any doubt that Pla was writing with a forced hand. Before judging the scope of the writer's subjective freedom, one should recall that censorship at this time, and for a long time thereafter, was total. Some time after Pla started contributing to *Destino*, the weekly was frequently fined or censored for expressing views at odds with the official slogans. The editors feared that the journal could be shut down, and to avert this prospect Pla recommended implementing ironical collaboration with the regime (cit. Vergés 45:38).

I am not implying that Pla was opportunistic in his retrospective attack on the Republic. His obsession with the decline of public order was real, suggesting that under the pressure of the moment he suffered a split between reason and emotion. He had narrowly escaped being arrested and possibly shot by an anarchist patrol in 1936. The nature of this patrol remains unclear, but it appears that it was composed of journalists designated by the newly appointed press commissar in the collectivized Catalan information industries, and that it was headed by Josep Navarro i Costabella, a former colleague and rival of Pla. Pla seems to have been protected by the local head of the anarchist militias, Pere Pey, of the CNT (Martinell, *Josep Pla vist per un amic* 116). The chaotic revolution that swept through Catalonia in the early days of the Civil War, leaving a wake of murder and destruction in every town and village, could not but leave emotional scars and troubled memories. And these necessarily contained the unassailable truth of personal experience. He believed that a regime that could not protect the life of its subjects had lost its legitimacy. In this he was at one with his patron, Cambó, who in 1917, in a context of sharp social struggle and mounting threat of revolution, had written: "There are moments when peoples have the right to revolution; but we must enquire when that right is born. Revolution means replacing right with violence, and that cannot be done, provoking that replacement is not just except in the case that right is no more than disguised violence" (*El pesimismo español* 40). That is why, under Cambó's influence, Pla was keen on showing that the Spanish Republic was a case of violence disguised as law; worse yet, it was a case of revolution disguised as democracy.

It can be objected that others who agreed with Pla's general assessment of the anarchist revolution did not condemn the Republican experience. Domènec de Bellmunt, a journalist of Pla's generation who remained loyal to the Republic, undergoing internment in the dismal French concentration camps and spending forty years in exile, shared Pla's assessment of the early days of the Civil War. Already on 19 July 1936, the day after the failed coup d'état, he understood that the armed workers' unions and revolutionary parties had no intention of consolidating a "bourgeois republic." He wrote in his memoirs: "On the Rambles antifascist volunteers marched with flags that were red, black, displaying skulls, with the hammer and sickle, etc., but not one Republican flag was to be seen. […] One had the impression that, if at the passage of the F.A.I., the P.O.U.M. or the P.S.U.C, someone had naively come up with the idea of shouting 'Long live the Republic!', he would have been lynched – so loaded with pepper and revolutionary social dynamite was the atmosphere of the country" (*Cinquanta anys de periodisme català* 163).

There is a persistent misrepresentation of the Civil War as a struggle between a legitimate government and a rebellious army. It is more accurate to say that, after 18 July, the constitutional government was attacked from both sides. On the rebel side, by a military directorate with Franco at the helm; in the Republican zone, by an anarchist and communist coalition using what remained of the democratic institutions of government to retain a shadow of international respectability. From the start of the war the democratic institutions had become a hollow shell, real power being in the hands of the revolutionary parties, which vied among themselves to define the terms and tempo of the revolution. On 16 July 1937, Cambó remarked in his journal: "In truth, no one except a naive, deluded Anglo-Saxon, believes that the debate in Spain is over freedom and democracy, because each of these will undergo a long eclipse whoever wins" (*Meditacions* 149). In the face of the events, this was undeniable. In Catalonia, the Generalitat was overpowered by the revolutionary upsurge, which "a naive, deluded Anglo-Saxon" like George Orwell found inspiring until it turned against him in May 1937. But this marvellous transformation, in which he saw the triumph of human dignity and social equality, hid the terror not just of the upper class but also of a large swathe of the middle class, which found itself trapped in an unruly, dangerous situation. The splendid exceptionality of a workers' city, where overalls had replaced suits and the peasant's beret the bourgeois hat, had a prosaic explanation: "To save their skin, everyone bought a beret and a mechanic's overall and rushed to obtain a union card from the C.N.T. or the U.G.T. And pretty much everyone tried to obtain a handgun, which was after all the best identity card" (Bellmunt, *Cinquanta anys de periodisme català* 164).

By the end of his sojourn in Spain, Orwell had come to see things in the same light as Cambó. After the Barcelona street-fighting of May 1937, he realized that the chances for democracy after the war were non-existent. "It would have to be a dictatorship, and it was clear that the chance of a working-class dictatorship had passed. That meant that the general movement would be in the direction of some kind of Fascism," by which Orwell did not necessarily imply a Franco regime, which, unlike Cambó, he saw as "an infinitely worse dictatorship" than one organized after a communist-Republican victory (*Homage to Catalonia* 181).

In *Uncertain Glory*, far and away the best novel about the Civil War, Joan Sales wrote that Catalonia had been crucified between two thieves. He meant the anarchists on the left and the fascists on the right, implying that these extremes were by and large non-Catalan. Less mystical, Bellmunt asserted that "the Catalan people wanted the Republic and Catalan freedom, but they *never* were excited by the struggles between marxists and anarchists, which were not part of their spiritual inheritance"

(*Cinquanta anys de periodisme català* 164). Orwell, an outside observer, corroborated Bellmunt's assessment when, in the midst of the fight to the death between anarchists and communists in Barcelona in May 1937, he estimated that "There must have been quantities of people, perhaps a majority of the inhabitants of Barcelona, who regarded the whole affair without a flicker of interest, or with no more interest than they would have felt in an air-raid" (*Homage to Catalonia* 148).

Pla agreed with the opinion that neither of these extreme-left ideologies elicited sympathies among the majority of Catalans, but he also blamed the Catalan democratic left for initiating an idealistic process that, in his view, played into the hands of the radicals. The fate of conscientious journalists in what Pla considered a de facto dictatorship of the left was epitomized by the assassination of his colleague Josep Maria Planes by an anarchist patrol one day after the publication of an article in which Planes denounced the anarchist murders. The Spanish Republic had become an impossible proposition from the moment its governments failed to identify the Republican regime with formal democratic procedures but rather identified it with specific attitudes and policies. "The Republic, in hands other than theirs – notwithstanding the perfectly democratic and liberal legality of this fact in its origin – was no longer the Republic" (*Historia de la Segunda República* 3:127).

In his consistently negative account of the five-year Republican experience, Pla rescues the moderating role played by the Catalan Lliga of Cambó. After recounting the dramatic events of 6 October 1934, when the Catalan government of Lluís Companys cast its lot with the revolutionary movement kindled by the socialists in Asturias and proclaimed Catalonia's statehood within an imaginary Spanish federal republic, he recalls the proposal advanced by the extreme right wing and seconded by all traditional and monarchical parties in the Spanish Parliament to derogate the Catalan autonomy and repeal all the laws and by-laws emanating from its statute. Then Pla, in words that reflect a view similar to that of moderate Catalanists,[4] disengaged mainstream

4 See, for instance, Gaziel's dejected reporting of the events of 6 October in *La Vanguardia*. Despair led Gaziel to speculate on a metaphysical disposition of Catalans to make the wrong decisions at every historical turn (*Tot s'ha perdut* 256). But beyond this overdetermination, he blamed the political disaster on the confusion of the roles of head of government and president of Catalonia in the Generalitat. The lack of a moderating figure had allowed a hothead like Companys to gamble the institution of self-government in an irresponsible wager. This aberration was not the fault of Catalans but of their flawed constitutional tool (*Tot s'ha perdut* 255).

Catalan opinion from the Catalan government's suicidal rebellion and presented the Lliga as the voice of reason attempting to discriminate between a reckless government and the institutions (*Historia de la Segunda República* 4:13).

Again, it is crucial to contextualize passages like this, which surface amid the wreckage of the Republican experience as remembered by Pla. On 5 April 1938, as soon as his army entered Catalan territory, Franco had derogated the statute of autonomy. It would not be reinstated until his death thirty-seven seven years later. In 1940, when Pla published the *History*, persecution of the Catalan identity was brutal and indiscriminate. By commissioning this vindication of the coup d'état at a time when Franco had achieved military supremacy but lacked effective legitimacy, Cambó was rendering what would be in effect his last service to Franco. The ostensible purpose of this commission was to denigrate the Republican regime, in particular the leftist parties. More speculative, but not to be ruled out, is the possibility that Cambó may have hoped to moderate Franco's post-war policies towards Catalonia and perhaps procure a degree of respectability for the Lliga. However the case might be, Pla, who was writing the first volume in Rome, benefited from documentation supplied by Cambó. Pla, in other words, wrote again under Cambó's influence, but it is quite likely that he shared Cambó's hopes of improving Catalonia's fate by writing a pronouncedly biased account of Spain's pre-war political life. This would explain his shining a sympathetic light on the leader of Falange Española, José Antonio Primo de Rivera. Between 1939 and 1942, Falange was at the height of its influence within the Franco government. It worked closely with the German embassy and, through Ramón Serrano Suñer, first Minister of the Interior in Franco's government and then Minister of Foreign Affairs and president of Falange's political council, it had privileged communication with the Nazi hierarchy in Berlin. Serrano was received with honours there and met with Hitler on 17 and 25 September 1940. Inspired and trained by the Gestapo, the Falange was responsible for a great deal of the repression in Catalonia. This is the frame of events in which Pla's deferential portrayal of Falange's founder and martyr, José Antonio, must be read. In 1940–1, the potential readers of the *Historia de la Segunda República Española* could only be the new masters of the situation. The others were locked in prisons while awaiting trial or execution, or were in French concentration camps or wasting away in Nazi extermination camps. The lucky ones were refugees in Mexico, Chile, Venezuela, Argentine, or the Soviet Union. In such circumstances, a passage like the following takes on its historical relevance. Pla recounts the necrological session in the Spanish parliament on the death of Catalan president Francesc Macià. The meeting occurred on 4 January 1934. There was uproar after a shout of "death to Catalonia" came from the right-wing side of the isle. The racket was indescribable, says Pla, and the commonplaces the delegates flung at each other not worth recalling. Worth remembering, however, "because they contained a *potential* politics," wrote Pla, were the words uttered by José Antonio Primo de Rivera:

> In the midst of this confusion, I rejoice that Catalonia's problem has been obliquely put forward, so I can no longer put off asserting that if anyone agrees with me in this Chamber or outside the Chamber, he must feel that Catalonia, the land of Catalonia, must be treated from now on and forever with a love, a consideration, an understanding it did not get in all the discussions. Because when the problem of Spain's unity was posited in this Chamber and outside this Chamber, a series of minor aggravations against Catalonia were blended with the noble defence of Spain's unity; a series of exasperations in matters of small importance, which were nothing but separatism fostered on this side of the Ebro River. (*Historia de la Segunda República* 3:83–4)

I have emphasized the word "potential" in Pla's phrase above, because I think that it reveals his intention of highlighting a contradiction between José Antonio's rejoinder to a call to destroy Catalonia that came from his own ranks and the victors' post-war behaviour. Recalling that unfulfilled potentiality in the post-war context amounted to an appeal to the Falangists to put into practice the magnanimity enjoined on them by their hallowed founder. Yet, in light of the ongoing repression, José Antonio's relativism with regard to the aggravations inflicted on Catalans took an ominous perspective, while his protestations of love, qualified by the explicit goal of assimilation, could also be interpreted – and were – as compatible with a policy of eradication. "We love Catalonia insofar as it is Spanish, and because we love Catalonia, we want it ever more Spanish, like the Basque country, like the other regions," the leader had said (*Historia de la Segunda República* 3:84). Ernesto Giménez Caballero, one of the Falange's co-founders, illustrated the nature of that love in his pamphlet *Amor a Cataluña*. Catalonia – wrote the Falange's most "avant-garde" writer – had chosen to follow the French Popular Front. Barcelona had become an Asian city with the colour of mud, snow, and garbage. It was like a bewitched country, with viragos climbing on men and on trucks like monkeys, and men, in their majority, no longer men (40). Luckily, a fearless leader riding a white horse and wielding a flaming sword broke the spell and led wayward Catalonia back to the Spanish altar. "And in this resides once more the fabulous *Future* of Catalonia: in its wedding with Spain. In the *Empire*. Under Yokes and Arrows [the Falange's emblem] – as in the amorous and generous time of Ferdinand and Isabel: when Boscán was born in Barcelona to proclaim the Unified Destiny – between Catalonia and things Spanish – in Language, in Poetry and in History" (161–2).

Pla's judgment on the deterioration of civil life under the Republic did not change during his lifetime. In 1978, two years before his death, and in the midst of Spain's monarchic restoration, he wrote: "Now the thing is to distort history, to make us believe that the Republic was a placid pond and the Republicans were in charge during the war. This is false: first the F.A.I. was in charge, then the communists. The Republicans, and above all the Catalanists, were never in charge" (45:109). It is fair to say that the picture he painted with broad strokes in the *Historia de la Segunda República* corresponded in its essentials to his experience of that period. And yet, in his chronicles of the parliamentary debates – the basis of the *Historia* – later incorporated in his Collected Works, the tone was more restrained and objective. There is no trace of identification with the right wing or the inspirers of the coup d'état. Above all, the reports are written from a perspective that is contemporaneous with the events. Conspicuously absent from the parliamentary chronicles are the long lists of casualties, attacks on property or institutions, and petty criminality that peppered the *Historia*. But one finds in them alarm at the degeneration of the political life and the prescient feeling that the Republican experiment could end in dictatorship. In the chronicle of 5 December 1935, for instance, during the period of right-wing majority in the government, Pla warned that dictatorships emerge from the excesses committed by the institutions and recommended renewing the Parliament to avoid disaster (42:522). Nevertheless, the year had not been bad. "Crime went down, according to the statistics; the number of social conflicts was noticeably smaller; there was, positively, a little *venticello* in the sense of commercial, industrial, and banking activity, without this implying the return to previous figures, but being a good symptom nonetheless.

Public order, in general, was guaranteed" (42:566). This is far from the hysterical denunciation of gloom and impending disaster for the same year in the *Historia*.

Certainly, Pla looked with apprehension on the period following the victory of the Popular Front in the February 1936 elections, and reported that the right-wing parties were convinced that the legal parliamentary mechanism was exhausted, "due to the dominant left-wing fascism." Pla seems to be merely reporting these words, but he adds on his own: "Indeed, if democracy is no more than a word to disguise the dictatorial attitude of the left-wing groups, then democracy is hardly good for anything" (42:662). Pla was increasingly alarmed by the growing influence of the anarchist FAI within the trade unionist CNT and the triumph of its thesis that the Republic implied the consolidation of bourgeois order and must be overcome through revolution. This was on the last day of March. Since the February elections, everyone could see the regime's instability, although attitudes towards the constitutional framework differed. Pla remained in Madrid until mid-April. The Civil War was in the air. In his last chronicle, dated 13 April, he reported an attempt on the life of Jiménez de Asúa, a socialist deputy, adding that most people associated this attempt with recent feuds between fascists on one side and socialists and communists on the other (42:665). He ended the chronicle by listing the certificates of appointment to the new parliament. Observing that some were still missing, he added laconically: "and there are some dead" (42:666).

Pla was hostile to the left-wing coalitions of the first Republican governments. He believed that they had institutionalized corruption and compromised national life. But in so doing, adds Pla, the Republic had merely extended the vices and shortcomings of the monarchy, which had been abolished only nominally (42:189). In his chronicle of 13 December 1934, Pla expressed an opinion that he would later omit from the post-war *Historia*: "In Spain there is never legality; only vanquishers and vanquished" (42:128). This cynical generalization by a liberal who feels crushed between uncompromising extremes describes Pla's politics much better than the label of reactionary slapped on him by left-wing sympathizers. Even now, as that prejudice has been waning for some years while Pla's recognition has increasingly grown, the ideological ticket has been revived among anti-Catalan intellectuals, some of whom paradoxically distil Francoist nostalgia in the form of literary revisionism.

The occasion was the publication of a chaotic book by Josep Guixà in which, embedded in a storm of unwieldy prose, are alleged proofs of Pla's early association with Falange Española and confirmation of his spying on behalf of Franco during the Civil War. The glee with which such "discovery" was received in Madrid media requires some comment. Pla's association with the Servicios de Información de la Frontera Nordeste de España (SIFNE), an organization financed by Cambó and run by Josep Bertran i Musitu with the objective of producing propaganda in favour of Franco during the war, has been known for a long time. He was in touch with this office during his stay in Marseille between October 1936 and June or July 1937, and his partner, Adi Enberg, was employed as secretary and collaborated in various ways. On the other hand, the nature of Pla's collaboration is unclear and remains a matter for speculation. And speculation there has been aplenty. A rumour circulated for years that he had shown up one night at a dock in Marseille and given a sailing order to the captain of a Greek ship that was loaded with weapons for Republican Spain. Subsequently that ship was sunk before it reached its destination (Badosa 217). Guixà chalks up the consolidation of this rumour to the gullibility of Pla's biographer (50). And certainly, the anecdote lacks evidence. Badosa herself recognized that Pla's usefulness as an agent of SIFNE was very limited. He simply could not keep secrets (216). And Guixà refers to a comment by fellow journalist and confirmed SIFNE agent Carles Sentís about Pla's questionable collaboration: "Pla only knew how to be Pla; it was difficult for him to do anything else" (Guixà 48). Sentís described his and Pla's task in Marseille as collecting information from Catalan refugees. They submitted their findings to the SIFNE to be used for counter-revolutionary propaganda (Guixà 48). Guixà suggests that Pla continued to collaborate with the SIFNE in Paris, but bases this assumption on nothing more than Pla's relative silence about this period in his life. That silence and a wealth of acquaintances in what was after all a tight social world mean nothing. A nosey journalist like Pla was bound to meet nearly everyone of any social significance. His acquaintance with Falangist ideologues in pre-war Madrid is unexceptional, since most of them moved in the intellectual and journalistic circles that Pla frequented as a matter of course. The fact is that Pla was also acquainted with and friendly towards left-leaning journalists and politicians.

It is not always clear that critics of the "fascist" Pla have the right Pla under their lens. Contemporaneous with Josep Pla i Casadevall was José Pla Comas. This other Pla, who also hailed from the Empordà region in Catalonia, was an aristocrat and committed Falangist who in 1940 worked for the Press and Propaganda Delegation in Girona and published inflamed articles in praise of Franco in the newspapers *El Pirineo* and *Los Sitios*. Yet a third José Pla, José Pla Cárceles, moved in Falangist circles in Madrid. This Pla, also a journalist, authored neo-imperial books such as *La misión internacional de la raza hispánica* (The international mission of the Hispanic race [1928]). It is not always clear, given the confusion of Guixà's narrative, whether he mixes up the various Plas in certain passages of his book. That Josep Pla was acquainted with José Antonio Primo de Rivera is unquestionable. Or that he felt respect for the personality of the young aristocrat turned fascist. But from this respect to ideological fraternity there is a very long stretch, which Pla filled with his mordant irony.

"Mr Primo de Rivera," he wrote, "is, among the people I met in Madrid, one of the most elegant, cultivated, passionate, and displaced" (44:175). As so often with Pla, the adjectives are chosen very carefully. José Antonio was a dandy with a better than average education. That polish was, however, offset by a passion that Pla, who did not approve of emotional outbursts, noted clinically. That trait revealed a certain psychological unevenness, the lack of repose that led a wealthy land-owner to embark on a quixotic project of violent rejuvenation of the empire. Hence the adjective "displaced," thrown casually like a flare that illuminates the entire context. Pla has explained that he met with José Antonio at a meeting of intellectuals in the office of the news-paper *El Sol* in Madrid. In his account of that meeting, José Antonio asked right away if Pla sympathized with Falange, and the answer was unambiguously negative. Pla defined himself as a conservative liberal in words suspiciously similar to those he used in later life to produce a ready-made vignette of himself for immediate, gullible consumption. "Are you interested in my politics?" José Antonio would have asked point-blank. "Hardly, not much. Your movement is vitalistic, illusionis-tic, illuminist, complex, feverish. I am a small rural landowner – I will be when my parents die. My obsession is the tax the state levies every quarter; an inefficient state at that. I am in favour of the silly era that Cánovas set up after the liberal and anarchic craze of Carlism in the last century. What I need is peace, calm, inanity" (44:175).

Regardless of the considerable muddling and displays of schadenfreude after the supposed revelations in Guixà's book, there never was a fascist Pla. Had there been one, the Falangist censorship would not have hassled him as persistently as it did during the Second

World War, when he became *Destino*'s most censored contributor, and the journal itself was the object of frequent raids by the censor. In later years, Pla told his friend Josep Valls: "They say I am fascist. But I am the man who lost the most money during Francoism, on account of the many articles of mine that were directly scrapped" (*Josep Pla oral* 52).

Destino had been founded in Burgos during the war by a group of Catalan Falangists and it resumed publication in Barcelona in June 1939. The journal's Falangism was, by the party's standards, feeble and short-lived. The main editor, Ignasi Agustí, was a monarchist, and the administrator and eventual owner, Josep Vergés, a liberal anglophile. Pla met them casually while walking on the Passeig de Gràcia in Barcelona, and they asked him to contribute to the weekly. He submitted "La sonrisa española" (The Spanish smile), an article commending Franco for his neutrality in the European war that had just broken out. Starting in February of the following year, Pla would be a regular contributor, while the journal veered towards an anti-Falangist, independent orientation. Its noticeable detachment from the government's ideology earned it the Falange's hostility.

In March 1944, Santiago Nadal published an article criticizing Mussolini's execution of his son-in-law Count Ciano and that of a minister in the Pétain government of Vichy. Barcelona's Falangist governor Antonio de Correa Véglison arrested Nadal and sent him to prison. In April, Pla wrote to Vergés asking if he had telegraphed Mossèn Joan Bonet I Baltà to enlist his aid on behalf of Nadal. Father Bonet had played a role in overseas Catholic propaganda during the Civil War. He must have intervened, because Nadal was freed a few days later, on Good Friday. By 1944, weakening of the Axis had altered the balance of power within the Spanish government, and the Church increased its influence as the Falange's declined. Pla explained the strategy to Vergés: "We must present the case on grounds of Catholicism and anti-Communism, as it can in fact be supported with the Perpignan and Toulouse dossiers. That's how I see the matter. Agustí, right now, is he not too obviously monarchical to carry out the negotiation? In this country, well-administered skill has always proved effective. Don't you agree?" (45:365). These are not the words of a man who is on good terms with the Falangist hierarchy. Or who is known for his fascist sympathies.

Pla's pro-Allies stance during the Second World War did not endear him to the government. Mention has already been made of the pro-Mussolini article he was forced to write as a corrective for his inability to conceal his sympathies. Now he recommended dosing the journal's ideological resources to navigate a thorny situation. But, in connection with his willingness to play that game, on 15 November 1942 he had written to Vergés: "I have no intention of submitting anything to *El Español*. The nuisance, if not over yet, is about to be over, and we'll see very big things. Be mindful" (45:360). The allusion is to a new weekly about "politics and the spirit," which *Destino*'s co-editor Ignacio Agustí directed between 1942 and 1947. Pla had just contributed one non-committal article, "Las ciudades y los hombres. Eugenio d'Ors y Barcelona" (Cities and men. Eugenio d'Ors and Barcelona), which would appear on 3 December. If anyone tried to read political significance into this article, it could only be as indirect criticism of the Falange, since d'Ors was at this time its foremost cultural idol. The date is significant, because the fate of the Wehrmacht in Russia had not yet been sealed. Pla, however, was convinced that the totalitarian regimes would not prevail and refused all collaboration from the start, warning Vergés to keep *Destino* on a liberal course.

In 1946, after his prediction had been fulfilled, Vergés asked the director of press and propaganda, Juan Aparicio, the very man who had censored and mutilated Pla's articles systematically, to grant Pla a reporter's credential, without which newspaper work was illegal in Spain. This time, Aparicio relented and even expressed admiration for Pla, to the point of offering to travel to Catalonia to personally present the credential. Vergés was anxious that the loose-tongued Pla might commit an indiscretion and begged him to be cautious. Aparicio was still powerful and capable of shutting down the journal. Pla dismissed his friend's anxiety as groundless; then, as soon as Aparicio walked into his house and they were shaking hands, Pla asked: "Would you explain to me, Mr Aparicio, why you were such a damned Germanophile?" "Look, Pla," replied Aparicio, "things have turned out this way and they could have turned out differently." Then Pla, condescendingly: "Well, don't worry. That is over now. The English have won the war, and that is all that mattered" (45:45).

Destino's divergence from the party line did not sit well with the Falange. On 18 July 1944,[5] after the annual commemoration of the coup d'état, four armed individuals in Falange uniforms attacked the office

5 Josep Vergés dates this attack in 1943, but it seems that his memory skipped one year. Guixà provides a reference to the report made to the police by Vicente Obiols on 21 July 1944.

of *Destino* and destroyed the furniture and documents (Vergés, in Pla 45:351). Later that year, Pla and his brother Pere were arrested in a raid for collaborating with the US intelligence service. They were part of a network that smuggled fugitives from German detention centres and channelled military information from occupied France (Clarà 2). Since the Allies were clearly winning the war and Franco was hedging his bets, this episode was muted, all the more so because the members of the group were identified as politically conservative. Interestingly, in connection with Guixà's innuendo, the report the Guardia Civil sent to the Civil Government associated Pla with the Lliga Catalana without mentioning any Falangist contacts or indeed any activities on behalf of Franco. Had Pla been as close to the Falange as Guixà suggests, or been active in Franco's service, it would have been odd not to report such connections under police interrogation. The collaboration with the Allies must have been significant. It appears that, after the Second World War, the US government offered Josep and Pere Pla decorations, which the two brothers, however, turned down (Dalmau 14).

In his hastily cobbled book, Guixà asserts that Pla had contributed to Falange journals between 1934 and 1936 (390). This is a surprising statement, because not a single one of the thirty-four issues of *Arriba* published since its inception until its suppression in March 1936 carries any article by Pla, either under his name or under his customary pseudonym of X.X. Not only is the signature missing, but none of the articles displays his style. In the entire run of the journal, only the unsigned editorial article in the issue of 18 April 1935 might raise suspicion due to a respectful reference to Cambó, of whom the writer says: "If anyone in Spain represents the Western European politics with a mark of excellence, that person is Mr Cambó." But then, the Falange's models were not the Western European democracies but the new authoritarian regimes of Italy and Germany. And sure enough, after that show of deference, the editorialist proceeds to throw Cambó's liberalism into the dustbin of history: "His conference in the Goya Cinema was an evocative delicacy, like the hats of England's Queen Mary. These hats, like Mr Cambó's polemic elegance, recall the pleasant years before 1914; those years when the cinema had not yet displaced the theatre and the automobile did not fully compete with the *grands Exprèss Européeens*. But what can be done, if things have occurred since those years; things like the Russian revolution, the March on Rome and Hitler's triumph! It would be desirable that none of these things had shaken an atmosphere that already jars a bit with Queen Mary's hats."

The wish that none of these political novelties had taken place is clearly ironical. The intention is to charge Cambó, a realistic politician, with old-fashioned idealism. The article closes with an allusion to Cambó's wisdom, declared obsolete in the fateful atmosphere of the 1930s, and followed by a reference to the martial legions of fascist youth preparing to save Europe by remaking it from the ground up ("Política española" 1). What is the likelihood that Pla was hiding behind the anonymity of an editorial to pile derision on his political idol and supporter? *Arriba*'s editorial articles were generally written by José Antonio Primo de Rivera. As a rule, these were doctrinal pieces setting forth the Falange's policy; to delegate them to a journalist who was not a party member and was known for his liberal views was unthinkable. Pla had in fact disparaged the notion that liberalism was a Victorian piece of junk. In an article published in *La Publicitat* nine years earlier, he had written that a defective parliament is better than a good tyranny, and that "among us a rumour circulates that all these truths are old and foolish nineteenth-century things. What a mistake! The people's bewilderment, the general perplexity, the inexistent civic dignity and determination are due to the lack of basic political culture" ("El perfecte demòcrata") (The perfect democrat).

In 1940, when *Arriba* veered from being a combat broadsheet to become a vehicle for Francoist propaganda, Pla contributed a few non-political articles without making any concession to the journal's ideological high pitch. The only exception to this muted tone were the above-mentioned articles, in which Pla was compelled to praise Mussolini. Writing under compulsion signals coolness towards the Falange's politics. But even in these articles, he managed to slip forms of double entendre and farcical exaggeration, which could pass undetected or at least unquestioned against the backdrop of the Falange's rhetoric. Thus, in "Trascendencia de la revolución italiana" (Transcendence of the Italian revolution), he wrote: "In Spain there has always been a picturesque kind of conservative gifted with an inborn incapacity to conserve and with a brilliant penchant for being easily devoured. Since ultimately to be conservative consists in the art of preventing the roof from falling on us intermittently, it is necessary to see and to figure out, and as far as possible to popularize this art for the enormous importance it has, not only for those who have something but, above all, for those who have nothing. In our time, this art has a generic name: it is fascism" (3). He went out on a limb when he capped the article with the following paragraph, in which the assertion of memory against propaganda could and did apply to the immediate context: "It seems to me that it is worth recalling these facts, because things are as they are, and not as wished by the dictates of a propaganda that clashes with our immediate memory in the strongest possible way" (3). But the closing sentence dangerously smacked of mockery: "Without Mussolini, without Fascism, half of Europe would have disappeared as a land fit for human habitation" (3).

In the course of the year, Pla published thirteen articles in *Arriba*. Most of them were descriptions of his travels in Italy, where he had lived in 1938, or of earlier stays in Munich and London; in other words, recycled material with no discernible political significance. The ostensible detachment from the immediate circumstances and from the daily's raison d'être had the value of a gesture, tantamount to the distancing effect of his refusal to use the informal form of address standard among Falangists when speaking with Falangist intellectuals. Guixà describes Pla keeping a safe distance from José Antonio's comrades (145). But Pla went further than mere aloofness. In these ostensible collaborations he managed to introduce occasional irritants, small witticisms that show, at the acme of Spain's fascist fervour, a poker-faced writer practising the form of ironical collaboration that he would soon recommend as a survival strategy for *Destino*.

In an article published on 20 February, the first of a series, he reported hearing an old dirge from the mouth of the municipal secretary in the Sardinian town of Alguer. The song, which the censor probably assumed to be in Italian dialect, was in standard Catalan, a language preserved in Alguer since medieval times. However that may be, the censor's red pencil did not come into action and Pla managed to get a Catalan poem printed in a Falange publication at the peak of the language's repression:

> Sailor, good sailor.
> May God give you fair weather.
> Have you seen or met
> My lover from France? ("Cagliari")

Moreover, was not the dirge's mourning tone expressive of the general emotion of the time? Would it be far-fetched to suggest that Pla was ventriloquizing the poem's ancient voice to ask about the fate of France, the paradigm of a democratic republic, in the war that had broken out the previous September? Pla was anything but a casual writer. But if this inference seems unacceptably belaboured, would it also be pushing the idea of a cunningly provocative Pla to interpret his use of the expression "my country" as a reference to Catalonia in the following passage, also published in *Arriba*? "I remember hearing the old men in the coastal villages of my country tell the adventures of coral fishing" ("Recuerdos de Ulises") (Memories of Ulysses). Nothing is innocent in Pla. And the allusion to the memory of a people, coupled with a reference to the shipwrecked Ulysses, man of many wiles, tips off the reader about his intentions. Granted, these are small, innocuous things, but they flash and flicker against the darkness of the times, like phosphorescent glow-worms in the night. The suspicion that Pla was introducing a micrometric program of disaffection at the heart of the fascist propaganda machine grows stronger when, in the third and closing article of the Sardinia series, he discusses Cavour's plan to unify the former Italian kingdoms by means of a railroad, and explains that to fuel the trains Cavour deforested the entire island. The article begins with the assertion that Italian unity was more important than Sardinia's landscape, a statement that was music to Falangist ears; but before the article is over, it develops into this incredible slap to fascist dogma: "Of course, it hurts to see the arboreal wealth of such a large island as Sardinia sacrificed to a secondary ideal whatsoever" (3). Political unity, a secondary ideal whatsoever! Pla was attacking the first article of faith, indeed the axiomatic core of Falange politics. He even allowed himself a sarcastic climax: "But this can be remedied, and Benito Mussolini, promoting the large-scale reforestation of Sardinia, will put things in order *also* in this matter" (3, emphasis added). The parallelism between Cavour's politically motivated railways and the radial design of Spain's railroad system, incompatible with the European track width, could not have passed unnoticed. But the censor probably chose to ignore the allusion, considering Pla's quip sufficiently indirect as to be removed from Spanish circumstances.

This modus operandi, this critique on the sly, looms in almost every article of Pla's in *Arriba*. Writing about cuisine, he took the opportunity to speak about "traditions that have followed naturally different directions" and represent "absolutely different things." The article concluded by denying the possibility that a cookbook can be "nationally complete" ("Para un libro de cocina del pescado" [For a fish cookbook], 3). Flying in the face of the Falange's assimilationist goals, this last phrase could easily be extrapolated from the kitchen to the state. It clinched the argument against the Falange by refuting its delusion of having achieved overarching national unity by removing internal differences.

Some phenomena, Pla was saying in effect, cannot be homogenized; they are "absolutely different things," the product of divergent historical trajectories.

At the beginning of July, in an article on Syracuse (an ancient kingdom ruled by a tyrant), and on the pretext of some archaeological findings, Pla leapt from the mention of ancient coins to lamenting "the degeneration of modern coins," that is, currencies. Since the irony was transparent, he hastened to add: "I mean their aesthetic degeneration" ("Siracusa"). This pro forma qualification did not cancel the swipe at the Falange's economic policy. The gibe about the loss of value of the peseta was unmistakable, and its passing clear under the censor's vigilance is somewhat of a mystery. Another example of Pla's embedding of irony occurs in an otherwise bland review of a Spanish translation of August Messer's *History of Philosophy*. Under the pretext of criticizing philosophical idealism, Pla took a shot at the regime's glossing over the realities of the post-war period: "People want things to be presented without spots, without cracks, without wrinkles, conveniently idealized" ("Una historia de la filosofía" [A history of philosophy]). This is followed by a reference to Lent, a period of fasting and abstinence, in connection with an exhortation to modesty and humility that contrasted starkly with the military swagger and imperial pomposity of the publication. And while the Falangists waxed lyrical about the dawning of the era of totalitarian societies, Pla soberly noted: "Our time will count with the greatest, most spectacular, most painful catastrophes of the human race's passage on this planet" ("El progreso" [Progress]).

Pla was never a regular contributor to *Arriba*, where, in addition to the Falange's political leadership, the names of Álvaro Cunqueiro, José Antonio Maravall, Samuel Ros, Eugenio Montes, Dionisio Ridruejo, Pedro Mourlane Michelena, and Román Escohotado were customary. In comparison with the frequency of these names, Pla's contributions to *Arriba* pale into insignificance. The pseudo-scandal arising from the "discovery" of his participation in the periodical has less to do with Pla's political outlook than with the opportunity to tarnish his reputation. Still, the question of why Pla agreed to publish a string of articles in a Falange paper begs for answers. One is rather simple. He needed money. Since May of the previous year, he had resigned his position as vice-director of *La Vanguardia* upon learning that the Falangist Luis de Galinsoga had been nominated as new director. The nomination had been made by the all-powerful Falange President and Minister of the Interior Ramón Serrano Súñer. Pla resigned his position and ceased contributing to the newspaper, retiring to his family's farm in Llofriu and leaving behind any involvement in public affairs. In 1943 he began contributing to *El Diario de Barcelona*, and later, between 1960 and 1965, he wrote regularly for *El Correo Catalán*, which, under Manuel Ibáñez Escofet's leadership, had become a liberal publication.

Between 1939 and 1943, Pla, convinced that for a long time the only constructive activity possible consisted in shoring up the ruins of the Catalan language and culture, was reduced to practising a literature of local customs and manners. In 1941 he published a travel guide of the Costa Brava (*Guía de la Costa Brava*); in 1942 a book on the painter Santiago Rusiñol crammed with turn-of-the-century anecdotes; a book on humour (*Humor honesto y vago*) (Honest and vague humour); and the important *Viaje en autobús* (Journey by bus), which did not escape the censor's scrutiny. Certain passages were expurgated, but he still managed to allude to the deprivation of the popular classes while the black market thrived, tolerated by the authorities. Pla never yielded to any temptation emanating from the New Spain, not even when a chair in the Spanish Academy of the Language was offered him by former Falangist and prominent Francoist novelist Camilo José Cela, the 1989 Nobel laureate, who travelled to Llofriu to sound him out about his interest in the offer.

If all of this does not suffice to lay to rest the myth of a Falangist-friendly Pla – a myth built on innuendo, such as Guixà's reference to Pla's "contacts with the José Antonian [in reference to Falange's founder] old guard" ("contactos con la vieja guardia joseantoniana") (341), perhaps the indirect testimony of his stringent, inflexible anti-fascist friend Eugeni Xammar will. Always well informed, Xammar would have never forgiven a soft spot for fascism in Pla or anyone else. Xammar, who barely escaped internment in a Nazi concentration camp, never forgave Carles Sentís, a fellow Catalan journalist, for spying on behalf of Franco. After the war, Xammar blasted Pla and the *Destino* group for writing in Spanish, a way of accommodating to the regime. Yet Xammar never accused Pla of espionage, and when he returned to Catalonia in the 1960s, he resumed their friendship. In contrast, he would never speak again to Sentís, a "sewer rat, devoted to the vilest tasks of spying for the enemy" (211). Xammar was quite capable of distinguishing tactical compromise from full-fledged collaboration, an ability that many Pla critics seemingly lack.

Pla's liberal conservatism prevented him from sharing the regime's hopes for a victory of the Axis in the Second World War. In 1947 he reacted to an article in which Joan Estelrich lamented the retreat of the Latin countries before a now hegemonic Anglo-Saxon world in unequivocal terms: "if the rise of Germany had continued, if it had not been stopped by civilization itself, you and I would now be in a concentration camp, because it is unthinkable that we should have changed our profoundly liberal, moral, and individualistic character" ("A los pesimistas" [To pessimists]). His Anglophilia was not opportunistic. In 1956, when defending Great Britain could no longer have any tactical value or social consequence, he lost his temper when the spouse of an acquaintance attacked that country during a dinner conversation. In Pla's own description, the discussion nearly turned violent. The couple left, the wife proffering insults. Pla, it is safe to assume, retaliated in kind. Another guest came out in her defence, opining that she had not been entirely wrong, and the infuriated Pla expelled the interloper from the restaurant (*La vida lenta* 134–5).

Pla was never well disposed towards Franco, but being staunchly realistic, he was averse to all forms of imaginary heroism. After Franco's death, he noted acrimoniously: "All right, Franco was a rather moronic, cagey general who distrusted everyone and who knew the army quite well and knew how to corrupt people. All right, Franco was one of many bloodthirsty creatures in this country, with the small detail, however, that he won the Civil War. As long as he was strong, everybody remained quiet. Then he got into bed and died attended by twenty-seven doctors. How shameful for the excited socialists and revolutionaries of the day, that they let the dictator die in bed!" (45:109). He knew that the regime lasted as long as it did not because of Franco's physical endurance but because of its pervasive demoralization of society. Many who accused him of collaborationism during the Civil War may have been objectively more complicit with the ensuing state of affairs than he was. In his journal of the year 1956, which remained unpublished during his lifetime, Pla noted down on 21 December: "Impressive country of madmen corrupted by Francoism" (*La vida lenta* 166).

After Pla's death, Josep Vergés observed in his portrait of the writer that "he was so conservative that agreeing with him was strenuous, so much did he exaggerate and distort things. But this should not surprise anyone, because he was conservative from the moment he started writing until his death" (45:42). Then he added: "But nothing could break his lifelong liberalism" (45:44). The oxymoron is accurate. Pla was a conservative liberal, or a liberal conservative. His quarrel with the Catalan left in the late 1920s had its roots in a different concept of freedom. The cries of "death to Cambó" in 1931 affected Pla so deeply that he could never again reconcile himself with the progressive parties. The Republican parties that won the elections in 1931 campaigned on principles that went back to the spirit of the French Revolution. In the traditional articulation of the social order, progressives perceived a hindrance to liberty and equality, two virtues that only a state that was hostile to that order could embody. From Pla's viewpoint, progressives were bent on destroying the existing traditions for the sake of utopian pipe dreams. Conservative liberals like him saw in those very traditions the guarantee of freedom, shielding individuals from the voracious intervention of the state. His anti-dogmatism precluded him from espousing political notions on principle. Democracy was only as good as the democrats who embodied it: "Democrats are people who want to give power to those who play cards at the Cafè de l'Oli." Liberals, on the other hand, want someone to rule but also want this ruler to have less power every day. "I am a liberal," adds Pla (Valls, *Josep Pla oral* 130).

Pla was a hard-core individualist, in John Stuart Mill's sense. Shortly before his death, he passed judgment on his society. "Catalans, generally speaking, do not believe in anything ... except for personal things. A Catalan is a permanent, sure-fire individualist. In my humble opinion, people like this are admirable" (44:600). Pla was no reactionary; he never wished for a return to the past, which was glorious only in the hallucinated minds of fanatics. He acknowledged the imperfections of the status quo, but refused the wisdom of wiping the slate clean, for that could only bring misery and bloodshed. "There is no situation without some defect or other. Eliminate it! Keep, however, what is indispensable. What is to come will be just like what preceded it – maybe worse. [This] country has nothing but words. To think [here] consists exclusively in talking – in talking without foundation, thoughtlessly. Thinking is more than talking. To think consists in keeping what is indispensable. To regress, never" (44:510). Pla understood that change is necessary for conservation and societies need to adapt to new circumstances. But unlike utopians, he did not believe that change for the sake of change was desirable or that a revolutionary tabula rasa facilitates the construction of a virtuous state. Recognizing and preserving the indispensable, this was the core of Pla's political philosophy. His Anglophilia was rooted in the perception that Great Britain was the only European country where change was committed to tradition, where adjustment was undertaken in view of the concrete conditions of life, not for the sake of rationalistic schemes and intellectual geometry. The indispensable is another name for necessity. It implies recognition of the realities (anthropological, geographic, cultural, historical) that shape life as it actually happens, and cannot be eliminated in the name of liberty without liberty being compromised. The liberal conservative rejects the impulse to vindicate one dominant principle and vindicates instead the multiplicity of competing, non-total principles from whose balance liberty ensues.

Pla belongs to the family of European conservatives. The similarity with Edmund Burke is striking. Burke's reactionary reputation stemmed from his rejection of the French Revolution. Pla repeatedly voiced anti-revolutionary intransigence. He was an acerbic critic of utopianism, which he saw always culminating in bloodbaths. One citation will suffice:

> What has fascinated me the most in my reading are the writings having to do with revolutionary periods. In the short run, and sometimes in the short and the long run, these periods produce misery, hunger, confusion, disorder, and complete sterility. Usually they produce a fabulous increase in human pain, which is intolerable in my view. They produce victims, extraordinary idealists, authentic saints. But at the same time, they usually let out the most abject, vulgar, and repugnant criminals of our species, which has always been so lavish in this sort of production. (38:173–4)

Pla's programmatic realism recalls Burke's urging the House of Commons on 22 March 1775, apropos the conflict with the American colonies, that policy should be formulated with a view to actual circumstances, not abstract ideas of right and general theories of government (Berkowitz 20). With the conservative school, Pla had in common the idea of a limited political intervention in human affairs. Today this idea is often ascribed to liberalism under the guise of neo-liberalism. But as Noël O'Sullivan observed, the history of liberal ideology is the story of a retreat from the idea of a limited style of politics. In the nineteenth century, with the emergence of faith in progress, liberals increasingly came to think that government interference on behalf of mankind's improvement took precedence over limited government (13). Thus liberalism and conservatism appeared increasingly incompatible.

John Stuart Mill thought that government had the right to inculcate a "religion of humanity," in effect politicizing the inner life of citizens.

Conservatives might agree with Mill on the need to supervise the people's spiritual life, while disagreeing on the nature of the religion to be instiled. But not all conservatives are of the same persuasion. Those O'Sullivan calls "moderate conservatives" would balk at the notion that governments ought to be permitted to colonize the subjective life of individuals. This type of conservative may be more usefully called a "liberal conservative," namely, someone concerned with preserving the distinction between the public and the private sphere, which he sees threatened by the advocates of radical change, whether from the left or from the right. It would be wrong to identify conservatism with right-wing politics, although this identification increasingly established itself after the socialist attack on private property caused its defenders to be confused with the guardians of the status quo. The conservative is not, however, someone who opposes social transformation. He is someone who prefers reform to radical change, because change, in the best of cases, not only disposes of the contingent evil but risks eliminating the essential good as well; at worst it recreates evil in the very struggle to alter the conditions intrinsic to social life.

Reformists had bad press in the twentieth century, the period that, as Pla liked to point out, was responsible for the worst man-made catastrophes in history. They are accused of protecting vested interests by slowing relief to oppressed sectors of society, but as Burke observed in *A Letter to a Noble Lord* (1795), his goal had been "in endeavoring to screen every man, in every class, from oppression." Although by adding "particularly the high and eminent," who are vulnerable to confiscation by the "jealousy, avarice, and envy of demagogues" (684), he exposed himself to being denounced as a minion of the ruling class, a liability that Karl Marx made use of when he called Burke a "sycophant […] in the pay of the English oligarchy" (*Das Kapital*, vol. 1).

Pla appreciated Marx's sarcastic style and, notwithstanding his loathing of revolutions, felt a certain fellowship with the theoretician of communism as a realist writer. On 17 December 1956 he wrote in his diary: "Marx's sarcasms are extraordinary, and this man is among those who are close to reality. What an impressing figure, my God!" (*La vida lenta* 165). Pla admired Marx on account of his acerbity, believing that excellent writing (and sound political doctrine) rests on recognition of human imperfection. This anti-Rousseauian position is the essence of conservative thinking.

There is no contradiction between Pla's attacks on the left during the Second Republic and his observation at the height of the dictatorship that "the left parties are easily managed by means of social concessions. The right-wing parties are insatiable and extremely dangerous" (*La vida lenta*, 157). They are dangerous because, unlike the conservatives, the radical right subscribes to an ideology of redemption to be achieved through expiation. It presents enslavement as purgation of social sins and assigns the mission of regenerating society to aggressive mass movements. Pla saw this ideology close at hand in the convergence of National Catholicism and the Falange during the Franco regime. The former produced its own variation on the Nazi slogan "Work sets you free" in the forced labour camps created after the Civil War, and in the false compassion with which it ministered to the Republicans who were incarcerated or purged in sweeping acts of political violence. The latter whipped the masses with the vision of renewed world dominance pinned on Spain's great reserve of moral power in a decadent Europe. Inspired by José Ortega y Gasset's sanguine prophecies about Spain's opportunity with the decline of modernity, Falangists concocted an inflated rhetoric of empire. One example of this rhetoric, commonplace in the 1940s, was the radio speech by José María Alfaro, Franco's undersecretary for Press and Propaganda, on the first anniversary of the "liberation" of Madrid: "Think only that it is not impossible that, amidst the madness and delirium of Europe, someday it falls to us to be the Old World's moral reserve and, possibly – united with our sons of America – arbiters in the steering of this delirious world" (*Arriba* 29 May 1940: 4).

As O'Sullivan points out, liberal democracy accommodates a variation on the rejection of human nature's imperfection in the idea of self-imposed limits, that is, the restraints decided by a majority legitimized through the notion of popular sovereignty. Whether Pla embraced this notion is hard to answer in a manner that is valid for all his life. He mistrusted populism and abstractions of all kinds. And in fact, the traditional conservative objection to the radical democratic idea that only self-imposed restraints are democratically acceptable had Pla's assent. If only laws reflecting the individual's will are acceptable, institutional destabilization will follow, not only because people's opinions and desires differ widely, but also because constantly shifting majorities can undo today what was done yesterday. Basing government exclusively on self-imposed restraints can lead in opposite directions: towards anarchy, leaving government open to attack by groups that refuse to acknowledge any principles other than self-imposed ones, or towards tyranny, where government can defend any policy, no matter how destructive or oppressive, by claiming to act on behalf of the people and justifying this with reference to electoral mandates. Worst of all, government based on the rejection of all external restraint ensures intolerance against previously existing institutions, customs, or principles, on the grounds that because they are not self-imposed they must be contrary to human nature. Pla rebutted such form of political self-production, insisting that nature not only is immoral but also blind to subjective determinations. A politics that isolates the political consciousness from natural constraints is not only false but also downright dangerous, because it replaces the individual's sober adaptation to the reality principle with dependence-producing fictions that reinforce the paternalistic state:

> Men of today aspire to believe that nature should reflect the morality we carry inside – sometimes we do not carry any – and should reflect and impose happiness, well-being, pleasure, hedonism, and security. This current is powerful, and the state, which grows more powerful by the day, wants to project onto men and women one kind or other of hedonism of state, since nature is always distant and indifferent. But all of this is deliriously grotesque, because these prodigious words have never had any real existence. (38:91)

To the idealized account of fifth-century Greece, Pla opposes the view of the comedies of Aristophanes, Menander, and their Roman imitators, principally Plautus. It is there, he says, that one learns the truth about the Parthenon, the Platonic dialogues, Thucydides's observations, or Aristotle. The comedies permit us to grasp the nature of Athenian politics. Pla calls Athens "the greatest political catastrophe of the ancient world" (38:336). This severe judgment owes a great deal to Nietzsche, from whom Pla gained the impression that Athenians had been nature-denying rationalists. And rationalism in politics implies self-imposed restraints. For Pla nature is unaccountable and it is better not to enclose it in forms of willed limitation. "Better to abstain from forecasts and prophecies regarding nature, whose march has nothing to do with our incipient and grotesque rationalism" (38:78).

Time and again he asserts the need to limit expectations and allow for human imperfection and fallibility. Happiness is a boon that one has no right to expect, much less demand. There is no divine plan and the state cannot supply one. Attempts to create Paradise on earth result in carnage and the demise of liberty. Sceptical of prophecy, he refused all truck with those who get their bearings from a philosophy of history, and those who enthrone absolute values of any kind. Like other liberal conservatives, a term by which one ought to understand individuals whose ruling concern is to preserve liberty, Pla set great store by experience. It was from direct knowledge of life that he derived the limited but solid virtue of prudence. Or shrewdness, as it is called in practical, everyday affairs.

To reject the natural limitations and replace them with an alternative reality articulated by means of generalizations manifests a hubris that is historically specific to the West. It is the hubris of the being that keeps life at arm's length in order to isolate a mental sphere grown out of a rarefied form of existence called "philosophical." German idealism was the link between that historical hubris and the twentieth-century totalitarianisms. Defining liberty as autonomy from natural constraints, idealism set the scene for the glorification of the state as the objectivation of freedom. In 1795, at the apex of romantic idealism, Johann Gottlieb Fichte asserted that, "as the French nation liberated men from external chains, my system liberates him from the chains of [...] external influence" (O'Sullivan 64). Such chains, Pla asserts, are unbreakable or nearly so. In his rejection of idealism, he came very close to a form of positivistic determinism, positing the pre-eminence of the natural forces, or the cosmic conflict, as the phenomenal paradigm from which humans derive their concepts, much as mythical thinking made gods out of natural phenomena. The meteorology of Empordà appeared to him as a gigantomachia: "Between these two storm-cloud systems, which are permanent and can be seen by anyone looking up at the sky, a struggle ensues, a cosmic dialectic of unprecedented fierceness. From this struggle, which I got to know when I was young, emerged the human, historical, and political dialectic, about which Hegel, Karl Marx, and Lenin have spoken, and which is now posed everywhere" (38:74).

As a conservative, Pla would have rather lived in a geographical area subject to few upheavals: in a stable country, say, or, since this was impossible, in a country with a marked tendency to stability. Such countries are more pleasant, he thought, because it is easier to adapt to their conditions. "How can one adapt to a country whose climate changes wildly and abruptly all the time?" (38:75). Pla used the weather to talk politics at a time when censorship forbade any open discussion of it. Ostensibly, he was describing an erratic wind pattern in Empordà, but pertinence of the description to Spain's political history did not escape anyone. At other times he was more explicit: nineteenth-century

Spanish history had been a roller coaster of revolutions and reactions. The country was ungovernable, and the relative calm and prosperity at the end of the century had been shaken by the insane war with the United States, which precipitated the end of the Spanish Empire. The twentieth century began under the shadow of this loss. Then, the crises of capitalism and the attendant difficulties of the democracies in the 1920s and 1930s inspired revolutionary movements in the Iberian Peninsula, with the corresponding reaction fuelled by the initial success of fascism on the continent. Such abrupt changes of the political climate, Pla suggests, made it very difficult for a liberal to adapt to the constant dialectic of extremes. The broad view that should have facilitated a continuous process of gradual change, i.e., adaptation to changing circumstances, was missing.

When the Spanish monarchy was overthrown at the polls in 1931 and a republic established, Pla considered that the new political order was hostage to demagogues who incited the people's hedonism, promising economic buoyance. In Spain, he asserted in 1932, money is dictatorial, inseparable from public order (26:61). He maintained this opinion till the end of his life. In 1979, shortly before his death, he wrote in view of the monarchical restoration: "Without public order the currency cannot be stable. Fools! They will pay dearly for this when it is too late for remedy" (45:108). A few years earlier, however, reading Joan Sardà's study of the Bank of Spain during the Second Republic gave him a lead to the problems that crushed the parliamentary regime, forcing him to revise his earlier account in *Historia de la Segunda República Española.* After 1932, Sardà explained, the Bank of Spain restricted its principal lines of credit, and the restrictions increased in 1934 and 1935. This policy had a marked deflationary effect on the economy, greatly contributing to the social malaise. Because the Republic inherited external debt from the monarchy and itself took a new credit from the Bank of France, the government maintained a tight monetary policy and increased its reserves to prop up the national currency. Spain's monetary policy ran counter to other countries that devalued their currencies in order to stimulate their economies. By doing this, Spain exacerbated its internal problems and gravitated towards civil war:

> One could see that the Republic was powerless against the Bank of Spain. That is, the regime was drawn into the ultraconservative ideas of the Emission Bank. The Republic, in spite of its revolutionary dimension, was ineffectual with regard to the Bank of Spain, the military party, the large

> landowners, and the Church, notwithstanding the fact that Mr Maura expelled Cardinal Segura, primate of Spain, from the country. Ultimately, it could not resolve [those problems]; it was not skilful enough. Spain is a devilish country. (A:387)

Pla's liberalism could overcome his conservatism. For someone who lived meagrely from newspaper work, who had witnessed the devastation brought to Germany by interwar inflation, accepting occasional inflationary policy was a substantial concession, a sign of mental flexibility. Pla was never an apologist of Franco. He would have preferred that the Civil War had been averted, but once it started, love of order and stability dictated his position. He could not accept a situation that had only the appearance of legality. Towards the end of the dictatorship, he wished that the Republican government could have swayed the Bank of Spain to adopt a looser monetary policy and let credit flow by raising the inflation target. "I am not in favour of inflation, but politics consists in fixing things, a little more or a little less. To keep going. I have always believed that the currency is the key to everything" (A:387).

As a liberal conservative he might be expected to admire Friedrich Hayek, with some of whose postulates he clearly agreed. For instance, the idea that "socialism" was to be defined by its methods rather than its aims, and that "it must always be remembered that socialism is a species of collectivism and that therefore everything which is true of collectivism as such must apply also to socialism" (84). Pla would in fact refer to Franco's state-directed economy as a form of socialism, since the market was profoundly skewed by political intervention and productivity was impaired not only by the existence of state industries and monopolies but by protectionism as well. Tariffs on imported products compensated business owners for the virtual impossibility of firing workers. Being a realist, Pla was not carried away by any theory or by the application of principles without regard for the conditions of the society in question. Although no friend of central planning, Pla never went so far as to claim, like Hayek, that once planning gets under way, government does not stop short of totalitarianism. That was, however, the situation during the autarky of the 1940s. And at the time Pla allowed himself sarcastic allusions to the dire consequences of politically controlling the economy. In *Viaje en autobús*, published as a series of articles between 1941 and 1942 in *Destino*, he called attention to the hunger suffered by the population while the black market flourished alongside the Falange-directed economy. Rationing and capping of prices pushed a large part of foodstuffs off the official trade. Stiff penalties for marketeering inevitably raised the prices, while production tumbled due to insufficient or non-existent profit in the regulated market.

As a result a brisk accumulation of wealth took place among party officials and their protégés, while a commensurate want spread among the population. In a passage that he later incorporated into *Viatge a la Catalunya Vella,* Pla described the travellers on a bus in awe at the sight of a potato field. On hearing the word "potato," the entire bus falls into a state of excitement; people leave their seats and move towards the windows to admire the scenery. A passenger tries to reach the door, but the bus is already on its way. A discussion about bucolic poetry and the classic love of the land follows. Was that gentleman "a pastoral, rustic poet, one of those who, inspired by the shapes of the earth, come into bacchic, Dionysian contact with their favorite muse?" Then, the lyrical flight nosedives: "the conception of the landscape depends on how hungry one is" (9:71).

But if Pla agreed with Hayek about the negative consequences of tampering with the economy, he was also aware of the need for strategic intervention when laissez-faire proves pernicious. "Entwined with laissez-faire are some of the causes of the most conspicuous misery. Of misery and joblessness" (33:288). Socialism is deadly to economic freedom. So, he concludes that in order to salvage freedom after laissez-faire has wreaked devastation, the principle of the lesser evil should apply. For him, this is the Keynesian principle of measured intervention. "State control is essentially an evil, but a little state control, especially if it is intelligent and based on economic reality, is preferable to the total loss of freedom devoured by state socialism" (33:288).

In a lengthy article about John Maynard Keynes, Pla defined the British economist as a "*sui generis* liberal" (33:288). There are moments when Pla seems to be describing himself as he draws the portrait of Keynes: "He never despised the reality of each moment, he never got sidetracked in unreal musings, he always acted on reality. In this sense, he was a complete Englishman, a prodigious dosage of theory and practice, an embodiment of the highest, superior, unbeatable, and unbeaten qualities of the Anglo-Saxon genius" (33:289). Keynes was aware that economic principles are refracted in the social medium, and knew how to go about the imperfect copies of ideas. He knew that logic works smoothly only in the empyrean of theory. With the deterioration of the Spanish economy in mind, Pla discusses Keynes's theory of unemployment and the limitations of considering the problem from a narrowly national point of view, asking: "What would political problems have mattered, if they had been the object of general collaboration on the economic front?" To this question, he replies: "They would have had no importance whatsoever, because political problems that separate countries are mere phraseology, ill-understood self-esteem, scarecrows of empty diplomacy. What truly hurts, what causes bloody pain in relations between countries is the political economy they pursue" (33:304). Keynes had revolutionized economic theory by pointing out that industrial production is driven by consumer demand, and for demand to exist, money in the pockets of workers is a precondition. The necessary inference is that capitalism, to avert crises, requires high salaries rather than austerity. "The purchase power of the citizens of a given country takes the form of a vicious circle [...] looping back to these citizens' productive capacity" (33:307). Previously he had clarified that such "vicious circles" were improperly named, because they were nothing more than the circularity typical of everything that is essential in life.

Pla wrote these words in 1955, at the dawn of Spain's conversion to the market economy. Transferring political economy from Falange hierarchs to the so-called technocrats, Franco placed Spain on a developmental path, without as yet lifting the tariffs or allowing workers' unions. Consumption of industrial products was still embryonic, while salaries ranked among the lowest in the Western world. Faced with the ravages of artificial full employment and state monopolies, Pla understood that Keynesianism was inapplicable there. "It is absolutely notorious that these theories of Keynes are inapplicable in those countries that have installed the general progressive laziness at the base of their political economy. In countries like ours, which base their economy on the increase of the number of consumers and the decrease of the number and quality of their producers, these theories are useless. If there is no production, how can consumption exist?" (33:306–7). His lifelong preoccupation with the value of the currency, his conviction that morality depends on price stability – a lesson drawn from his experience of German hyperinflation – found confirmation in Keynes's observations in the "Social Consequences of Changes in the Value of Money" (1923). The English political economist pointed out that devaluation can trigger social upheavals and is always the source of unjust alterations in the relations among the classes, because the change in the value of the monetary unit does not operate uniformly or affect all transactions in the same way. A change affecting society uniformly would remain without effect. However, Keynes observed that historically and at the time of writing, when money changed it did not do so equally for all persons and intents. Because of that, an alteration in the value of money produces "the vastest social consequences" (80). It "transfers wealth from one to another, bestows affluence here and embarrassment there, and redistributes Fortune's favors so as to frustrate design and disappoint expectation" (80–1).

Although the most dramatic effects of the alteration of the value of money still lay in the (near) future, Keynes's warning could not have been clearer: inflation and deflation, "each has an effect in altering the distribution of wealth between different classes, Inflation in this respect being the worse of the two" (82). Pla, who in March 1975, a time of renewed inflation in the West, counselled the future king Juan Carlos I to maintain the value of money and to fight inflation by all means (45:82), understood nonetheless that politics had to be a factor of moderation and that falling prices, as Keynes had warned, could also spell disaster in the form of unemployment. Despite his obsession with the need to avoid oscillations in the value of the currency, he advocated a judicious application of the principles to the circumstances, as he always had. On 20 February 1971, observing an inflationary mindset becoming entrenched, he admitted that under certain conditions moderate inflation could be salutary (A:387). Pla was a *sui generis* liberal in that, while he advocated the freedom of the individual, including the freedom of *homo economicus*, he was aware that an unbridled free market destroys the traditions and ultimately the very ecosystem from which the individual derives his freedom in precarious adaptation to the natural milieu and the integrating institutions: family, village, profession.

Pla's model of freedom was an older friend from his native Palafrugell: the self-reliant, individualistic, and sceptical gamekeeper Hermós. Sebastià Puig, alias Hermós, turns up in several of Pla's books and is the object of an eponymous essay ("Sebastià Puig (A) Hermós" 43:663–703). Illiterate, this Renaissance man of manual professions belonged to a dying species. From the 1950s on, the tourism-driven development of the Costa Brava eradicated this native species, just as Mellors, D.H. Lawrence's famous gamekeeper, could not have survived the socialist politics capped by Thatcherism in the United Kingdom. Hermós's freedom was predicated on the survival of a liberal conservative outlook, personified in his employer, the lawyer, economist, and Lliga Catalana politician Joan Ventosa, whom Pla in 1935 considered "the most all-around, most European, and most universal Catalan of all living Catalans" (cit. Bellmunt, *Homes de la terra* 109). Ventosa owned the Aigua Xellida cove where Hermós worked as a private rural guard. "Work" does not capture Hermós's relation to the place. He lived as he saw fit in a natural domain of crisp, unblemished beauty.

This paradise began to fade in the European post-war period, when new prosperity in the formerly belligerent countries contrasted with the foundering of Spain's centrally planned economy. After 1958 the Spanish government dropped its isolationism, grasping the potential of tourism as a source of sorely needed foreign currency. Pla described the boom soberly but without nostalgia. "The state could have harvested the same amount of foreign currency it now obtains with a tourism less copious but endowed with more substantial possibilities. The state has promoted mass tourism with the consequence that the landscape has been destroyed" (7:221). The ruthless exploitation of the landscape to the point of endangering this natural resource proved to him the inapplicability of Keynesianism in Spain. The country combined the worst aspects of free enterprise with misplaced regulation. The state promoted the massive influx of tourists and creamed off the revenue, while developers drove up the price of the land, creating a speculative bubble. Pla asked rhetorically: "If regulated tourism is incapable of eliminating the greatest amount of risk possible from the business, that is, to set it on stable and durable bases to the extent that this is humanly possible, then it is natural to ask what's the good of regulation?" (7:221–2).

Tourism, added to the waves of migrants from outside Catalonia, altered the coast beyond recognition. Pla experienced the flood of rootless people as a constraint upon his freedom. The presence of a new type of human being unrelated to the history of the place, its traditions, its language; a creature reduced to the vegetative functions and driven by primitive instincts, willing to live in termite hills that occluded and ultimately destroyed the landscape, clashed with Pla's conception of human existence as life adapted to both the natural and cultural ecosystems. In a putative conversation with a school friend, Pla discussed the new phenomenon:

> The sheer quantity of people today has robbed us of the freedom we had in this country. How we knew to have fun in our teens! Today it is no longer possible. Do you remember?
>
> – Of course I remember. People, the mass, have sullied everything to an incredible degree. How are your feelings with regard to this invasion? Do you have any?

> – I have one: they are ungrateful; they are ignorant of the most elementary things. They don't know anything at all. They never know where they're going, or the path they walk on, neither do they know the birds that fly nor the names of the plants they trample, nor where the wind is coming from, nor the colour of the sky, nothing. (35:551)

From the early 1960s to the mid-1970s, Catalonia's population doubled through successive waves of migrants from all corners of the Iberian Peninsula. To these masses of people, strange to the country, were added hundreds of thousands of seasonal visitors from central and northern Europe. Most of them concentrated on the narrow strip of the coast, especially in the area where Pla grew up and where he spent the second half of his life. The swift, spasmodic nature of this deluge of people with no interest in the natives or their culture was the harbinger of things to come. Without leaving his house, Pla could see a future unfolding in which the masses would govern by sheer strength of numbers. Moving freely around the world, like capital and information, they would fall like swarms of locusts upon local communities, devouring them until nothing remained but the bones of commercial skeletons. The millennial accumulation of labour necessary to produce a landscape is thoughtlessly consumed in a moment, laid to waste without concern for its renewal. Pla saw the mass as a reckless, craving, insensitive, and thankless monster. Infatuated with its own uncontrolled movement, it perseveres in its voracity until its energy is spent, like the wind or the currents of the ocean (35:552).

Pla's stark opinion about the masses resembles José Ortega y Gasset's. In *The Revolt of the Masses*, the Spanish philosopher had described this new phenomenon as the full-house effect ("el lleno"). The masses had taken over the spaces previously reserved to the privileged few. Pla's horror of the mass, however, did not exhibit the class overtones of Ortega's, an intellectual Pla did not much respect. His aversion to the mass was not a defence of class entitlement but an objection to government by the insensitive and uninformed. He bears closer resemblance to a liberal conservative like Walter Lippmann, to someone, that is, who, without turning his back on democracy, denounced the hypocrisy that made voters the ultimate authority on truth or falsity, right or wrong (14). The voter is the political tourist. He visits the polls at certain intervals for the purpose of imposing his will, but remains aloof from public duties in the intervals between elections. By the power of a fluctuating majority, voters exert their will in the name of an abstract totality (*the people*, or *the nation*) whose embodiment they arrogate by virtue of a fiction, just as interlopers arrogate the right to redefine the character of a historical place by virtue of their casual presence.

With regard to the violent political fluctuations of the Second Republic, Pla would have endorsed the following pronouncement of Lippmann's: "A prevailing plurality of the voters are not *The People*. The claim that they are is a bogus title invoked to justify the usurpation of the executive power by representative assemblies and the intimidation of public men by demagogic politicians. In fact demagoguery can be described as the sleight of hand by which a faction of The People as voters is invested with the authority of *The People*. That is why so many crimes are committed in the people's name" (34). These are crimes that correlate with the so-called enfranchisement of the masses, with the elevation of the standard of living, with the generalized acceptance and simultaneous debasement of the idea of liberty into unbound desire. Lippmann made the point that the liberties were given to the masses by the liberal state before the masses obtained the right to vote, that their liberties were not a democratic conquest at the polls but the gift of people who were convinced that not being able to vote was incompatible with the human dignity of their co-citizens (40). But what the new mass electorates did with the votes was unexpected. In many places the masses used their voting power to attack liberal ideas and to impair or destroy the liberal institutions that guaranteed their liberties. Lippmann found it disconcerting that "in this century, [...] the enfranchised masses have not, surprisingly enough, been those who have most stanchly defended the institutions of freedom" (40). Pla's summary of his time endorsed Lippmann's unromantic view of mass democracy, passing a hard judgment on the stretch of history that he witnessed during his lifetime:

> I have lived in the most horrible period of history, and what I find most surprising is that I am still alive. This is probably the most bloodthirsty, most lethal, most fanatic, most horrible age that ever existed. It has been the age of the greatest progress, in every sense of the word. All that is new today, which is literally prodigious, stems from the last few decades. Socialist man is gradually being created. This new being will consist of eating, defecating, sleeping, not having any responsibility, and working as little as possible. [...] Personal freedom – which is the only freedom that exists – is breathing its last. [...] Mechanic standardizing is general and relentless. One can see it at a glance. (35:552–3)

One year before the Civil War, when Pla was still sending his political chronicles from the Spanish Parliament to Barcelona, Bellmunt described him as an ideological turncoat, who managed to inspire nearly universal benevolence because people could not take his extreme about-faces seriously:

> Josep Pla is a picturesque character, intelligent, with a great deal of personal sympathy. To a different kind of man people would not have forgiven the enormous contradictions incurred by this writer from Empordà. But Pla is extraordinarily sharp, a conversationalist of inexhaustible humour, and no one has ever taken his doctrinal and ideological metamorphoses seriously. This may have sensibly damaged his prestige as a public person, but it has saved him from many an enemy and spared him a series of poisoned attacks. (*Homes de la terra* 105)

After the civil war, his pre-war dalliance with Falangist intellectuals and his ambiguous involvement in wartime anti-Republican activities did not meet with the same extenuations. Among Catalans in exile and those active in the cultural resistance, he was considered a collaborator. This reputation stuck. For a long time, those who see the world in black and white vilified him, including people who had not read him or, if they had, failed to go under the surface of his apparent dogmatism. Pla was opinionated, but his radicalism should not be rashly ascribed to fickleness, callowness, or diffidence. It has its source in the fitfulness and contradictions of Catalan and Spanish politics in the twentieth century. He rejected the charges of volatility levelled against him. The alleged wavering and unreliability were an optical illusion, a trompe l'oeil produced by the mutability of the background, by the levity and frivolousness of those whom he saw as dupes of ephemeral ideologies. "I have been attacked for my vagaries. This is false. I am one of the men in Catalonia who has changed the least. It seems, though, that in our country the men who never change are those who change every two weeks" (Bellmunt, *Homes de la terra* 111).

10 Of Women and Days

In a television interview conducted in 1976, one year after Franco's death, host Joaquín Soler Serrano asked a seventy-nine-year-old Josep Pla about love. The writer replied tersely: "I do not know what love is, I've already told you." And he added: "I have had some vague, vague, very vague affaires" (Soler Serrano). This statement is striking. Pla had been de facto married to Adi Enberg,[6] daughter of the Norwegian consul of Denmark in Barcelona, and the couple lived together for more than ten years. In fact it was Pla who was rather vague about this "affaire" as well as others that lasted even longer. There was nothing new in this posture. As a writer, he had always practised a paradoxical realism, focusing objectively on all sorts of externalities as a way of drawing a curtain between his intimacy and his writing. He was probably truthful when he declared to Soler Serrano: "I have never written anything with emotion."

Since the publication of his first book, *Coses vistes*, he had given away the secret of his autobiographical writings in the short story "Bulevard Saint Michel, París." In this tale about life in a Parisian boarding house, the narrator, a boarding guest himself, studies not so much the actions, conversations, and gossip of the other guests as the psychological mechanism of boarders relating to each other in shared space. Being forced by imposed proximity to reflect on the character traits of his housemates, the narrator finds himself reflecting also about himself, "about how I am made" (6:183). And through his effort at introspection he discovers that the mental apparatus of reflection

6 Cristina Badosa's biography of Pla provides a great deal of information about Enberg.

performs reasonably well when observing others but poorly when turned upon oneself. "When I observe myself, the logic of my organ of introspection veers instantly from the heart of the matter and tends to focus on marginal issues, on unimportant aspects that are often far from the real question" (6:183). The literature of the "I," the personal diary, and the autobiographical chronicle for which Pla is primarily known, is vitiated by this mechanism of dispersal whose secret purpose is to save face. Pla speaks about an invincible tendency to self-justification. Autobiographical writing is less an exercise in self-exposure than a strategy for self-protection. "I do not deny, a priori, that an absolutely authentic confession is possible. All I say is that every confession is also part of our instinct for self-preservation – of which amour propre is one of the most important chapters – and that every confession is weighted by justifications of assured plausibility" (6:185). Readers of Josep Pla would have done well to heed this warning, because his work is a skilful dancing around the spontaneous sources of his personality, so much so that his public figure, like that of his friend Salvador Dalí – who was also native to Empordà – was meant to hide his innermost feelings. Pla, many who were on familiar terms with him agreed, was hard to know. Jaume Pou Girbal, a younger journalist who had access to Pla's home, described him as "a man who does not know himself, a mystery person" (Amir 66).

The mystery with regard to his love life has been barely lifted. The vagueness of his affaires, to put those relations in his own terms, had less to do with the quality of his interactions with women than with his deliberate attempt to diffuse them, to reduce them to physical encounters devoid of emotion. Although in the case of Adi Enberg, Pla's use of the adjective "vague" for the relation may have been correct. Strictly speaking, the marriage, if it actually took place – and there is no document to prove it – was invalid, since Adi was already married and her estranged husband had not granted her a divorce. Pla and Adi announced their wedding to their families and invited them to join the couple in Narbonne in February 1927 seemingly for a ceremony that has not been confirmed. Shortly after, they embarked in Marseille for a honeymoon in Corsica.

When Josep met Adi in Paris in February 1926, he was struck by the tall, blue-eyed, cultivated blonde who spoke Catalan in addition to several other languages. They started a relationship almost right away, and soon decided to marry in London in December. In his memoirs, journalist Domènec de Bellmunt wrote that all Catalans living in Paris

Figure 7. Adi Enberg and Josep Pla at the wedding of Pere Pla. Sant Sebastià (Palafrugell), 1927.

Photographer unknown. Courtesy of Fundació Josep Pla, coll. Ed. Destino

at the time were in on the secret of the love affaire between Pla and Enberg. Bellmunt recounts that for months the couple played cat and mouse with each other, making their Catalan acquaintances suspect that both were afraid of marriage (*Cinquanta anys de periodisme català* 67).

Whether or not the wedding took place, Josep and Adi moved in with the Pla family for a while. In 1931, when Pla became political correspondent for *La Veu de Catalunya* at the Spanish Parliament, she followed him to Madrid and both stayed there until shortly before the beginning of the Civil War. In the revolutionary summer of 1936, Pla had good reason to fear for his life. His conservative views were widely known and journalists who had been critical of the anarchists were targeted. In the event, his connection with Adi proved useful, as his father-in-law, the consul of Denmark, provided him with a Danish passport that allowed the couple to leave Barcelona on a French ship bound for Marseille. Passengers' documents were scrutinized by anarchist patrols, since many of the upper class – the natural prey of anarchist committees – tried to escape Republican territory under false identity. Even safe conducts provided by the Catalan government did not guarantee safe passage, but a middle-aged man provided with a Danish passport and a Danish-speaking wife did not arouse suspicion.

Pla's relationship to Adi probably saved his life. Despite assurances by Jaume Miravitlles, secretary of the Committee of Anti-Fascist Militias and wartime Propaganda Commissar of the Catalan government, that Pla's life was not in danger, an anarchist patrol had showed up in Palafrugell looking for him. The chief of the local militia protected him on this occasion (Martinell, *Josep Pla vist per un amic* 116), but whether he would have been able to do so in the long run was uncertain. Pla did not stay to find out. In Marseille, he and Adi worked for SIFNE . This would be the last period of Pla's life with Adi, since in 1937 he went to Italy while she stayed in Marseille. In 1938 they reunited in Biarritz and from there crossed into Spain to Franco-held territory. Soon after the end of the Civil War the relationship soured and ended abruptly in Fornells, the village to which Pla had withdrawn to gain distance from the new political order. Pla would never see Adi again and would never mention her in his writings. The only woman with whom he maintained something like a formal relationship and with whom he had an unrecognized daughter simply dropped out of his life.

Adi was not the only woman to be denied a mention in Pla's voluminous oeuvre. His romantic life (to use a term that he would have derided) began somewhat precociously. As a teenager, he maintained a five-year-long love affair with Esperança Suquet, the daughter of his family's neighbours in Palafrugell, whose physical charms Pla used to rave about to his friends. When he moved to Barcelona to study at the university, her place was taken by Mercedes, daughter of the landlady at the boarding house where he lodged in 1919, during his last year of college. Although *The Gray Notebook* is allegedly a diary of this period, it does not mention this liaison, which ended when Pla moved to Paris as correspondent for *La Publicidad*. Other flings included Rosetta Lagomarsino, a beautiful newsstand salesgirl whom Pla met in Genoa in 1922. She lived in Portoria, a depressed neighbourhood, and Pla seems to have planned to marry her, because he invited her to Palafrugell and introduced her to his family in 1923. But his parents disapproved and sent her back after a few days. Pla remembered Rosetta in the volume *Notes disperses*, where she is the "R ..." who taught him Italian by reading from *Il Corriere della Sera* at the newsstand, while he made "absolutely ineffective and totally useless declarations of love to her." Many years later, on a trip to Genoa, Pla approached the newsstand with the morbid desire to see her again, but instead saw her brother and turned away without saying anything.

The following year, in Berlin, he met Aly Herscovitz, an eighteen-year-old Jewish-Russian émigré whom he mentions in several letters to his brother Pere, the first one dated 6 October 1923 (*Cartes a Pere* 65–6]). Later, in *Notes disperses*, he wrote that she was twenty-one when they met at the Romanisches Café in the Kurfürstendamm, and that after a few dinners she moved to the room he was renting in a private apartment. She was, he says, quite patriotic and had a taste for military music. He describes her line of work as interpreting for foreigners and keeping company to provincial merchants on business trips to the capital, a blend of tourist guide and call girl. After he left for Paris, she wrote to tell him that she had been diagnosed with syphilis but was reluctant to seek treatment at a local hospital for fear that her family would be notified. Pla invited her to Paris and arranged for her admission to a hospital there. After the treatment she stayed, working as a model for sculptors. When Pla returned to Paris after an extended absence, he found out that she had gone back to Germany. He writes that, during the Second World War, he learned of the existence of concentration camps with crematoria intended especially for Jews and that he had an intuition that Aly Herscovitz had been cremated. When the war was over, he tried to trace her through an international organization based in Switzerland (probably the Red Cross), but they were unable to help. He then considered seeking information from Leipzig, the city where the Herscovitz family had lived, but he did not know how to contact the Russian zone. For ten years, he lived with the uncertainty about her fate and then "the passing of time confirmed everything" (12:247).

Then Adi came along. She would be the partner who came closest to a formal relation, living with him from 1926 to 1939, with brief

Figure 8. Aurora Perea.

Photographer unknown. Courtesy of Biblioteca de Catalunya. Josep Vergés Matas Archive.

interruptions. In the summer of 1932, while she was in England, he cheated on her with a twenty-year-old Swiss vacationer named Lilian Hirsch. Hirsch would meet with the writer again on a couple of occasions, and she visited him in 1978, three years before his death. On Lilian's suggestion, Josep Vergés published their correspondence in the posthumous "A" volume of the Collected Works under the title "Un amor de Josep Pla al Canadell" (A love of Josep Pla at Canadell).

Vergés thought that Pla's tendency to fall in love with young women was an outlet for his concealed tenderness, a giveaway of the sentimental core behind the cynical attitude he had adopted to protect himself (A:914). He may have been right, although Pla's reticence with respect to his love affaires applies only to his written work. In real life he did not hide them; it even appears that he made them seem more vulgar than they actually were. As Xavier Febrés points out: "He only hides these affairs literarily, as if he found it harder to overcome his shyness and prudishness in writing, and as if he wished to prevent these relations from unmasking the allegedly anti-romantic, sceptic loner, which he presented as a narrative image [of himself] for external purposes" (33–4). Towards the end of his life, Pla authorized his publisher to print the rough draft of a journal for 1967 through October 1968, *Notes per a un diari* (Notes for a diary), which came out after his death in volume 39 of the Collected Works. This logbook contained a stunning image of an old man's prurience and his emotional, largely imaginary dependence on a certain A., the only woman mentioned repeatedly and with such intensity in the bulk of his oeuvre. Hers was a disturbing representation, as he admitted to himself: "Night spent with the obsession of A." (39:643). Plainly, the letter did not stand for Adi. It was the initial of Aurora. But who was Aurora?

Eleven years later, Vergés published another set of diary notes, corresponding to 1965 and 1966, in the supplemental volume A. Aurora was very much present in these new "Notes for a diary." But it was not until the publication outside the Collected Works of *La vida lenta* (Slow living), a volume with Pla's diary notes for 1956, 1957, and 1964, that it became apparent that he had been corresponding with Aurora at least since 1964. The notes for this year are full of references to her. At times he merely jots down the initial without comment, as in the entry for 13 January, which ends: "I spend the night in any which way. A." (*La vida lenta* 207). Clearly, he suffered from insomnia and was thinking about her in bed. On 17 January, he writes: "First letter from A." (*La vida lenta* 208). This entry would seem to be the beginning of the correspondence, although it cannot be ruled out that the ordinal "first" referred to a series marked by some event, possibly Pla's recent visit to Aurora in Buenos Aires, where he stayed between December 1963 and March 1964 (Febrés 124). In the absence of the diaries for the years 1958 to 1963, it is impossible to know exactly when the correspondence started. What we know for sure is that, from the first reference to her, Aurora is already a fixation for Pla, as he confesses in his diary. "The obsession of A. is permanent" (*La vida lenta* 210). Pla lives in expectation of her letters: "No news from A." (*La vida lenta* 212). When he receives one, he succinctly records the fact: "Letter from A. Nothing" (*La vida lenta* 213). The "nothing" that nullifies the letter suggests disappointment. It is a frequent reaction. What he expected from their communications is unclear, but the confluence between memories of Aurora and anticipated verbal tokens of those memories suggests that Pla refused to let the past be. From this refusal emerges a dramatic scenario with the age-conscious writer fighting the onset of a future in which he can discern only the tedium of absolute disenchantment. "Physical love is the single human defence against vital boredom" (12:185). This late burgeoning of sexual imagination is a well-known phenomenon, which he designates with the French expression *retour d'âge*. The correspondence with Aurora appears to have stirred up old memories and reanimated the physical pleasure in the form of erotic fantasies. Entries like that of 16 February bear out this hypothesis: "I think of A. Eroticism" (*La vida lenta* 219).

Few people knew who A. was until Argentine lawyer Beltrán Gambier investigated her identity, and Anna Caballé and Arcadi Espada revealed the name of the mysterious woman in an article in *El País* of 8 March 1998. Her full name was Aurora Perea Mené. She was born in Bielsa, in the Spanish province of Huesca, in 1910 and died in Buenos Aires on 18 July 1968. Pla had met her in ambiguous circumstances after the Civil War. To his friends he intimated that he had met her in a bar-girls parlour,[7] but people who knew her disputed this statement. She appears to have been a seamstress and to have inspired the character of the same name in Pla's short novel *L'herència* (The inheritance; vol. 23 of the Collected Works). They lived from 1943 to 1945 in the fishermen's town of L'Escala; then she left him for an unknown reason, perhaps because of his incapacity to commit to a formal relationship. In those years of enforced Catholic morality, extramarital relations were frowned upon, and living in unholy union often had negative consequences for the woman. Or perhaps she went away due to the difficulty of living with Pla. There was a sombre side to his sociability and conversational charm. In L'Escala some old people still remember his bad manners, especially when drunk. On these occasions he could behave abusively towards Aurora. The relation seems to have been passionate, but publicly he feigned indifference to her. In his profile of Pla, Vergés cites a witness who remembers her sitting quietly and ignored during the all-male chats at the Sport Bar in Figueres. "No, Aurora does not say anything, she only looks like a

7 Arcadi Espada, obsessively hostile to Pla's publisher, will claim that it was the latter who made up the rumour of Aurora's dubious sexual life when Pla could no longer refute him (114). Vergés had in fact described Aurora as a "poor prostitute full of eroticism" (45:57).

caged bird and listens to the strange conversation, quiet, with a half smile, almost agape" (45:57).

After she left L'Escala, they continued to see each other regularly at the Viena Hotel in Barcelona until 1948. That year she immigrated to Buenos Aires, where she found work as a dressmaker. Her family would follow her the next year. On the day the ship departed, Pla came back to the hotel in a state of disarray, blurting out to the doorman that he had lost "the love of his life" (Febrés 78). If the doorman's testimony is accurate, this must have been one of few occasions on which Pla used the word "love" to describe his feelings. However, when Aurora left Barcelona, Pla was already living with another woman. Consuelo Robles was a young brunette with a dark gipsy complexion. The by now fifty-year-old Pla had been living with her in Cadaqués since 1945 before he invited her into his house at Llofriu in 1947. There he introduced her to his acquaintances as the maid, until Pla's mother objected and Consuelo had to go. She went to live in a small house that Pla had bought in Cadaqués, where he visited her intermittently. Although the relationship lasted twenty years, Consuelo, like others before her, left no trace in Pla's work. There exists, however, an unpublished correspondence, which passed through her mother, since Consuelo was illiterate. As he had already done with Aurora, Pla told his friends that he had met Consuelo in a brothel (Martinell, *Josep Pla vist per un amic*). But long after Pla's death, she told a journalist that they had met on a train and that the next day Pla had turned up at her house (cit. Febrés 79).

Since his youth, Pla had patronized brothels. In *El meu poble* (My town), he recalls going at night "to greet the girls in the 'Maison Tellier'." To the meanness of these institutions he attributed the maintenance of "peninsular Senecism," which he describes as "the general, progressive bad mood" of Spaniards (7:605). Given the fear of women, which he attributes to the images deposited in men's memories by their visits to these establishments (7:604), his penchant for associating significant women in his life with such environments begs the question. Whence this need, real or imaginary, to assimilate love to fornication? A series of aphorisms on love in the volume *Notes disperses* is the closest he came to a sustained reflection on the subject of eroticism. And several of the aphorisms are about prostitution. One mentions Tolstoy's *Resurrection*, adding the evidently self-inclusive comment: "Many have frequented the institution thinking about the redemption of a Maslova or other – which generally has turned out (the redemption) to be a totally false alarm" (12:186). Plainly, he was writing from experience, but there is no way of knowing whether he had in mind any of the known women in his life or others he had met in brothels and left behind. But it is certain, in any case, that, like Dostoevsky's Underground Man, Pla experienced love as an oscillation between lofty feelings and abjection (12:186), and that his wavering became acute in his later years, when he yearned for a frank, unbridled eroticism which enthralled him to an absent Aurora.

What unifies the aphorisms is the conviction that love is, in its essence, physical attraction. He quotes from Victor Hugo's *Les Rayons et les Ombres*: "To love is to understand heaven. / It is, whether one is asleep or awake, to install a light in his eyes, / a music in his ears," and then he comments: "One must really be a great romantic poet to transfer the things of life to this scale of catastrophic madness" (12:179). The choice of a paradigmatic romantic poet is not casual. Pla derided romanticism in love as much as he did in literary matters. Accordingly, he applied his programmatic realism to the relations between the sexes. For him, to idealize a physical instinct and to indulge in a flight of fancy were equivalent foibles. "Regarding this point, perhaps we should put ourselves inside life's reality, in its limitation and inevitable miseries. If one has the strength to place oneself there, then it is easy to understand that one of the most real, authentic, and truthful things that can occur between a man and a woman is physical, sensual love – pleasure" (12:179). If narcissism finds a pretext in the diversity of existential conditions – of class, religion, nationality, or race – physical love is the single universal bond capable of transcending these expressions of self-absorption. "Physical love is perhaps the single force capable of breaking the tragic and exceedingly frequent narcissism, which is a natural phenomenon and can find, in the aforementioned divisionary factors, an inexhaustible fount of existence" (12:189).

Such bluntness is often met with scandal, but Pla's cynical view of love was an aspect of his merciless tearing of embellishing illusions. This brusqueness regarding the facts of life goes back to Nietzsche and Schopenhauer, both widely read at the turn of the century. Pla's belief that the essential relation between men and women is sensual will strike feminists as reductive, if not downright misogynistic. But unlike those forerunners, Pla did not deny the possibility of genuine tenderness. He simply thought it impossible without the foundation of physical love. "Real, preserved, persistent tenderness originates in physical love. It is its well-founded, understandable, and normal consequence" (12:188). In other words, desire can transmute into love, but not the other way around.

The true forerunner of this position, although an unlikely direct source for Pla, was Duns Scotus. Against the grain of standard medieval theology, Scotus asserted that the intellect is subservient to the senses, and that its function is to interpret sensory data. Likewise, the will is natively locked with the sensual instinct in order to enjoy itself, a phrase (*condelectari sibi*) that Hannah Arendt understood in a literally reflexive mode, as the will finding delight in its own activity (*The Life of the Mind* 143). From the original phrase, it appears, though, that the will's enjoyment derives from its primary attachment to sensory desire, so that it is the desire itself that, by pervading the will, produces the latter's enjoyment. The distinction is significant. It is a question of a human function being capable of reflexive self-sufficiency or being determined by the body and, through it, by the objects of experience. However, what matters, for the purpose of identifying a distant precedent to Pla's notion of the primacy of erotic attraction, is Scotus's understanding that "no mental delight can compete with the delight arising from the fulfilment of sensual desire, except that this delight is almost as transient as the desire itself" (Arendt, *The Life of the Mind* 143). But then, if desire is transient and disappears with its satisfaction, only the will remains. And will can be transformed into love, an active desire that the object *be*, that it has Being (Arendt, *The Life of the Mind* 144).

Scotus postponed the perfection of love to the afterlife, to the condition of beatitude, which "consists in the full and perfect attainment of the object as it is in itself, and not merely as it is in the mind" (cit. Arendt, *The Life of the Mind* 144). But if we refuse the metaphysical projection of an afterlife, as Pla did, we are left with the experience of the love object in its intimacy rather than in the vagaries of the lyrical or the theological imagination. In the earthly realm, desire may be transient and as such unquenchable in its aspiration, but the object *as it is in itself* can be attained only in physical intimacy, not in the phantasy that accompanies self-gratification, which is the bodily expression of the will's alleged capacity for self-enjoyment.

Pla considered onanism a normal form of erotic activity, the recourse of people who can't express their erotic feelings for lack of "fit" with a partner. The sexual drive does not leave room for alternatives. He did not believe in abstinence as an option. "Ultimately there is either love physically resolved or onanism that can have an immense diversity of mental or oneiric nuances, whether based on reality or purely fantastic" (12:188). The lack of sexual "fit" may be caused by separation, as Mellors, the gamekeeper, writes to Connie Chatterley, revelling in the forced chastity that comes from her absence rather than, as he claims, from fulfilling intercourse. But that chastity is in reality a form of craving, in which writing replaces possession: "Well, so many words, because I can't touch you," and with the recognition of a newly developed dependence: "Now I can't even leave off writing to you" (Lawrence, *Lady Chatterley's Lover* 365).

In his later years Pla also suffered from epistolary dependence, relying on erotic correspondence as an aid to mental stimulation and, quite possibly, onanism. These were years in which the "little flame," as Mellors calls the sexual force, revived in the solitude of the farmhouse at Llofriu. The object of that flame was the distant Aurora Perea, the only woman whose loss Pla appears to have regretted. And the only one he tried to retrieve. Beginning with a letter to his publisher in 1956, in which he aimed to convince Vergés of the importance of sending him to Argentina to write an extensive article for *Destino*, Pla sought all manner of pretexts to visit Aurora in the suburb of Buenos Aires where she lived with an older husband whom she had married in 1952. He finally succeeded in January 1958, and between then and January of 1967, he crossed the Atlantic five times, each time ending up at the suburb of Ramos Mejía, where Aurora lived in a prefabricated wooden house. From there, Pla recounts a chaotic existence with salacious conversations and furtive sexual encounters that Aurora's husband pretended not to notice. Pla had been sending her money for years and continued to do so for a long time. In return, he demanded that she write to him and impatiently awaited her letters, eager for something that the poor, uneducated woman could not give him. Not in words. Even so, the volume of their correspondence seems to have been considerable. Pla's friend Josep Martinell guessed that it must have run close to one thousand letters (Febrés 103). But none have been found, although Pla preserved every scrap of paper and several people, including Consuelo, claimed to have seen them at some point.

Their disappearance seems to be the doing of Frank Keerl, Pla's nephew and heir. Keerl owns the bulk of Pla's papers and denies access to any documents of a personal nature. So far, he has refused to publish these documents, reasoning that, since the writer did not mention such things in his work, his decision to remain silent on aspects of his private life must be respected. In short, Keerl's zeal presents the opposite case of a Max Brod breaking faith with the wishes of his friend Franz Kafka and giving the world the work of one of the greatest writers of the twentieth century. Keerl has been accused of hoarding his uncle's papers for speculative gain. If this is true and the correspondence has not been destroyed, Pla's readers may still come into possession of an unprecedented collection of texts making up new volumes of the Collected Works. Unprecedented, of course, in the context of Catalan literature, since precedents exist in European literature, including Joyce's letters to Nora Barnacle, which Pla could not have known because they were first published in 1975, or Paul Léautaud's *Journal particulier*, which he almost certainly knew, since he read Léautaud's *Journal littéraire* with great interest and recommended it to his friends.

The *Journal particulier* came out in two volumes in 1956. It described Léautaud's relations with various lovers and included the erotic letters he sent them. The *Journal* is supplemented with aphorisms on sensual pleasure written by a sixty-year old man in a matter-of-fact style bearing a similarity to Pla's pages on the brisk sexual reawakening in old age that he referred to, not coincidentally in French, as *retour d'âge*. Sometimes Pla's reading of Léautaud and his writing to Aurora overlapped. The entry for 19 December 1967 is explicit on this point. Pla says that he has written a letter to "A." before dinner. "Perhaps too shy," he adds (39:551), meaning of course not too spicy. Next he writes down the time he had dinner and what he ate and drank: sausage with kidney beans and wine from Begur. Some time after dinner, he annotates: "I read Léautaud. Tolerable. Quite good." Then, without transition: "I like writing to A. The mental erotic game" (39:551). The game, mental enough, had physical consequences. Pla did not write to the distant lover in a mood of nostalgia. Through the language of desire, he invoked her physical presence in a ghost-like manner for the purpose of stimulation. "I start a letter to A., which produces the desired effect" (39:361).

A volume by Pla gathering one thousand letters in graphic language would have been the equivalent of Picasso's pornographic drawings, reminiscent of his excursions to Barcelona brothels. Picasso sublimated such experiences in *Les demoiselles d'Avignon*, which does not refer to the southern French town best known as the diocese of the anti-Pope Benedict XIII during the fourteenth century, but to a narrow street in the old district of Barcelona where nightlife concentrated in the years Picasso spent in this city.

In the absence of the letters it is preposterous to assume that Pla experienced difficulty with writing obscenities in Catalan, a language, according to Espada, with "problems in the writings of notary publics and in the idiom of whores" (86). Espada's book is a suggestive combination of fact, speculation, and prejudice. He is a writer with several axes to grind.

But his book is useful in revealing a side of Pla that more hagiographic works tend to gloss over. Pla wrote to Aurora in Catalan as a matter of course. It was the language in which the two of them had grown up and carried on their relationship. In addition, it might have proved advantageous in keeping Aurora's Spanish husband unaware of the compromising aspects of their letters, if he should ever peer into them.

With the correspondence missing, Aurora might have remained unknown to Pla's readers, were it not for the posthumous publication of his diaries, where Aurora's name glimmers spectrally, suggesting the existence of a background psychodrama. Indecisive, Pla wonders whether he should stop or go on with the correspondence, adding "despite her pure and simple egotism" (A:528). Egotism? What was he referring to? Had she asked him for money again? Was she demure in writing? Or did her letters seem irrelevant to his desire? Were they not piquant enough? As a rule, he appraises her letters on precisely those terms. On 6 August 1965, he observes, mollified: "I find two letters from A. – some interest" (A:611). Then, on 9 August, he notes, satisfied: "Letter from A., tasty" (A:612).

Whatever the reason for his frequent disappointment, Pla was captive to his erotic imagination and needed her to keep the illusion of active sexuality. On 14 January 1965, two days after complaining about her egotism, he writes that he can't sleep. He thinks about A. intermittently. And thinking about her keeps him awake (A:528). One year later, on 28 February 1966, he writes an unusually extended and callous reflection couched in general considerations about the psychology of prostitution. The passage is worth quoting at length:

> The difference between an honourable woman and one from prostitution is memory. In prostitution memory does not exist. [...] A. A case for the books. She is the typical instance of what we were just saying; she has no memory. Sometimes she has a little and becomes sad right away. But everything goes away with the first sensual craving. Given their economic situation, how can one fathom her erotic humour, her language, her food ingestion? She devours like a locust, says her husband. It's exactly like that. It's the lack of memory. She's like a bird with its brain incapable of staying focused on anything, looking from one thing to another. It's the clearest case I have been able to observe. On the other hand, all her pneumotechnic sediment is a superposition of erotic images seen in the course of her life – I have seen it – which perhaps present themselves to her as her appreciable psychic life. She must have had very good teachers in

> this respect. Her memory is nothing more than this. From the erotic point of view, she is unbeatable. Her other defects, though, persist. Nothing has changed, and some things may have worsened. (A:714)

The spite oozing from this passage should not deter us from trying to understand it in light of Pla's position on sensuality. It bears repeating that in his scale of values sensuality is always positively accented. In another passage, he writes in praise of sensually savvy women. They are rare, he says, and they are the real thing. "If chance permits you to enter into the life of a sensually intelligent woman, one who is effective and not exceedingly foolish, do not lose sight of her. There aren't many of those. The more or less sentimental literary forms of love are either child's play or doddering" (12:180). On this account Aurora leaves nothing to be desired, says Pla. So, what is the connection between sexual savvy, which Pla suggests is a learned ability, and weak memory? Sensual pleasure is – can only be – a transient experience, as Scotus asserted. It easily becomes the experience of transience itself. Hence concentrating on grasping the volatile present is destructive of the past, reduces memory to the immediacy of the moment just before the climax, a minimal remembrance required by the feeling of intensified sensation, without which there is no pleasure. A life reduced to the activity of procuring (or giving) pleasure must be light like a bird's, turning hither and thither in search of the nectar of experience. Such a life is necessarily devoid of memory, because pleasure is impossible where regret exists. Aurora shows the incompatibility between pleasure and recollection at those moments when a flash of memory sinks her into despondency. It could well be that her alleged lack of memory was simply a resistance to linger in the past, a past that, whether or not it included the experience of the brothel, had been far from happy.

To be given over to pleasure, human life must be free from the conscience that binds it to the idea of guilt (or of shame), an idea inseparable from the concept of debt. From Pla's viewpoint, Aurora was indebted to him through his remittances of money. If she did not mention those handouts while he stayed in Ramos Mejía, this would explain his annoyance at her "lack of memory." Pla had been sending money regularly through Miquel Bigas, an acquaintance from his native Palafrugell who lived in Buenos Aires. One thousand pesetas every month was not a negligible amount in the 1950s and even the 1960s. But if she was as Pla described her, her lack of memory would have had deeper roots than the generic anti-romanticism that Pla attributed to women.

"Woman is the anti-romantic being par excellence," he asserted in the television interview. If Aurora was truly one with her body, if she lacked the split consciousness characteristic of mental life, then a collection of sensory images would indeed be the authentic expression of her being. Everything else, all that pertains to honourable women – the ambition of wealth, career, family, and social reputation – would have fallen away from her as so much inessential ballast. The nervous energy spent on intensifying sensory experiences would explain her fondness for food, scandalous to someone with a poor, fastidious appetite like Pla's, as his cook, Lola Carreras, reported (Amir 44). Unlike a writer who burned the midnight oil and stayed in bed until midday, someone living at the tip of her senses would require nourishment, just as a bird needs large amounts of food to sustain its flight.

In these metaphors (locust, bird, lack of memory) we are dealing, of course, not with realistic comparisons but with a sign game. Pla writes abut sexual attraction as illusion. In the middle of a passage discussing broad beans in Mediterranean culture, he compares the appetite for this legume to sexual enticement. "Broad beans are like women: they soon bore you, but they are at the permanent root of human illusion" (15:115). Metaphor, like the linguistic sign, is always arbitrary. It is the root of all illusion, the taking of something for something else. In this case the illusion that a particular appearance will allay the pulsing of desire and satisfy the craving inherent to life. If illusion is what entices individuals to come out of their constitutive solitude and enter the social bond, beginning with the smallest social unit, the mother-child, or its adult reproduction in the couple, then disillusion is a falling back to the narcissistic life of the individual. When boredom, fatigue, or irritation dispels the illusion, compatibility breaks down. "It is like a house of cards falling spectacularly as a result of a word uttered in a tone that gets on one's nerves" (12:181). Jean Baudrillard calls this experience "the vertigo of nullity" (54). Like a house of cards held upright by the composite balance of the cards' weight, erotic illusion uses the body's impulse to transcend the gravity of desire. The illusion remains in force as long as the signs interlock with each other, defying natural law. However, it will collapse when the least incident gives away the game and dispels the charm. The woman's body, says Baudrillard, "becomes pure appearance, an artificial construction to which the other's desire adheres" (119). In the struggle to maintain her seductiveness, she refuses to be described in natural terms. She knows that the surest way to awaken desire is to reject all determination, to mask her raw physicality with the froth of illusion. In one of her letters to Pla, known through the testimony of Consuelo Robles, Aurora admonished him: "Do not ask if I am fat or skinny" (Febrés 80).

Was she, in feminist fashion, forbidding Pla to impose on her a masculine ideal of beauty? Was she claiming sole ownership of her body? Or was she rather stirring him away from the objective physicality of her body, the better to plunge him into the image of his own desire? Was she resisting him or rather confirming Baudrillard's argument that "in seduction, woman lacks a body of her own, lacks her own desire"? (119). Baudrillard's idea is that woman does not believe in the substantiality of the seductive body or the objectivity of desire but merely plays with it. His thesis is all the more suggestive in the context of Pla's years-long pen-pal affair, a sexual relation from which the desired body was literally absent though literarily invoked, and in which his was the only desire marshalled. All along, the desiring body knew that the desired body was out of touch. Hence, it craved for its signs; more precisely, for their symbolic encoding. This desire desired to be seduced; it begged for seduction. On 31 July 1965, he wonders: "Started a letter to A. My obsession. If I had her, would I like her so much as I do now? Sometimes I doubt it. Now she's an erotic obsession" (A:608).

There could hardly be a higher victory of appearance or stronger seduction than the pretence of enacting the rituals of the flesh in writing. And the ruse was all the subtler for being sustained by an unliterary woman over a long period of time. Like Baudrillard, Pla felt that male desire is duped in the game of seduction. In the television interview with Soler Serrano, he declared: "Woman rules man. Without a doubt, because she rules in bed." Sex is the original battleground and the primal source of ideology. Freud *dixit*. Hence, control of sexuality is the ultimate stake, the lowest common denominator in power struggles. If, as feminists claim, the social is the domain of patriarchy and the heaven that women must take by storm, then social structures, the very foundation of culture, must be seen as defensive bulwarks erected by the forces of *production* to contain the challenge of *seduction*. Pla detects such defensiveness in the most rudimentary of masculine havens, the tavern and the café:

> It seems to me that the tendency of the male population of Palafrugell to fill the cafés and the taverns – especially the taverns – is due to the need to escape produced by women's dominating instinct. We all know people who had to fight for years in order to obtain the right to leave the house

> whenever they please. Some enjoy this right in never-never land. To live in the reticence of domination is a little vexing and tiresome in the long run. In every man from Palafrugell there is a scared runaway who is fond of everything that is free and comfortable. It is women who produce the anarchists. (7:556–7)

Baudrillard concurred: "The feminine is not only seduction, it is also challenge to the masculine for being *the* sex, for assuming the monopoly of sex and its enjoyment; challenge to go to the end of its hegemony and to exercise it unto death. It is under the pressure of this challenge, constant through the entire sexual history of our culture, that the phallocracy crumbles today, lacking the power to meet it" (36–7). As a political conservative and a philosophical utilitarian, Pla understood seduction as a purposeful game. In his thinking about sexuality there is no trace of Baudrillard's vertigo of the signifiers, nothing about artificial games consisting of reversible challenges. Instead there is a suggestion of a (possibly unconscious) reproductive strategy marshalled through nature's economy of means. Just as desire dies through its satisfaction, once the male is trapped in a reproductive institution the seductive game is over. Women, "after the wedding, cease to fascinate. That is because they've already got what they wanted" (Soler Serrano).

Pla made this statement in a social context in which divorce did not exist and in which women's professional marginalization made marriage almost their sole path to financial security. But it would be wrong to leave things at that banal level of explication. The matter goes deeper than a trivial remark about the consequences of patriarchal dependence. Pla is almost certainly making a statement about the relation between fascination and the invisibility (rather than the repression) of the biological urge to reproduction. In all cultures, women fascinate by deploying signs that transcend signification. Seduction relies on the body to suggest without explicitly displaying sexuality's biological function. In seduction there is no hint of reproduction, or even pleasure; rather elusiveness of purpose and gratuity of the image. Sex is blind, whereas fascination assaults the imagination. In Latin *fascinare* means to charm or bewitch, especially with the eyes. It highlights the power of the gaze, which exerts its influence without committing to any meaning in particular, exactly like the coquette, a special case of the fascinating woman. The *fascinum* was a phallic amulet worn around the neck. Thus, the charm was sexualized from the beginning by referring to the phallus's implicit representation/embodiment of desire. Transferred to the eyes, and *mise en abyme* in the soul, the black hole of the unmarked sex, the phallus draws male desire out of itself into unknown territory. The active, positively marked sex is trapped by its reflection in the mirror of the passive, unmarked one, and in this way narcissism transcends its self-circumscription. In Pla's words, "narcissism is a titillating and dramatic longing for physical love" (12:196).

The fascinating charm is less an invitation than a challenge. But how could the challenge survive its reduction to the "merely" sexual, once the uncertainty of the feminine gives way to the predictability of male desire? The answer is: it cannot survive it. In Buñuel's *Cet obscur objet du désir*, female mastery hinges on the perpetual deferral of intercourse. The sexual sign is preserved qua sign, while its meaning is constantly deferred. Conchita's inscrutability, her elusive appearance and shifting features, her turning up when most unexpected and her going away without notice, her indefinable, hard-to-pin-down determination, in short, her mysteriousness, follow from her refusal to be identified with a piece of her anatomy that she knows can only fail to anchor Mathieu's desire. Unrelated to morality or prudishness, her refusal is part of the game that plunges Mathieu in the abjection of his irrational dependence on a metonymy.

When a woman proves incapable of sublimating "possession" into the elusive signs of a mystery, the challenge disappears and she is reduced to the truth of her body. At this point, if they do not renounce sexuality altogether, men must either accommodate themselves to crude, disenchanted pleasure, or restart the game through infinitely renewed self-delusion: the Don Juan principle. Striking in Pla's correspondence with Aurora Perera is her ability to sustain the fascination indefinitely by removing her body from the exchange ("do not ask if I am fat or I am skinny"). Equally arresting is Pla's perennially hopeful/hopeless renewal of the erotic liaison, despite his irritation at the inanity of her writing.

Like Mathieu, Pla is aware of cutting a ridiculous figure. He is less conscious, though, that his obsession with keeping up a pornographic correspondence mimics his "devilish mania of writing" (1:451). Seduction, as Baudrillard asserted, withdraws something from the order of the visible – in the case at hand, Aurora's physical body. Only her ghostly body counts, a sign of her real presence. Production, on the other hand, turns everything into evidence (Baudrillard 55). Male desire strives to fix what is elusive or secret and ends up fetishizing the absence, the cleavage. It tries to penetrate the impenetrable, transfixed by the slit in the surface, like Mathieu mesmerized by a seamstress mending a torn, bloody nightgown behind a shop window. An allegory of rape? Of deflowering? At any rate, it is the inverted image of his yearning to objectify the inscrutable, forever thwarted by the insurmountable wall of his own desire. A utopian will to close the gap between the object and its representation governed Pla's aesthetic of surfaces. It underlay his dogged pursuit of the one adjective that renders the elusive essence of things. It was also at the root of his belief in the superiority of description to imagination, of his preference for an intrusive, masculine writing over a seductive, feminine one.

Being trapped in a pornographic masquerade would have been ludicrous at any time, but it was particularly bizarre in an aging man, and Pla was painfully conscious of the gap between feasible and purely imaginary desire:

> All persons with some experience of life have abundant documentation about the phenomenon which the French call *retour d'âge* ... in others. Love, the so-called love passions, fills up life from beginning to end with more or less intensity but with real force. Life's degradation does not extinguish anything. The impossibility of physical contact, by intensifying the imagination in a certain way, can give rise to ridiculous, absolutely grotesque situations of a sinister doddering that is often repugnant. (12:183)

Given Pla's awareness of the preposterous aspects of his correspondence with Aurora, the question arises, not of why he kept it up for so long (the answer is obvious) but why he left a record of it in his diary. All his life, Pla annotated his experiences. The notes were the quarry from which he carved the materials for his books. From the fact that he did not publish them during his lifetime, should we conclude that he wished to keep the contents secret? All we can say with certainty is that he did not come around to working up the notes into literary diaries. Apropos private diaries, the Israeli philosopher Avishai Margalit asks whether it is psychologically possible to write a truly private one; that is, one not intended to be ever read by anyone other than the author. His opinion on this matter: "The universal hope of anyone writing a diary is that it will be read – perhaps posthumously – by a sympathetic reader" (158). If we accept this view, we may reasonably assume that Pla expected his erotic correspondence to be eventually read by others, as a supplement to the diaries that he never got around to writing and have come down to us in a raw state. It seems rather likely that he toyed with the idea of publishing an erotic diary like Leautaud's after working up the notes into readable texts. Like Stendhal, whose *De l'amour* he knew well, Pla in all probability intended to write a volume on eroticism, of which the aphorisms finally inserted in *Notes disperses* would have been a part.

In those aphorisms Pla chose to consider the subject in general terms, rather than present his observations in light of his own experience, as he always had. In this decision there was probably an attempt at self-concealment. But there were also formal reasons. This is one of the subjects on which Pla sought to rise to a modest level of generalization, as if he had caved in to the ambition to philosophize. Then, from an aesthetic point of view, elaborating on the "vague affaires" – as he would call them on TV – by means of autobiographical anecdotes would have hardly added anything substantial to Pla's reflections of love. The women in Pla's life do not seem to have provided him with the occasions for casuistry in such matters. If he viewed them, or pretended to view them, as accidents in a life deprived of love, as he asserted in the interview with Soler Serrano, we must take this statement at face value, as his final truth on the matter.

Even so, these women embodied, under different circumstances, an intimacy that the writer protected by adopting a defensive cynicism. Yet he was no seducer. He did not serialize his sexual encounters, as Don Giovanni does, nor was he satisfied with a psychological triumph, in the supercilious style of Johannes in Kierkegaard's *Either/Or*. Pla was subjectively monogamous. He believed that a fulfilling relationship was proved by its sufficiency. In *Notes disperses* he declared free love incompatible with a mutually fulfilling sexual relation (12:185). One of love's conspicuous symptoms is the indifference of those affected by it to everything else. Love makes people more limited and monographic, yet this limitation accounts for the happiness love provides (12:153). This passion extricates its victim from the plane of ordinary existence, leaving it alone with the loved object. The totalized object and the lover are exempted from mundane rules but subjected to the iron law of happiness. Their strange coexistence replicates the ancients' idea of consciousness as a dialogue between the "I" and the "self." Love is a special case of reflexivity, in that the "self" has displaced its narcissistic tendencies onto an "other" that mirrors back the individual's self-love as other-directed love. "Physical love is perhaps the only force capable of breaking the tragic and very common narcissism, which is a natural phenomenon and can find in said separative factors an inexhaustible source of existence" (12:189).

Childish happiness in the suspension of worldly concern resembles the pleasures of philosophy as the classical age understood it, namely, as withdrawal from practical matters and into the recesses of the mind. It may have been this association that prompted Pla to follow his thoughts on the lover's apathy towards everything except the loved object with a reflection on stoicism's inadequacy to modern life. From *Much Ado About Nothing* he quotes Leonato's dismissal of the idea (derived from Epictetus) that the mind can master the self's reactions to events. "For there was never yet philosopher that could endure the toothache patiently, however they have writ the style of gods, and made a push at chance and sufferance" (Act 5, scene 1, 31–8). Shakespeare's phrase, says Pla, is exact but has no meaning for modern life. These days, philosophers do not even attempt to live according to philosophical principles. And that is a significant departure from the ancient world (12:153). "Ataraxia" is just an archaic, fossilized word.

What could Pla mean by pointing out the inconsistency between philosophers and philosophy? A first answer could be that he was indulging in his customary anti-academicism. This sounds convincing but leaves us in the dark. To give the question its due, we must assume that he took seriously antiquity's endeavours to use the power of the will to manipulate impressions. Expressed in different ways by the various schools of thought, the ancient ideal of wisdom was to free the self from the vagaries of fortune. The rational, discursive self was not otherworldly; it merely trained itself to shut off the sluices through which the world flooded the soul. Ataraxia was not absence of impressions, merely indifference, equanimity, steadiness of the soul. Modern rationalism split the world in two, so that the objective world became an unfamiliar externality, knowable only through representations. With Hegel mind came to rule the world and history became rational, but in its grandeur the mind that comprehended and was identical with the becoming-conscious of the Idea was incompatible with the puny figure of a state-appointed philosophy professor.

When Pla remarked that the original pursuit of philosophy has been debased to a split between academicism and ordinary life, he intimated that there was something more serious in the ancient enterprise than is envisaged by the contemporary institution of philosophy. The Shakespeare quotation could well be a clue to the terse comment that baffled Espada in the notes for a diary of the year 1965, when on 4 July, right after the initial "A.," Pla entered the question "As neopaganism?" (A:597). He repeated the term on the next day, adding a supplement that is hardly less mysterious: "I finish a letter to A. Material neopaganism – a large amount of food. The bed is comfortable. Delightful hotel" (A:597). And once again, on 9 July: "The obsession of A. persists: the idea of a down-to-earth but real neopaganism. The problem lies in finding out if I am capable of it" (A:598–9). The mention of food – large amounts – is clearly an allusion to the service at the hotel. It has nothing to do with Aurora's appetite, with "her voracity," as Espada calls it (76). Juxtaposed with the coziness of the hotel, the allusion to a large meal leaves no doubt that Pla is referring to bodily experience, his own. Undeniably, thoughts of Aurora mingle with this experience. They even enhance it. The letter he has just written to her galvanizes the representation of an absent object, testifying to the will's impotence in controlling sensation. In contrast to the difficulty of conjuring up a shadow, the food and the other causes of physical contentment are immediately given. Then, pausing in his vain pursuit of a phantom, he wonders if it may be possible to oppose to ethereal desire a simple but real culture of the senses. Real in the sense of efficient, of producing tangible effects. He, a memory-sick animal, who once associated Aurora with prostitution due to her alleged lack of memory, now yearns for a neopagan dilution of memory in physical impressions. Lack of memory was precisely what sustained Aurora's sexual prowess. A consciousness free of remorse supported her living from one moment to the next submerged in a flow of shifting mental images.

Paganism had intrigued Pla since a much earlier date. In his "Notes sobre Sicíla" (Notes on Sicily), published in 1951 in the volume *Pa i raïm* but based on observations made during his previous travels in Italy, he asked: "But does anyone know what paganism was? What aspect of paganism one wishes for?" (15:336). He knew that paganism was a cultural construct, that for centuries it had been a pretext for art and academicism, but he looked upon it as an indubitable factor in human behaviour, a mythopoetic climate sought after by modern men and women, and thus as an anthropological reality associated with a geographic space:

> The point is not to find out if the ideal conception of paganism is true or false, but whether it can be accepted by enlightened people or is a sheer invention concocted with the help of admirably chosen texts. It is factually certain in any case that this graceful, sunny scenery has enormously influenced the most excitable areas of female romanticism and the most morbid segments of male imagination.

> What one asks from the South is, ultimately, this: freedom, naked forms, sun, light, easy engagement of the senses, nature's collaboration in the cultivation – or wasting – of the marrow, accessible voluptuousness. To sum up: people dream of a normal hedonism that is accepted and without strings attached, a comfortable, fulfilling "bad life." (15:337)

Pla associated contemporary paganism with André Gide, who undertook to live as a pagan with "apologetic purposefulness" (15:337). He could have mentioned D.H. Lawrence, a writer whose second Italian sojourn (November 1919–February 1922) might have overlapped with Pla's first.[8] Lawrence was attracted by a culture "so primitive, so pagan," that he found it pervaded by the "mysterious gods of the early Mediterranean," by "Proserpine, or Pan, or even the strange '[…] gods' of the Etruscans" (123). One of Gide's literary heirs, the Albert Camus of *Noces* (Nuptials) (1939), also contributed to a reformulation of the Mediterranean myth. The academic paganism that Goethe had taken from Winckelmann and that Ulrich von Wilamowitz-Moellendorff defended against Nietzsche and Wagner was transplanted to Catalan gardens by the *noucentistes*. Venus became the *Ben Plantada*, "the well-planted one," in Eugeni d'Ors's fable of the transfiguring of a vacationer's community by the presence of a young woman who embodies the classic *nomos*. *Noucentisme* promoted a homespun version of Mediterranean sobriety, a paganism conveniently tamed by Christian virtues of humility and obedience.

In this pseudopaganism there was little room for sensual rapture. Vines and olive groves there were, and agave-sprinkled cliffs overlooking a sleepy cove centred by a boat with a lateen sail dangling from its mast. A distilled landscape like this was a perfect rostrum for family picnics, a habitat for scenic shepherds and fishermen practising their trade. But it was not a theatre for renewed Eleusinian mysteries, such as Camus experienced them in Tipasa: a spousal of the senses with the earth: "At the mysteries of Eleusis contemplating sufficed. And here I know that I will never come close enough to the world" (*Noces* 18).

8 In *Cartes d'Itàlia* he asserted that he visited Italy for the first time in late winter of 1921, probably meaning in early 1922. "I think I arrived in Italy for the first time at the end of winter 1921." But in the corresponding volume of the Collected Works he advanced the arrival by one year: "When I first arrived in Italy in 1920" (37:164). This latter date is probably a lapse of memory. He went to Italy to cover the International Conference in Genoa, which took place from 10 April to 19 May 1922. If he went in advance of the conference, he would have arrived in Italy toward the end of the winter of 1921.

Pla had famously rejected the *noucentista* mythography and satirized its neoclassic pretensions. What could he mean when he wondered if he was still capable of a "down-to-earth but real neopaganism"? For the sixty-eight-year-old Pla, neopaganism, even if homespun, could not mean a return to the placid sensuality of a bourgeoisie who epitomized their Mediterraneism in opulent villas built by *noucentista* architect Rafael Masó along the cliffs of S'Agaró in the Costa Brava. Rather, the old man's tragic doubt – tragic because it called his entire life into question – referred to the possibility of embracing Epicureanism in the spirit of Camus's "I know that I will never come close enough to the world" (*Noces* 18). Pla considered neopaganism a method of redemption through the senses. Wondering if he would prove capable of it was inextricable from his avowal that he could not rid himself of his obsession with Aurora. He would actually visit her two more times the following year.

The fact that he presented this neo-vitalism as a challenge: "let us see if I am capable of it" suggests that he was turning over in his mind a new life program, one at odds with his established routine. All his life, Pla had been, or tried to be, more Stoic than Epicurean. Now he considered the possibility of putting into practice a systematic nihilation of time, by plunging into physical sensation as a way of steadying the inexorable *durée* that he felt speeding up towards the inevitable outcome. Earlier that year, his mother's death had prompted him to write, on 31 May: "This has been the month of my mother's death. Soon it will be a month since she entered eternity. It's a curious idea that while we're alive we're not in eternity and after we die we are. But is living anything other than a bungled form of frenzied present?" (A:582). A bungled form of frenzied or raving presentness. Could his mother's death have triggered in him a sense of futility crystallizing in some form of *carpe diem*? Did Pla, looking back on his own life, discern only the cinders of passion that had failed to live up to its promise?

His view of the Mediterranean basin as an area characterized by sadness long preceded the *Notes per un diari*. This view recurs throughout his oeuvre. As a sample, the following passage from *Cadaqués*, written in 1946 and published the following year, will do. Here, Pla associates the Mediterranean with what he calls the "romanticism of limitation" and claims that this "fever of limits" throws "the veil of resigned sadness" (27:171) over every individual. To which must be added "the sediment of earthly disillusion and bitter oppression felt on the shores of this sea through the popularization of the doctrine of the soul's immortality" (27:171). The Nietzscheism of this paragraph recalls the German philosopher's assertion, in the preface to *Beyond Good and Evil*, that Plato was the most beautiful but diseased flower of antiquity (566). Plato had poisoned the legacy of pagan thinkers with his doctrine of the soul's immortality and the attendant debasement of the senses. Christianity exported this outlook throughout the ancient world. The striving of consciousness to transcend the body's temporality demeaned life in the *saeculum*, turning it into "a bungled form of frenzied present." Neopaganism entailed reversing the millennial cast of Mediterranean societies, their eternity-oriented and present-denying universalism, and undoing the culture of death, which set limits on the capacity to experience the fullness of time.

When the elderly Pla expressed reservations about his capacity to undertake a neopagan regime of life – "The problem lies in finding out if I am capable of it" – he was not questioning if his physical condition would support some form of debauchery. He was wondering if he would have enough presence of spirit to counter two millennia and a half of religious denial of the senses. As he felt the approach of death, the decision to turn his gaze away from the Medusa to focus on the certainties of a dwindling present required an emotional strength that Pla was not sure of commanding. He subscribed to Paul Valéry's dictum that nothing is deeper than the skin ("L'idée fixe" 215),[9] but he was also part of a culture that, from earliest childhood, taught people to renounce the surface of life for the depth of the beyond. Another poet, Joan Maragall, had famously challenged God on the question of the senses in the beyond. In "Cant espiritual," he had asked: "With what other senses will you make me see this blue sky above the mountains, and the vast sea, and the sun which shines everywhere? Give me eternal peace in these senses and I shall wish for no other sky than this blue one" (176). But if Maragall asked God for eternal peace through the senses, it was because he knew that he could not reasonably expect it; that experiencing the world keeps the soul in motion; that there is no Faustian moment to which one can say: "Linger on, you are so beautiful!" (Goethe 57). That the only instant when time freezes is the instant of death.

Maragall wished to swap the static moment of perfection for a totality of such moments without exiting from the present: "He who to no moment said 'Linger!' save to the one that brought him death, I do not understand him, Lord, I who would like to arrest so many moments of each day and make them eternal in my heart ..." (176). Pla, on the

9 In *Notes disperses* he wrote: "Considering that the skin is the deepest thing in the human body, the incompatibility between skins is a sure fact. Incompatibility of skins is narcissism" (12:196).

contrary, never gave vent to metaphysical demands. He knew that to be alive is to be immersed in variation and movement, and that the contemplation of appearances is the thread that keeps consciousness attached to the world. Watching that same Mediterranean over which a pall of eternity had been hanging for millennia, he mused:

> For someone who is contemplative, motion rules the spirit, magnetizes sight, arouses an unconscious, blind, spontaneous attachment. For the contemplative person, it is like coming back to life, the flavour of the contrary. Movement engenders novelty and diversity. Diversity, siren of the world ... Mobility fascinates animals, makes them play with their own shadow's fugacity, live on their hope, the eye permanently open, the ear alert, in a state of wakefulness that blends with their own life. (27:172)

It is unclear how much Pla's neopaganism owed to Camus, a recognized contemporary source for an immanent religion of the senses. Pla certainly thought along the lines of the following excerpt from "Summer in Algiers":

> These measly and essential belongings, these relative truths are the only ones that move me. As for the others, the "ideal" truths, I do not have enough soul to understand them. Not that one must behave like an animal, but I find no meaning in the happiness of angels. I know simply that this sky will last longer than I. And what shall I call eternity except what will continue after my death? (*Noces* 61)

Not that he was indebted to Camus for his view of the Mediterranean as a space governed by limits. *Noucentisme* was, after all, a doctrine of definition and self-limitation, and the young Pla had come under its influence. But *Noucentisme* was lopsided in its worship of the goddess reason and its demonization of the Dionysian side of Mediterranean life: the joy of the senses, the interplay of the lesser divinities, the passions. So, he cast this deflection as a conflict between neopagan innocence of the senses and the bad eternity responsible for destroying beauty and afflicting nature on the Mediterranean shores.

In his commentary on *Cadaqués*, Miquel Pairolí pointed out the incongruence between the original edition and the version published in volume 27 of the Collected Works, *Un petit món del Pirineu* (A small world in the Pyrenees). The incongruence refers to an interpolated text of seventeen pages that was not part of the original. It is a short story about a young woman named Aurora who commits suicide after facing her family's and the village's rebuke for having an affair with a stranger. Pairolí was mystified by the inclusion of this narrative in a descriptive book. The text was in the manuscript that Pla submitted for the Collected Works and was titled "Mort d'Aurora" (Aurora's death), a detail that Pairolí interpreted as meaning that the short story was meant to remain autonomous within the volume, which contained two other unrelated books. Inexplicably, it was finally embedded in *Cadaqués* without the title. According to Pairolí, the ad hoc inclusion suggests a belated composition, probably in 1973, when Pla was preparing the volume for the Collected Works. The suggested date is quite possible, but the story's inclusion in *Cadaqués* is far from incongruent. Aurora's suicide was clearly an exemplum for Pla's theory of the Mediterranean curse, a vivid illustration of neopaganism tragically stillborn and of sin wrecking the glory of nature under an indifferent sky.

Pla points in this direction: "The destruction of a human body, so young, so well made, so beautiful, so attractive, is a terrible thing. Who realized it truly? Perhaps her father, who had spent so many hours dreaming the wonderful olive groves of these mountains" (27:197). In the story, the cosmic elements overpower the petty human will. The *mestral*, the imposing northwesterly wind, blows over Cadaqués while the villagers cower in their homes. "Six days of the bluest sky, empty and remote, who can endure them? The wind unravelled the memories related to Aurora's death. Oblivion covers everything – if I am not mistaken" (27:197). Who can endure the deepest blue, the emptiness of a remote transcendence? Is this not what Pla had in mind when he expressed misgivings about being able to convert to an honest neopaganism?

In 1974 Pla brought out another volume of his Collected Works, *Notes per a Sílvia* (Notes for Sílvia), which contained a poem about the death of Aurora:

> While Aurora lay dying,
> a glowing sun was rising.
> Everything seems like fiction to me.
> The blue swelling of the evening,
> the memories from the past and the memories
> of the imminence of pleasure – so uncertain, those!
> While Aurora lay dying,
> a glowing sun was rising.
> But Aurora is nothing – I think.
> She was a ghost of life. What more could we ask for? (26:448)

This poem is the twin of another included in the posthumous *Darrers escrits* (Last writings). Since that poem is cited in full on page 281, there is no need to reproduce it here. Found among Pla's last papers in the so-called death folder, that other poem was, according to Vergés, written shortly before Pla's death. But Arcadi Espada asserts that the poem was written more than a decade earlier, contemporaneously with those published in *Notes per a Sílvia* (46–7). He based his opinion on a comparison of the poem's handwriting with that of the other items in the folder (47). To the calligraphic proof we may add the thematic and tonal proximity between the two poems. One might ask, of course, why Pla did not include the second poem in the earlier volume, but an answer is not hard to find. He wrote two versions of an essentially identical poem and chose to publish the most economical one. This would be in character with his preference for simple, unassuming expression.

Baffled by the profusion of Auroras, Pairolí asked whether these poems referred to the Aurora featured in *Cadaqués* or to the Aurora with whom Pla maintained a correspondence well into old age. He concludes that they could not refer to the real-life Aurora who had lived in Buenos Aires but to the young suicide of the Cadaqués story. In the latter poem, as in the story, Pairolí observes, Pla bemoans the disappearance of a young, beautiful body and foregrounds the clash between spirit and matter (163). I believe that this very argument holds the clue to the identity between all these Auroras. The sarcasm about philosophical dualism in the poem from the "death folder" relates this text to Pla's allusion to neopaganism in the context of his obsession for A. "Down-to-earth but real neopaganism," he had called it then. That was in 1965. The real, earthly Aurora died in 1969. Pla wrote the poems and the story about the young suicide sometime before 1973. How likely is it that he would write impressive dirges about a non-existent woman shortly after the death of the only one for whom he had felt an irrepressible passion for a quarter of a century? Or is it rather the case that, reticent about his feelings, he projected his pain on a literary substitute, a young Aurora whose beautiful body he had once known and whose loss could only be assuaged through recourse to metaphysical cynicism? Did he not blame the real Aurora's departure on the rigid morality of a small town, which almost certainly had turned up their noses on Aurora for living with him out of wedlock? To erase his tracks, he placed the story not in L'Escala, where he had once lived with her, but in nearby Cadaqués. Even so, he situated Aurora's encounter with her seducer in Castelló d'Empúries, a small village in the vicinity of L'Escala. From the comments he made to the doorman of the Viena Hotel on the day she left for South America, it was evident that he considered her departure a tragic event. And this feeling could only grow in retrospect, when the past had set and become as unalterable as the slate of the terraces on the slopes overlooking the bay of Cadaqués. The desire to raise a lament against the destruction of happiness through infatuated morality would explain the insertion of the story in a previous text about a place where the natural and human scenarios clash with tragic results.

One more detail: Pla included the poem about Aurora's death in the series of poems that he called "of *retour d'âge*" (26:448). This decision suggests that in his mind the poem was interwoven with the senescent eroticism that he had channelled through his correspondence with Aurora Perea. If any doubts remain about the identity between the young body in the story and in the "death folder" poem with the actual Aurora's, these verses from the published version of the poem should lay them to rest:

> The blue swelling of the evening,
> the memories from the past and the memories
> of the imminence of pleasure – so uncertain, those! (26:448)

The blue swelling of the evening recalls the hard-to-endure "bluest sky, empty and remote" (27:197), which the northwest wind had cleared of memories after Aurora's death in *Cadaqués*. But here, in the verses, the memories are not about her death but about the past and about the expectation of pleasure remembered by the poet. Not memories of the pleasure itself (if any such there be), but of its expectation, as keen as Pla's anticipation of A.'s letters and their uncertain reward. It had all become like fiction, the young woman's seductive body a ghost of life, a pretext for the illusion that keeps life spinning in cycles beyond its provisional shapes. The perpetual rising of the sun god being the only eternity that an honest neopagan can be certain of. "What more can we ask for?"

11 Encroaching Death

The image of death was contracting like the diaphragm of a photographic lens being stopped down.

– Philippe Ariès, *The Hour of Our Death*

Reading Pla, one feels in the presence of someone inhabiting a two-fold cosmos. On one side are things, so-called reality; on the other, the words corresponding to those things. He writes, or pretends to write, as if everything could be said precisely and without circumlocution. What cannot be said in a direct, honest way either does not exist or is not worth saying. Obscurity, the deliberately artistic or philosophical expression of subjectivity, is for him a dishonest affair. Kierkegaard had asserted: "Everything subjective, which through its dialectical inwardness eludes a direct form of expression, is an essential secret" (*Concluding* 74). Pla would have added that it is a worthless secret, and its expression through the artistry of negative dialectic – such as Kierkegaard advocated – a disingenuous hoax.

He wrote about every conceivable thing, spurred on by an insatiable curiosity, intense social activity, and great sensitivity to detail. He managed to create a complete image of his country (so far as completion goes in the realm of circumstantial, or as Sartre might have said, situational consciousness). Catalonia – not the concept but its sensuous image – is Josep Pla's invention. He is the most omnivorous Catalan writer to date. In comparison, every other writer seems limited in scope. One turns to Pla for encyclopedic information of the quality and amenity that one does not find in academic historians. He is an inexhaustible source for the kind of information that can be found only in local histories, but then often in the dismal prose and lack of perspective typical of the guardians of local memory. When Scottie Ferguson in the film *Vertigo* wants to find out about a nineteenth-century woman named Carlotta Valdés, he asks his assistant about an authority on San Francisco history. When she mentions a professor at Berkeley, he replies, "not that kind of history. The small stuff! About people you never heard of!" Pla wrote about famous people, some of whom he had met, but he wrote a great deal about the small stuff, making people come alive in much the same way the ghost of Carlotta comes alive in Hitchcock's movie. He makes us feel in the presence of those people, local celebrities or simple acquaintances, that gave density to what would otherwise remain threadbare accounts of political or economic history.

Pla was not a specialist, just an observer, a man with his eyes permanently trained on reality and with a brain capable of processing the information. This is to say, capable of putting it through the grinder of his irony and the quarantine of his scepticism. He produces the impression of a complete writer; yet, among the flotsam and jetsam of his "human comedy," one theme is conspicuously under-represented, the theme of death. It is as if Pla, while listening to the variations and scales of life's music, had not perceived the silences. He seems to have fled the intellectual confrontation with life's finality and missed the cultural implications of this fact. But just as in a previous chapter I claim that amid the froth of Pla's journalism it is possible to discern a structured sensibility, I will argue here that Pla's vitalism was the reverse of a sober concern with death.

Xavier Pla conveys a different impression when he asserts that in *The Gray Notebook*, "little by little, page after page, death becomes the key concept of the entire journal" (*Josep Pla. Ficció autobiogràfica* 159). He repeats this idea in the preface to his edition of *El primer quadern gris*, where he considers "meaningful that his earliest reflections about literature take place so significantly under the sign of death" (ix). He bases this opinion on Pla's decision to start *The Gray Notebook* with a reference to the flu pandemic that devastated Europe in the fall of 1918. The epidemic forced the University of Barcelona to close, causing the young Pla to go home for a period of enforced leisure during which he decided to start a journal. In *Viatge a Catalunya*, first published in 1934, Pla had already related his earliest attempts at writing to the dread instilled in him by the flu pandemic. "It was probably the lucidity produced at times by the fear of death that made me see the marvel in front of me. […] One day, without knowing how it happened, I found myself with a pencil and a notebook in my hand. I started placing adjectives after each pine grove, each field, each piece of sea" (7:475). The older Pla certainly remembered having lived during this time in the grip of fear. In *Barcelona, una discussió entranyable* (Barcelona, a fond discussion), he recalled: "In that confused period between the closing stages of adolescence and the beginning of youth, which is the time of feverish sensuality, I was lucky to be intermittently swayed by the idea of death […] The obsession of death presented itself without mitigations, in a primitive, violent fashion" (3:313). In view of this obsession, common at that stage of adolescence when life suddenly unveils its limited horizons, it is remarkable that Pla introduced the subject of death so obliquely in his principal book. The original journal, the *Primer Quadern*, a mere notebook with entries intended for later elaboration, starts with this laconic phrase dated 13 October 1918: "At least now people are unanimous in Catalonia: we all have the flu" (4). And two days later, mentioning the funeral of an old neighbour who had died from alcohol abuse, he adds: "These days I have attended several funerals and I feel that death moves me less and less. It would be most convenient if no one else died for now" (4). A correction in the manuscript shows the reason Pla hopes for a reprieve of death: he does not want to go to more funerals (4).

Wishing to strike a cynical note, the young Pla treated death as merely a disruption, rather than something capable of stirring his emotions. The reference to his neighbour's funeral and his own blasé response to death have disappeared from *The Gray Notebook*, which Pla brought out when he was sixty-nine years old. In this elaborated text, Pla split the incipit of the original notebook into two separate entries. Advancing the date from 13 October 13 to 8 March, so as to make it coincide with his birthday, he begins the book with the news that the university has closed on account of the flu. There is, however, no mention of death. Reporting the infection at the beginning of *The Gray Notebook* merely serves to establish his presence at home before the end of the academic term and his provisional status as an idle student (1:87). Only a few days and many pages later, on 14 March, he retrieves almost verbatim the notebook's first entry: "Now, finally, it's a real joy to live in Catalonia. That's unanimous. Everybody agrees. Inevitably we all have, have had, or will have influenza" (1:104). But still no suggestion of death, unless we assume that Pla expected readers to remember that the influenza pandemic of 1918–19 was one of the deadliest on record, having caused between fifty and one hundred million deaths worldwide. Whatever one thinks about this point, Pla's removal of the allusion to the high rate of deaths from the published journal bespeaks a decision *not* to engage the subject overtly.

On the face of this reticence, Pla would appear to confirm Philippe Ariès's thesis that in the twentieth century Western society banished death (560). During this time, said Ariès, death ceased to be a public event subject to rituals intended to heal the community and to facilitate the work of mourning for the bereaved. Gradually it became a private affair and its handling was turned over to professionals, releasing family and relatives from their secular involvement in the final-stages and post-mortem care of the dying. And certainly, Pla's pronouncements on death are rare in his work. Thus, it is above all the meaning of his reserve on this subject that needs to be analysed for clues not only to his attitude on the ultimate question but also to what it tells us about the status of death in the second half of the century.

Of the thousands of pages Pla published during his lifetime, few deal explicitly with death. To be sure, characters die in his narratives. Roby, in the story "Roby i la deflació" ("Roby or Deflation"), or Tintorer, in "El moribund intermitent" ("Intermittently Moribund"), both from the trilogy "El cercle de Berlín" ("The Berlin Circle"), included in *La vida amarga* (*Life Embitters*),[10] are cases in point. And there are, needless to say, allusions to people passing away or having died in his biographical portraits and historical accounts. But none of this amounts to a confrontation with death in any depth. If one leaves aside the story "Un mort a Barcelona" (Death in Barcelona), from the same volume (6:69–126), as dealing not really with death but with the entanglements, jealousies, and petty interests in a boarding house, the yield is rather meagre. Only one brief article from 1973, appropriately entitled "La mort" (Death), is devoted explicitly to the subject. It recounts a conversation with a doctor. "It appears – says the doctor – that life is a circumstantial, fleeting phenomenon, a mere distraction of nature, and that death is the return to a state of universal equilibrium, to which everything inexorably gravitates" (36:497–8). In this professionally detached opinion, it is not difficult to recognize the influence of Freud, who, in *Beyond the Pleasure Principle*, claimed that life strives to return

10 Peter Bush has translated the title of this volume as *Life Embitters*. "The bitter life" is perhaps more literal. The original permits both translations, depending on whether one reads "amarga" as verb or adjective. To a native speaker, the former is less intuitive, since "life" is more often the object than the subject of "embitter." I have always read the book's title as Pla's intended contradiction of the shibboleth "the sweet life."

to its previous inorganic state. In the same article, a friend asks Pla to accompany him to a doctor's office to pay for the care received after a severe car accident. At the office, the friend blames the doctor for reviving him after he had already crossed death's threshold and stepped into a world that was "so languishingly pleasurable!" (36:501).

"Languishingly" recalls the state of no tension that Freud considered the ultimate goal of every living substance. Higher forms of life, says Freud, are unities that have developed complicated and circuitous paths to return to the inanimate state. Curiously, desire – which is usually considered life enhancing – is a polymorphic disguise for the basic instinct and thus a complicated way of furthering organic dissolution. Freud explains these convoluted detours as the result of repression: the backward path that leads to complete satisfaction is blocked by the repressions built into social life. In the scenario created or reported by Pla, the patient blames the doctor for impeding the total satisfaction that only death can provide and reacts aggressively to the frustration of that goal. Pla is aware that a taboo has been violated. That is why he adds: "We left without taking leave, because among the three of us an atmosphere was produced that resembled that which condenses when the elemental sense of shame is broken" (36:501). Something was revealed that wasn't meant to be. As a result, society's idea of health as the cornerstone of happiness foundered and the intrinsic "sickness" of the will was exposed. Exposure of the "sickly" will may well be what the contemporary "banishment of death" is meant to hide. The doctor is speechless when his patient knocks the bottom out of the fiction on which his social role depends. The patient remains silent because he knows that life's purpose is not its own maintenance but its extinction. And Pla is embarrassed at having to adjudicate between the irreconcilable claims of Eros and Thanatos.

Pla is embarrassed but curious too. "I would have loved, positively loved, to get my friend to explain in some detail what he felt before, just before the injection. But I was unable to bring him out of his silence" (36:501). If pleasure is defined, with Freud, as the relief of accumulated tension, then Pla's curiosity about the state of utter relief goes as far as he ever did in confessing any metaphysical curiosity. For the most part, he looked on death with the ideological poverty that Albert Camus attributed to the natives of the Mediterranean shores: "We don't know how to discuss death or colours" (*Noces* 37). Once, during the TV interview, Joaquín Soler Serrano asked Pla if he believed in the existence of God. The writer replied that, if we knew about that, all our problems would be resolved. Two years earlier, in *Notes per a Sílvia*, published when Pla was seventy-seven, he had written, "God is the unattainable future" (26:447). A future beyond reach amounts to an inapprehensible experience of time.

Our lives are mutable because they are not grounded in anything timeless. And faith, Kierkegaard's paradoxical anchor in self-motivated certainty, was too passionate a proposition for the unromantic Pla, who wrote in *The Gray Notebook*: "thinking about it soberly, the only moment in life when it must be impossible to deny the existence of Providence must be the instant of death" (1:136). His publisher, Josep Vergés, interested in ranging Pla in orthodox Catholicism, is unconvincing in his efforts to gather evidence of religious sentiment (45:98–100). It does not amount to much: a passage from *The Gray Notebook* on the inevitability of sin (which is strongly reminiscent of Kierkegaard) and the fact that Pla accepted the last rites. But then, he did so on condition that they be administered by the abbot of Poblet, the twelfth-century Cistercian monastery and burial place of the Catalan kings. Finally, the abbot anointed him, ceremonially assisted by hooded monks.

Was Pla indulging in patriotic grandiloquence or was he being ironic to the very end? At the close of the sullen verses included in *Notes per a Sílvia*, he inscribed the words "Laus Deo" (Praise be to God). But, as if to deny any devotional intention, an ambiguous statement, which could be taken for a disclaimer, preceded those words: "In this country, on the last page of poetry books, people often write Laus Deo. I do so too, for the sake of discipline" (26:448). There is irony in this compliance, as there is in his acceptance of the last rites. Observance of religious custom – exceedingly rare for Pla – proves nothing more than his enduring reverence for social institutions. It would be rash to mistake his thespian concession to tradition for genuine devotion. Years earlier he had described the Sicilian cult of death, remarking on its poetic, grandiloquent style without any trace of sentimentality. The sheer materialism of Mediterranean mortuary rites and the scenes of desolation they comprise, he speculates in "Notes sobre Sicília," are "a dramatic complaint against the belief that death is the ascent to a world different from this one" (15:344). In the social organization of the transit, Pla recognized an ancient form of behaviour surviving with accretions and modifications the ebb and flow of civilizations. The mildness of the sky and the air, the quality of the light and the smiling sea, the smooth, amiable shape of the land, everything conspired to arouse a vivid, concrete life of the imagination. Death could only be envisioned as continuation of earthly existence, and this regret of the feast of the senses precipitated the belief in a bodily afterlife:

> Such inner tension, such disconsolate wailing in the face of death, which ancient Mediterranean civilization gave rise to, created the consoling dogma of the ressurrection of the flesh, which is a truth of Holy Mother Church. Those great lords of Palermo who had themselves transported to the cemetery in a coach as if they were still alive, did it to prove that they were marvellously prepared for the day when the trumpet shall sound. (15:345)

Church dogma, specifically Paul's insistence on the centrality of bodily resurrection to the Christian faith, is presented as a late variation on a millennial attachment to this world. Pla neither affirms nor denies this belief, but in the face of such relativism, can it be maintained that his demand for the exequies of a Catalan king was any different from the lords of Palermo having their corpses arranged so as to drive their coaches to the graveyard? Vergés pushed his case when he intimated that Pla may have played a comedy all his life, hiding his religious faith under a veneer of materialism, rationalism, and indifference (45:99). But if Pla played a comedy, why assume that the performance stopped when it suited social convenience?

It seems more sensible to compare his attitude to that of Montaigne, his chief literary reference and a model for his literary persona. Montaigne lived and died formally a Catholic. By his deathbed stood a priest. He abhorred disturbance and did not believe in purchasing improvement with revolt. For this reason he did not sympathize with the Huguenots. Pla was sceptical of paradise in general and averse to any paradise located at the far end of revolution. He loathed the attacks on churches, not out of devotion to the cross but because the Catholic Church was heir to the Romanization that had structured Catalonia physically, legally, and practically. In *Escrits empordanesos*, he wrote about the numerous Romanesque churches built in Carolingian times. He explains that a certain Gotmar, Bishop of Girona, consecrated the new places of worship. "Before this man," says Pla, "I take off my hat" (38:72). He saw Gotmar's work as initiating the necessary articulation of the territory.

Erich Auerbach said of the *Essais* that they are totally un-Christian, because they treat death as if there was no redemption and no immortality. His remark apropos Montaigne, that one cannot imagine him at prayer, befits Pla, as does the observation that what he writes about religion are the comments of a decent, tactful person, not of a believer (28). In Pla's case, as in Montaigne's, one finds a recurrent expression of uncertainty and of the provisional nature of knowledge. For instance, the first paragraph of

Notes del capvesprol reads as follows: "To believe is much more comfortable and easier than learning, than knowing. Verification of this fact could lead us to think that religious conceptions are permanent, at all levels" (35:11). Starting a book of old age with this statement leaves little doubt about Pla's position on the matter of faith. According to him, mental laziness accounts for the popularity of religion. This may not be the last word of a sceptic, of course. His irony vis-à-vis dogmatism of all kinds, including the modern faith in science, may jar with his emphasis in judging certain attitudes, but it is always an expression of his refusal to step outside the bounds of his subjective certainty. In his work religion finds a place as an element of society, never as piety or metaphysical concern. His subject matter is at all times the observable facts of life and of death.

An explicit reflection on the reasons advanced for God's existence is found in the original *Gray Notebook*, the so-called *Primer quadern gris*. On pages 95–7 of the manuscipt he says that he has been thinking about God for three hours and observes that on this matter one can propose various hypotheses corresponding to different viewpoints. God can be considered as a working hypothesis, a premise that permits initiating and maintaining an argument. Or as a metaphysical hypothesis, a cause necessitated by logic, such as the watchmaker implied by the mechanism of the watch. One may also consider God as an intervening force responsible for all that occurs, as Providence. Finally, God can be identified with the infinity of matter, or energy, as in Pantheism. As for himself, Pla declares that he lacks all sensibility to conceive God (194). He raises the issue of the contradiction between Providence and suffering, disease, inequality, misfortune, dissatisfaction, melancholy. The explanation of humanity's Fall and original sin, he says, would be perfect if animals and all sensitive life in general were not also subject to the same misery and decay as humans, and wonders if the theory of original sin must be expanded to include cats and dogs, tomato plants and green beans (196). "Whosoever does not have religion must suffer from syphilis in order not to look ridiculous" (196).

The Pla who wrote these propositions in 1918 does not come through as a religious transvestite. And although these passages were left out of the edition of *The Gray Notebook* published forty-eight years later, the older man's discretion does not prove his conversion. In fact, the evidence points the other way. In an interview with Salvador Pániker the year before, when Pla was sixty-eight, he replied to the query about his religious attitude with his usual scepticism:

– Up till now I have no religious sensibility. I feel like any other Mediterranean person, and you know that we Mediterraneans have no religious sensibility. We believe that life is an adventure, often unpleasant, situated between an initial nothingness and a final nothingness. This phrase is silly, but it is an immortal phrase. We use religion when we are sick and when we are about to die. I don't know why. (Pániker 3)

In the above-mentioned article, "La Mort," Pla discovered the overlap between death and desire. If only death can fully satisfy desire by consuming it, it follows that desiring, even when redirected to substitutes that will always disappoint, leads the organism ever farther on the path of regression. Pla believed that thoughtlessness preserved organic life: "Faith! To have faith! What best preserves the human body is inanity pure and simple" (44:622). Mindlessness, absence of care, places the body on the vegetative state. Pla is, of course, not speaking about happiness but about duration. And duration may be long-lived, carry on, and hold out, but it inevitably comes to an end. Pla's expletive about faith, a glaring cry of despair over the undeniable fact of physical deterioration, stems from a keen awareness of the incongruity between mind and eternity.

Death is the finality of life but it is not part of life. It is exterior to life and thus inconceivable except as the spectacle of the death of others. In relation to death things stand as with Achilles and the tortoise. By means of this paradox Zeno demonstrated the logical inconsistency of completing an action that has no conclusive moment and thus opens up an infinite series of approximations. Achilles cannot catch up with the tortoise, despite the fact that with every stride he reduces the distance between the two. This is because at every segment of the race, the tortoise advances simultaneously, resetting Achilles's goal at no matter what infinitesimal difference. As a result of the slippage, repeated an infinite number of times, the target cannot be comprehended in the segment in which Achilles would catch up. Death is that slippery target for the understanding, and Pla observes that although old age is death-like, death itself remains beyond its intellectual grasp: "The old man is nearly dead, but he's still alive" (44:586).

The approximation of death, biologically intuited or statistically calculated, does not change the terms of the paradox. Until death is, it is nothing, and as nothing it cannot displace any volume of experience. This means, in effect, that death constantly recedes from consciousness. In Pla this paradox takes the form of the absence of thoughts about death despite the abundance of death occurring during his lifetime. Only in the articles written in old age does death make a reflected appearance, as if Pla were closer to catching the tortoise. And yet, the thing itself slips away, opening a gap between the pursuing consciousness and the pursued finality. Such a gap cannot be spanned; it reopens as soon as it is on the point of closing, and will reopen time and again until death is and Pla is not: "The inevitable proximity of death, if one has a minimal capacity for observation, is absolutely certain, but this proximity is systematically rejected. Old age is a genuine way of living, like any other, although it consists of nothing more than dragging on for as long as the rope – or the string – holds" (44:585). The semantic false step in the choice of verb, "holds," where logic required "breaks," is an obvious case of inadvertent censoring of the finality of death. Something snaps and gives way, and the two parts cannot be rejoined. No mediation, certainly no rational mediation, can do the trick. This rejection of the irreparable from consciousness means nothing less than the absolute, undialectical distinction between life and death, one that cannot be mediated, because life asserts itself relentlessly, "pulling the string" until the Parcae cut the thread. Until, that is, something external annuls the slippage and undoes the paradox.

But even the state of consciousness that affirms life against the backdrop of adjoining death turns out to be uncertain. In his last article, significantly titled "Més enllà" (Beyond), Pla writes: "In this world, even old age is uncertain, but the day will come when it will be over. We will die, go down, and oblivion will cover all, as it always has" (44:587). The phrase "in this world" suggests the existence of other possible worlds and the implicit belief in a beyond. It replaces, but also replicates, Pla's more frequent use of the locution "in this country" as a spatial circumscription of the writer's experience. Both are popular apothegms that quickly establish a tacit understanding of the intended meaning. Coud Pla be using the popular phrase "in this world" free of metaphysical implications? It is possible. As possible as the fact that he is revealing a dimension of his spirit previously entrusted to silence.

The article follows up with a brief dialogue in which a friend says to him: "I'd like to tell you something. Would you believe that in the course of my life I have never thought about what you call to go down, that is, about death? On the other hand, no one has talked to me about it, do you understand?" Pla comments: "It's a typical fact everywhere. It's very rare that someone thinks about the beyond, about death. If someone thinks about it, the reserve is absolute. And even more rare is to begin a dialogue about it. Everyone, or nearly everyone, wants to live – this is the truth" (44:591).

Utter reserve with regard to the most universal experience, personal extinction, confirms Philippe Ariès's thesis about the privatization of death and its banishment from public space in the twentieth century. It also suggests that the scarcity of reflection on this universal event transforms death into an external and utterly alien phenomenon. Expelled from the inner self-relation of the subject, death becomes a mute and incomprehensible object. Lack of thought and lack of talk, the forms taken by the social repression of death, rob it of its image. Even the corpse, starved of meaning, becomes blurry and fades from memory.

In *L'herència* (The inheritance), one of Pla's rare narrative works, he tells the story of an office clerk who is favoured in the will of an aunt whom he hardly remembers. To take care of the formalities, he travels to the village in time for the burial and on the way is assaulted by the thought that he has no ready image of death. "I did not remember having seen a dead person either by chance or in the street. I had forgotten the corpses of my parents through sheer inertia. Inertia has a huge power over memory. Despite living in a period during which the number of dead used in conversation was fabulous – revolutions, wars, accidents, etc. – the corpse as such was for me a totally unprecedented image" (23:16).

Pla describes society's repulsion of natural, ordinary death, to the point of blurring its image. Death is talked about as an extraordinary, accidental, or eye-catching phenomenon, part of the spectacle of world history that one observes at a distance from an impossible outside. Only abstract death has social currency and is discussed as collateral damage of world events that one comes to know through the press or from history books. Never is it discussed in the concreteness of the individual dead, the cadaver. The latter is shrouded in an image specific to itself, if one accepts the romantic presupposition of a death all of one's own. It is this image that, according to Robert Harrison, the funeral rites assist in removing from the corpse, so that the survivors can begin to detach themselves from the dead by committing their images to the imagination (148). But what happens when not enough force of imagination is available to retain the image? Inertia, resistance to change, is the antithesis of life, which is permanent becoming. Inertness is the same as deadness: permanent stasis in a given condition. Paradoxically, in the clerk's reflection, inertia, a force that weighs on memory, turns not against life but against death, or rather against the memory of death, of what death looks like. Death covers itself with a sense of shame; it secretes a sort of modesty around the corpse, screening it by means of the image. But as the clerk fails to appropriate it, he thwarts the ritual exchange of the body for its symbol. As a consequence, the experience of death slips from his mind, and a new decease presents him with an unprecedented image.

That the aspect of death is unprecedented may come as a surprise, given the profusion of deaths that the clerk recalls from conversations about the great upheavals of the twentieth century. But its irruption has the effect of casting a different light on existence, as if a piece that had been missing were unexpectedly found but it turned out not to fit and one had to scramble the entire puzzle. Elsewhere, apropos the demise of the painter Marià Llavanera, Pla describes the experience of death as a personal revelation. "The death of that man made a great impression on me. Before this death I was a blissful fool, of the bumpkin sort. After the burial, I became a different thing" (44:506). This is a strange confession for someone who, as a young journalist working for *Las Noticias,* was assigned to the crimes, accidents, and disasters section. This was during the years of class warfare in Barcelona, and Pla saw a good number of corpses within hours or even minutes of the assassination. But these violent deaths seem to have left the young Pla relatively indifferent. They were part of the urban landscape, a prelude to the revolution that would eventually break out, but hardly conveyed the sense of irretrievable loss lurking at the core of life.

Llavanera's death was different. Through its contact, Pla experienced something like a rebirth. Death, meaningfully perceived for the first time, revolutionized his existence. The blissful foolishness of a rural youth, as Pla deprecatingly described his previous self, stood for the naiveté of natural man. Its interruption by the introjection of the consciousness of death amounted to discovering one's own mortality, the presence of death as the immanent condition of living. In this enlightenment through death there is a faint intimation of Heidegger's being-towards-death and of its conscious acceptance as the touchstone of authentic existence. Although it is unlikely that Pla read Heidegger to any meaningful extent, he mentions him as the foremost exponent of existential philosophy, adding that this philosophy, which emerged "from peasant feet" and replaced the philosophy of essence, was the only contemporary philosophy. "Today there is no other," he said (44:519). In all likelihood, Pla was seduced by the idea that the twentieth-century's dominant philosophy arose "from peasant feet," recognizing a certain parentage to his own peasant extraction. But when he describes existentialism as a "philosophy with peasant feet," he does not have Heidegger or his Black Forest retreat in mind, but the somewhat more urban Kierkegaard, on account of Copenhagen's provincialism in the nineteenth century.

Pla shared the Dane's rejection of Hegel's axiom of history's rationality, a belief that, in its Marxist and Bakuninist reformulations, had blasted away the world of Pla's youth with an explosion of instinctual blindness. In old age, Pla restated his lifelong conviction that uncontrollable forces are in charge of human destiny. "Nature is irrational, history is irrational, and politics is irrational; the relation between men and women is irrational. It all depends on fortune or chance. Everything turns out well or badly depending on chance. Yet, according to Aristotle, mankind is rational. You decide ..." (44:616). Chance and fortune are the same pagan divinity, Tyche or Fortuna, one of the Moirai, the Fates. Pla is far from the Christian belief in the transcendent management of the world. If there is a divinity ordering human affairs, it is an immanent one, not subject to the Hegelian laws of world history but acting wilfully in inscrutable ways. He expressed the same idea in response to the question whether he was for or against the Church:

> – Mr Pla, are you in favour of the clergy?
>
> – Yes, sir. I am in favour of the clergy, but sometimes I am not. I have great respect for our Church. It has existed for centuries ... Where would our country be without all the things the Church has built? I never liked vulgarity. However, to speak generically is very difficult. What happens at any moment are the details, the situations, that which is in front of us. [...]
>
> – Mr Pla, are you anticlerical?
>
> – Sometimes no, sometimes yes ... It depends on what I just told you ... on what is in front of me. What I find hard to believe is that man is always a rational animal. Aristotle was too kind. (44:628)

What this imaginary interlocutor asks Pla is not whether he believes in God, or in the afterlife, but how he feels about the clergy. Pla's protestation of respect for the Church as a historical and socializing institution is, from the religious viewpoint, non-committal. It has no more meaning than honouring the crown, property registries, or banks, all pillars of social stability. In the interview with Soler Serrano, Pla says that the Church is a bureaucratic institution that performs three necessary functions: recording births, marriages, and deaths. Then he adds, "in the face of death, I take off my hat" (*Josep Pla A Fondo*). Death is the truly solemn reality, the Church merely a useful establishment for the bookkeeping of the biologically determining facts. In the previous dialogue about the clergy, it would be wrong to attribute his conditional reply to ambiguity or hedging. He insists on withholding abstract opinions, the kind of blanket statements that make unconscious fanatics of most people. Instead, he defers to the authority of the senses, the only witnesses he trusts. His reply does not prove that Pla was an atheist or a materialist, since it leaves room for a truth that can be apprehended through a pure act of consciousness. However, this act requires the decision that Kierkegaard called the leap. And while the rebuttal of rationalism as a defining human trait seems to point to the possibility of just such a passionate move, Pla's scepticism militates against it. He is much closer to the post-Cartesian sobriety of Camus than to the puritanical conscience of the lofty Dane, haunted by the exaction of earthly sacrifice in the flame of a single-minded love of the eternal.

When he describes the feeling of the absurd at the beginning of *Le mythe de Sisyphe* (*The Myth of Sisyphus*), Camus says that what counts is not so much the evidence of man's mortality per se as the consequences that each person derives from it. Few people draw the extreme conclusion from that evidence; most live in the self-deception of what we imagine we know rather than within the limits of what we really know (33). And what is it that we know with absolute certainty? Not the Cartesian "I," says Camus. "If I try to capture this 'I' of which I am certain, if I try to define and summarize it, it is no more than water running through my fingers. I can sketch one after another all the faces that it assumes, and all those that have been given to it: this education, this origin, this eagerness or these silences, this greatness or this baseness. But one does not add up faces" (34). One is forced to choose between a description that is certain and hypotheses that purport to teach, but which are uncertain (36). The protagonist of his best-known novel, Mersault, is charged with atheism and lack of principles when he is merely one of those few who draw the extreme consequences from the evidence presented to their senses. He refuses Kierkegaard's leap into the unknown as a betrayal of his miserable certainty within the narrow space of his cell (a metaphor for the death sentence hanging over every human consciousness).

Pla also refused to cross the line dividing certainty from hypothesis. He conceded ontological value only to phenomena that conflate instinctual satisfaction with the reality principle. He can speak of "a fish fry of absolute reality" (44:617), because it is not the product of wishful thinking but of the art of fishing and the effort to apply it, which Pla described with gusto in several of his books and in old age reaffirmed as an indubitable possession of his spirit. He shared the French writer's love of the sensuous presence of nature. Camus often attributed the passionate traits of his personality to his "Spanish" descent, embodied in the memory of his stern grandmother, who still spoke the Minorcan dialect of Catalan with her sister, an idiom that Camus – too French to recognize the linguistic dignity of a non-state language – calls "le patois mahonnais" in his autobiographical novel *Le premier homme* (88). Ironically, Camus, who felt keenly about the Spanish Civil War and denounced the Franco regime, never expressed the slightest concern about the persecution of his grandmother's tongue, whereas Pla – an enemy of the revolution and a circumstantial adherent of the Franco reaction – devoted his life to preserving and dignifying that language. Yet both delighted in the perception of the actual. "The perception of an angel or a god has no sense for me," Camus declares in *Le mythe de Sisyphe* (66–7). Pla would have agreed. Still another similarity reconciles the Catalan and the Algerian authors, otherwise so dissimilar: a somatic consciousness that could manage without the illusions of transcendence.

A few hours before Mersault's execution, the prison chaplain asks him how he envisions the other life. Mersault shouts: "A life where I could remember this one" (*L'étranger* 168). Then he asks the priest to leave. Mersault knows that he will be immediately forgotten by the world, but in the time that remains he does not wish to forget the life he knows, the only life of which he can be certain because it has burned itself into his consciousness. Similarly, Pla refused to embellish death with romantic notions of sublimity. In April 1981, days before dying, he told the son of his editor: "Here, touch my arm, it's all bones. Death is like this" (45:126).

Like Mersault's, Pla's idea of an afterlife was contingent on memory. He knew that the wish for total recall, for experiencing it all over again, was of the order of utopia. In one of his very last notes, he regrets the impotence of memory: "I have spent half of my life thinking about memory; it is the one thing that matters in life. To have memory! Easier said than done!" (44:631). A perfect memory is a divine attribute, and Pla admitted the limitations of human consciousness. Desire for memory, a variant of the yearning for eternity, was the mainspring of his writing: "The days are so short, everything flies away! Memory is the essence of life, the highest thing, especially if coupled to accounting! Memory is so important that it tends irrevocably to be written!" (44:632). Memory was for Pla the sole guarantee of order in an irrational universe. Man is perhaps not absurd, but he confronts the absurd constantly and inescapably. This is to say that he is the measure of the absurd, that the absurd is nothing but the incommensurability between his fleetingness and the *longue durée* of the natural forces.

On 29 November 1980, during the last autumn of his life, Pla reflected on the perennial struggle of the winds at the climatic crossroads that was his region. "The combat of these winds has been going on for thousands of years. It's not a struggle. It's irrational and brutish Nature. We must be patient. There is no other way" (44:615). There is no sense in cosmic phenomena. It is the same inconmensurate Nature that pits life against death in eternal oscillation without purpose or respite. From the viewpoint of a consciousness seeking a reason or even minimal intelligibility, the spectacle is absurd. It is also tragic. It enfolds the human speck of lucidity in its midst and hurls it to its annihilation before it can obtain a sense of order, method, or meaning. It is, in short, nothing but blind repetition. Contrasted with the millennial recurrence of the cosmic gigantomachy, the rush to extinction that was his own life revealed to Pla the inadequacy of language, that is, of consciousness, in the face of the irrational: "Our language is precarious, thin. I must use the word 'hatred' – a purely human term – to signify the eternal battle fought, in this country, between the north and the south winds" (44:615).

Although it is not possible to escape the absurd, one can at least dignify it. This is Sisyphus's stance, as he descends yet again to take up the task that he can never complete. This is the hour of consciousness, says Camus, and in the consciousness of his torment without end, Sisyphus is superior to his destiny (163). Pla also renewed ceaselessly, and to the end of his life, the task of collecting materials for a complete memory. He did it in full awareness of the hopelessness of the goal. Memory, the highest thing there is when coupled with accounting, he said. How does the accounting come into play? Quite simply, accounting is the management of memory. Its answerability. It selects the relevant information and brings it to bear on decisions. Memory, subject to accounting, is justice itself. "Memory is inseparable from justice. In the world we live in, absurd things are constantly happening" (44:632).

And most absurd of all is the striving after justice that condemns us to a futile, ever recommenced work of memory. Camus chose Sisyphus as representative of absurd man, a being condemned to exert himself without finishing anything. Says Camus: "It is the price one has to pay for the passions of this earth" (162). Summing up his life, Pla saw nothing but years of obedience to the iron law of repetition. He had been pushing up the slope a mass of articles that added up to a feeling of shame, inadequacy, and incompleteness. "Now I am nearly eighty-four years old. I have worked as a journalist more than sixty years. I have done what I was told. The amount of papers I had to send make me ashamed of myself" (44:621).

Since John Locke, memory has been the seat of identity. To be sure, the Christian understanding of eternity was also based on memory. Images of past life anchored the soul to its eternal torment, as in Dante's *Inferno*. Or they melted away in the heat of eternal love, as in *Paradiso*. Loving life passionately was typified as a sin by Saint Bernard, who called those enamoured of this world *avari*. *Avaritia* was not only or even primarily the love of riches but attachment to this world and what it contains, the *temporalia*. Memory was the attachment, the lime that glued the sinner through sensual representation or repetition of momentary enjoyment. Pla uses the term "avarice" in the modern sense of a desire to accumulate wealth, but he suitably relates it to the illusion of duration, as if life could be prolonged indefinitely by the enhancement of material fortune.

In answer to the question why avarice is a passion that tends to develop in old age, he considers: "At this age we are biologically dominated by an illusion that makes us believe in our permanence and endlessness. This illusion governs us, and in spite of being so close to the ending line, it makes us perpetrate all the acts through which the urge to go on living manifests itself" (36:129). The obsession to live forever goads the old person to provide beyond the natural life expectancy. Such passion to secure life by clinging to its material conditions eclipses the imminence of death and its attendant fears. It is an instinctual substitution of the mediate for the immediate. This irrational self-delusion, says Pla, is an admirable ruse of the vital impulse. Physical decline steeped in thoughts about death would be intolerable. Luckily, as soon as the organism begins to decline, the expectation of the end is lifted. There is no reprieve, of course, but a happy oblivion of the execution of the sentence. In this phenomenon Pla identifies an argument in favour of philosophical dualism, of the split between spirit and matter (36:128).

Affirmation of dualism suggests the presence of a hidden dimension in Pla's oeuvre. If the observing consciousness is engrossed in the spectacle of the world and in a language that was developed in order to socialize the experience, then that language acts as a fence, keeping the spiritual off limits. Pla, a brilliant writer and a sparkling conversationalist, seemed to adhere to Wittgenstein's proposition 4.002 in the *Tractatus*, which holds that "Colloquial language is a part of the human organism and is not less complicated than it." Speaking and writing are vital functions, like breathing and digesting; as such they cannot deal with the antithesis of life, with death, of which they are the obverse. If dualism holds up, and Pla believed that death furnishes incontrovertible proof thereof, then language and thought stand for the same split as body and spirit. Proposition 4.002 continues: "Language disguises the thought; so that from the external form of the clothes one cannot infer the form of the thought they clothe, because the external form of the clothes is constructed with quite another object than to let the form of the body be recognized. The silent adjustments to understand colloquial language are enormously complicated" (63). Here the dualism of body and spirit takes the form of the language/thought distinction, but not in such a way that language is the proximate, imperfect embodiment of thought, one that can be made more precise to produce an increasingly better fit. On the contrary, language comes into play for an entirely different purpose than revealing thought. That purpose, whatever its other determinations, includes the concealment of thought.

Pla admitted that his literature had a secret intention, but then proceeded to reveal it, or pretended to do so. As revealed by him, this secret purpose was rather overt, even unexceptional: to produce an eminently readable literature and facilitate the popular reimmersion in the Catalan language, which had fallen on hard times. But he also claimed not to be part of a coterie in favour of facile writing (44:287). We would do well not to take Pla at face value. He could be sublimating necessity into purpose, law into will. It is possible, indeed quite likely, that this so-called secret purpose was conceived retroactively, coming after the fact of a language already shaped by lifelong adaptation to the journalistic requirement of clarity. Journalism imposes censorship of style before it imposes the more circumstantial forms of censorship. After a lifetime of this kind of writing, Pla confused teleology with purpose. The secret of his literature, of his obsession with writing, was not language but something equally primordial: the thought that animated his search for words, for the adjective, to clothe and disguise his naked Being. In Eden God gave Adam the power to name all the animals, gave him the repertory of substantives, but refrained from giving the adjectives, the qualifiers that modify, vary, enhance, and distort the forthright determination of "substances." The noun is the given; adjectives are the supplement, the creative, enhancing power of language. Finding the adjective, tweaking language to regain the direct vision of paradise, is a form of labour, hard labour, which supervened to Adam after he discovered his essential lack in his nakedness. That lack, that partiality of Being, that interfering of consciousness and splitting of experience, is another name for the negative work of the spirit coming to face itself in the disclosure of one's own mortality. This awareness is what we call thought, and because thought shies away in the pre- or proto-linguistic depth of conscience, where the call "where are you hiding?" resounds, it cannot be truly disclosed in language. It must be exposed obliquely, by approximation, coming upon it noiselessly and pouncing on it in one fell swoop of intuition.

In Pla there is a Wittgensteinian conviction that "everything that can be said, can be said clearly" and that "everything that can be thought at all can be thought clearly" (*Tractatus* 4.116). But between the thinking and the saying there is a link that cannot be represented in words. Thought is reflected in language and is thus not of language. "That which mirrors itself in language, we cannot express by language," says Wittgenstein (4.121). Which is not to say that it does not exist. Only that it belongs to the sphere of the unspeakable, a sphere that Pla, having no metaphysical inclination and no patience with mysticism, prudently left alone.

But the fact is that we will never discover an author's intimate thought only by reading. Interpretation is an infinite and ultimately futile task. The elements of his spiritual activity remain concealed, perhaps even to himself. It is not a question of depth – Pla often asserted the primacy of surfaces – but of incommensurability. Language may be animated by thought but it is not itself thought. Like the soul, which the early anatomists were unable to locate in the body, thought eludes the analytics of language, which, as part of the organism, as a projection of sight, sound, feeling, and taste – the basic components of Pla's descriptions – will decay in time and die a cultural death. Pla had completely shaken off the romantic myth of literary immortality.

Writing, as much as living, of which it is a pale modality, is a transitional form of becoming, a falling from thought into the ontical disclosure of Being (to use Heideggerian jargon). It actualizes (and thus limits) the possibility of Being as Being-there, opening the gateway not to immortality but to supersession. It shows the remnant of untapped possibilities in the forward movement of becoming:

> – So, you do not believe in anything, not even your own literature?
>
> – That's what I least believe in. If thirty years after my demise people still talk about or read my literature, it will be a curious thing. No more than curious. For what reason should I believe in it? It is all stories about the present, in other words, made up stories …
>
> – What you say is quite different from what people in this profession assert … They believe in their immortality.
>
> – I believe the opposite. I believe in my absolute mortality. I have said and written it many times. Everything I have written, which is vulgar, insignificant, but one might say fair, is only to stimulate those who come after me to do it better. (44:336)

Pla's awareness of mortality took the form of an omnivorous curiosity. He was always keen on recasting the primary impressions into structures of feeling, into mnemonic articulations of the phenomena in their everyday authenticity. On this level, his literature has few rivals, regardless of the truth content or his often opinionated but never frivolous remarks. On the other hand, whatever cannot be grasped empirically or deduced from ultimately material human interest he cast into the dark pit of "abstraction" and inane confusion. What makes Pla so "unphilosophical" may well be a form of philosophical prudery. Not that he denied the ultimate questions but rather that he derided the verbal affectations that feed off those questions. His theory of knowledge was uncomplicated: everything we know is based on sensation. The mind can aspire, with the help of language, to reflect reality, which for all practical purposes is the reality certified by the body or experienced at a distance through acts of communication. These, however, can only give a proximate idea of the original event. Hence Pla's absolutism with regard to sensation and his scepticism vis-à-vis opinion. For him, knowing was not based on theory but on doing: travelling, talking to people, taking part in their activities, learning the tricks of various trades, eating and drinking, writing.

If death is the unspeakable, if the *logos* is necessarily the logic of life and nothing can be said outside this logic, then nothing can be said about death, only about dying. In a posthumously published poem of uncertain date,[11] Pla underscored the absurdity of death:

> Thus, Aurora died.
> Now, to prevent this fact from falling prey to amnesia,
> which is the end of all things in life,
> I would like to say one thing
> to preserve the memory
> for five years perhaps, which is a lot.
> We are dualists.
> We believe in matter and spirit.
> Death, so well explained,
> consists in the separation of these elements.
> Spirit departs.
> Death is inexorable.
> How is it possible, though,
> that spirit has left
> such a graceful, beautiful body,
> a young woman – eighteen years – as prodigious
> as Aurora was?
> Where is the spirit now? Where did it flee?
> How sad and lonely it must be
> disembodied from a virginity! (44:614)

The poem's poignancy is enhanced by the evocation of Aurora at the height of her physical splendour, a virgin of eighteen years whose spirit has departed the flesh. Like Dante, who wrote "that which has never been written of any woman" to eternalize the angelical Beatrice, Pla writes this "down-to-earth" poem to preserve the memory of Aurora. More modestly than the Florentine poet, he hopes to secure her memory for five years, which he considers a feat of human loyalty. And he does so, almost as an afterthought, in lame verses written late in life, when he himself is at the gates of death.

---

11 The poem was dated in or around November 1980 by Pla's publisher, Josep Vergés, who claims to have found it in a folder containing the last texts written by Pla, the so-called death folder (45:57). But this dating is problematic. See page 259 of this book for a discussion of this matter.

Or at the behest of an inner demon, like Socrates learning to play the flute while waiting to drink the hemlock. For just as Socrates had neglected the musical art in his lifetime, Pla had failed to write about his moments of happiness with Aurora Perea, except allusively in the notes for diaries never written and perhaps in their unpublished and possibly lost correspondence.

The dualism affirmed in the poem does not identify Pla's metaphysics. It is asserted by a social subject, by a "we." This "we" corresponds to Heidegger's "they," the master of the general situation (Heidegger 346), a subject defined by "publicness" (Heidegger 165). Pla mocks dualism. Traditional belief in the resolution of the composite of body and spirit fails to ensure even the memory of a wonderful youth. In Pla's hierarchy of value, the tangible body of a young woman vastly overshadows the disembodied spirit, whose ethereal existence Pla denounces as a pious tale. Why should the spirit, pure mind, exist apart from the beauty of triumphant flesh?

Aurora's death must have made an impression on Pla. That it disturbed him is attested by the existence of a cognate poem, published with the "poems of *retour d'âge*." These are the closing lines:

> While Aurora was dying,
> a bright sun was rising.
> But Aurora was nothing – I think.
> She was a spectre of life. What else could one ask for? (26:448)

Aurora was no emanation of the divine light. She was no *Donna angelicata*. Her epiphany is an illusion that evaporates as the physical sun rises, indifferent to the passing away of forms and the subjective pain caused by their disappearance. Her insubstantial epiphany was good while it lasted. One must learn to do with the chimera of happiness without unreasonably asking for a consoling transcendence.

There is more than resignation in Pla's "what else could one ask for?" It is a sober and sobering question that contains its own answer. He had left behind Maragall's pantheistic nostalgia. In "Càntic spiritual" (Spiritual hymn), Maragall wished to arrest the process of becoming and asked God for an afterlife, if not identical to this life, at least based on the emotions of its beauty. He asked God "what more can you give us in another life?" (76), implying the world's perfection. To this rhetorical question Pla replied with his own. Beauty is transient. And to ask for its eternity is fatuous, excessive, insensate.

A Mediterranean tottering on the verge of paganism, Maragall asked for an indefinite extension of present sensations in a body-immanent eternity. At the end of the poem he asks God to grant him eyes large enough to contemplate his "immense face," hoping that death will be a rebirth to greater things. In contrast, Pla did not look on nature in divine tranquillity, or expect rebirth into some higher revelation. He rejected "eternity's enormous tediousness," and rather than admission to the sublime spectacle of the infinite, he begged respite from eternity through occasional coffee breaks: "won't you let me out ever again … Not even for coffee?" (26:435). For mortal man, timelessness is as incongruous a medium as infinity. Hence he asks God if he will be allowed to see once more the friends whose roll call makes up the central part of the poem. Finally, he asks:

> Was it worth to be born
> just to end so badly?
> Will it no longer be possible
> to speak with anyone?
> I would love to know
> what you all think about that. (26:436)

The poem juxtaposes the assurance of eternity with the petty pleasures that Pla indulged in his lifetime: café conversations in non-mystical communion with friends. Providers of actual interlocution, those chatting associates have replaced God as the poem's apostrophic addressee. Withdrawal from the absolute to the relative, from the one to the many, marks the redirection of those pressing questions from the mute source of dogmatic confidence to the mundane bearers of opinion. As he used to, after holding forth on politics before a café audience, he now challenges his imaginary listeners to venture an opinion on the uncertain things of the beyond. A diffident Pla asks the divinity for occasional respite from the timeless monotony of the grave. This modest desire is not strong or delusive enough to defuse the affliction of necessity:

> I couldn't ask for more.
> I could not ask for resurrection
> pure and simple. It would have been too much,
> Because necessary things
> encumber me profoundly.
> I cannot understand that we were given

an ounce of intelligence
and must end life
in such irreparable fashion. (26:436)

Necessity is stronger than hope. Again we meet Camus's intuition of the absurd: a conscious being confronting the inevitability of his disappearance, which is also the disappearance of consciousness:

The dead lack memory,
ears, touch. (26:437–8)

To have faith in resurrection is to desperately hold on to the particularity of this life through the escalation of the same consciousness that is the source of present affliction:

When we resurrect – it's quite normal –
we will have memory, ears
and touch. And if we don't know
everything, gossip will tell us.
Then a complete bedlam will break lose
all the way until blood is spilled.
I am not in favour of useless bedlams.
Will you heed what I say?
Let us forget these carnal,
awesome resurrections:
we want to be left in peace once and for all! (26:438)

Pla, who did not envision a hereafter except in precarious memory (five years at most before the memory of Aurora's bodily perfection would decay), was gloomy on this point. "The human species has a fantastic gift: forgetfulness. Forgetting is more important than memory. [...] The generic, universal gift is forgetting. [...] The question of living is placed on the gift of forgetting – which is probably not a consequence of sensibility but of pure mechanics" (44:362).

Forgetting is the second and definitive death, and yet death in the service of life. Because life is constantly bringing forth new forms, the old ones must disappear to make room for the recent ones. The annihilation of the self takes place in the midst of a festival of life. The mechanism of forgetting is also the mechanism by which life is permanently reconstituted. One can revolt against this truth and adopt a tragic garb, like Camus's absurd hero, or accept obliteration, knowing that the individual's separateness is accidental and death reunites us with a whole that can be visualized, as it always was in most cultures, in the line of the ancestors. Pla accepted this traditional representation of death. Combining lineage with territory, ancient societies have honoured the local cemetery where the ancestors lie in tenuous mnemonic contact with the living. He saw himself bound in life and in death to the land that he could take in with the naked eye, an expanse proportional to his human measure, a sector of the earth to which he referred as "my country." Its chronotope, to use familiar jargon, was shaped by the boundary cross that he projected onto it by using the village cemeteries as cardinal points and himself, standing on the lookout of Sant Sebastià, as the centre of a system of coordinates circumscribed by his ancestry. Village cemeteries were places of genealogical continuity, and this is the non-mystical, intuitive eternity that Pla acknowledged and identified as a sensory vision:

> One day, sight led me to draw four cardinal points on the land in front of me. At every point there was one village of the plain. Of every village I saw the cemetery – which was a familiar cemetery for me ... On that day I felt that I stood before this boundary cross of death, bound to this land with immortal ties. Of all the days of my life, this one has been perhaps the more profitable one. On that day I saw that Sant Sebastià was eternity for me. (7:477)

In death he sought the same concision and concreteness that he cultivated in life. Familiarity was inextricable from memory and continuity, the only eternity he knew. Abstraction amounted to evanescence, insubstantiality, and neglect. He refused the anonymous death in a hospital ward, the "hidden death" that was becoming widespread in the 1950s, as European societies modernized (Ariès 570). Reporting a conversation with a friend after falling at home in April 1979, Pla revealed his plans for the disposal of his body:

> – Hospitals and medical centres are indispensable ...
>
> – I will do all I can to go to the other world without visiting them. Perhaps I won't be able to, what's to be done ...? But for the time being my intention is clear.
>
> – You have thought about many things, I see ...
>
> – About some, yes! I will ask to be buried in the Llofriu cemetery, if possible next to my grandmother Marieta, who is the only immediate

> ancestor I ever met. I have not met any of my male ancestors, and among the female grandmother Marieta is the one I have met. What a good woman that impressive and managerial peasant was! I wish to be buried by her side, if I can. (44:338)

In hoping to bypass the anonymous, concealed death in a hospital and asking to be tucked away with his ancestors in a village cemetery, Pla was rebelling against the modern form of death, as much as he had rebelled against other forms of "progress," such as universal education, the tourist industry, or the ravages of "socialism," mass culture, and the immorality of inflation. It is in light of this revolt against the dictatorship of the urban and the bureaucratic that his emphatic adherence to tradition must be understood. His insistence in adopting the garb of a peasant was a consciously outdated affirmation of a form of life that he had barely known; just as of all his ancestors he had only known his grandmother Marieta. The histrionic demand that the abbot of Poblet administer the last rites to him should be understood in the same vein as the affirmation in extremis of a cultural memory against the despair provoked by the certainty of its evaporation.

Pla's ironic query about the destiny of the spirit and its loneliness after the loss of its material companion bespeaks scepticism about the continuity of mind or even the existence of mind as an immaterial entity. Under the indiscretions of the scalpel, the long-held belief in the soul's location in the body gave way to its dematerialization. Whether in the recesses of the blood, as a *rete mirabile* or wonderful net (a network of veins and arteries believed to be at the base of the skull and to serve the transformation of the vital spirits of the heart into the animal spirits of the brain), or in the pineal gland, one by one the alleged physical locations of the soul fell away, and with them the possibility of opening to scrutiny the immortal aspect of human existence. At the height of the disputes arising from anatomical explorations of the human body, in particular after Locke's new conception of the self, the soul was recreated as mind (Sugg 209). But the mind turned eventually into the brain and a complex of neurological functions, and these, alas, are as finite and as mortal as flesh and bones. The result of this "progress" was to reduce the funeral rites to minimal expression or to entirely do away with them and with centuries of a culture of death, turning over the handling of the moribund and of the corpse to medical professionals and licensed undertakers. As a result, death rituals, wherever they subsist, acquired a merely symbolic and no longer sacramental meaning. It is significant that just before stating his wish to lie next to his grandmother, Pla recalled her virtues as an efficient landed peasant. Hers were the virtues that the old Pla reverenced and wished to embody. But these were not spiritual virtues, unless we understand spirit as Pla did, as the principle that shapes and organizes human existence, creating order out of chaos. But then, in recalling those ancestral virtues and wishing to make them contiguous to himself in time and space, Pla was not envisioning death so much as life, the life that he would have liked to live in a second term. Short of that option, he transformed it into the life that he wished to project into an afterlife in the form of memory: a life worth remembering for as long as memory prevailed.

Works Cited

List of Josep Pla's Collected Works

In the body of the text, citations from Pla's *Obra Completa* are indicated by volume number followed by the page number. To facilitate consultation of the passages, a numerical list of the volumes cited follows. Translations of the quotations are my own.

1. *El quadern gris. Obra completa*. Barcelona: Destino, 1977.
2. *Aigua de mar. Obra completa*. Barcelona: Destino, 1969.
3. *Primera volada. Obra completa*. Barcelona: Destino, 1966.
4. *Sobre París i França. Obra completa*. Barcelona: Destino, 1967.
5. *El nord. Obra completa*. Barcelona: Destino, 1967.
6. *La vida amarga. Obra completa*. Barcelona: Destino, 1967.
7. *El meu país. Obra completa*. Barcelona: Destino, 1968.
8. *Els pagesos. Obra completa*. Barcelona: Destino, 1975.
9. *Viatge a la Catalunya Vella. Obra completa*. Barcelona: Destino, 1968.
11. *Homenots. Primera sèrie. Obra completa*. Barcelona: Destino, 1969.
12. *Notes disperses. Obra completa*. Barcelona: Destino, 1981.
13. *Les escales de Llevant. Obra completa*. Barcelona: Destino, 1983.
14. *Tres artistes. Obra completa*. Barcelona: Destino, 1981.
15. *Les illes. Obra completa*. Barcelona: Destino, 1970.
18. *En mar. Obra completa*. Barcelona: Destino, 1983.
21. *Homenots. Tercera sèrie. Obra completa*. Barcelona: Destino, 1972.
22. *El que hem menjat. Obra completa*. Barcelona: Destino, 1972.
23. *Àlbum de Fontclara. Obra completa*. Barcelona: Destino, 1972.
24. *Humor, candor ... Obra completa*. Barcelona: Destino, 1973.
25. *Cambó. Materials per a una història d'aquests últims anys. Obra completa*. Barcelona: Destino, 1973.

26. *Notes per a Sílvia. Obra completa*. Barcelona: Destino, 1974.
27. *Un petit món del Pirineu. Obra completa*. Barcelona: Destino, 1981.
28. *Direcció Lisboa. Obra completa*. Barcelona: Destino, 1975.
33. *El passat imperfecte. Obra completa*. Barcelona: Destino, 1977.
35. *Notes del capvesprol. Obra completa*. Barcelona: Destino, 1979.
36. *Per passar l'estona. Obra completa*. Barcelona: Destino, 1979.
38. *Escrits empordanesos. Obra completa*. Barcelona: Destino, 1980.
43. *Caps-i-puntes. Obra completa*. Barcelona: Destino, 1983.
44. *Darrers escrits. Obra completa*. Barcelona: Destino, 1984.
45. *Imatge Josep Pla (a cura de Josep Vergés). Obra completa*. Barcelona: Destino, 1984.
A. *Per acabar. Obra completa*. Barcelona: Destino, 1992.

Bibliography

Aguiló, Anna. "*El carrer Estret* de Josep Pla, Premi de novel·la Joanot Martorell, 1951." In *La poètica de la banalitat*, edited by Anna Aguiló and Xavier Pla, 7–9. Actes de la Jornada d'Estudi Cinquanta Anys d'*El carrer Estret*. Girona: Universitat de Girona, 2003.

Albert, Caterina (Víctor Català). *Solitude*. Translated by David H. Rosenthal. London: Readers International, 1992.

Alcoberro, Ramon. *Contra Josep Pla*. Barcelona: Barcanova, 1993.

Alfaro, José María. "Discurso por Radio Nacional de Madrid en la conmemoración de la liberación de la capital." *Arriba*. 29 March 1940: 4.

Amat, Jordi. "L'alliberament de França. Un 'petit raport' de Joan Estelrich a Francesc Cambó." *L'Espill* no. 47 (Fall 2014): 116–25.

Amir, Xavier. *Josep Pla: L'home*. Barcelona: Editorial Mediterrània, 1981.

Anderson, Benedict. *Imagined Communities*. London: Verso, 1991.

Antón, Jacinto. "El sumergible de Josep Pla." *El País*. 15 January 2006.

Arendt, Hannah. *The Life of the Mind*. New York: Harcourt Brace Jovanovich, 1978.

– "Lying in Politics: Reflections on the Pentagon Papers." In *Crises of the Republic*, 1–47. New York: Harcourt Brace Jovanovich, 1969.

Ariès, Philippe. *The Hour of Our Death*. Translated by Helen Weaver. New York: Alfred A. Knopf, 1981.

Aristotle, *De Anima*. Translated by Robert Drew Hicks. Cambridge: Cambridge University Press, 1907.

Assmann, Jan. *Das kulturelle Gedächtnis: Schrift, Erinnerung und politische Identität in frühen Hochkulturen*. Munich: C.H. Beck, 2013.

Auerbach, Erich. *Philologie der Weltliteratur. Sechs Versuche über Stil und Wirklichkeitswahrnehmung*. Frankfurt am Main: Fischer, 1992.
Augé, Marc. *Non-Places: Introduction to an Anthropology of Supermodernity*. Translation by John Howe. London: Verso, 1995.
Badosa, *Cristina. Josep Pla. Biografia del solitari*. Barcelona: Edicions 62, 1997.
Barthes, Roland. *S/Z*. Paris: Seuil, 1970.
Baudrillard, Jean. *De la séduction*. Paris: Galilée, 1979.
Bellmunt, Domènec de. *Cinquanta anys de periodisme català (1923–1975)*. Andorra La Vella: Edicions Mirador del Pirineu, 1975.
– *Homes de la terra*. Barcelona: Llibreria Catalònia, 1935.
Benjamin, Walter. "The Work of Art in the Age of Mechanical Reproduction." In *Illuminations*, 217–51. Translated by Harry Zohn. New York: Schocken, 1976.
Bensman, Joseph, and Robert Lilienfeld. "Phenomenology of Journalism." *Diogenes* 17, no. 68 (1969): 98–119.
Bergson, Henri. *Matière et mémoire. Essai sur la rélation du corps à l'esprit* (1896). *Oeuvres*. Paris: PUF, 1963.
Berkowitz, Peter. *Constitutional Conservatism: Liberty, Self-Government, and Political Moderation*. Stanford, CA: Hoover Institution Press, 2013.
Blackmore, Josiah. *Manifest Perdition: Shipwreck Narrative and the Disruption of Empire*. Minneapolis: University of Minnesota Press, 2002.
Blumenberg, Hans. *Schiffbruch mit Zuschauer*. Frankfurt am Main: Suhrkamp, 1979.
Bonada, Lluís. *"El quadern gris" de Josep Pla*. Barcelona: Empúries, 1985.
– "Una lectura del carrer Estret." In *La poètica de la banalitat*, edited by Anna Aguiló and Xavier Pla, 55–60. Actes de la Jornada d'Estudi Cincuanta Anys d'*El carrer Estret*. Girona: Universitat de Girona, 2003.
Burke, Edmund. *Selected Writings and Speeches*. Edited by Peter J. Stanlis. New Brunswick, NJ: Transaction Publishers, 2009.
Cambó, Francesc. *El pesimismo español*. Madrid: Hesperia, 1917.
– *Meditacions: Dietari (1936–1946)*. Vol. I. Barcelona: Alpha, 1982.
Camus, Albert. *L'étranger*. Paris: Gallimard, 1953.
– *Le mythe de Sisyphe*. Paris: Gallimard, 1942.
– *Le premier homme*. Paris: Gallimard, 1994.
– *Noces*. Paris: Gallimard, 1950.
Carbonell Camós, Eliseu. *Josep Pla: El temps, la gent i el paisatge. Una etnografia de l'Empordà franquejant la literatura*. Barcelona: Edicions de 1984, 2006.
Carey, John. *The Intellectuals and the Masses: Pride and Prejudice Among the Literary Intelligentsia, 1880–1939*. New York: St Martin's Press, 1992.
Casajuana, Carles. *Pla i Nietzsche: Afinitats i Coincidències*. Barcelona: Edicions 62, 1996.

Casasús, Josep Maria. *Lliçons de periodisme en Josep Pla*. Barcelona: Destino, 1986.

Casellas, Raimon. *Dark Vales*. Translated by Alan Yates. Sawtry, UK: Dedalus Books, 2014.

Casey, Edward S. *Representing Place: Landscape, Painting and Maps*. Minneapolis and London: University of Minnesota Press, 2002.

Castellanos, Jordi. "Josep Pla i la novel·la." In *Josep Pla, memòria i escriptura*, edited by Glòria Granell and Xavier Pla, 35–64. Actes del col·loqui de l'any Pla. Universitat de Girona (October 1997). Girona: Universitat de Girona, 2001.

Castellet, Josep Maria. "Aspectes estilístics de Josep Pla." Actes del Quart Col·loqui Internacional de Llengua i Literatura Catalanes. Basilea, 22–7 de març de 1976. A cura de Germà Colon. Publicacions de l'Abadia de Montserrat, 1977: 459–73. Reprinted in Castellet, *Josep Pla o la raó narrativa*, 129–46.

– "De la objetividad al objeto: a propósito de las novelas de Alain Robbe-Grillet." *Papeles de Son Armadans*. 15. June 1957: 309–32.

– *Josep Pla o la raó narrativa*. Barcelona: Destino, 1978.

– *La hora del lector: notas para una iniciación a la literatura narrativa de nuestros días*. Barcelona: Seix-Barral, 1957.

Cherno, Melvin. "'Man is what He Eats': A Rectification." *Journal of the History of Ideas* 24, no. 3 (July–September 1963): 397–406.

Clarà i Resplandís, Josep. "Josep Pla, fitxat com a espia americà." *Estudis del Baix Empordà* no. 11 (1992): 261–7.

Cohen, Jeffrey Jerome. "Monster Culture (Seven Theses)." In *Monster Theory: Reading Culture*, edited by Jeffrey Jerome Cohen, 3–25. Minneapolis: University of Minnesota Press, 1996.

Connery, Thomas B. *Journalism and Realism: Rendering American Life*. Evanston, IL: Northwestern University Press, 2011.

Coromina, Xavier. "Sobre l'aprenentatge de l'ofici literari." In *Josep Pla, memòria i escriptura*, edited by Glòria Granell and Xavier Pla, 225–33. Actes del col·loqui de l'any Pla. Universitat de Girona (October 1997). Girona: Universitat de Girona, 2001.

Cowley, Malcolm. *Exiles Return: A Literary Odyssey of the 1920s*. New York: Penguin, 1954.

Cramerotti, Alfredo. *Aesthetic Journalism: How to Inform without Informing*. Bristol: Intellect, 2009.

Dalmau, Francesc. "Josep Pla i el seu germà Pere." *Punt Diari*, 23 April 1982. Supplement: 14.

Debray, Régis. *L'emprise*. Paris: Gallimard, 2000.

– *Le pouvoir intellectuel en France*. Paris: Editions Ramsay, 1979.

D'Ors, Eugeni. *Glosari 1906–1907*. Edited by Xavier Pla. Barcelona: Quaderns Crema, 1996.

– *Gualba, la de mil veus*. Edited by Xavier Pla. Barcelona: Quaderns Crema, 2012.
– *La Ben Plantada*. Edited by Xavier Pla. Barcelona: Quaderns Crema, 2004.
– *Oceanografia del tedi*. Barcelona: Selecta, 1948.
Emerson, Ralph Waldo. "Nature." *The Complete Works of Ralph Waldo Emerson*. Vol. 3. Essays. Second Series. Boston and New York: Houghton, Mifflin and Company, 1903: 167–96.
Espada, Arcadi. *Josep Pla*. Barcelona: Ediciones Omega, 2005.
Esslin, Martin. *The Theatre of the Absurd*. Revised edition. Harmondsworth, Middlesex: Penguin, 1968.
Febrés, Xavier. *Les dones de Josep Pla*. Barcelona: Edicions 62, 1999.
Fernández de Oviedo, Gonzalo. *Misfortunes and Shipwrecks in the Seas of the Indies, Islands, and Mainland of the Ocean Sea (1513–1548)*. Book 50 of the *General and Natural History of the Indies*. Translated and edited by Glen F. Dille. Gainesville: University Press of Florida, 2011.
Ferrater, Gabriel. *Tres prosistes. Joaquim Ruyra, Víctor Català i Josep Pla*. Barcelona: Empúries, 2010.
Finn, Michael R. *Proust, the Body and Literary Form*. Cambridge: Cambridge University Press, 2004.
Fontbona, Francesc. *El paisatgisme a Catalunya*. Barcelona: Destino, 1979.
Ford, Edwin H. "The Art and Craft of the Literary Journalist" (originally published in 1937). In *New Survey of Journalism*, edited by George Fox Mott, 304–13. New York: Barnes, 1950.
Fradera, Josep Maria. *Cultura nacional en una sociedad dividida: Cataluña 1838–1868*. Madrid: Marcial Pons, 2003.
Frye, Northrop. *The Educated Imagination*. Bloomington: Indiana University Press, 1964.
Fumaroli, Marc. *La diplomacia del ingenio. De Montaigne a La Fontaine*. Translated by Caridad Martínez. Barcelona: Acantilado, 2011.
Fuster, Joan. "Amenitats del camp." In *Causar-se d'esperar*, 36–43. Barcelona: Editorial A.C., 1965.
– "Notes per a una introducció a l'estudi de Josep Pla." In Josep Pla, *Obra completa* 1, 11–83. Barcelona: Destino, 1966.
– *Viure per viure*. València: Publicacions de la Universitat de València, 2005.
Gallofré, Maria Josepa. "Un llibre inèdit: El carrer Estret." *La poètica de la banalitat. Actes de la Jornada d'Estudi Cinquanta Anys d'El carrer Estret*. Edited by Anna Aguiló and Xavier Pla. Girona: Universitat de Girona. Servei de Publicacions, 2003: 33–43.
Gaziel (Agustí Calvet). *Història de La Vanguardia 1884/1936*. París: Edicions Catalanes de París, 1971.
– *París, 1914. Diari d'un estudiant*. Barcelona: Aedos, 1965.

– *Tots els camins duen a Roma. Història d'un destí 1893–1914*. Barcelona: Aedos, 1958.

– *Tot s'ha perdut. El catalanisme polític entre 1922 i 1934*. Barcelona: RBA La Magrana, 2013.

Geertz, Clifford. *The Interpretation of Cultures*. New York: Basic Books, 1973.

Giménez Caballero, Ernesto. *Amor a Cataluña*. Madrid: Ruta, 1942.

Goethe, W.J. *Faust*. Goethes Werke. III. Hamburg: Christian Wegner, 1964.

Grabolosa, Ramon. *Olot, en les arts i en les lletres: L'aportació comarcal als moviments artístics i literaris de Catalunya*. Barcelona: Editorial Dirosa, 1974.

Granell, Glòria, and Xavier Pla, eds. *Josep Pla, memòria i escriptura. Actes del col·loqui de l'any Pla*. Universitat de Girona (October 1977). Girona: Universitat de Girona, 2001.

Guixà, Josep. *Espías de Franco. Josep Pla y Francesc Cambó*. Madrid: Fórcola, 2014.

Gustà, Marina. *Els orígens ideològics i literaris de Josep Pla*. Barcelona: Curial, 1995.

– "Plasticitat i visualització. L'expressionisme planià." In *Josep Pla, memòria i escriptura*, edited by Glòria Granell and Xavier Pla, 101–15. Girona: Universitat de Girona, 2001.

Halbwachs, Maurice. *La mémoire collective*. Paris: Albin Michel, 1997.

Harrison, Robert Pogue. *The Dominion of the Dead*. Chicago: University of Chicago Press, 2003.

Hartsock, John C. *A History of American Literary Journalism: The Emergence of a Modern Narrative Form*. Amherst: University of Massachusetts Press, 2000.

Hayek, Friedrich A. *The Road to Serfdom*. Edited by Bruce Caldwell. Chicago: University of Chicago Press, 2007.

Heidegger, Martin. *Poetry, Language, Thought*. Translated by Albert Hofstadter. New York: Harper and Row, 1971.

Heller, Agnes. *Everyday Life*. Translated by G.L. Campbell. London: Routledge and Kegan Paul, 1984.

Hemingway, Ernest. *A Moveable Feast*. New York: Charles Scribner's, 1964.

Homer. *The Odyssey*. Translated by Richard Lattimore. New York: Harper Perennial, 2007.

Husserl, Edmund. [1900/1901]. *Logical Investigations*. Translated by J.N. Findlay. Edited by Dermot Moran. 2nd edition. 2 volumes. London: Routledge, 2001.

Iribarren, Teresa. "Josep Pla i James Joyce o el diàleg entre gegants." *Serra d'Or* 534 (June 2004): 47–50.

Italia, Iona. *The Rise of Literary Journalism in the 18th Century: Anxious Employment*. New York: Routledge, 2005.

Katvan, Zeev. "Reflection Theory and the Identity of Thinking and Being." *Studies in Soviet Thought* 18, no. 2 (1978): 87–109.
Keynes, John Maynard. *Essays in Persuasion*. New York: Norton, 1963.
Kierkegaard, Søren. *Concluding Unscientific Postscript*. Translated by David F. Swenson and Walter Lowrie. Princeton, NJ: Princeton University Press, 1944.
Laplace, Pierre-Simon, Marquis de. *A Philosophical Essay on Probabilities*. Translated by Frederick Wilson Truscott and Frederick Lincoln Emory. New York: John Wiley, 1902.
Lawrence, D.H. *Lady Chatterley's Lover*. NewYork: Grove Press, 1959.
– *Sea and Sardinia*. In *D.H. Lawrence and Italy*, edited by A. Burgess, 137–326. Harmondsworth: Penguin Books, 1981.
Lejeune, Philippe. *Écrire sa vie. Du pacte au patrimoine autobiographique*. Paris: Éditions du Mauconduit, 2015.
– *Le pacte autobiographique*. Paris: Seuil, 1975.
– *Signes de vie. Le pacte autobiographique* 2. Paris: Seuil, 2005.
Lewis, Sinclair. "Self-Conscious America." *The American Mercury*. October 1925.
Lippmann, Walter. *The Public Philosophy*. Boston: Little, Brown and Company, 1955.
Locke, John. *An Essay Concerning Human Understanding*. Edited by Raymond Wilburn. London: J.M. Dent, 1947.
Lohmar, Dieter. "Husserl's Type and Kant's Schemata. Systematic Reasons for Their Correlation or Identity." In *The New Husserl*, edited by Donn Welton, 93–124. Translated by Julia Jansen and Gina Zavota. Bloomington: Indiana University Press, 2003.
Lottman, Herbert R. *The Left Bank. Writers, Artists, and Politics from the Popular Front to the Cold War*. Boston: Houghton, Mifflin, 1982.
Luhmann, Niklas. *Art as a Social System*. Translated by Eva M. Knodt. Stanford, CA: Stanford University Press, 2000.
– *Observations on Modernity*. Translated by William Whobrey. Stanford, CA: Stanford University Press, 1998.
Lule, Jack. *Daily News, Eternal Stories: The Mythological Role of Journalism*. New York: Guilford Press, 2001.
MacLeish, Archibald. "Ars Poetica." *Poetry* 28, no. 3 (June 1926): 126.
Maftei, Micaela. *The Fiction of Autobiograph: Reading and Writing Identity*. New York: Bloomsbury, 2013.
Maragall, Joan. *Poesies. Obres Completes* I. Barcelona: Sala Parés Llibreria, 1929.
Margalit, Avishai. *The Ethics of Memory*. Cambridge, MA: Harvard University Press, 2002.
Marí, Antoni. "Josep Pla i les arts plàstiques." In *Josep Pla, memòria i escriptura*, edited by Glòria Granell and Xavier Pla, 117–26. Girona: Universitat de Girona, 2001.

Martinell, Josep. *Josep Pla vist de prop*. Barcelona: Pòrtic, 1972.
– *Josep Pla vist per un amic de Palafrugell*. Barcelona: Destino, 1996.
Mitchell, W.J.T., ed. *Landscape and Power*. Chicago: University of Chicago Press, 1994.
Morand, Paul. *Ouvert la nuit*. Paris: Gallimard, 1987.
Nietzsche, Friedrich. *Jenseits von Gut und Böse*. In *Vorspiel einer Philosophie der Zukunft*. *Werke in Drei Bänden*, vol. 2, 563–759. Munich: Carl Hanser Verlag, 1955.
Nogué, Joan. *Paisatge, territori i societat civil*. València: Tres i Quatre, 2010.
Oller, Narcís. *L'escanyapobres*. *Obres completes de Narcís Oller*. Vol. 1. Barcelona: Gustau Gili, 1928.
Orwell, George. "Charles Dickens." In *An Age Like This. 1920–1940*, 413-60. Vol. 1 of *The Collected Essays, Journalism and Letters*. Edited by Sonia Orwell and Ian Angus. Boston: Nonpareil Books, 2000.
– *Homage to Catalonia*. Boston: Beacon Press, 1952.
O'Sullivan, Noël K. *Conservatism*. New York: St Martin's Press, 1976.
Pairolí, Miquel. *La geografia íntima de Josep Pla*. Barcelona: La Campana, 1996.
Pániker, Salvador. "El mundo según Josep Pla." *La Vanguardia*. Revista, 8 May 1997.
Péguy, Charles. *Note sur M. Bergson et la philosophie bergsonienne*. In *Oeuvres en prose (1909–1914)*, 1311–45. Biliothèque de la Pléiade. Paris: Gallimard, 1961.
Perejaume. *L'obra i la por*. Barcelona: Cercle de Lectors/Galàxia Gutemberg, 2007.
Pla, Josep. *Aigua de mar*. *Obra completa* 2. Barcelona: Destino, 1969.
– *Àlbum de Fontclara*. *Obra completa* 23. Barcelona: Destino, 1972.
– "A los pesimistas." *Destino*. 4 October: 8 and 15.
– *Barcelona, una discussió entranyable*. In *Primera volada*. *Obra completa* 3. Barcelona: Destino, 1966: 213–462.
– "Cagliari". *Arriba*. 20 February 20, 1940: 3.
– *Cambó. Materials per a una història d'aquests últims anys*. 3 vols. Barcelona: Edicions de la Nova Revista, 1928, 1929 and 1930. Re-edited in *Obra completa* 25. Barcelona: Destino, 1973.
– *Caps-i-puntes*. *Obra completa* 43. Barcelona: Destino, 1983.
– *El carrer Estret*. In *Els pagesos*. *Obra completa* 8. Barcelona: Destino, 1975. 437–671.
– *En mar*. *Obra completa* 18. Barcelona: Destino, 1983.
– *Cartes a Pere*. Barcelona: Destino, 1996.
– *Cartes d'Itàlia*. *Obra completa* 13. Barcelona: Destino, 1982: 7-234.
– "Cerdeña y Cavour." *Arriba*. 3 March 1940.
– *Coses vistes 1920–1925*. Barcelona: Edicions Diana, 1925.
– *Darrers escrits*. *Obra completa* 44. Barcelona: Destino, 1984.

– *Direcció Lisboa. Obra completa* 28. Barcelona: Destino, 1975.
– *El meu país. Obra completa* 7. Barcelona: Destino, 1997.
– *El pagès i el seu món.* In *Els pagesos*, 7–259. *Obra completa* 8. Barcelona: Destino: 1975.
– *El passat imperfecte. Obra completa* 33. Barcelona: Destino, 1977.
– "El perfecte demòcrata." *La Publicitat*. 27 January 1926.
– *El primer quadern gris. Dietaris 1918–1919.* Facsimile edition. Edited by Xavier Pla. Barcelona: Destino, 2004.
– "El progreso." *Arriba*. 21 April 1940.
– *El quadern gris. Obra completa* 1. Barcelona: Destino, 1977.
– *El que hem menjat. Obra completa* 22. Barcelona: Destino, 1972.
– *Escrits empordanesos. Obra completa* 38. Barcelona: Destino, 1980.
– "Georges Simenon y la técnica de la novela." *Destino* 643 (3 December 1949): 5, 22.
– *The Gray Notebook.* Translated by Peter Bush. New York: New York Review Books, 2013.
– "Hemingway." In *Darrers escrits*, 187–191. *Obra completa* 44. Barcelona: Destino, 1984.– *Historia de la Segunda República Española.* 4 vols. Barcelona: Destino, 1940–1.
– *Homenots. Tercera Sèrie. Obra completa* 21. Barcelona: Destino, 1972.
– *Humor, candor ... Obra completa* 24. Barcelona: Destino, 1973.
– *Imatge Josep Pla (a cura de Josep Vergés). Obra completa* 45. Barcelona: Destino, 1984.
– "Interviú con Simenon." *Arriba*. 17 March 1940.
– "James Joyce." *La Publicitat*. 19 February 1927.
– "Joan Estelrich o la dispersió." In *Homenots*, 473–516 . *Primera sèrie. Obra completa* 11. Barcelona: Destino, 1969.
– "John Maynard Keynes (Lord Keynes)." In *El passat imperfect*, 286–318. *Obra completa* 33. Barcelona: Destino, 1989.
– "L'adjectivació." In *Darrers escrits*, 291–5. *Obra completa* 44. Barcelona: Destino, 1984.– *Madrid – L'adveniment de la República.* In *Notes per a Sílvia*, 29–149. *Obra completa* 26. Barcelona: Destino, 1974.
– "La meva literatura." In *Darrers escrits*, 286–90. *Obra completa* 44. Barcelona: Destino, 1984.
– "Las ciudades y los hombres." *El Español*. 3 December 1942.
– *Les illes. Obra completa* 15. Barcelona: Destino, 1970.
– *Notes del capvesprol. Obra completa* 35. Barcelona: Destino, 1979.
– *Notes disperses. Obra completa* 12. Barcelona: Destino, 1981.
– *Notes per a Sílvia. Obra completa* 26. Barcelona: Destino, 1974.
– "Para un libro de cocina del pescado." *Arriba*. 24 March 1940: 3.

– *Per acabar. Obra completa* A. Barcelona: Destino, 1992.
– *Per passar l'estona. Obra completa* 36. Barcelona: Destino, 1979.
– *Un petit món del Pirineu. Obra completa* 27. Barcelona: Destino, 1981.
– *Primera volada. Obra completa* 3. Barcelona: Destino, 1989.
– "Recuerdos de Ulises." *Arriba.* 25 February 1940: 3.– "Reflexions sobre l'Empordà." In *El meu país*, 7–223. *Obra completa* 7. Barcelona: Destino, 1968.
– *Relacions.* Barcelona: Edicions Diana, 1927.
– "Sebastià Puig (A) Hermós." In *Caps-i-puntes. Obra completa* 43. Barcelona: Destino, 1983: 663–703.
– "Siracusa." *Arriba.* 2 July 1940: 3.
– *Sobre París i França. Obra completa* 4. Barcelona: Destino, 1967.
– "Trascendencia de la revolución italiana." *Arriba.* 26 December 1940: 3.
– "Una historia de la filosofía." *Arriba.* 4 August 1940: 3.
– "Un home fatal." In *La vida amarga*, 227–54. *Obra completa* 6. Barcelona: Destino, 1974.
– *Viatge a Catalunya.* Barcelona: Ancora, 1946.
– *Viatge a la Catalunya Vella. Obra completa* 9. Barcelona: Destino, 1968.
– *Viatge a Rússia el 1925.* In *El nord*, 453–633. *Obra completa* 5. Barcelona: Destino, 1967.
– *La vida amarga. Obra completa* 6. Barcelona: Destino, 1967.
– "Vida de Manolo, contada per ell mateix." In *Tres artistes*, 9–279. *Obra completa* 14. Barcelona: Destino, 1981.
– *La vida lenta. Notes per a tres diaris (1956, 1957, 1964).* Barcelona: Destino, 2014.
Pla, Josep, and Josep Maria Cruzet. *Amb les pedres disperses. Cartes 1946–1962.* Edited by Maria Josepa Gallofré. Barcelona: Destino, 2003.
Pla Comas, José. "Banderas que volvían." *Los Sitios.* 14 February 1940.
Pla, Xavier. *Josep Pla. Ficció autobiogràfica i veritat literària.* Barcelona: Quaderns Crema, 1997.
– "Josep Pla: Madrid 1936." *El País.* Cultura. 6 October 2014: 17–31
– "La prehistòria literària a *El carrer Estret*: dos capítols inèdits de la relació de Josep Pla amb la novel·la." In *La poètica de la banalitat*, edited by Anna Aguiló and Xavier Pla, 00–00. Actes de la Jornada d'Estudi Cincuanta Anys d'*El carrer Estret.* Girona: Universitat de Girona, 2003.
– *Simenon i la connexió catalana.* València: Edicions Tres i Quatre, 2007.
"Política española." No author. *Arriba*, no. 5. 18 April 1935: 1.
Proust, Marcel. *Swann's Way.* Translated by C.K. Scott-Moncrieff. New York: Vintage, 1989.
Puig, Valentí. *L'home de l'abric.* Barcelona: Destino, 1998.
Puig i Ferreter, Joan. *Servitud (Memòries d'un periodista).* Barcelona: Llibreria Catalònia, 1926.

Pujals, Joan Maria. *Presència de Catalunya*. Proa, 1999.

Pujols, Francesc. *La solució Cambó*. Barcelona: L'esfera dels llibres, 2005.

Quart, Pere. *Vacances pagades*. Barcelona: Proa, 1981.

Riba, Carles. "Pla." In *Clàssics i moderns*, 200–18. Les Millors obres de la literatura catalana. Barcelona: Edicions 62, 1979.

Ricoeur, Paul. *Memory, History, Forgetting*. Translated by Kathleen Blamey and David Pellauer. Chicago: University of Chicago Press, 2004.

Rilke, Rainer Maria. *Die Sonette an Orpheus. Sämtliche Werke*. 6 vols. Frankfurt am Main: Insel Verlag, 1955.

Riquer, Borja de. "Cambó i Pla, El 'Mecenes' i el 'Convers.'" In *Josep Pla, memòria i escriptura*, edited by Glòria Granell and Xavier Pla, 147–83. Girona: Universitat de Girona, 2001.

Rorty, Richard. *Contingency, Irony, and Solidarity*. Cambridge: Cambridge University Press, 1989.

Santana, Mario. *Foreigners in the Homeland: The Spanish American New Novel in Spain, 1962–1974*. Cranbury, NJ: Associated University Presses, 2000.

Schama, Simon. *Landscape and Memory*. New York: Vintage, 1995.

Schmitt, Carl. *Land und Meer. Eine weltgeschichtliche Betrachtung*. Stuttgart: Klett-Cotta, 2008.

Seremetakis, C. Nadia S. "The Memory of the Senses, Part I: Marks of the Transitory" and "The Memory of the Senses, Part II: Still Acts." In *The Senses Still: Perception and Memory as Material Culture in Modernity*, edited by C. Nadia Seremetakis, 1–18 and 23–43. Chicago: University of Chicago Press, 1994.

Sloterdijk, Peter. *Literatur und Organisation von Lebenserfahrung. Autobiographien der Zwanziger Jahre*. Munich: Carl Hanser Verlag, 1978.

Soler Serrano, Joaquín. *A Fondo. Entrevista a Josep Pla*. Radiotelevisión Española, 1976. Video recording.

Stendhal. *Le rouge et le noir*. In *Romans et Nouvelles*, vol. 1, 193–699. Bibliothêque de la Pléiade. Paris: Gallimard, 1952.

Sugg, Richard. *Murder after Death: Literature and Anatomy in Early Modern England*. Ithaca, NY: Cornell University Press, 2007.

Toulmin, Stephen. *Return to Reason*. Cambridge, MA: Harvard University Press, 2001.

Trilling, Lionel. "Manners, Morals, and the Novel." *Kenyon Review* 10, no. 1 (Winter 1948): 11–27.

Underwood, Doug. *The Undeclared War between Journalism and Fiction: Journalists as Genre Benders in Literary History*. New York: Palgrave MacMillan, 2013.

Valéry, Paul. "L'idée Fixe." *Oeuvres*. Vol. 2. Paris: Gallimard, 1960.

Valls i Grau, Josep. *Josep Pla: Converses a l'Empordà*. Barcelona: Blume, 1986.
– *Josep Pla oral*. Barcelona: A Contra Vent, 2011.
Verdaguer, Jacint. *Antologia poètica*. Edited by Carles Riba. Barcelona: Edicions 62, 2002.
Vergés Coma, Josep C. "L'espia José Pla." *Diari de Girona*, 23 November 2014.
Vergés Matas, Josep. "Records de Josep Vergés." In Josep Pla, *Imatge Josep Pla (a cura de Josep Vergés)*, 11–138 *Obra completa* 45. Barcelona: Destino, 1984.
– "Unes notes explicatives." In Josep Pla, *Polèmica. Cròniques parlamentàries (1929–1932)*, 7–10. *Obra completa* 40. Barcelona: Destino, 1982.
Vidal Olivares, Jaime. "Spanish business in Argentina and Chile since 1880." In *The Impact of Globalization on Argentina and Chile: Business Enterprises and Entrepreneurship*, edited by Geoffrey Jones and Andrea Lluch, 135–50. Cheltenham, UK: Edward Elgar Publishing, 2015.
Virgil. *The Aeneid*. Translated by Robert Fitzgerald. New York: Vintage Classics, 1990.
Wang, Qi. *The Autobiographical Self in Time and Culture*. Oxford: Oxford UP, 2013.
Weber, Ronald. *News of Paris: American Journalists in the City of Light Between the Wars*. Chicago: Ivan R. Dee, 2006.
Wickes, George. *Americans in Paris 1903–1939*. New York: Doubleday, 1969.
Winfield, Betty Houchin, *Journalism 1908: Birth of a Profession*. Columbia: University of Missouri Press, 2008.
Wittgenstein, Ludwig. *Tractatus Logico-Philosophicus*. Translated by C.K. Ogden. London: Routledge & Kegan Paul, 1971.
X., X. "Les teories de Josep Pla sobre la novel·la." *La Publicitat*, 8 May 1927: 1.
Xammar, Eugeni. *Cartes a Josep Pla*. Edited by Xavier Pla. Barcelona: Quaderns Crema, 2000.
Zola, Émile. *La fortune des Rougon*. In *Les Rougon-Macqart*, volume 1, 1–315. Bibliothèque de la Pléiade. Paris: Gallimard: 1960.
Zweig, Paul. *The Adventurer*. New York: Basic Books, 1974.

Index

TORONTO IBERIC

1. Anthony J. Cascardi, *Cervantes, Literature, and the Discourse of Politics*
2. Jessica A. Boon, *The Mystical Science of the Soul: Medieval Cognition in Bernardino de Laredo's Recollection Method*
3. Susan Byrne, *Law and History in Cervantes' Don Quixote*
4. Mary E. Barnard and Frederick A. de Armas (eds), *Objects of Culture in the Literature of Imperial Spain*
5. Nil Santiáñez, *Topographies of Fascism: Habitus, Space, and Writing in Twentieth-Century Spain*
6. Nelson Orringer, *Lorca in Tune with Falla: Literary and Musical Interludes*
7. Ana M. Gómez-Bravo, *Textual Agency: Writing Culture and Social Networks in Fifteenth-Century Spain*
8. Javier Irigoyen-García, *The Spanish Arcadia: Sheep Herding, Pastoral Discourse, and Ethnicity in Early Modern Spain*
9. Stephanie Sieburth, *Survival Songs: Conchita Piquer's* Coplas *and Franco's Regime of Terror*
10. Christine Arkinstall, *Spanish Female Writers and the Freethinking Press, 1879–1926*
11. Margaret Boyle, *Unruly Women: Performance, Penitence, and Punishment in Early Modern Spain*
12. Evelina Gužauskytė, *Christopher Columbus's Naming in the* diarios *of the Four Voyages (1492–1504): A Discourse of Negotiation*

13 Mary E. Barnard, *Garcilaso de la Vega and the Material Culture of Renaissance Europe*
14 William Viestenz, *By the Grace of God: Francoist Spain and the Sacred Roots of Political Imagination*
15 Michael Scham, Lector Ludens*: The Representation of Games and Play in Cervantes*
16 Stephen Rupp, *Heroic Forms: Cervantes and the Literature of War*
17 Enrique Fernandez, *Anxieties of Interiority and Dissection in Early Modern Spain*
18 Susan Byrne, *Ficino in Spain*
19 Patricia M. Keller, *Ghostly Landscapes: Film, Photography, and the Aesthetics of Haunting in Contemporary Spanish Culture*
20 Carolyn A. Nadeau, *Food Matters: Alonso Quijano's Diet and the Discourse of Food in Early Modern Spain*
21 Cristian Berco, *From Body to Community: Venereal Disease and Society in Baroque Spain*
22 Elizabeth R. Wright, *The Epic of Juan Latino: Dilemmas of Race and Religion in Renaissance Spain*
23 Ryan D. Giles, *Inscribed Power: Amulets and Magic in Early Spanish Literature*
24 Jorge Pérez, *Confessional Cinema: Religion, Film, and Modernity in Spain's Development Years (1960–1975)*
25 Joan Ramon Resina, *Josep Pla: Seeing the World in the Form of Articles*

www.ingramcontent.com/pod-product-compliance
Lightning Source LLC
LaVergne TN
LVHW090150080826
844660LV00013B/747/J
* 9 7 8 1 4 8 7 5 0 1 8 4 6 *